THE TYPOGRAPHIC IMAGINATION

STUDIES OF THE WEATHERHEAD EAST ASIAN INSTITUTE,
COLUMBIA UNIVERSITY

STUDIES OF THE WEATHERHEAD EAST ASIAN INSTITUTE, COLUMBIA UNIVERSITY

The Studies of the Weatherhead East Asian Institute of Columbia University were inaugurated in 1962 to bring to a wider public the results of significant new research on modern and contemporary East Asia.

For a complete list of titles, see page 315.

The Typographic Imagination

READING AND WRITING IN JAPAN'S AGE OF MODERN PRINT MEDIA

Nathan Shockey

Columbia University Press
New York

Columbia University Press wishes to express its appreciation for assistance given by the Wm. Theodore de Bary Fund and by Bard College in the publication of this book.

Columbia University Press
Publishers Since 1893
New York   Chichester, West Sussex
cup.columbia.edu

Paperback edition, 2023

Library of Congress Cataloging-in-Publication Data
Names: Shockey, Nathan, author.
Title: The typographic imagination : reading and writing in Japan's age of modern print media / Nathan Shockey.
Description: New York : Columbia University Press, [2020] | Series: Studies of the Weatherhead East Asian Institute, Columbia University | Includes bibliographical references and index.
Identifiers: LCCN 2019018559 (print) | LCCN 2019981086 (ebook) | ISBN 9780231194280 (cloth) | ISBN 9780231194297 (pbk.) | ISBN 9780231550741 (ebook)
Subjects: LCSH: Book industries and trade—Japan—History—19th century. | Book industries and trade—Japan—History—20th century. | Printing—Japan—History—19th century. | Printing—Japan—History—20th century. | Books and reading—Japan—History—19th century. | Books and reading—Japan—History—20th century. | Japan—Intellectual life—19th century. | Japan—Intellectual life—20th century.
Classification: LCC Z463.3 .S437 2020 (print) | LCC Z463.3 (ebook) | DDC 381/.45002095209034—dc23
LC record available at https://lccn.loc.gov/2019018559
LC ebook record available at https://lccn.loc.gov/2019981086

Cover design: Chang Jae Lee

CONTENTS

ACKNOWLEDGMENTS

Having spent more than a decade researching and writing this book about the materiality of books, it is with deep gratitude and some disbelief that I prepare to witness at last the transubstantiation of these writings into a material object possessing physicality and, I hope, some form of value. At the same time, I am confronted with the limits of the printed word to express all the personal and professional debts and thanks that I owe to so many people who have made the present volume possible. At Columbia University, Tomi Suzuki taught me in the deepest sense what it means to read and to write; it feels somehow ironically appropriate that I find myself at a loss for words with which to convey my profound gratitude as she continues to be a boundless source of guidance, support, advice, and insight. Paul Anderer has likewise been encouraging and inspirational since day one, through his teaching and his involvement in the research, writing, and revising of this work as he challenged me to always strive further. Haruo Shirane's careful critical eye and his penetrating and indispensable advice have pushed my work to a higher level than I thought possible. Also at Columbia, Lydia Liu, David Lurie, and Stefan Andriopolous gave crucial input that informed my approach to the histories and theorization of media and script.

The majority of the research for this book was conducted over the course of several extended stays at Waseda University, Tokyo, where I had the exceedingly good fortune to benefit from the guidance, support, and sponsorship of Toeda Hirokazu. Countless were the times in which I learned that my "discoveries" had been made by him long ago, and boundless is my appreciation for everything he has shared with me. As an attempt to repay my deep debt of gratitude, I can only hope to live up to the standards he has set as a scholar.

I have also been lucky enough to benefit from the advice and intellectual support of a range of scholars in both Japan and the United States who provided interlocution, inspiration, encouragement, and opportunities to share my research and ideas throughout the many stages of this project. My thanks go out to Heather Bowen-Struyk, Michael Bourdaghs, Jim Dorsey, Michael Emmerich, Norma Field, Sarah Frederick, Jim Fujii, Fujii Sadakazu, Aaron Gerow, Harry Harootunian, Hirasawa Gō, Marilyn Ivy, Seth Jacobowitz, Sabu Kohso, Kishikawa Shuntarō, Kōno Kensuke, Tom Lamarre, Seiji Lippit, Hoyt Long, Tom Looser, William Marotti, Anne McKnight, Max Moerman, Naitō Mariko, Ōkawachi Natsuki, Ōsawa Satoshi, Ozaki Natsuko, Mark Pendleton, Sakasai Akito, Ann Sherif, Satoko Shimazaki, Shihono Kaori, Tanaka Yukari, Toba Kōji, Tokinoya Yuri, and Wada Atsuhiko.

This research has been made financially possible through the generosity of a number of foundations, institutions, and organizations. Early phases were supported by the Weatherhead East Asian Institute and the Columbia Department of East Asian Languages and Cultures; the Japan Foundation and the Shinchō Foundation for the Promotion of Japanese Studies allowed for an extended research stay in Tokyo from 2008 to 2010; in the final stages of the project, grants from the Japan Society for the Promotion of Science and the Andrew W. Mellon Foundation (via Bard's Center for Experimental Humanities) made possible crucial additional time at Waseda and return trips to the archives.

Papers and presentations on portions of the work that would become this book were given at meetings of the Association of Asian Studies, the Association of Japanese Literary Studies, and the American Comparative Literature Association, as well as at the Censorship, Media, and Literary Culture in Japan Symposium, the Kimuspo Seminar on Narratology, the Media Histories / Media Theories and East Asia Conference, and the Histories of the Japanese Book Japan Foundation Summer Institute; I am grateful to all those who organized, attended, read papers, and asked questions. A special thanks also goes to the faculty and students at Northwestern

University, McGill University, and University of California, Los Angeles, for hosting me, and for their questions and comments on presentations that contributed to important late-stage rewriting of chapter 1 in particular.

I am deeply grateful for the work of the staff and librarians at the Waseda University Libraries and at the C. V. Starr East Asian Library at Columbia University; those at the latter heroically saved the irreplaceable collection from catastrophic loss to water damage in 2018. I would like to express a special thanks to the librarians, staff, and archivists at the Ōhara Institute for Social Research, the Japanese Esperanto Institute, the Meiji Shinbun Zasshi Bunko at the University of Tokyo, the Tokyo Paper Museum, the Tokyo Photographic Art Museum, the Printing Museum of Tokyo, and the National Diet Library for working with me to access invaluable and otherwise unavailable materials, often on short notice. Likewise, it would be disingenuous to write so extensively about the history of Japan's used-book trade without mentioning the booksellers and traders at work in Jimbōchō and at assorted *furuhon'ya* and temple fairs across Tokyo, which so often supplied unexpected materials and made visible unanticipated connections.

My most heartfelt thanks go to the many friends, colleagues, and comrades who were available for conversation, questions, reading drafts, drinking drafts, and solidarity in all forms at all hours of the day and night across many years, including Dan Abbe, Ariel Acosta, Ramona Bajema, Adam Bronson, BuYun Chen, Anatoly Detwyler, Chad Diehl, Pau Pitarch Fernandez, Tom Gaubatz, Gal Gvili, Phil Kaffen, Andy Liu, Nan Ma Hartmann, Brian Hurley, Andrew Leong, Hiroaki Matsusaka, Jenny Wang Medina, Pat Noonan, Greg Patterson, Daniel Poch, Franz Prichard, Chelsea Szendi Scheider, Miryong Shim, Seiji Shirane, Ariel Stilerman, Myra Sun, Christophe Thouny, Takuya Tsunoda, Max Ward, Tim Yang, Anri Yasuda, Christina Yi, Hitomi Yoshio, Yurou Zhong, and many others whom I am sure to be inadvertently forgetting to list but who know who they are.

When I first began teaching at Bard College, I could not have imagined how incredibly lucky I would be to have such a wide community of brilliant colleagues that make it such an exciting and enjoyable place to work. My understanding of my own work has expanded immeasurably through the opportunity to work with scholars in such a wide variety of disciplines. The colleagues to thank here are perhaps too many to list but include Alex

Benson, Nicole Caso, Ben Coonley, Maria Cecire, Christian Crouch, Rob Culp, Deirdre d'Albertis, Richard Davis, Adhaar Desai, Miriam Felton-Dansky, Alex Kitnick, Peter Klein, Marisa Libbon, Patricia Lopez-Gay, Allison McKim, Susan Merriam, Amir Moosavi, Keith O'Hara, Gabriel Perron, Dina Ramadan, Miles Rodriguez, Wakako Suzuki, Yuka Suzuki, Drew Thompson, Dominique Townsend, Eric Trudel, Olga Voronina, Robert Weston, Thomas Wild, Tom Wolf, Marina van Zuylen, Li-hua Ying, and most especially Mika Endo for our years working together.

Before any of this, as an undergraduate at Stanford, Yoshiko Matsumoto, Adrienne Hurley, Jim Reichert, and Steven Carter inspired me to pursue a career in the study of Japanese literature. Sincere thanks is also due to all the faculty and staff in the Japanese language program at Stanford; now that I teach the language myself, I have a newfound appreciation for their work that made it possible for me to do my own. Jim Fujita taught me my first words of Japanese, and it thus no exaggeration to say that his teaching changed the course of my life for the better. In Kyoto, Ueda Haruka continues to be a source of conversation and friendship; I feel privileged to have inherited her family's vintage edition of the *Sōseki Zenshū*. I also want to acknowledge the lasting hospitality of the Shima, Kosugi, and Matsukura families, through whom I learned Japanese of a different kind. In Shinjuku, I am thankful for the many late-night interlocutions with Kotetsu, Eri, Kazue, Asami, Toba-san, and most of all the dear departed Yōko, which helped keep the world outside the archive in perspective.

Elsewhere beyond the academy, special thanks go to Ryan Sands, Jessica Flores, Leopold Lambert, Hiroko Nakatani, Aram Kim, Erin Chun, Roxann Stafford, Roopa Mahadevan, and Ming Wong for their everlasting and ongoing friendship. The memory of Eric Larose lives on in spirit and conscience.

Having completed a book about the important work of editors and publishers, I feel incredibly lucky to have worked with my amazing editor Christine Dunbar at Columbia University Press, who deserves many thanks for her work both on this project and toward opening exciting new scholarly horizons in the study of East Asian literatures more broadly. I also would like to thank Leslie Kriesel, Christian Winting, and the rest of the staff at the press who took part in the formatting, layout, and design processes that give this book its materiality. I am also sincerely grateful for the penetrating and helpful comments of the anonymous reviewers, whose feedback doubtlessly improved the manuscript. This book has been the beneficiary of the support of the Weatherhead East Asian Institute, whose decision to take on the project helped it definitively toward completion. I extend my thanks in particular to Ross Yelsey for his incomparable support in shepherding the book toward publication.

A special thanks goes to Jillian Tamaki, who graciously permitted me to use a page of her work as this book's concluding image, one which so perfectly captures its theme. A portion of chapter 5 has previously appeared in print as "Toward a New Word Order: Early 20th-Century Orthographic Reform and Its Discontents" in the journal *Japanese Language and Literature*.

Finally, and most deeply of all, I would like to thank my family, in every sense. I am lucky enough to come from a large and close extended clan who have always been incomparably supportive; to list them all would put me well beyond any reasonable word count for these acknowledgments. This book is dedicated to the three most important women in my life who are my past, present, and future—to the memory of my mother, Erie Arbisser Shockey, to my wife, Felicia, and to our daughter, Mira, who was born into the world along with this book.

A NOTE ON ROMANIZATION AND TRANSLATION

The romanization of Japanese script in this book generally follows the Modified Hepburn convention, which I employ in transliteration and citation. In some cases, alternative romanization schema and script systems are used, such as the array of conventions referred to under the name of *Nihon-shiki rōmaji*, or "Japanese-style roman script." Idiosyncratic variations in otherwise standardized conventions also occur. These alternative conventions appear frequently in chapter 5, which considers the unfixed quality and contestation of romanization and orthographic approaches in early twentieth-century Japan. In all such cases, I have reproduced the romanization exactly as it appears in the relevant original texts when it deviates from contemporary common usage. Unless otherwise indicated, all translations from Japanese are my own.

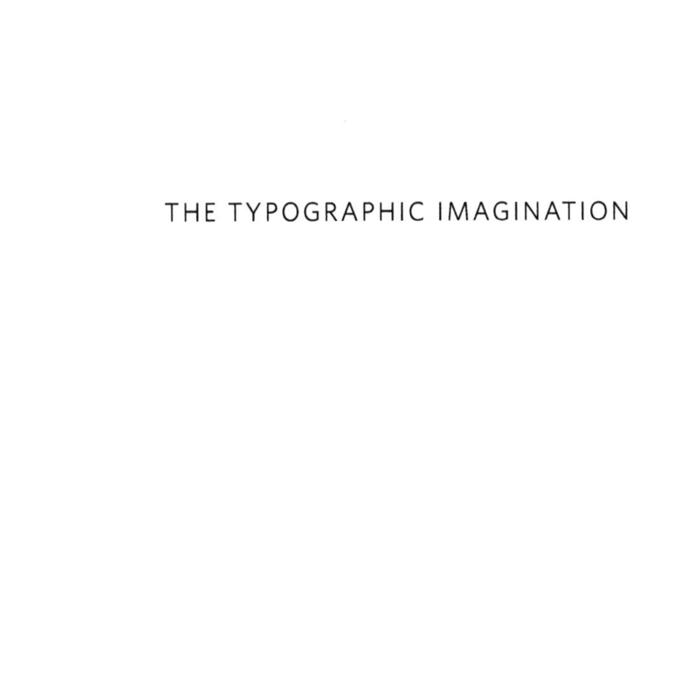

THE TYPOGRAPHIC IMAGINATION

INTRODUCTION

The World Made Type

A book is a machine to think with, but it need not, therefore, usurp the function either of the bellows or the locomotive.

—I. A. RICHARDS, *PRINCIPLES OF LITERARY CRITICISM*[1]

One day in August 1915, when he was not quite fifteen years old, Ōya Sōichi (1900–1970) wrote in his diary that he took a break from brewing soy sauce on his family farm outside Osaka to read some magazines. A few days later, he came home from a long day at work in the potato fields to lie under the electric light and quietly pass the time flipping through books, magazines, and a modern edition of the *Kokinshū* (*Collection of Ancient and Modern Poems*), a tenth-century anthology of classical Japanese verse. After school, where he studied English and Chinese as well as Japanese, Ōya would stop by the library to browse photographic gazetteers, then spend the afternoon reading more newspapers and magazines before his evening bath.[2]

The scene of a teenage boy in the suburbs lolling around and reading after his daily chores may seem entirely unremarkable; its interest lies precisely in how unremarkable it is. Ōya, who would grow up to become an important cultural critic, belonged to the first generation of modern Japanese readers to come of age in a world where cheap typographic print media was a normal and naturalized part of everyday life. Much about Ōya's habit of quietly reading after tending the eggplants was in fact quite new; several decades earlier, far fewer books and magazines were accessible and affordable to provincial students, and the act of reading was likely to have involved voicing the text aloud in a group setting. Books might have been string bound, woodblock printed, and borrowed from an itinerant book peddler rather than purchased for a few coins at the local shop by the train station.[3] For Ōya, books and magazines were exciting new forms of media, but they were also always already there, cheap, and available. On another day in August 1915, Ōya walked into a bookstore:

> In the evening, I went on an errand to Ibaraki, and on the way back I stopped off at Toratani bookstore to buy a map. The new magazines had arrived. I calmed the excitement in my pounding chest and swiped a copy of *Shōnen Sekai*. Without pausing to look at the beautiful frontispiece or read the no-doubt-interesting articles, I flipped through the pages until my eyes landed on the submission section. Heaven and earth fell away. I looked at the next page and joyfully saw my name and the name of my story . . . My heart began pounding even harder . . . My name was in type [*katsuji to natte*].[4]

Ōya learned to write from what he read, practicing his vernacular prose by mimicking the style in popular periodicals. Like the other boys and girls his age who would go on to become the renowned authors, critics, and artists of twentieth-century Japan, Ōya was raised on a diet of cheap magazines and books—the same media that he and his generation would use to transform their minds, their language, their writing, and their world. At this moment, Ōya saw for the first time his name inscribed and reflected in the typographic print that shaped that world. When he and all those other readers and writers opened a book or magazine to find themselves shaped by print, what did they see?

This book explores the habituation of modern forms of reading and writing in Japan from the last years of the nineteenth century through the first decades of the twentieth as the rapid growth of the typographic publishing industry made mass-produced print media an inexorable part of everyday life. In this period, industrially produced print achieved the status of a practically ubiquitous medium for all manner of literary, cultural, and social discourse. The same period saw the rise of new types of visual and auditory media, the integration of Japanese thought into global intellectual currents, the emergence of new styles of prose writing, the restructuring of literary and philosophical canons, extended debates over script and language reform, the rise of radical political movements, and the popularization of social thought. This book argues that this new media ecology precipitated a consciousness of the typographic text as a material medium and economic artifice with the power to critique and remake the modern world. Mass-produced books and magazines, the texts they contained, and the discourses that they generated through their circulation came to be staple commodities for modern life. As Japanese citizens were, to borrow the words of Friedrich Kittler, "engulfed in paper," and as reading and writing became "common property," authors, critics, publishers, politicians, linguists, scientists, activists, and others became deeply interested in the ontological status of typographic text and its functions as a technology with the ability to affect the material and social realms.[5] Rather than render vernacular language somehow immediate, transparent, or invisible, this typographic transition generated an array of attitudes concerned with the materiality and mediality of printed writing. The medium of mass-produced type produced a generation of intellectuals who understood their subjectivity to be constructed through the circulation of printed language and thus took typographic print as a powerful heuristic means and method for their efforts to reconstruct the modern world, regardless of ideological orientation. I call this consciousness the typographic imagination. Just as type was an inexorably physical medium for discourse, these writers assayed the power of print never as merely conceptual but always also as a practical and economic matter inextricably linked to the realities of the commercial market.

This reconstruction of reading, writing, and thinking began as Japan expanded its empire via military victories over first Qing China (1894–1895) then Russia (1904–1905), spurring domestic industrial and financial booms. The rise of typographic print culture was intimately integrated into imperial Japan's burgeoning consumer economy, and writers and publishers understood that any form of literary, linguistic, or intellectual experimentation was necessarily carried out in negotiation with the marketplace. In 1894, just at the cusp of Japan's publishing boom, the young critic Uchida Roan (1868–1929) presciently and humorously sketched the position of the would-be writer within the emergent modern publishing industry in his parodical masterpiece *Bungakusha to Naru Hō* (How to Become a Literatus). His style is informed by Edo-era satire but perfectly captures how the modern reader and writer situate themselves vis-à-vis the world of commercial print:

> Before becoming a literatus [*bungakusha*], one must be an observer and connoisseur [*tsū*] of the literary realm [*bungakukai*] . . . For newspapers, the connoisseur takes the *Kokumin*, *Yomiuri*, and *Asahi* . . . For magazines, he must read *Kokumin no Tomo*, *Jogaku Zasshi*, *Waseda Bungaku*, *Sanrai*, *Bungakkai*, and *Shigarami Zōshi*. Strictly speaking, he does not have to actually read these magazines—it is more than enough to simply look at the advertisements and the table of contents . . . The best way to tell who is important is by the font size in which names appear in advertisements . . . One must not shirk reading newspapers and magazines. No matter how boring they are—and of course they are boring—one must endure that boredom as the ascetic discipline of the literary connoisseur . . . One should look carefully at the covers of all the new releases from the publishers Shun'yōdō and Hakubunkan on the bookstore racks . . . The best way to learn what fiction [*shōsetsu*] is any good, which magazines sell, and other such matters of present-day literary reputation is to learn from the booksellers.[6]

In the age of mass media, Roan's aspiring writer begins by performing readership through savvy consumer behavior. In his satirical vision, to know the literary realm is less to understand its content in any critical sense than to grasp the business of literature in the age of modern advertising by purchasing the latest releases from the right publishers. This would-be man of culture lives fully immersed in the world of modern print media as he seeks to make the transition from reader to writer and become part of the literary industry himself. Roan's cynical sketch vividly limns the contours of modern Japanese literature's discursive field through the circulation of magazines, newspapers, and cheap mass-produced books.

PRINT MEDIA AS STAPLE COMMODITY

As different forms of typographic text transitioned from new to normalized, commercialized, and ubiquitous media for discourse, we see a consciousness toward mass-produced type as a material artifice able to span, link, and transform diverse ideologies and modes of expression. Authors, readers, intellectuals, and activists imbued mass-produced printed type with great potential for linguistic, literary, philosophical, and social change, from the advertising of paperback books as bearers of transcendental knowledge, to the role of typesetters in fomenting international revolution, to the remaking of the Japanese written language itself. *The Typographic*

Imagination asks, how did writers and readers understand the nature and power of new media like modern books and magazines? How did they perceive the ways in which their own senses of self, language, and society transformed in tandem with the usage of these media? In seeking to answer these questions, this study considers each of book historians Thomas Adams's and Nicholas Barker's schema of events in the life of books—publishing, manufacture, distribution, reception, and survival—but at the core of my analysis is less the books themselves than the circumstances of their use and the accompanying reimaginations of reading, writing, knowledge, and mass culture. I likewise find it helpful to complicate Robert Darnton's classic model of the communications circuit of author, publisher, printer, shipper, bookseller, and reader. In early twentieth-century Japanese publishing, we see not a one-way trajectory from author as producer to reader as consumer but myriad ways that the circuits between these stages intersect, loop back, disconnect, and reconnect as the topography of the publishing world was reconstructed via forces of industrialization and commercialization. This book examines the productive and generative roles of printers, publishers, editors, archivists, advertisers, agents, copywriters, typesetters, collectors, booksellers, and others in this epochal shift in the history of Japanese media and mass culture. Here, the concept of "the book," bearing the definite article, cannot encompass the diversity of simultaneously circulating forms of print in this period, including string-bound woodblock-printed volumes, paraffin-wrapped pocket paperbacks, sumptuously jacketed hardcovers, thousand-page compendia, newspapers, illustrated commercial photography magazines, coterie journals, political pamphlets, mimeographed handbills, strike bulletins, advertising circulars, catalogs, archival indexes, and more. Further, the uses of these bibliographic documents were by no means limited to reading as such; they produced meaning as they circulated—as they were printed, advertised, sold, displayed, traded, stored, indexed, and even as they were destroyed and forgotten.[7]

I believe that we can and should think of modern Japanese mass-produced typographic print as a kind of staple commodity, the wide circulation and everyday usage of which rewrote the horizons of social discourse. I draw these concepts of staple medium and circulation from the work of Harold Adams Innis (1894–1952), the proto–media historian and colleague of Marshall McLuhan (1911–1980) at the University of Toronto. An economic historian by training, Innis spent the first part of his career tracing how the needs for staple commodities such as codfish, beaver pelts, and coal structured the expansion of the British Empire in Canada along networks of waterways and railroad lines.[8] In his final years, Innis pivoted to study the role of communications media across the history of civilization in two seminal works, *Empire and Communications* (1950) and *The Bias of Communication* (1951), in which he traced a narrative from Sumerian cuneiform clay tablets through papyrus, parchment, the codex, and the typographic printing press to explore "the implications of the media of communication for the character of knowledge."[9] Implicit in Innis's pivot, and central here, is the reimagination of the medium of communication as a staple commodity—a crucial product for both trade and everyday subsistence—a category expanded to encompass not just wheat, fish, or firs but also paper, printed text, and information.

The quality of a medium as a staple is not located solely in the material strata of the technology of inscription and the inscribed surface, such as stone, chisels, parchment, pens—or in the case of early twentieth-century Japan typographic print on wood-pulp paper—but also includes the content of that medium. In *The Gutenberg Galaxy*, McLuhan considers how the naturalization of typographic text as a ubiquitous commodity constitutes a new horizon of shared social life: "Typography is not only a technology but is in itself a natural resource or a staple, like cotton or timber or radio, and like any staple, it shapes not only private sense ratios but also patterns of communal interdependence . . . Print was in itself a commodity, a new natural resource which also showed us how to tap all other kinds of resources, including ourselves."[10] In the present study, the relevant staple commodities are not just the books and magazines proliferating across Japan but also the historical form of the Japanese script and the literary and cultural discourses that circulated in tandem as new necessities for modern literates. Per Innis and McLuhan, the forms and technologies of media through which people read, write, communicate, and think have a profound effect on the structures of consciousness and patterns of social organization and cultural expression. Staple media—here modern Japanese mass-produced typographic books and magazines—do not exist in a vacuum but are integrated into larger circuits of trade, culture, commerce, and capitalist exchange. It is thus crucial to analyze the complex sets of institutions, economic systems, and discursive paradigms within which those media move and function and which are in turn constituted by the movement of those media.

In the late nineteenth century, Japan was in transition neither from an oral to a literate society nor from scriptural culture to print culture but from one regime of print culture to another, as the Edo-era xylographic economy gave way to new structures of publishing and written expression with their own distinct patterns for the production, circulation, and consumption of text. Innis's approach, in which the material properties of a medium map to a set social structure, teeters on the edge of technological determinism, a specter that has haunted the study of print media at least since Elizabeth Eisenstein's *The Printing Press as an Agent of Change* (1980). It is possible to take seriously Eisenstein's suggestion that "changes in book format might well lead to changes in thought patterns" while understanding that process dialectically, with those changes in format and production themselves emerging through a nexus of material and social factors.[11] As per book historian Adrian Johns, "a large number of people, machines, and materials must converge and act together for [a book] to come into existence."[12] The stories of print's impact on society and society's impact on print are by no means mutually exclusive, and the history of typography in Japan is particularly well suited to dispel the shibboleth of technological determinism. Typographic print had arrived in Japan twice prior to the nineteenth century but with relatively small effect on literature, thought, and society at large. In the early 1590s, Portuguese Jesuits imported printing presses from Europe to outposts in Amakusa and Nagasaki, and in 1592 the warlord Toyotomi Hideyoshi (1537–1598) brought back sets of copper type from his invasion of Korea.[13] In these instances, typographic technology was never successfully integrated into the early modern Japanese publishing industry and did not become the basis for an ongoing print culture distinct from the xylographic regime. It follows that we must consider the media in question within a broader historical context that then becomes much more than context, following Roger Chartier's reminder that "reading is not uniquely an abstract operation of the intellect" but rather "is always a practice embodied in acts, spaces, and habits," as well as, I would add, historically specific economic systems.[14]

PRESS, STATE, EMPIRE, WORLD

In his work on the early history of writing, Innis describes how Athenian society's adoption of the alphabet came hand in hand with urbanization, the standardization of writing conventions, and the "rapid expansion in the variety and volume" of books. Likewise, in the decades after Gutenberg, Europe saw the rise of "smaller portable volumes," an increased popularity of vernacular literature, and "the mobilization of a market for a commodity which could be adapted to a variety of consumers."[15] We can witness all these phenomena at play in Japan around the turn of the twentieth century. Such parallels to Japan's modern print revolution can be found not just elsewhere in time but also in other parts of the world at a roughly contemporaneous moment. In mid-nineteenth-century Britain, as in Meiji Japan, books were expensive, but technological advancements in periodical publishing facilitated a boom in magazine publishing and the serialization of literary works for a common audience. In England and Japan alike, the 1880s and 1890s saw the expansion of a discursive system increasingly centered around mass-produced magazines as affordable commodities and important components of everyday life.[16] Meanwhile, in neighboring China there were active centers of commercial publishing such as Sibao in Fujian Province as well as a robust system of circulation across the southern mainland, albeit one still based upon xylographic woodblock printing.[17]

Perhaps the most salient locus of comparison is Germany, where educational reform, state support of publishers, and the industrialization of a craft-based bookmaking system into a factory process were tied to tremendous growth in literacy, reading, and bookselling across the latter part of the nineteenth century. The modern Japanese pedagogical system was explicitly modeled on the German one, and German publishers were important antecedents to Japanese bookmakers in promoting a culture of widespread reading for education, entertainment, and self-cultivation.[18] The place of publishing in Enlightenment Europe, and the age of German Romanticism in particular, shone like a beacon for Japanese publishers and critics, some of whom self-consciously understood their work in historical parallel. In other aspects, the history of print in Japan ran ahead of, rather than behind, the curve of foreign nations—Japan's cheap paperback revolution, modeled on German publisher Reclam's *Universal-Bibliothek*, began in 1927 with Iwanami's *bunkobon*, while Britain's Penguin paperback series only began in 1935, and the paperback phenomenon in the United States was largely a postwar phenomenon.

In 1894 and 1895, Japan fought its first modern international war against Qing China, marking a moment transformative for both the expansion of the empire and the power of print in public life. Compared with Innis's interest in the role of media in the rise and fall of empires, *The Typographic Imagination* is less explicitly concerned with questions of imperialism. Yet imperialism hangs on the margins and hums in the background throughout this period in which Japan's empire and ambitions expanded in tandem with the growth of the print industry. The Japanese newspaper industry developed rapidly throughout the 1870s and 1880s, during which many papers were closely linked to political parties and various organs of the state bureaucracy. The press played a role in fomenting public support for the First Sino-Japanese War, and a dramatic expansion of the market for Japanese typographic print unfolded with that war. A new generation of magazines, beginning with the photographic gazetteer *Nisshin Sensō Jikki* (Record of the Sino-Japanese War, 1894–1896), produced an intense desire for battle coverage. New media technologies such as telegraphy, photography, and industrial printing were internal and necessary to the war effort, both as it was fought and as it was perceived on the home front as a media event in the mass mind. Alongside this modern war-media complex, we see the reproduction of discourse in print at a previously unthinkable scale as the wartime readership explosion provided a capital injection that funded a new generation of commercial literary and intellectual magazines.

The first chapter of this book considers the dialectical complexities at play between the growth of the industrial print realm, the expansion of the Japanese empire, and the reorientation of the senses in the reading process. In the chapters that follow, the question of empire features less overtly; I hope that the reader will understand this not as an omission but as an acknowledgment that Japan's imperial economy structurally but sometimes invisibly underwrote the possibility of publication and cultural production on a mass scale. Beginning in the late 1870s, the Meiji state actively supported (sometimes overtly, sometimes not) the development of the publishing industry as an organ of modern social life and national consciousness, despite the sometimes oppositional stance of the press and the government.[19] An ongoing encouragement to literacy via a nationalized education system and textbook program, along with protracted attempts to standardize spelling and writing conventions, helped create the conditions of possibility for mass-produced print as a ubiquitous medium. In turn, the government saw in privately published newspapers, magazines, and books the means by which to execute state goals of universal literacy and regular reading by national subjects.

The linkages between the publishing realm and the imperial state were intertwined at the most practical and material levels: the lion's share of the nation's paper supply was produced by the Ōji Paper Company (Ōji Seishi), which maintained acres of forests under government contract in the colonies of Sakhalin and Korea that were harvested for pulp to print millions of books and magazines in the metropole.[20] The relationship between the state and the publishing industry was in some ways structural and productive, thanks to patronage by bureaucratic functionaries and political parties as well as linkages between government organs, editorial rooms, and publisher's offices. As scholars like Yamamoto Taketoshi, Kōno Kensuke, James Huffman, and Jay Rubin have demonstrated, it was the state bureaucracy and the Home Ministry that established the boundaries within which an ostensibly free publishing sphere could thrive, boundaries limned by the ever-present, if often implicit, threat of censorship.[21]

The ways in which the private publishing industry and the state were interlaced appear intermittently throughout *The Typographic Imagination*; my hope is that these instances evoke a set of multivalent interrelations between readers, publishers, and various manifestations of governmental power. Viewed positively, the state encouraged the development of literacy through standardized textbook contracts; made postal allowances for the cheap shipping of print and thus its availability via local booksellers and mail-order services; supported the development of libraries and schools to institutionalize reading practices across all classes and regions; encouraged publishers to sell magazines supplementing official education policy; promoted bibliographic exhibitions and archival practices to craft a history of Japanese print; and worked with writers and scholars to institute modern linguistic and orthographic policies. At the same time, the state's attitude toward the publishing industry and an ideologically diverse reading public could be pernicious: works considered politically problematic were censored or banned from publication; socialist texts were suppressed while publications espousing a moralistic and imperialist vision of mass culture were promoted; political and linguistic movements misaligned with the state's ideological orientation were surveilled at large; left-wing and proletarian authors and critics were jailed, sometimes tortured, and even killed; and strikes demanding labor rights at printers and publishers were crushed.

These specters of oppressive political currents flicker throughout both the period and the book, never too far distant. We know with the hindsight of history that Japan's mass society would be mobilized in the service of ultranationalism and totalitarian war in the late 1930s and early 1940s, but for those living through this earlier period the future was still very much unwritten. The first decades of the twentieth century were characterized by competing functions and futures for print in modern Japan. As these new media helped structure the self-conscious subjectivity of the Japanese reading masses, the fall toward fascism was only one of several possible futures, albeit the one that ultimately and tragically came to pass.

THE XYLOGRAPHIC CONFIGURATION

The history of print in Japan is remarkable in that a highly developed system of early modern print culture existed prior to and largely distinct from the popularization of typography and industrial printing in the late nineteenth century. This historical circumstance makes it all the more important to understand the functions of print media within broad circuits of cultural, economic, and discursive contexts. Beginning in the early 1600s, the commercialization of woodblock printing (xylography) gave rise to a robust, diverse, and dynamic urban print culture.[22] Around the turn of the seventeenth century, xylography moved out from under the eaves of sutra-printing Buddhist temple complexes to the milieu of urban commoners, in what Konta Yōzō and others have described as a transition from printing (*insatsu*) to publishing (*shuppan*), in the sense of making public for a commercial audience.[23] The Japanese publishing industry was originally concentrated in Osaka and Kyoto, where houses like Hachimonjiya helped precipitate an explosion of styles and formats of books and a diverse range of literary genres and themes, before shifting toward the metropolis of Edo around the Genroku period (1688–1704).[24] As Peter Kornicki, Haruo Shirane, Elizabeth Berry, and others have shown, the publishing trade in the Edo period was characterized by advanced forms of early modern capitalism and commercialism, whereby printing houses utilized complex marketing strategies to advertise books via signs, flyers, performances, handbills, and other types of printed visual media. Urban Japan in the early modern period was very much a world richly saturated with all manner of print, including illustrated books, calendars, maps, guides, almanacs, and more.[25] The form and content of literary expression were closely linked to different book formats and genres as authors and publishers crafted works for a wide readership, all while highly self-conscious of the economics of the print business.

The line dividing the early modern xylographic publishing regime and the typographic industry that would emerge in the late nineteenth century is far from neat, but the two systems were significantly distinct in their patterns of production, circulation, and consumption. Under the woodblock-print system, the production and sale of books were intimately intermingled under the auspices of firms that vertically controlled the process, from the writing and copying of manuscripts, through the carving of the text and illustrations onto blocks, to the advertising and distribution of the finished volumes. Beginning in the early eighteenth century, publishers were organized under guilds called *toiya nakama*, which controlled production, mediated between bookmakers and the government, and managed publication rights.[26] Starting in the late seventeenth century, itinerant book lenders called *kashihon'ya* served as the primary vectors for the circulation of books by renting out releases for a small fee, as purchasing a book was quite expensive. This complex, artisan-based system of early modern xylographic bookmaking engendered a broad commoner readership but did not allow for production on a truly mass scale. By the early nineteenth century, although some exceptionally popular works like Ryūtei Tanehiko's (1783–1842) *Nise Murasaki Inaka Genji* (A Fraudulent Murasaki's Bumpkin *Genji*, 1829–1842) sold more than ten thousand copies, a thousand copies sold was considered worthy of celebration in the teahouses of the Yoshiwara licensed quarter.[27] But texts reached a far wider readership than that belied by the low circulation numbers, as *kashihon'ya* lent their books out countless times, and readers who borrowed from them did not read solo and silently but often aloud to groups of families and friends. Edo alone boasted eight hundred book lenders with ten thousand subscribers, and a robust distribution network allowed books to travel from the publishing centers in the downtown Nihonbashi and Kyōbashi districts to Kyoto, Osaka, and castle towns across early modern Japan's feudal domains.[28]

Typography arrived on Japan's shores twice prior to the industrial age, in distinct but contemporaneous circumstances just before the start of the Edo era and the institutionalization of commercial woodblock publishing. In the 1590s, Jesuit missionaries from Portugal printed Christian texts in Latin and roman-script transliterations of classics like the thirteenth-century *Heike Monogatari* (*Tales of the Heike*), as well as cut Japanese type resembling handwritten script for translations of works like *Aesop's Fables* (as *Isoho Monogatari*, 1593).[29] The Jesuits printed about one hundred different books between 1590 and 1614, now known as Christian editions (*kirishitan-ban*), but most were lost or burned following Tokugawa Ieyasu's suppression of Christianity. In 1592, Toyotomi Hideyoshi returned from his invasion of Korea; one of the spoils of war was cut typography like that used for court documents in Korea since the late fourteenth century.[30] The shogun Ieyasu became smitten with typographic printing and commissioned the production of several sets of type, the basis for editions later known as Fushimi-ban and Suruga-ban, named for the locations of their production. About one hundred thousand pieces of type were produced in Fushimi between 1599 and 1606 and were used primarily to print records, historical documents, and Confucian writings. It is unclear if Ieyasu read the books himself or just saw their creation as the symbolic duty of a ruler and an expression of political authority, as per his formal presentation of a set of copper type to the emperor.[31] Aesthetically accomplished early seventeenth-century typographic publications of classics like *Tsurezuregusa* (*Essays in Idleness*, 1329–1333), *Ise Monogatari* (*Tales of Ise*, ca. 947), and the *Hōjōki* (*Account of a Ten-Foot-Square Hut*, 1212), known as Sagabon, informed the production of later xylographic editions of the same, but typography remained a historical curiosity until the mid-nineteenth century, as it was expensive and ill-suited to the production of the illustrated genres and running script that remained popular throughout the early modern period.

A NEXUS OF NEW NETWORKS FOR READING

Aside from assorted experiments in the 1850s, the father of modern typography in Japan is generally considered to be Motoki Shōzō (1824–1875), who worked as a translator of Dutch in Nagasaki before importing printing tools from Europe and developing type-cutting and foundry techniques.[32] With the guidance of William Gamble (1830–1886), who had modernized electrotyping for Chinese characters as a missionary in Shanghai, Motoki succeeded in his quest in 1869, making the era of modern Japanese typography nearly concomitant with the history of the Japanese nation-state following the Meiji Restoration of 1868.[33] In the early 1870s, Motoki standardized and industrialized his process, eventually setting up the Tsukiji Type Foundry (Tsukiji Kappan Seizōsho) not far from the active locus of xylographic printing in Nihonbashi, where he taught the technology to others and took on jobs printing the first generation of modern Japanese newspapers.

Yet we should resist the temptation of neatly bifurcating the early modern xylographic era from the typographic modern, as the transition between the two was complex. Woodblock printing and its associated systems of circulation and reading practices continued well into the Meiji period; Itakura Masanobu estimates that it was not until the mid-1880s that type surpassed woodblock printing in volume, and traditionally printed and bound books continued to circulate well beyond that.[34] The uneven transition between the two print regimes is exemplified in the history of one of the great best sellers of the early Meiji period, Fukuzawa Yukichi's (1834–1901) *Gakumon no Susume* (*An Encouragement of Learning*), a series of seventeen pamphlets outlining the roles of education in modern civilization, released between 1872 and 1876.[35] The first pressing of the first pamphlet was printed with metal type that Fukuzawa had purchased from Motoki for his press at the Keiō Institute school in February 1872, but demand quickly outstripped the press's ability to print, so a woodblock edition was published in June the same year. The second and third pamphlets were pressed on woodblock, while the fourth and fifth saw a switch back to type. The sixth and seventh pamphlets were released in both type and woodblock editions to maximize the print run, while the tenth pamphlet was printed in woodblock only. The eleventh pamphlet was type only, while the twelfth through sixteenth were woodblock only, and the concluding volume was type only. Xylographic printing was still faster and was used to help stave off piracy, which was by all accounts rampant—an estimated two hundred twenty thousand copies of the first pamphlet were sold, only a portion of which were printed by Fukuzawa at Keiō.[36] This iconic work of modern enlightenment thought thus shuttled back and forth multiple times between old and new publishing systems and distribution channels.

Fukuzawa identified efficient reading as a crucial need for modern subjects in the first pages of his pamphlet: "We should put aside impractical scholarship [*jitsu naki gakumon*] and instead promote practical learning [*jitsugaku*] with value for everyday human needs. One should learn, for example, the forty-seven-unit *iroha* kana syllabary, how to write correspondence, handle accounting and the abacus, weights and measures—these are the crucial principles to study."[37] Fukuzawa deemed scriptural literacy a necessity for human affairs and sought to move reading pedagogy away from recitation and toward reading as an integral ability to advance knowledge and the development of modern self and society. Fukuzawa, who later founded the popular *Jiji Shinpō* (News of the Times, 1882–1936) newspaper, saw the promulgation of literacy as indispensable in the creation of a public and promoted print media as a key technology for making sense of and remaking the modern world.[38]

The 1870s and early 1880s saw the establishment of a newspaper industry that was increasingly independent, if never fully distinct from bureaucratic and party interests, as broadsheets transformed into commercial dailies, beginning with the *Yokohama Mainichi Shinbun* (Yokohama Daily, 1871–1879); some of these, such as the *Yūbin Hōchi Shinbun* (Postal Report, 1872–1894) and the *Tōkyō Nichinichi Shinbun* (Tokyo Daily, 1872–1942), found it more efficient to use xylographic printing before switching to first wood then metal type in the mid-1870s.[39] By the late 1870s, newspaper circulations were in the millions, and diverse, independent content paved the way for commercial papers like the *Kokumin Shinbun* (The Nation's News, 1890–1942) and *Yorozu Chōhō* (Morning Report, 1892–1940), which built a middle- and working-class readership.[40]

This same period saw the restructuring of the distribution networks by which print reached readers. *Kashihon'ya* lenders were active into the final decades of the nineteenth century but changed their model from itinerant vendors of woodblock books to fixed rental shops and mail-order businesses for readers to borrow books and magazines.[41] The *kashihon'ya* network would soon be replaced with a modern postal distribution system based on the new national railway system; trains were supplemented by horses, carriages, rickshaws, boats, and later cars and trucks to move across every corner of the country.[42] The national postal service, headed by Maejima Hisoka (1835–1919), who studied shipping, weights, and measures in the United States and Europe, facilitated the spread of print media by fixing a special discount rate for newspapers and magazines. At the same time, undersea telegraph lines integrated Japan into broader global information circuits.[43]

On the production end, printing, publishing, and binding processes were separated out into individual businesses, and the last of the Edo-era *nakama* guilds dissolved to be replaced by modern corporate concerns. Major distribution conglomerates (*toritsugiten* or *urisabakiten*) such as Tōkyōdō constituted new circulation networks whereby books and magazines were sent from the printing nexus in central Tokyo to regional distribution centers, then to individual bookstores in nearly every town.[44] The spread of printing techniques beyond the old industry center of downtown Tokyo, as well as the advancement of machine technologies likes rotary and offset presses, allowed for increased competition and a rapid drop in the price of printing costs in the 1880s.[45] Trade magazines like *Insatsu Zasshi* (Printers Magazine, 1891–present) shared strategies for typesetting, mediated professional knowledge of new technologies, and introduced scholarship on the history of print from Asia and Europe.[46]

The other key factor in the formation of this new regime of typographic publishing and its associated readership was the establishment of a modern educational system. Through the Edo period and into the early Meiji era, the primary sites of formal pedagogy were *terakoya* (so-called temple schools), which focused on recitation, memorization, and the Chinese classics. The Ministry of Education, founded in 1871, aimed to eliminate illiteracy and founded twenty thousand primary schools in the following decade.[47] The new school system eschewed Sinitically focused methods and traditional *ōraimono* primers in favor of modern textbooks printed by private firms under government contract. As school attendance grew in the 1880s, textbooks became important commodities contracted and sold on the order of hundreds of thousands of copies, with sales further spurred by the 1890 Imperial Rescript on Education (*Kyōiku Chokugo*). In the years following, the government worked together with private textbook publishers to create the first true mass-produced books of the modern era. The transition from woodblock to machine-type printing and the advent of domestically produced Western-style paper led to fervent competition between publishers.[48] The circulation of textbooks as market commodities played a crucial role in institutionalizing modern bookselling networks, before graft and scandal led to regulation and the establishment of the national standardized textbook (*kokutei kyōkasho*) system in 1903–1904.[49]

A turning point for both Japan's imperial ambitions and the growth of a broad national readership was the war against Qing China in 1894 and 1895. The typographic print publishing complex was an essential part of the war itself, with newspapers inciting prowar sentiment and magazines heralding new techniques and technologies of representation through which metropolitan readers perceived the conflict. The war was a media event, and the public's new need for news, text, and images was created through the expanded circulation of print, which in turn propelled subscriber and readership numbers ever higher. According to Nagamine Shigetoshi, in 1889 the total annual circulation of newspapers and magazines was about 27 million copies, with about 2 million books printed. By 1896, following the end of the war, that number had increased to 86 million periodicals and 6.6 million books; in 1911, periodical circulation was 192 million copies per annum with 46 million books printed, an increase by a multiple of more than twenty in about as many years.[50] This publishing boom also constituted a sense of shared simultaneity between Japanese domestic discourse and global intellectual currents. Starting in the late 1890s, we see Japanese literary, critical, and social writing become ever more integrated into a modern world discursive system same as news wire services and the translation of foreign ideas in popular magazines allowed for a temporal congruency of thought and experience between Japan, the United States, and western Europe. In sum, the coterminous development of printing technology, industrial publishing economics, transportation infrastructure, corporate distribution networks, and pedagogical institutions constituted a nexus for the circulation of typographic print media at a mass scale by the early 1890s and laid the groundwork for the rapid expansion of print culture in the years to follow. This is the moment at which our story begins.

Over the past decade or two, the importance of print media in Japanese literary history has become a topic of lasting academic interest. In English, books such as Seth Jacobowitz's *Writing Technology in Meiji Japan*, Edward Mack's *Manufacturing Modern Japanese Literature*, and Sarah Frederick's *Turning Pages* have explored the functions of print capitalism in the birth of modern Japanese literature. Jacobowitz's book is a sweeping study of the intersections of technological and ideological networks in the transformation of modern writing practices; Mack's work probes the business of publishing, printing technologies, and the interlocking systems of literary and economic value in the early twentieth century; Frederick gives critical attention to magazine readers, editors, and advertisers as constitutive forces in the expansion of discursive horizons for fiction and criticism. *The Typographic Imagination* posits that modern Japanese intellectuals and the mass public alike came to reflexively understand their subjectivity as constituted through the commodification and circulation of typographic media. By demonstrating the connection between print as a staple commodity and the rise of a materialist consciousness of language, this book makes evident just how profoundly reading and writing practices and concepts of language and expression were restructured. My ability to make this argument is in no small part thanks to the robust body of existing work by Japanese-language scholars such as Toeda Hirokazu, Kōno Kensuke, Nagamine Shigetoshi, Shibano Kyōko, Satō Takumi, Obi Toshito, Kuroiwa Hisako, Yamamoto Taketoshi, and Ōsawa Satoshi, among others too numerous to list here. Their work achieves a diversity of method and a depth of detail to which I can only gesture; I cite their research throughout and strongly encourage interested readers to seek out their studies.

This book is divided into two parts of three chapters each, with each chapter covering an approximately congruent stretch of time, from roughly the 1890s through the early 1930s, to provide a synchronic, prismatic examination of this period through a variety of interlocking lenses. Part 1, "The Making of a Modern Media Ecology," details how mass-market typographic print became ubiquitous and examines how that process transformed the meanings and functions of magazines and books. These chapters explore the dramatically expanded horizons of literary and cultural discourse via analyses of visual and oral media in magazine publishing, the popularization of philosophy and paperbacks by the company Iwanami Shoten, and the used and antique bibliophile book trade. Part 2, "Prose, Language, and Politics in the Type Era," investigates the vicissitudes of literary writing, linguistic thought, and political action vis-à-vis the rise of the media complex detailed in part 1, with chapters on the literary experiments of Yokomitsu Riichi (1898–1947), debates over script reform, and the interplay between the prewar leftist movement and the publishing industry. Viewing them together, we witness a shared typographic imagination—a consciousness of printed language as a material quality both shaped by and able to shape the course of history and structures of self and society.

Chapter 1 traces the emergence of a market-oriented discursive space for literature, intellectual writing, and popular culture in magazines during and following the Sino-Japanese War of 1894–1895. The new technology of the reproducible photographic print in the magazine *Nisshin Sensō Jikki* precipitated major capital inflows to the publisher Hakubunkan, which would release Japan's first general interest magazine and biggest mainstream commercial literary magazine. The chapter examines the legacies of Hakubunkan and the popular entertainment publisher Kōdansha to argue that the integration of print images and oral-performance genres into late-Meiji magazine pages played a pivotal role in the elevation of typographic print to a staple medium for literary discourse, communication, and cultural expression.

Chapter 2 moves from magazines to the birth of books as a mass-market commodity, focusing on the bookstore-cum-publisher Iwanami Shoten's projects to popularize philosophical knowledge. I show how Iwanami marketed once-elite literary and intellectual canons to the reading masses in the magazines *Shichō* (Trends in Thought, 1917–1919) and *Shisō* (Thought, 1920–present), then turn to Iwanami's pocket paperback (*bunkobon*) format, the revolutionary competitor of the one-yen volume (*enpon*) that has been the object of extensive analysis by scholars like Obi, Mack, Toeda, and Kōno. I argue that Iwanami's negotiation of the double bind of cheap commodity and transcendental ideology through these small books shows how new forms of media can be imagined as objects bearing political and ontological significance. This dynamic is manifest in the work of philosopher Miki Kiyoshi (1897–1945), who wrote advertising copy for Iwanami's popular edition of Marx's *Capital* in 1927 and saw the paperback book as a politicized medium with the power to critique capitalist forms of social life.

Given this new reality of print as a cheap commodity, chapter 3 explores the changing meanings of books and magazines as they were bought, sold, traded, collected, and archived. As mass-market books became affordable, the trade in antique volumes heated up, and new bibliographic anxieties emerged concerning the materiality of print media and the necessity of organizing and preserving typographic ephemera. I read the writings of cantankerous collector-critics like Uchida Roan, which reveal a materialist tendency of bibliophilic thought critical of the instrumentalization of books as useful containers for content through their place in capitalist consumer culture. The chapter unfurls the cartography of the book trade in Tokyo as I argue that bibliophilic collecting, indexing, and cataloging practices opened new horizons for the writing of literary and media history in Japan.

Part 1 provides a picture of how books and magazines became inexorable parts of everyday life, and what they meant to those who read, wrote, made, bought, and sold them; part 2 asks whither language, prose, and politics in this new discourse network and social milieu structured by mass-produced print media. Chapter 4 focuses on Yokomitsu Riichi and the Shinkankaku-ha (Neo-Sensationist or Neo-Perceptionist) group to consider how a generation of writers born into this print media economy and ecology explored new possibilities for prose and negotiated the fault lines of critical discourse. This coterie, associated with the journal *Bungei Jidai* (Literary Age, 1924–1927), theorized the role of the text in mediating sensations and perceptions of the material world via experimental writing practices that challenged accepted norms of grammar and narrative structure. Yokomitsu's early short stories demonstrate a concern for how the movement of language, bodies, and commodities can disrupt and transform practices of reading and writing, and debates over formalism in the late 1920s evince competing concepts of literary materialism held by an array of contemporaneous critics.

Chapter 5 continues tracking this materialist attitude toward language through linguistic reform debates. Protracted arguments over kana orthography (*kanazukai*), romanization (*rōmaji*), and the international auxiliary language Esperanto reveal a shared ideology of script as a physical artifact, the manipulation of which has the power to restructure human consciousness and the social order. Literati argued over phonetic versus historical script conventions and expressed anxiety over the instrumentalization of writing in the service of efficiency. At the same time, linguists, politicians, publishers, scientists, and socialists all experimented with ideas of the Japanese language as a material, measurable quantity to be rationalized for the sake of Japan's autonomous participation in the global production of knowledge. I argue that script reform served as a multivalent site for the negotiation and contestation of the ontological nature of printed type and the place of the Japanese language in the international order.

The final chapter considers the complex relationship between the prewar proletarian movement and the publishing industry. The leftist movement in Japan grew coterminously with the consumer print market, as socialists, communists, anarchists, and others engaged in a complicated dialectical dance with print capitalism. Publishing could make the movement a popular political phenomenon, but leftists were wary of commodification by the very culture industry they critiqued. Proletarian thinkers like Sakai Toshihiko (1870–1933) and Hirabayashi Hatsunosuke (1892–1931) were involved in the publishing business, and major firms like Kaizōsha and Heibonsha capitalized on public interest in socialist themes to increase circulation. I argue that the prewar leftist movement was inseparable from the publishing business, while the simultaneous integration of radical political themes into popular magazines was equally critical for the expansion of Japanese print capitalism. The chapter concludes with a discussion of the writer Tokunaga Sunao (1899–1958), who learned to read and write while working as a typesetter, and whose position in front of the type tray and on the front lines of printing-press labor strikes provides a unique view of what it means to possess the typographic imagination.

I choose these subjects because they all exemplify a sensibility of script as an irrevocably physical capacity with a structural function in the imagination of human consciousness and social form. Whether intellectuals were debating experimental prose, linguistic reform, or political organization, their attitudes toward print transcended discursive fields and ideological orientations to exemplify this materialist typographic imagination. This imagination spans categories of knowledge and dialectically unites seemingly opposing factions; as such there are any number of other authors or texts from early twentieth-century Japan that might have found a space in this study as exemplars of the typographic imagination. Yokomitsu Riichi and his clique were not the only authors to be born into this new media ecology and understand their writing in regard to the consumer economy as a condition for literary production, but I do believe that the Shinkankaku-ha most explicitly expressed the newness of their moment, most self-consciously marketed their work in a commercially oriented critical framework, and most deeply probed the physiological relationship between the human body and the printed text. Likewise in the realm of linguistic thought—another entire book could be written about other contemporaneous linguistic technologies, including modern dictionaries and encyclopedias, grammar manuals, writing implements, the adoption of disciplinary academic linguistics, diverging strands of philological analysis, and the study of oral literature in tempo with the universalization of mass-produced print. I focus on kana orthography, romanization, and Esperanto as three contrapuntal responses to the question of script reform, which share in their deeper structure an assumption of type as an atomistic building block for thought and expression. Similarly whither the question of politics; this book focuses on an admittedly narrow slice of the socialist movement at the expense of a complex array of figures, journals, and factions from elsewhere on the left, and with little reference to those aligned with ideologies of liberal democracy or rightist imperialism. That said, I believe this material dialectically demonstrates both how modern print was pivotal to political action in prewar Japan and how new political horizons helped make possible the ubiquity of print.

A brief conclusion considers the closing of this phase of Japan's print revolution and contemplates correspondences between early twentieth-century Japan and our present moment. We might think of the uneven edge of the early 1930s as the period when typographic print ceased to be new media and succeeded in fully becoming part of the infrastructure of everyday life. At the same time, the early 1930s marked a fading of the open expression of ideas, as state suppression and censorship constrained the horizons for political discourse, leaving many of the issues raised throughout this study unsettled for decades to come. Today, we find ourselves in the early phases of an epistemological shift out from McLuhan's Gutenberg galaxy and toward postprint digital media systems. There are, in my opinion, profound parallels between Japan's rapid movement into the typographic era and our own embrace of networked electronic communications technologies as ubiquitous media for reading, writing, and social discourse. These include the reorientation of the relationship between text and image, the widespread adoption of portable formats, the radical opening of access to archives, the reimagination of the canon, the advent of experimental forms of prose, the reconfiguration of written grammar and syntax, the problematics of script and legibility in an age of global interconnection, and the contingencies of political possibility on new social media platforms.[51] At the same time, we can perceive phenomena inverse to the association between typographic print and the materiality of language of Japan a century ago. Today, as our lives and language migrate online, our concepts of reading and writing on digital devices are replete with metaphors of immateriality, immediacy, transparency, and disembodiment that contrast with the physicality of the typographic era.

PART I

The Making of a Modern Media Ecology

Chapter One

PICTURES AND VOICES FROM A PAPER EMPIRE

In the early 1890s, literary discourse in Japan was confined mostly to a rarified world of educated intellectuals. Smallish fiction journals were published to be read and debated mostly by other literati. Discussions of prose, philosophy, and criticism were robust but by no means the purview of the average Japanese citizen. By the end of the same decade, interested readers could follow fiction in newspaper serials, buy a codex edition at a local bookstore, or pick up a general interest magazine at a newsstand to keep up on the latest in poetry and philosophy or geography and home economics. Within a few decades, a dizzying array of books and periodicals sold on the order of hundreds of thousands of copies for less than the price of a taxi ride or a beer. This chapter traces the evolution of mass-market typographic print media across this period as the rapid growth of the publishing industry precipitated the emergence of market-oriented discursive spaces for literature, intellectual writing, and popular culture.

By the 1880s, Japan boasted an active newspaper-publishing scene, with major newspapers in Tokyo and Osaka reaching robust circulation numbers. Likewise, smaller literati journals such as *Garakuta Bunko* (Library of Odds and Ends, 1885–1889) and *Shigarami Zōshi* (Bound Together Magazine, 1889–1894) provided opportunities for authors and intellectuals to debate modern language and literature, and readers enjoyed a growing trade in Western-style bound codices. In the early 1890s, most magazines remained low in circulation, though "practical magazines" (*jitsugyō zasshi*) offering business advice sold well. Even *Kokumin no Tomo* (The Nation's Friend, 1887–1898), the so-called giant of magazines (*zasshikai no kyōjin*) that sold about twenty thousand copies an issue, was closer to a thin pamphlet.[1] At several yen a piece, books were prohibitively expensive to the average citizen. The critical turning point in the expansion of print capitalism in Japan came hand in hand with the nation's first modern imperial war against Qing China in 1894 and 1895. The First Sino-Japanese War marked a new phase in the empire's entrance into the modern global economy and provided a huge boon to domestic industries. Coverage of the conflict in magazines like the publisher Hakubunkan's *Nisshin Sensō Jikki* (Record of the Sino-Japanese War, 1894–1896) exploded on the scale of hundreds of thousands of copies as Japanese citizens clamored to learn everything they could about the war. Sales of wartime periodicals provided a huge capital injection to the publishing industry, which in turn helped set the stage for a mass market for literary fiction and other forms of modern culture in print.

Rather than understand the war as an event a priori and external to Japan's mass media explosion, with the latter a mere effect of the former, we can think of print as internal to the war and its representation. In the 1880s and early 1890s, the Japanese newspaper industry developed dramatically in terms of size, reach, readership, and political power; newspaper journalism was intimately integrated with government discourse, actively stoked nationalist sentiment, and rallied public support for the war effort.[2] New technologies like telegraphy and photography that connected the front lines to the metropole were logistically integral to both the war effort and its production as a spectacle for the public at home. To those witnessing the conflict from afar, periodicals, photographs, lithographs, maps, and woodblock prints constituted the war as a media spectacle. This continually unfolding discursive event produced both the desire to see the process of imperial expansion and the desire to consume more of the media that made seeing it possible. These new media thus also produced the war that produced them.

In the period immediately following the war, we see the rise of profitable literary and general interest magazines and critical discourse rendered in the form of high-circulation typographic text. This wide popular readership was predicted on a variety of factors, including a drive for mass education following the Imperial Rescript on Education (*Kyōiku Chokugo*) of 1890 and the associated rise of textbooks as big business, as well the growth of Japan's industrial economy through the empire's integration into circuits of global trade. Like many new nation-states in the nineteenth century, the Meiji government encouraged the development of a phalanx of institutions, including a postal system, a military, and an active press, all seen as necessities for a modern empire. The Meiji state supported the production of print at a practical, industrial level and played a structural role in the emergence of the ostensibly free press. Beginning in the late 1870s, a system of sometimes implicit, sometimes explicit patronage facilitated the rapid growth of newspapers, which were considered a means by which to create an educated, literate citizenry. The press was considered by the state to be a vital force and active partner in nation building, although Meiji publishers were compelled to operate within bounds limned by the Home Ministry and codes like the Press and Publication Regulation (Shinbunshi Jōrei) of 1887 and the Publication Law (Shuppanhō) of 1893.[3]

Crucial for the next stage of modern Japanese print capitalism were industrially reproduced photographic and lithographic images. Citizens bought hundreds of thousands of copies of *Nisshin Sensō Jikki* not just to read the latest from the front lines but also to see the war in photographs, paintings, prints, and etchings. Photography had arrived in Japan in 1848, but only in the late 1880s did developments in camera technology and collotype printing allow pictures to be taken in the field and reproduced on newspaper and magazine pages. In addition to the appeal of seeing naval ships, distant vistas, and famous persons, there was the attraction of the new technology of the reproduced photographic image itself, regardless of subject. High-quality reproductions of photographs and other visual media became a selling point for magazines, with many featuring photo inserts and illustrated covers. At the same time, limitations on the photographic representation of war encouraged new modes of literary reportage.

The company that best seized the wartime boom was Hakubunkan, which had been known for publishing textbooks and business magazines. After the war, publishers scrambled to find ways to compel readers to buy their products. With the *Nisshin Sensō Jikki* proceeds, Hakubunkan began publishing genre-defining magazines like the highbrow yet commercial literary magazine *Bungei Kurabu* (Literary Club, 1895–1933), the general interest magazine *Taiyō* (The Sun, 1895–1928), and the children's magazine *Shōnen Sekai* (Boys' World, 1895–1933). These magazines were among the first to market literary writing, social discourse, and popular entertainment on the order of hundreds of thousands of copies, selling fiction and criticism as commodities for mass consumption through the strategic use of visual images. Developments in distribution systems, marketing practices, and rail and postal networks allowed magazines to be read across Japan, and Hakubunkan's magazines outlined a shared sense of national culture inclusive of trends in art, culture, politics, entertainment, and intellectual life.

The second half of this chapter turns from Hakubunkan to the popular-entertainment publisher Kōdansha; if Hakubunkan achieved success by the integration of the reproduced image, Kōdansha succeeded through the integration of popular oral performance arts into printed text. An early magazine, *Yūben* (Oratory, 1910–1941), made a case for the role of orality in modern life, and the company's flagship, *Kōdan Kurabu* (Kōdan Club, 1911–1962), brought popular genres of narrative, comedic, and musical storytelling like *kōdan*, *rakugo*, and *naniwabushi* to the printed page. Kōdansha's founder, Noma Seiji (1878–1938), a supporter of state-publisher relations, saw the interfacing of print with oral and visual forms of entertainment culture as a means to promulgate an ideological program of moral education and national duty, culminating in the staggeringly successful *Kingu*, the first Japanese magazine to sell one million copies of a single issue in January 1927.

In essence, Japanese print media in this period can be seen as at once universal and particular. Universal in that magazines become pervasive, omnipresent, and able to incorporate all manner of other media and ideas as typographic print became the medium by which nearly all writing and thought circulated. At the same time, typographic print became increasingly particular in that mass-produced printed text sat side by side with photography, music, and eventually film and radio as only one of many forms of modern media. Significantly, it is precisely the integration of these auditory and visual media into the register of print that allowed modern Japanese typographic media to become affordable and ubiquitously accessible.

FIGURE 1.1 Cover of *Nisshin Sensō Jikki* (Record of the Sino-Japanese War), no. 30 (July 17, 1895), featuring an engraving of a naval battle.

DEVELOPING A PAPER EMPIRE

The publishing house Hakubunkan was founded in Tokyo in 1887 by Ōhashi Sahei (1835–1902), having grown from a regional bookstore with an Edo-esque structure wherein firms both made books and sold them retail. Many of Hakubunkan's early releases were genres popular in the early modern period, such as heroic biographies, Chinese dynastic histories, and primers for women's education.[4] By the early 1890s, however, Hakubunkan had begun to reorganize both its production system and its list of titles in accordance with Meiji market interests. The promulgation of the Imperial Rescript on Education in 1890 precipitated a new era of the national education system, and Hakubunkan began printing textbooks for lower schools. Textbook contracts were a golden ring for Meiji publishers, a guarantee of orders on the scale of many thousands as the government sought to universalize literacy. Hakubunkan's other moneymakers were "practical magazines" (*jitsugyō zasshi*) and trade periodicals that sold briskly to a populace looking to succeed at business.[5]

The watershed moment for Hakubunkan arrived with the start of the Sino-Japanese War in 1894 as an intense desire among Japanese citizens for information and images helped trigger a nationwide publishing boom. Founder Ōhashi had returned from a trip to Europe and the United States to study publishing and telegraphy, having visited the 1893 World's Columbian Exposition in Chicago and spent time at Reuters news service. Telegraphy increased the speed by which messages could be sent from the front lines, and every newspaper and magazine publisher embedded reporter corps in military units. After hostilities commenced, Hakubunkan began publishing *Nisshin Sensō Jikki*. Released thrice monthly, it was the first true best-selling magazine of the modern print era in Japan; the inaugural issue alone went through twenty-three pressings and sold three hundred thousand copies, and by the end of its fifty-issue run, the magazine had sold more than five million copies, a number staggering even by the circulation standards of later decades. Print journalism thus heralded the advent of the war, which in turn stoked a simultaneous printing boom.[6]

Nisshin Sensō Jikki was the first magazine in which the public could regularly behold high-quality photographic prints. The appearance of the photographic image on the printed page was a relatively recent phenomenon in Japan, newly made possible by advancements in gelatin, collotype, and zinc dry-plate printing technologies.[7] Photography had first come to Japan in 1848 via a daguerreotype process imported from the Dutch. For the first few decades, most photo production in Japan was carried out by foreign studios in Yokohama as an export industry catering to Western desires for orientalist images of geisha, samurai, and chrysanthemums. As late as the 1880s, photography remained the purview of the elite, even after Japanese photographers began opening domestic studios.[8] The first printed newspaper photograph in Japan, depicting the eruption of Mount Bandai, appeared in the August 9, 1888, edition of the *Yomiuri Shinbun* newspaper and was such a phenomenon that the newspaper published the same photo for weeks. Previously, photographs had been pasted, rather than printed, onto newspaper pages, or indirectly reproduced via woodblock copies. Newspaper photographs later became common at the time of the Russo-Japanese War (1904–1905) thanks to advances in cylinder printing. Crucially, printing and photographic technologies were increasingly comparable with those in Europe and the United States as the form and content of Japanese magazines came to resemble those overseas.[9]

It was thus both the ability to see the war from afar and the attraction of technologically reproduced photographic images that drew readers to *Nisshin Sensō Jikki*. These techniques were pioneered by Ogawa Kazumasa (also known as Isshin, 1860–1929), who studied photography in Boston from 1882 to 1884, then returned to industrialize domestic photo production. Ogawa ran a photography studio, translated writings on light sciences, and advanced the dry-plate and collotype processes necessary for shooting moving objects outdoors and printing high-quality images on a large scale. These technological advancements dramatically expanded the range of photographic subjects, and Ogawa taught field photography to army survey corps and served as chief photographer for the *Nisshin Sensō Jikki* photo brigade, as well as edited the official photographic record of the war for the Imperial Army and Navy.[10]

So, what did readers see when they opened up an issue of *Nisshin Sensō Jikki*? The majority of the magazine was dense with text, including dispatches from the front by soldiers and reporters. Each issue's cover boasted a high-quality etching of a naval battle scene, followed by several pages of photographic plates, including portraits of military officers, squadrons in full dress, battleships at sea, and landscapes in Korea and Manchuria, allowing the viewer to mentally situate the terrain of the war. Most photos were straightforward shots of vistas, people, and boats—the work of Ogawa and his fellow war photographers does not figure significantly in historiography of art photography in Japan. Later issues contained more varied subject matter, including mounted guns, scenes of daily life in camps, and conquered villages. These photographs of distant lands and vanquished people in *Nisshin Sensō Jikki* and competing graphic periodicals like *Sengoku Shashin Gahō* (War Photography Gazetteer, 1894–1895) allowed Japanese readers to witness their empire's territorial ambitions. Photography in this period thus not only recorded the expansion of the Japanese empire but also actively facilitated that expansion by making conquest visible to domestic viewers and mobilizing support for the imperial project. This type of photographic practice had immediate precedent in the British Empire, as field photography in Victorian-period colonial expeditions helped bring home images of landscapes, troops, and humans on the frontier, so that those in the metropole could bear witness to ever-extending imperial power.[11] *Nisshin Sensō Jikki* and other Sino-Japanese War gazetteers, the first true

FIGURE 1.2 Photo insert from *Nisshin Sensō Jikki*, no. 30, featuring formal portraits of fallen Japanese soldiers.

mass-market modern print magazines in Japan, both brought images of the empire at war to a national reading populace and expanded that reading populace by an order of magnitude.

REPRESENTATION ON THE FRONT LINES

Ironically, the one thing that could not be shown in photographic periodicals covering the Sino-Japanese War was the war itself. Photographers could shoot preparations for and the aftermath of battles and everyday life on the front, but never actual battles; even Ogawa, official photographer to the Imperial Army and Navy, could not directly cover the fighting. This lack of access meant that photographs could never fully represent the war to the domestic reader; as a result, they remained a single component of a complex system of representational strategies, both visual and textual, that produced what Paul Virilio calls "that spectacle" of war that is its "very purpose."[12] The appeal of staid war photographs lay in their content and the novelty of the medium as much as in any formal or aesthetic characteristics. The cover etchings of *Nisshin Sensō Jikki* are far more dynamic, with guns blazing, flags beating, smoke wafting, and soldiers charging. The strategic use of vivid images had played a crucial role in an earlier generation of popular Japanese news media made to appeal to a mass audience—namely, the sumptuously illustrated *nishiki-e shinbun* broadsheets popular in the mid-1870s. Brightly colored pictures of the Satsuma Rebellion of 1877 had pioneered how pictorial media could draw attention to war reportage, setting an important precedent for the pictorial magazines of the Sino-Japanese War era. These images are echoed in the full-color woodblock *nishiki-e* prints produced by the artist Kobayashi Kiyochika (1847–1914)—brilliant, vivid images of explosions in the sky, soldiers falling into the sea and bleeding out on land, and prisoners being bayoneted.[13] Like the lithographs, these color woodblock images represented what photographs could not, for reasons both technological and political—dramatic, subjectively tinged images of battle.

Photographs and prints worked in tandem with reportage that filled the pages of *Nisshin Sensō Jikki* and other war periodicals. Much of this writing is the textual equivalent of Ogawa's photographs—flat, straightforward, and objective, with little subjective commentary or attempts at literary expression. Yet as Kōno Kensuke has pointed out, these magazines were perceived as far more colorful and nuanced in coverage than the daily newspapers.[14] Every periodical was reporting on the same war, so publications competed by offering fresh kinds of coverage. One of the most popular newspapers, the *Kokumin Shinbun* (The Nation's News, 1890–1942), published by Tokutomi Sohō (1863–1957), touted its ability to "give our readers the most complete picture of the war on land and at sea."[15] One of Sohō's strategies was to hire a young aspiring writer and editor, Kunikida Doppo (1871–1908), who would later go on to become a major figure in the Japanese naturalist literary movement. In 1894, Doppo, then known as Tetsuo, was writing fiction and poetry and keeping his diary, *Azamukazaru no Ki* (An Unembellished Diary, 1893–1897, published 1908–1909), but had little luck publishing in literary magazines, so signed on to work as a reporter for the *Kokumin Shinbun*. His first major assignment was to board the battleship *Chiyoda* in November 1894 to provide color commentary from the front.[16]

Doppo, a twenty-four-year-old dropout from Tōkyō Senmon Gakkō (now Waseda University), became a journalist through his friendship with the writer and editor Yano Ryūkei (1851–1931). His early career as a war correspondent is poorly remembered in literary history, perhaps because it does not align with the image of the author as a lovelorn poet wandering the countryside and dying young of tuberculosis.[17] Doppo's correspondence, later collected as *Aitei Tsūshin* (Messages to My Dear Brother, 1908), proved popular as it provided readers with a more personal, philosophical view of the war, a counterpoint to more straightforward journalistic coverage. Doppo's writings contrasted with and complemented other modes of reportage and helped drive sales of the *Kokumin Shinbun* while subtly marking out a space for literary writing in mass-market mainstream publications. Doppo begins his first transmittance from the battleship *Chiyoda* to his newspaper audience by raising the question of literary voice and writing style, asking rhetorically, "Just how should I send these messages [*ika ni tsūshin subeki*] . . . the sending itself is easy, but choosing the method [*hō o erabu*] is hard."[18] Doppo's challenge was to find a writing style appropriate for conveying his own subjective experience of the war to hundreds of thousands of subscribers at home, and he lights upon the conceit of writing as if he were addressing his brother, beginning letters with the salutation *aitei*, "beloved brother," in a personal epistolary style. Kuroiwa Hisako has pointed out that the *Kokumin Shinbun* generally employed classically inflected *bungotai* style, and Doppo used colloquial vernacular language to convey the depth and interiority of his experience.[19] By writing to his brother as an imaginary yet specific reader, Doppo is able to, in his own words, "attempt objective depiction [*jissha o kokoromi*]" while still maintaining a poetic spirit as he describes the sea, moon, and stars in the night sky, and the laughter and tears of soldiers. Through this stylistic device of writing as if to his own brother, Doppo transforms his audience into something more than "just readers" (*tan ni dokusha*) and becomes able to "tell his tales freely" (*jiyū ni kataran koto*).[20]

It is an inventive solution to a problem not yet faced by many Meiji literati—writing for a mass audience. Doppo is not publishing in a small-circulation literary magazine but for a readership of hundreds of thousands. He tells his readers that he aims to be something more than "just a reporter" (*hōkokusha*) or a "dispassionate observer" (*reisei naru kansatsusha*).[21] The creativity in Doppo's experiment becomes clear by comparing his newspaper accounts with the record of events in his "unembellished diary." During this period, his diary is written in a Sinitic style and reads like a flat list of events. Doppo's entry for November 6, 1894, reads only, "Attack on Dalian [*Dairen kōryaku*]."[22] By contrast, his correspondence for the newspaper describes the day with more poesy, sketching how "the steam off the water vanishes into the mist and haze as the ships at the rear advance into the bay. As the sun dips down toward the horizon, the evening light turns resplendent, and all falls silent as the bright rays cast over the waves." Doppo balances his internal pathos (*aware ni kanjinu*) and conveys what he sees as the "incredible beauty" (*yūbi*) of the war. The view of the carnage at Dalian is such that "only an artist [*bijutsuka*] could paint it . . . and so as for the scene itself, I will leave it up to your imagination."[23]

Doppo's diary lists events, names, places, and dates, while his *Kokumin Shinbun* columns tell of details like barking dogs, strange trees, and pitiful locals. What strikes Doppo deepest is the experience of seeing the dead body of a fallen Chinese soldier for the first time: "In the past, I recited [*sodoku*] war chronicles, histories, fiction [*shōsetsu*], and poetry, but seeing a dead body on these wastelands allows me to imagine for the first time what it means to live . . . it gives me the sensation of understanding great mysteries. Like with poetry or paintings about the wars between the Minamoto and the Taira, I feel the profound truth of humanity."[24]

Doppo aestheticizes the war he witnesses at the expense of the dead enemy combatants, taking the opportunity to ruminate on how war lays bare life, death, and the spirit of the individual. Literature helps him make sense of this tableau of carnage, and the battlefield likewise instigates a new relationship with classical texts like the *Heike Monogatari*. Doppo, who notes in his diary that he was reading the poetry of Wordsworth and the writings of the Christian thinker Uchimura Kanzō (1861–1930) while deployed, sees his work as a war reporter as an opportunity to face death and thus confront nature, belief, and the contradictions of modern life. "I act [*katsudō su*], and then I act again. Life [*seikatsu*]! Life! Is [this war] not a departure from everyday life and an entrance into the realm of politics, religion, and philosophy?"[25] War reporting allows Doppo to make these conceptual abstractions immediate and transmit them back to the public via his epistolary style. His in-depth commentary and emotionally charged

FIGURE 1.3 Photographic scenes from the front line of the Russo-Japanese War, in *Nichiro Sensō Shashin Gahō* (Photo Gazetteer of the Russo-Japanese War), no. 34 (October 8, 1905).

reportage thus functioned in tandem with photographic coverage and traditional reporting to provide an image of war with depth as well as surface, making tentative steps toward an era of the newspaper as a space for expressive literary writing.

PICTURING A NEW ERA OF LITERATURE

In the years following, mass-produced magazines provided opportunities for new techniques of representation and modes of expression as calibrated for a wide audience. New media and technologies such as telegraphy, photography, and the reproduction of high-quality images helped precipitate the large-scale circulation of typographic periodicals. This possibility was itself tied to Japan's imperial expansion, as Taiwan's camphor industry provided a new source of raw material that facilitated the cheap large-scale production of celluloid camera film and thus photographic magazines.[26] Following the success of *Nisshin Sensō Jikki* and its imitators, the graphic magazine, or *gahō*, was established as a genre in Japanese publishing—there were illustrated gazetteers for women (*Fujin Gahō*), children (*Shōnen Gahō*), aspiring intellectuals (*Chishiki Gahō*), professionals (*Jitsugyō Gahō*), and others suited to every delineation of the reading populace. Doppo played a role in this graphic boom; he found critical but not financial success as a writer and sustained himself by working as an editor. Having seen the potential of the graphic periodical, he founded the magazine *Tōyō Gahō* (The Eastern Graphic, 1903), which specialized in photographs of foreign palaces, temples, and other exotic scenes. The magazine later became *Senji Gahō* (War Graphic, 1904–1905) during the Russo-Japanese War, and finally *Kinji Gahō* (Modern Graphic, 1905–1907).[27]

The first issue of *Tōyō Gahō* features a short foreword by Doppo's mentor, Yano Ryūkei, on the new relationship between reading and seeing engendered by graphic magazines:

> To only hear and not to see is not to truly know something. To only see and not to hear makes nothing clear . . . One must have both daily newspapers that are primarily "heard" [*kiku*] and illustrated magazines [*ega zasshi*] that are primarily "seen" [*miru*] . . . when hearing and listening happen together, that is when knowledge is first truly realized . . . then readers can stay in Japan and still witness events abroad, or be abroad and witness events in Japan.[28]

FIGURE 1.4 The October 1908 issue of *Tōyō Fujin Gahō* (The Lady's Graphic, 1907–1909), a popular illustrated magazine from the years following the Russo-Japanese War.

Yano's choice of "hearing" as the sense used to read newspapers is noteworthy, as well into the Meiji period the act of reading was likely to involve listening to a literate person read aloud. Here, however, "hearing" seems to imply a more modern sense of reading as hearing an imaginary voice produced by vernacular written text, in contrast to "seeing" or looking at pictures. In illustrated Edo-era woodblock-printed books, these two processes were more intimately interwoven but had become separated under the typographic regime and thus had to be realigned by the modern reader.

Perhaps the most profound way in which graphic periodicals affected the realm of Meiji literature is also the most simple—illustrated magazines' remarkable sales figures provided a massive influx of capital to publishers. The successes of magazines like Hakubunkan's *Nisshin Sensō Jikki* and Shun'yōdō's *Sengoku Shashin Gahō* allowed publishers to reorganize their businesses and create a new generation of popular, affordable magazines that ran high-quality literary and critical content ready for wide consumption. The new magazines founded by Hakubunkan in the wake of the Sino-Japanese War would set the template for multiple genres for decades to come. Hakubunkan inaugurated a new set of flagship magazines, including *Taiyō*, which was the prototype for general interest (*sōgō zasshi*) magazines, *Bungei Kurabu*, a highbrow fiction magazine, and *Shōnen Sekai*, a children's magazine. The editors did not forget the basis of the company's newfound success, and each issue featured pages of photo plates and illustrations using the latest image-reproduction and printing technologies. In 1897, *Taiyō*, *Shōnen Sekai*, and *Bungei Kurabu* held the respective ranks of first, second, and third best-selling magazines in the nation, with a combined circulation of more than five million copies sold between the three. Suzuki Sadami rightly identifies this moment as the beginning of magazines as big business in modern Japan.[29]

Of these three magazines, *Bungei Kurabu* had the lowest circulation—about fifty thousand monthly copies to *Taiyō*'s biweekly output of more than one hundred thousand—but nonetheless had a profound effect on the literary market. Any number of smaller literary journals provided opportunities for experimentation in and debates over fiction and poetics, but these were generally published by literati circles or attached to universities, such as *Teikoku Bungaku* (at Tokyo Imperial University, 1895–1920) or *Waseda Bungaku* (at Waseda University, 1891–present). Prominent literati journals of the previous decade, such as the Ken'yūsha group's *Garakuta Bunko* or

Mori Ōgai's *Shigarami Zōshi*, as well as contemporaneous magazines like Yamada Bimyō's *Miyako no Hana* (Flower of the Capital, 1897–1903), were low in circulation and plain in style, with simple covers, the occasional small black-and-white woodblock image, and little else to appeal to readers besides the texts themselves. By contrast, Hakubunkan's *Bungei Kurabu* was designed as an attractive, eye-catching commodity to signify literary value to a wide audience amid a diversifying print marketplace. The format of *Bungei Kurabu* was similar to its predecessors, but it was bigger, thicker, and more sumptuously illustrated, with multicolor covers and photo plates. *Bungei Kurabu* also regularly ran advertisements, not only for other literary journals or books but also for the latest fashionable commodities, like designer hats and Egyptian cigarettes. Proof of the magazine's broad appeal is further evident in its use of *sōrubi*, interlinear diacritics giving the readings for each kanji, making *Bungei Kurabu* accessible to readers at less-advanced levels of literacy.

Readers at the turn of the twentieth century were drawn in by *Bungei Kurabu*'s vivid covers, which were decidedly modern in execution but evoked Edo-era woodblock prints and traditionally bound *wahon* books. The early-modern aesthetic of flower brocades and running script was an editorial design choice made to conjure up literary associations. The opening pages were filled with layered, sophisticated photo collages of temples, exotic scenery, and beautiful women, as well as full-color reproductions of woodblock prints and oil paintings. All these images had little to no direct connection with the fictional content of the magazine and served primarily to attract readers and signify the presence of aesthetically evolved highbrow content. When the photographs and images were on rare occasion linked, the relationship between the two could be uncomfortable, as in the scandal that ensued when a picture of the young woman writer Higuchi Ichiyō (1872–1896) was featured in the *bijinran* (gallery of beauties) section alongside pictures of geisha.[30] *Bungei Kurabu* ran fiction by authors from the Ken'yūsha group, such as Ozaki Kōyō (1868–1903), Izumi Kyōka (1873–1939), and Oguri Fūyō (1875–1926), as well as by other prominent writers like Kōda Rohan (1867–1947) and Kosugi Tengai (1865–1952) and developed name recognition for writers that published books with Hakubunkan. If a story was a success, it helped increase circulation of the magazine and could be reprinted as a book to be advertised to the magazine's subscribers. *Bungei Kurabu* thus served to affix its publisher, Hakubunkan, with the sign of the literary and helped authors' popularity spiral upward, proving the viability of a wider market for literary writing at the turn of the twentieth century. Competing publishers soon followed Hakubunkan's lead; prominent book publisher Shun'yōdō used its journal *Shinshōsetsu* (New Fiction, 1889–1890, 1896–1926) to similar effect.[31]

The other prominent sites for publishing fiction were newspapers, whose daily circulations reached as high as one hundred fifty thousand in the golden age of "newspaper fiction" (*shinbun shōsetsu*) following the Sino-Japanese War. Seki Hajime has shown that serialized fiction was one of the primary strategies that newspaper publishers used to keep circulation high and subscribers reading following the end of the war. As Tsubouchi Shōyō (1859–1935) put it in 1890, newspapers were the media that "the whole of society, smart and dumb, old and young, men and women alike" all read. The most successful of these newspaper serial novels was Ozaki Kōyō's *Konjiki Yasha* (The Golden Demon, 1897–1902), which ran for six years in the *Yomiuri Shinbun* and helped that paper earn the name of "literary newspaper" (*bungaku shinbun*). The *Hōchi Shinbun* likewise had Murai Gensai's (1864–1927) *Hinodejima* (Island of the Rising Sun, 1896–1901), the *Kokumin Shinbun* had Tokutomi Roka's (1868–1927) *Hototogisu* (The Cuckoo, 1898–1900), and somewhat late to the game, in 1907 the *Asahi Shinbun* would hire Natsume Sōseki to help it compete.[32]

Newspapers encouraged readers to integrate themselves into the production of literary fiction by writing letters and postcards to authors and editors, thus creating a cycle of reader feedback that precipitated discourse between writers and readers and among readers themselves. Writers and publishers also sought ways to sell fiction beyond newspapers and magazines, which were typically consumed then thrown away. By contrast, a bound book had physicality and permanence and could continue to be reprinted and sold for years to come by preserving a work of serial fiction beyond an issue's expiration date. Ozaki Kōyō's *Konjiki Yasha* is the case par excellence; the first book installment was released by Shun'yōdō in 1899, and the novel went through dozens of pressings and remained a best seller well into the 1920s. Accordingly, a great deal of attention was put into the design and binding choices of books published in this era so as to distinguish them from their serialized formats. Kōno Kensuke has pointed out that books like Kōyō's were made in a way that reproduced the style and appearance of traditionally bound *wahon* books, even as printing techniques advanced and Western-style *yōshi* paper replaced Japanese-style *washi* paper.[33] As with the magazine *Bungei Kurabu*, it was important that these books looked and felt "literary" and presented themselves to readers as durable, aesthetic commodities for reading and consumption. Through magazines like *Bungei Kurabu* and *Shinshōsetsu*, newspaper novels, and a new wave of modern book publishing, literary fiction was made available to the masses and integrated into the economy of typographic publishing.[34]

A SHINING LIGHT OF COMMON CULTURE

If *Bungei Kurabu* and newspaper serial novels were a turning point in establishing a wider market for literary fiction, Hakubunkan's flagship magazine *Taiyō* was what Suzuki Sadami calls "the basis for a generalized national culture."[35] *Taiyō* was Japan's first true general-interest magazine and covered almost every imaginable subject in two-hundred-page biweekly issues sold at the low price of seventeen sen. In an introductory note in the opening issue, Hakubunkan head Ōhashi acknowledges that "the nation's need and desire for reading material have been proven by the sales of hundreds of thousands of copies of *Nisshin Sensō Jikki*," then notes that there is no magazine to draw together various specialized fields.[36] He laments that there are too many journals for any one person to read: "The goal of *Taiyō*," he continues, "is to collect and gather specialists and have them introduce their topics broadly, so that all can share in this exchange and gain knowledge from one another."[37] In these nascent moments of Japanese mass publishing, there is already a sense of overload and the need to organize new types of knowledge. If *Taiyō* was meant to help the modern reader manage an excess of information, it also contributed to that excess, as its appeal was based on sheer quantity as much as the quality of contributions. It is difficult to imagine the average reader memorizing and reciting it from cover to cover, the way the author Masamune Hakuchō (1879–1962) claimed to have done with the shorter magazine *Kokumin no Tomo*.[38]

Ōhashi pitches *Taiyō* as "a great step forward for our nation's publishing industry . . . we are no longer in our infancy and we must act accordingly."[39] To Hakubunkan, Japan's most powerful publisher, the goal of this new magazine was to unify all forms of knowledge under one corporate combine in an age of industrial mass production. The term *sōgō zasshi*, referring to magazines like *Taiyō* and its followers such as *Chūō Kōron* (The Central Review, 1899–present) and *Kaizō* (Reconstruction, 1919–1955), is typically translated as "general interest magazine," but given Ōhashi's thinking, it is perhaps more productive to translate *sōgō* as "synthesis"—the merging of distinct parts into a greater whole. The magazine's table of contents lists sections on history, biography, geography, fiction, arts, home economics, politics, law, poetry, science, business, agriculture, industry, society, foreign philosophy, and diplomacy, to name only a sampling. *Taiyō* attempted to integrate all manner of political, social, cultural, and literary discourse into one unified register, but the writing styles used by contributors were diverse; following the conventions of the time, political columns used a formal Sinified style, while articles on gossipy topics tended toward vernacular prose.[40]

With an annual circulation of around 2.5 million copies, it is difficult to overstate the importance of *Taiyō* in opening a discursive space in which different political, social, and literary ideas could come into contact with one another. These ideas circulated far beyond the metropolis, as an efficient train network and postal system meant magazines could be transported across the country. Although Tokyo constituted the single biggest market, about 70 percent of each issue's copies were delivered across the countryside to rural readers. This reach was owing to the strength of Hakubunkan's distribution network, which it also leveraged as a system to circulate magazines by other publishers.[41] At the same time, *Taiyō*'s content was international, and the magazine served as a vector for fin de siècle foreign ideas to enter into Japanese popular consciousness. Telegraphic technologies made it quick to get news from abroad, engendering a sense of contemporaneity in journalism and criticism between Japan and the West. *Taiyō*'s cover image, an etching of rays of sunlight spreading across the globe, gestures toward the international orientation of the magazine, and the cover's monumental style belies the influence of Anglo-American journalism in particular; the magazine maintained an ongoing contract with Reuters and regularly printed translations and original English-language articles from *Harper's Monthly*.[42]

Taiyō was also a site for a new wave of literary and philosophical translations. Takayama Chogyū (1871–1902) and Hasegawa Tenkei (1876–1950) played important editorial roles, running translations of works by the likes of Nietzsche, Poe, Hawthorne, Dumas, Balzac, Dickens, Gogol, Hugo,

Wordsworth, Tolstoy, and Rilke and pushing the Japanese sense of the canon of global thought and literature closer to the prevailing images held in Europe and the United States.[43] Even *Taiyō*'s "gallery of beauties" (*bijinran*) was international and featured French, German, and Turkish "belles" in contrast to the geisha of *Bungei Kurabu. Taiyō*'s internationalism evinces a sense of synchronicity between Japan and the rest of the modern world, just as exports and imports tripled in the years following the war, buoyed by the indemnity paid by China.[44] During this period, the systematic, rather than piecemeal, entrance of foreign texts, images, and ideas into Japanese domestic discourse and debate helped to produce the possibility of global intellectual exchange and modern cultural contemporaneity.

THE POLITICS OF ORATORY AND MODERNITY

Taiyō, *Bungei Kurabu*, and generation of magazines following the Sino-Japanese War helped position political, social, and literary discourse as commodities for mass consumption. As a result, topics that had been the purview of literati and intellectual elites entered into the consciousness of a broad national readership around the turn of the twentieth century. The level of literacy rose in tandem with the higher circulation of periodicals, and the publishing industry was spurred further by the Russo-Japanese War. Gazetteers again proved popular; Hakubunkan repeated its success of a decade before with *Nichiro Sensō Shashin Gahō* (Photographic Gazetteer of the Russo-Japanese War, 1904–1905) and *Nichiro Sensō Jikki* (Record of the Russo-Japanese War, 1904–1905). But as the years of Meiji waned, so, too, did Hakubunkan's primacy in the publishing industry. New rivals arose, including the general interest magazine *Chūō Kōron* and Shinchōsha's literary magazine *Shinchō* (New Tide, 1904–present). Hakubunkan remained powerful as a printer, and its corporatized, vertically integrated production process endured as a combine for papermaking, typesetting, printing, binding, and distribution for decades. The company would continue to constitute the underlying infrastructure through which newer publishers could carry out the complex industrial processes of making and circulating books and magazines. Hakubunkan's vertical integration constituted a primary circuit for publishers to achieve distribution to bookstores not only across the Japanese empire but as far away as diaspora communities in Russia, Hawaii, and the United States.[45]

Of the new publishers that came to prominence after the Russo-Japanese War, the one to have the most lasting effect on Japan's "generalized national culture" is without a doubt Kōdansha (founded in 1909 as Dai-Nihon Yūbenkai), whose name has come to be synonymous with modern Japanese mass culture and popular entertainment. Around the turn of the twentieth century, many popular forms of entertainment were based in a diverse spectrum of oral, musical, and theatrical performance genres, such as *rakugo* comic storytelling, *naniwabushi* (*rōkyoku*) balladry, and the narrative art of *kōdan*, from which Kōdansha took its name. Whereas Hakubunkan capitalized on the technological reproduction of visual images, Kōdansha succeeded by using typographic print to reconstitute oral and musical culture forms for mass consumption. Company founder Noma Seiji argued for the importance of oral performance genres in negotiating the experience of modernity and built a publishing empire by integrating these auditory media into the print register. It is thus the incorporation of not only the visual (as per Hakubunkan) but also the oral (as per Kōdansha) into the typographic regime that helped print in Japan achieve the status of a ubiquitous medium for modern discourse.

Born in Gunma in 1878, Noma was an aspiring intellectual who passed through the pre–national textbook era of Meiji education. Growing up in the 1880s and 1890s meant diverse reading material was available to supplement the formal education that Noma found dull and lacking. As a teen, Noma read English primers, Christian books, fiction, and the writings of Fukuzawa Yukichi and Tokutomi Sohō, both figures with a strong sense of the importance of education and duty to the nation. Noma entered the teacher-training course at Tokyo Imperial University, where he studied linguistics with Ueda Kazutoshi (1867–1937), literary history with Haga Yaichi (1867–1927), and national history with Mikami Sanji (1865–1939), all pioneers in their respective fields, before graduating in 1904 to become a middle-school teacher in Okinawa. In 1907, Noma moved to a clerk position at his alma mater, where he began thinking about methods for the self-cultivation of citizens beyond the national education system.[46]

Noma centered his mission on oratory and public speaking, known as *yūben* or *benron*, a trend among late-Meiji youth. He was disappointed that his school had no formal program in oratory to stand aside departments like law, literature, and science, though it did have a dedicated student club for oratory, the Yūbenkai.[47] The club, which included a young Tsurumi

Yūsuke (1885–1973), later the great advocate of Wilsonian democracy in Japan, inspired Noma to start a magazine to champion the necessity of oratory and public debate. The practice of modern oratory and lecturing (*enzetsu*) had been a part of public life since the early Meiji period, but the term *yūben* was more rarified; Noma would recall that people often misheard it for the more common *yūbin*, "postal."[48] Despite no prior experience in publishing, Noma leveraged connections and released the first issue of the magazine *Yūben* (Oratory, 1910–1941) in February of 1910, naming his company Dai-Nihon Yūbenkai (The Great Japanese Oratory Society). The core concern facing Noma was how to produce a print magazine based around an oral art. He first considered publishing well-known works of oratory in situ but realized that "shorthand transcriptions [*sokki*] of oral performances would not be enough for a magazine." Noma feared that the reduction of practiced and performed speech to printed text would fall flat and the magazine would fail.[49] Instead, he decided to use his new magazine to make a case for oratory through print, a medium by which he could reach a wider audience than could come hear a single speech in person.

Noma begins his editor's introduction in the inaugural issue—one of the few things he ever wrote for the magazine—with a plea for the necessity of oratory in the modern age. He invokes Plato and claims that "oratory is the light of the world [*yo no hikari*]" while lamenting that "public discourse [*yoron*] in a society not led by oratory is surely rotten." Noma worries that "despite advances in the past twenty years, there has been regretful backsliding in terms of oratory and political discussion in the Diet." His primary concern is the calcification of discourse in the modern age, a fear that unless citizens properly practice the arts of speaking, debate, and argumentation, then individual, nation, and society alike would fail to meet their full potential. To Noma, *yūben*, the art of speaking, is "the barometer of social righteousness" (*shakai seigi*), and so *Yūben*, the magazine, was an attempt to cultivate that oral art among the common people outside the formal strictures of bureaucratic state education.[50] For Noma, the universalization of cheap print was not a phenomenon that threatened the oral arts in modern society but a medium by which to popularize and develop those arts.

Noma's ideas found their mark. The inaugural issue of *Yūben* sold out in three days and went through multiple printings in a week, totaling fourteen thousand copies, huge for a private magazine printed outside a major publishing company.[51] *Yūben* resembled an intellectual journal in both form and content; there was little of the visual ornamentation of popular magazines, and its table of contents was dense with submissions by legal scholars and elite oratory clubs. But *Yūben* aimed not to be an inwardly focused coterie journal but a mainstream magazine, and Noma was savvy enough to know that "no matter how high the quality of contributions, without money there is no magazine." He began taking advertisements and advertising the magazine with exaggerated but not insincere claims that *Yūben* would "shed light on the future of Japanese civilization [*Nihon shōrai no bunmei*]"; the ad's overly dramatic catch copy reveals a belief that print journalism possessed the potential to affect social change in an age when reading was a part of everyday life.[52]

Even so, Noma had difficulty separating the medial concerns of producing a magazine from the content value of the subject at hand. In a memoir, he recalls that he had no patience for dealing with editorial issues like the order in which pieces ran, the size of the font, and the page layout. He believed that "if the content [*naiyō*] truly has value [*makoto ni kachi aru*]," then the rest would not matter; people would read it, see that it was good, and it would sell, regardless of the form in which it was presented. Noma understood magazines as a crucial means for the advancement of oratory and popular education, but his idea of the magazine as a medium remains somewhat abstract and detached from the specifics of its production; he wisely removed himself from editorial duties to focus on the business aspects of his project.[53]

For Noma, the goal of *Yūben* was to develop a print-based process for making educated, loyal "new citizens" (*atarashiki kokumin*) with a strong sense of moral rectitude and national duty.[54] This moralistic, nationalistic ideology would continue to be the backbone throughout the company's history. Noma died in 1938, but during the war years Kōdansha worked to mobilize Japan's citizenry in the service of empire, and the company's publications became propaganda vehicles for imperial ideology. Although a detailed discussion of the role of Kōdansha's publications in the wartime regime is beyond the scope of this book, it is worth noting that it is structurally consistent with the relationships cultivated between publishers and the state in the Meiji period and the orientation of Noma's company from its nascent moments. In 1910, however, *Yūben* was ideologically diverse, as Noma's idealized sense of oratory and debate was a formal mode in which all comers could participate regardless of political stripe. Early contributors included the aforementioned Tsurumi Yūsuke, the socialist politician Abe Isoo (1865–1949), and the liberal journalist Yoshino Sakuzō (1878–1933), provided the fledgling magazine with the feel of intellectual authenticity.

The mission of *Yūben* was to provide a place for metadiscourse on discourse itself and to make an argument for the relevance of the oral arts in the age of industrial print. In an essay in the second issue on "Oratory and Literature" (Yūben to Bungaku), the literary historian Haga Yaichi laments that Japan, despite a rich history of oral literature, has never had a culture of debate (*giron*), which he contrasts with the orators of Greece and sages of China.[55] As a result, he claims, "modern citizens [*waga kokumin*] are not used to oratory [*benron*] and feel that public speaking [*enzetsu*] is somehow impossible in Japanese." If, Haga asks, "the United States Congress is full of lively discussion like the fish market at Nihonbashi, how can we make that Nihonbashi fish market spread across all of Japan?"[56] Like Noma, Haga sees typographic print as possessing the potential to engender oral skills via the use of shorthand transcription (*sokkijutsu*) in recording oral performances (*enzetsu*) and storytelling (*kōdan*). Seth Jacobowitz has recently argued for the importance of the practice of shorthand (*sokki*) in the development of modern Japanese literature, with shorthand serving as a new technology of writing that helped mediate oral speech into literary forms.[57] Haga sees the cycle continue another step as printed transcriptions of orations develop oral skills as well as advance the written. The publication of transcriptions normalizes speaking and writing, and Haga sees a further phase wherein "those who become orators [*yūbenka*] will develop a deep interest in literature [*bungaku*]," as the oral arts fostered by the magazine might lead the masses back to their written heritage.[58] Haga's essay is thus a text on the oral origins of writing, for a print magazine aiming to promote an oral culture, so that modern orality can engender a new appreciation for the literary arts. This cyclical logic contains an implicit understanding of popular magazines as phenomena that do not foreclose the development of the oral but rather facilitate its growth at both the practical and conceptual levels.

ORAL PERFORMANCE AND THE BIRTH OF MODERN MASS CULTURE

The magazine to which Kōdansha owes its success and its name was Noma's follow-up venture, *Kōdan Kurabu*. Whereas *Yūben* was established to attract a popular audience to a topic of gravitas, *Kōdan Kurabu* was modeled as an entertainment magazine focused on performance genres of mass enjoyment. The core of *Kōdan Kurabu*'s content was transcriptions of performances of *kōdan* and *rakugo*, as well as *naniwabushi*, in addition to coverage of other kinds of popular entertainment. This included theater and cinema, which was inseparable from the sphere of oral performance as per the role of the *katsuben* or *benshi*, who narrated events on-screen and provided character voices in silent films.[59] Although *rakugo* is still regularly performed today, *kōdan* and *naniwabushi* have faded into relative obscurity, but they were some of the most popular forms of entertainment until well into the twentieth century. The deep roots of *kōdan* storytelling can be found in the early-modern recitational art of *Taiheiki-yomi*, and *naniwabushi* is derived from the Edo-era chanting genres of *chongarebushi* and *saimon*. However, Hyōdo Hiromi has made the important point that Meiji-era *kōdan* and *naniwabushi* are ultimately modern forms of urban mass entertainment; originally performed in urban slums, these performance styles gained general acceptance and came to be performed in hundreds of *yose* theaters across the country beginning in the mid-1870s, often selling out to huge crowds. The lasting popularity of these performance genres was such that they continued to be ranked as the most popular program categories on the radio from the beginning of public broadcasting in Japan in 1925 until well into the 1930s.[60]

As with *Yūben*, the editorial question for *Kōdan Kurabu* was how to present these oral genres in the form of a periodical print magazine. There was precedent in pamphlets transcribing *rakugo* and *kōdan* that had been published since the 1880s, and transcripts and performance scripts ran in newspapers. These published transcripts were made possible by phonographic shorthand recording and were not only consumed by fans but also served as important texts for performers, who learned new stories and content through script books known as *kōdanbon* and *netabon*.[61] The evolution of performance arts such as *kōdan*, *rakugo*, and *naniwabushi* in the modern period thus took place not only or even primarily through oral transmission but rather via the circulation of printed books and magazines in a cycle that moved between voice and writing. In *Kōdan Kurabu*, pieces are presented in a form resembling a play script, with lines assigned to each character in the story, although sometimes *kōdan* stories ran as uninterrupted narratives not dissimilar from literary fiction. The register of language in these transcriptions is decidedly vernacular, and the transcriber sometimes received equal credit with the teller of the tale in authorial attribution. *Kōdan Kurabu* also used images in tandem with the magazine's presentation of printed scripts; some *kōdan* transcripts are accompanied by a portrait photograph of the performer, a painted or woodblock picture of the storyteller performing, or illustrations depicting the content of the story. The texts in *Kōdan Kurabu* utilize all these components together to convey a sense of performance on the page and evoke Edo-esque patterns of reading between image and text, albeit in the entirely modern format of a mass-produced illustrated magazine. In terms of genre, *kōdan* storytelling provided an important basis for the evolution of so-called popular literature or mass literature (*taishū bungaku*) and *yomimono* (entertainment stories) in the coming decades.

For Noma, who kept the *Analects* on his desk and was a patron of the martial arts, personal and national morality were paramount, and he saw popular storytelling magazines as means to promulgate a vision of moral education for the masses; stories about heroism, endurance, duty, loyalty, and filial piety were excellent vehicles for ideology, especially when mixed with a healthy dose of humor and presented in the vernacular.[62] *Kōdan* and *naniwabushi* already had a long political history when the first issue of *Kōdan Kurabu* was released in 1911. *Seiji* (political) *kōdan* and *jiji* (current events) *kōdan* were commonly practiced in the Meiji period; the satirist Miyatake Gaikotsu (1867–1955), in his history of public speaking in modern Japan, notes that political *kōdan* was especially important in the Freedom and Popular Rights Movement (Jiyū Minken Undō) in the 1870s and 1880s, as the form and content of performance were closely linked in the struggle to speak openly about politics in public. The national government was likewise aware of the power of popular performance and supported the writing of patriotic songs and stories about each of Japan's modern wars.[63]

In Noma's memoirs, he writes that popular theater possessed great capability for instilling moral values, but that magazines were more powerful still, as they could reach an audience exponentially larger than even the

FIGURE 1.5 Illustration for "Ōishi Yoshio Yamaga Okuri" (Ōishi Yoshio Sent to Yamaga), by Ichiryūsai Teizan (1876–1945), a representative work of popular fiction in Kōdansha's *Kōdan Kurabu* 3, no. 6 (June 1913).

largest *yose* performance.[64] Further, magazines like *Kōdan Kurabu* could serve as tools to help the masses develop reading and linguistic skills; Kōdansha was seen as a sort of alternative "Ministry of Education" (*Monbushō*) that promoted literacy, service, and "education for the people" (*minshū kyōiku*). Noma's vision was not "to build a school and educate a small number of talented people but run a magazine and guide the masses" (*tasū no minshū*) in order to expand his particular vision of ideological education through cheap print media.[65] Given the moralistic nationalist ideology of Noma's project, the government actively encouraged and supported Kōdansha's work to supplement national education with popular culture to disseminate imperial ideology.

Kōdan Kurabu and Kōdansha's successor magazines like *Fujin Kurabu* (Women's Club, 1920–1988), *Shōnen Kurabu* (Boys' Club, 1914–1962), and *Shōjo Kurabu* (Girls' Club, 1923–1962) allowed readers to produce as well as consume content for the magazine. Issues called for submissions of "amateur [*shirōto*] *kōdan*" and "home [*katei*] *rakugo*," haiku, and *senryū* (comic verse), by which readers could send in work to be considered for publication. In addition to the honor of having one's name listed in the gallery of winners at the back of each issue and perhaps having their work printed in the magazine, Kōdansha offered monetary prizes. By basing a portion of each issue on reader contributions and submissions (*tōsho*), Kōdansha created a feedback cycle in which consumers could become producers and readers could become writers. Some literary magazines used similar strategies, and the submission processes continued across genres for decades as a method to discover new talent and cultivate devoted subscribers.[66] Kōdansha also solicited surveys and encouraged reading groups (*dokushokai*) associated with their magazines. All these techniques were effective means to quicken the circulation of what Hyōdo Hiromi calls "stories that everybody knows" and the creation of a shared sense of national mass culture.[67]

A *KINGU* IN EVERY KITCHEN: MAGAZINE, CITIZEN, HOME, NATION

Kōdansha's integration of oratory, music, and storytelling into the print register was only the beginning of a process in which Japanese magazines would become increasingly intermedial and ever more popular. After success with magazines like *Fujin Kurabu*, *Shōjo Kurabu*, and *Shōnen Kurabu*, Kōdansha's largest coup was the release of *Kingu* (King, 1925–1957) for New Year's 1925, publishing seven hundred fifty thousand copies for the first issue and becoming the first magazine to break the one million copy mark in January 1927. The goal of *Kingu* was to create a magazine commensurate with the masses across form, content, and readership. A generation earlier, Hakubunkan's *Taiyō* attempted to synthesize and make accessible every conceivable genre of knowledge. It folded in 1928; according to Kimura Ki (1894–1979), *Kingu* "ate" *Taiyō*. Magazines like *Taiyō*, *Chūō Kōron*, and *Bungei Shunjū* (Literary Chronicle, 1923–present) were at the time referred to as highbrow or upper-class magazines (*kōkyū zasshi*), as they peddled serious news and big ideas, rather than popular entertainment. *Kingu*, by contrast, was crafted from the first to be accessible to everyone and anyone—the first issue was dedicated to "the elderly, children, men, and women . . . students, entrepreneurs, salarymen, and housewives, so that they might enjoy reading what they want to read without regard to age, gender, profession, or position."[68] According to Noma, the name *Kingu*, an English loan word, was chosen because the editors felt that any Japanese word would come too loaded with the feeling of a particular demographic orientation, whereas the English "king" was both neutral and easy to understand.[69]

Kingu was designed to be a necessity for any member of the Japanese consumer masses. Kōdansha's goal was one copy of each issue in every household, to be "read together after dinner each Sunday evening as a family."[70] The ideological congruency of magazine, family, household, and nation is clear—the medium was made to be commensurate with the fantasy of a shared national culture across urban and rural Japan, and eventually the whole empire. Noma's brags of appealing to all ages and classes were in fact supported by survey data, which showed *Kingu* as most read among demographics spanning from middle schoolers to older adults and among farmers and urban workers alike. In a survey of 1934, *Kingu* was fifteen times more likely to be read by youth than *Kaizō*, and forty times more likely than *Chūō Kōron*.[71] The months leading up to the debut of *Kingu* necessitated extensive negotiations between Kōdansha and its distributors, who initially refused to take on an order so large, as they were unsure how to physically transport so many copies.[72] Kōdansha launched a carefully coordinated "American-style" (*Amerika-shiki*) multimedia advertising campaign involving direct mail, meetings with teachers, military leaders, housewives clubs, banks, and mayors, postcards passed out and mailed out across the country, regular newspaper ads, posters in public baths, and, famously, a *chindon'ya* marching band that paraded through city streets chanting the "Kingu Song" (Kingu no Uta): "Look up to the blue skies, the weather's clear / King King."[73] For those who wanted to sing along, the harmonica sheet music, lyrics, and photos of how to do the accompanying "King dance" were printed in the first issue.

Kōdansha reminded its audience of how cheap its magazine was—for the low price of just fifty sen, a typical newspaper ad for *Kingu* promised, the magazine would "make all our lives more truthful, good, and beautiful." This offer to rectify the contradictions of modern life through the purchase of a single magazine was open to all, "regardless of age, profession, or class" and available "to anyone who lives in the country or the city who needs the light of the sun [*taiyō*] to survive . . . it is necessary . . . for spiritual pacification [*seishinteki ian*]."[74] At the same time, the advertisement cautions, potential buyers should not "make the mistake of thinking that just because the price is cheap that the value of the content [*naiyō kachi*] is cheap as well." The magazine was pitched as an inalienable necessity for all modern subjects; an affordable, accessible, enjoyable commodity able to offer spiritual peace at a moment of rapid social change. Technological advancements in printing and formatting were a major draw; newspaper ads pushing *Kingu* mention little about the contents but make a point of the quantity of pictorial inserts, and even the quality of the domestically produced paper and ink. The arrival of new high-speed rotary letter presses in 1925 helped *Kingu* achieve such remarkable circulation numbers.[75] Kōdansha's attention to the quality of its industrial processes encouraged the reader to perceive *Kingu* not just as the sum of its parts but also as a milestone for the technological advancement of Japanese print culture and thus the Japanese empire.

Kingu's record-smashing circulation numbers were a selling point, and the table of contents of the inaugural issue emblazons in large font: "The highest circulation in Japan [*Nihon-ichi no daibusū*]! The most interesting magazine in Japan [*Nihon-ichi omoshiroi*]!" Prior to any editorial content of the first issue were nearly one hundred pages of advertisements; many of these were for modern commodities, like hair products and soy sauce, but a significant number came from other sectors of the publishing industry, congratulating Kōdansha on its milestone. These advertisements came from the production side of the industry and give a glimpse into the complex integration of companies, factories, and processes that made it possible to produce, advertise, and distribute a magazine on the scale of *Kingu*. Congratulatory notices came from other publishers, typesetters, printing presses, ink manufacturers, and advertising agencies and were followed by numerous ads hawking pens, all the better to use for writing submissions to Kōdansha's contests. There were congratulatory advertisements from newspapers from almost every city and prefecture, in addition to colonial Korea and Manchuria. The circulation of Kōdansha's magazines stretched across Japan's growing empire; an English note attesting to postal permissions in Los Angeles indicates that Kōdansha magazines were reaching Japanese diaspora communities on the other side of the Pacific as well.[76]

The contents of *Kingu* were a menagerie of diverse and incongruous material, selected for immediate appeal rather than intellectual coherency. A typical issue might include glossy full-color reproductions of European oil paintings, fairy tales foreign and domestic, gag manga, stories about

Abraham Lincoln, crossword puzzles, historical fiction, and photographs of tigers smoking pipes, circus freaks, and acrobats. There was the occasional bit of salubrious content, such as Noma's essay in the inaugural issue that sought to answer the ultimate question for modern consumers: "How to Get What You Want" (Ika ni Shite Kibō o Tassu ka). Noma's answer was experience, action, patience, and good manners; the essay was accompanied by drawings of proper bowing technique for a dozen different situations. The first issue of *Kingu* also contains a photo gallery of sixty-four famous people from all walks of life, including literati like Tsubouchi Shōyō, Kitahara Hakushū, Yosano Akiko, and Miyake Kaho, as well as linguists Ueda Kazutoshi and Hoshina Kōichi, editors Tokutomi Sohō and Miyake Setsurei, and numerous barons, viscounts, musicians, lawyers, educators, and politicians. These figures' involvement with *Kingu* was negligible, but the diverse array of supporters speaks to a sense that *Kingu* was seen as having more cultural import than a mere entertainment magazine, even while it ran photographs of dogs talking on the telephone.

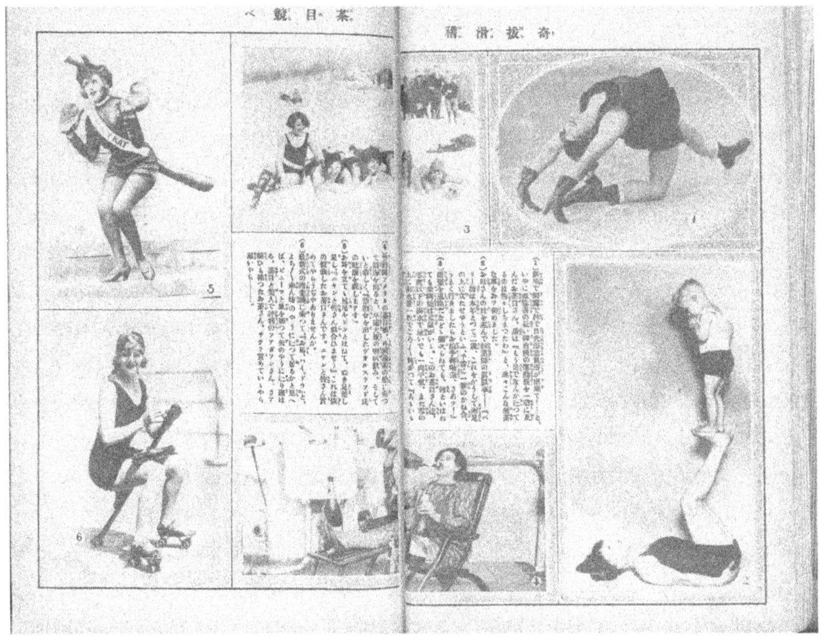

FIGURE 1.6 Photo collage from Kōdansha's *Kingu* titled "A Comparison of the Strange, Playful, and Humorous."

If this iteration of unconnected yet stimulating content mirrored the experience of modern urban consumer life, then the editors of *Kingu* promoted their new magazine by ascribing a sense of meaning that approached the transcendental. In an editors' introduction to the inaugural issue, titled "Santari Kingu no Shutsugen" (The Rise of the Radiant King), they call the new publication "the ideal magazine [*risō no zasshi*]," a piece of braggadocio worth taking seriously for what it reveals about the ideological structure of the medium. "*Kingu* is the king of magazines [*Kingu wa zasshi no kingu*]," they claim, announcing it to be equal to nothing but itself and thus able to become everything to everyone. *Kingu* was sold as a near cosmological substance with the potential to contain and become congruent with all of mass culture and the mass audience. The editors imbue *Kingu* with the magical powers of a shape-shifting fetish object; it is able to "take the form of a poet and sing hymns to the mysteries of life [*seimei no shinpi*] . . . it can then become a politician and lay out one hundred years of national policy." The magazine can alternately become a soldier, a merchant, an artist, or even a regular person (*bonjin*), taking the shape of the ideal version of any of its readers; since it contains all things, it can likewise become all things. *Kingu* is a "national park" of "mountains, fields, rivers, and seas" where birds chirp and animals sing, a fantasy consummate with the globe itself, a cosmic "wide world" that can provide "happiness for all mankind" (*jinrui zeppan no tame no kōfuku*).[77] *Kingu* is presented to the Japanese masses as an idealized mass-market commodity par excellence, not merely a benefit (*tame ni naru*) to the individual and the nation but also an object with the potential to save the world.

In another anonymous editorial essay in the same issue, "Our Pain in Bringing *Kingu* into the World" (*Kingu* ga Yo ni Deru made no Kushin), the editors insist that they labored "without sleep or rest" so that the magazine "would not be a simple commodity [*tannaru shōnin*]" like the makeup or soy sauce advertised in its pages.[78] But the commodity character of an object cannot be dispelled by fiat, and the editors' disavowal of *Kingu* as commodity merely affirms its character as such, as it takes on magical fetish powers even while obfuscating its own production process. Ultimately, however, *Kingu* was disposable, the proof of which lies in the present. Despite a circulation of one million monthly copies, today it is far more difficult to locate original copies of *Kingu* in archives or bookstores than literary magazines from the 1890s with much lower print runs. Unlike literary magazines, which were considered to have cultural value and thus be worth saving, most copies of *Kingu* were thrown away at the end of the month like any cheap product.

In the same way that Hakubunkan's *Nisshin Sensō Jikki* and *Bungei Kurabu* took advantage of new possibilities for photography and visual imagery and Kōdansha's *Yūben* and *Kōdan Kurabu* expanded print media through the incorporation of oral performance, *Kingu* would continue to interface with other forms of new media as the print realm and Kōdansha's publication empire expanded over the following decades. Satō Takumi describes *Kingu* in the late 1920s and early 1930s as a "radio-like magazine" (*rajioteki zasshi*), in which the oral performers that made *Kōdan Kurabu* so popular found a new home on the airwaves; Kōdansha also crafted cross promotions with vinyl recordings from King Records, still one of the country's largest record labels. The 1930s were likewise the era of *Kingu* as a "talkie-like magazine" (*tōkīteki zasshi*), where Kōdansha developed relationships between its magazines, film producers, and performers. In this way, Kōdansha's approach to print media and its relationship with the oral and visual that was developed in magazines like *Kōdan Kurabu* can be seen as a precursor to the highly integrated multimedia complex of Japanese publishing, mass media, and "media mix," or what Henry Jenkins calls convergence culture of the postwar period and the present.[79]

It is important to note in closing that this mass-media complex was actively complicit in Japan's road to fascist empire and total war. Noma Seiji would die in 1938, but his guiding ideology for the company was from the first tied to the cultivation of strong national spirit, individual sacrifice, and moral duty to the empire, and it is easy to imagine how a magazine like *Kingu* could contribute to the political project of the militarist far right. It would be hard not to see the parallels between the transmedia advertising blitz surrounding the release of *Kingu* and the transformation of public space into propagandistic space during the period of total war in the late 1930s and early 1940s. The structure of Kōdansha's mass-media complex made a ready framework for the dissemination of imperialist ideology; readers clubs organized for factory workers, farmers, and housewives were repurposed for the war effort. If the circulation of multimedia print publications like Kōdansha's helped readers imagine a shared national culture, then magazines were primed to play a key role in bolstering fascist attitudes among the populace.[80]

Over the thirty-plus years spanning from the early 1890s to the mid-1920s, the circulation of magazines in Japan exploded from the tens of thousands into the millions. The most important part of this story is not the increase in issues sold but how the maturation of print capitalism produced a nationwide market for literary writing, intellectual discourse, and mass entertainment. Changes in the production, form, and circulation of magazines created a Japanese mass public that could see itself reading, writing, and thinking in synchronicity with contemporaries around the globe. Crucial in this process was the integration of visual media and oral performance into the print register, which helped launch typographic media into a position of structural ubiquity through which future generations would produce, debate, and consume fiction, criticism, art, and social thought, all of it indivisible from the consumer market.

Chapter Two

IWANAMI SHOTEN AND THE ENTERPRISE OF ETERNITY

Today it is almost unthinkable to walk into a bookstore in Japan and not spy a shelf of little beige books wrapped in prismatically colored bands. Each book fits lightly in the palm of a hand but carries with it the weight of tradition and erudition, a pocket-size classic to carry with you. Surrounding shelves are sure to be filled with neatly lined-up little books of exactly the same size. Those books belong to the publisher Iwanami Shoten's long-running Bunko library, a series that has aimed since 1927 to bring "the classics of new and old, east and west" (*kokon tōzai*) to the broadest possible audience. Iwanami was the first to publish these pocket paperbacks, which take their name, *bunkobon*, from the company's initial project. The *bunkobon* format, measuring precisely 105 millimeters by 148 millimeters, remains the industry standard for affordable books in Japan, and every major publisher maintains an array of their most popular books in the size. Now ubiquitous, the *bunkobon* was birthed from a radical publishing experiment and a protracted plan to popularize philosophy for mass consumption. The Iwanami Bunko series was a culminating step not only in the crafting of a popular canon of world thought but also in the creation of the modern book in Japan as an affordable, mass-market commodity.

Since its founding as a used-book store more than a hundred years ago, Iwanami Shoten has gathered around it an aura of intellectual yet accessible sophistication and introduced a broad audience to many major works of thought and literature, both domestic and international. Through its canon-forming Bunko series, its weighty "lecture" (*kōza*) compendiums, and the still-seminal philosophy journal *Shisō* (Thought, 1921–present), the company has established itself as a premier publisher of popular and scholarly writings on all manner of metaphysical problems. In this chapter, I explore the early years of Iwanami Shoten to show how the company's ideology of philosophical idealism for the masses evolved through a series of publishing and marketing projects. An investigation into Iwanami's history also raises larger questions about how publishing as an economic endeavor can inform a sense of publishing as a philosophical practice. By tracing Iwanami's history, I show how the mass production and mass marketing of books in modern Japan allowed for the imagination of universal wisdom as an accessible commodity for consumption.

Rather than provide a comprehensive history of Iwanami Shoten, I focus on a series of points in the company's history in which the reading, writing, production, sales, and marketing of books took on outsized intellectual and conceptual significance. In doing so, I trace the processes through which Iwanami transformed the idea of "thought" itself into a marketable commodity and sold philosophy to the public. The chapter begins with a brief background of company founder Iwanami Shigeo (1881–1946), then turns to the short-lived journal *Shichō* (Trends in Thought, 1917–1919) and its editors' work to negotiate the heritage of nineteenth-century European philosophy. I examine the attempts of the editorial coterie of Abe Jirō (1883–1959), Abe Yoshishige (1883–1966), and Watsuji Tetsurō (1889–1960) to share their elite education with a wider audience and position their work within a comprehensive schema of world thought. Further publishing projects at Iwanami such as the Tetsugaku Sōsho (Library of Philosophy), the Iwanami Kōza Sekai Shichō (Iwanami Lectures on Trends in World Thought) compendium, and ultimately the Iwanami Bunko series facilitated the construction of a comprehensive genealogy of ideas and the fantasy of transcendent universal knowledge. Finally, I show how *bunkobon* paperbacks came to be understood as objects imbued with political and philosophical significance by addressing the competition between Iwanami and rival publisher Kaizōsha to release dueling translations of Marx's *Das Kapital* in 1927. Iwanami strategically wielded and dispatched socialist ideological discourse made accessible for average consumers as a successful strategy for market relevance; this association between the company's name and a progressive leftist intellectual tendency would continue through the postwar period and at least through the 1990s.[1] The philosopher Miki Kiyoshi (1897–1945), who worked as an editor at Iwanami, saw the paperback book as a medium that possessed a special power to critique the commodity form and transform the social logos. But paperback books nonetheless remained mass-produced commodities made by industrial labor, and the chapter concludes with the story of a 1928 strike at Iwanami Shoten that reveals the antinomies and contradictions inherent in the company's ideology of transcendental value.

THE EDUCATION OF AN INTELLECTUAL YOUTH

Iwanami Shigeo was born in 1881 in Suwa, Nagano, to a landowner family of better than average means. Shigeo was a model youth of the mid-Meiji period—individually driven and inspired by modern educational trends to bring idealistic personal and social goals to fruition. Shigeo matriculated into the local primary school in 1887 and belonged to the first generation of pupils to pass in full through Japan's modern education system.[2] He attended public school during the First Sino-Japanese War of 1894–1895 and was inspired to further his education by the lectures of the Christian thinker Uchimura Kanzō (1861–1930) and the writings of the pedagogical reformer Sugiura Jūgō (1855–1924), whose Nihon Chūgakkō school Shigeo transferred to Tokyo to attend in 1899.[3] In 1901, Shigeo continued his studies at the prestigious First Higher School (Daiichi Kōtō Gakkō; hereafter Ichikō), where in line with the intellectual trends of elite youth, he became enamored with the writings of Leo Tolstoy (1828–1910) and new concepts of self, faith, and platonic love. At Ichikō, Shigeo met many future collaborators who would play central roles in Iwanami Shoten's publishing enterprises. In 1905, after completing his course of study, he matriculated into the Department of Philosophy in the Faculty of Literature of Tokyo Imperial University.[4] Shigeo was a representative member of a generation of rising intellectual elites, a product of Japan's new education system inspired by his teachers, the writings of modern thinkers foreign and domestic, and by his eager schoolmates. Upon completing university studies in 1908, Shigeo took a position as a progressive pedagogue at the nearby Kanda Women's Higher School. The position allowed him to propagate his self-consciously modern ideals through the burgeoning field of women's education, and he was well liked by his students for introducing his personal favorite texts in addition to the formal curriculum.[5]

In 1913, Shigeo left his teaching position to open his eponymous bookstore, Iwanami Shoten, in Jimbōchō. Although Iwanami Shoten has come to be mythologized as a symbol of aspirational middle-class culture, Shigeo's resolution to go into business for himself was spurred as much by his dissatisfaction with his low teacher's salary of thirty-five yen and his long daily streetcar commute as by any intellectual ideals. The founding of Iwanami Shoten should likewise be understood as a choice more complex than simply the next step in a mission to educate the masses. High-flung notions of freedom, knowledge, and education for the common man would come later; at the time Shigeo wanted "a house in the city and a job that wasn't too stressful"—Iwanami was very nearly a candy shop instead of a bookstore. When Shigeo decided to go into business selling books, a key adviser was Sōma Aizō (1870–1954), founder of the famous Nakamura-ya curry shop in Shinjuku.[6] We can also understand the opening of the Iwanami Shoten bookstore as part of a process in which the potential to educate the people moved out from under the eaves of institutions of formal higher education such as Shigeo's own alma mater. In fact, Shigeo's seemingly contrasting aims of popularizing philosophical education and making money were by no means contradictory; it is precisely the potential for books to be sold as commodities like candy or curry that allowed for Iwanami's transition from the realm of elite education to the sphere of popular publishing. To open the shop was both to act out of individual financial incentive and to grasp that selling books was a way to stimulate the broad consumption of knowledge and intellectual culture.

THE PRICE OF THE UNIVERSAL

Iwanami Shoten opened its doors in August 1913, but prior to the sale of a single book the shop was already rooted in the transformation of fixed capital into books as circulating commodities. Shigeo had raised the necessary funds by selling inherited farmland he held in absentia, and he took the capital influx and invested in a stock of used books for the fledgling store. At age thirty-two, Shigeo began traveling by bike across Tokyo to buy used editions from dealers, collectors, and other shops to accumulate stock.

As a fledgling bookseller, Iwanami needed to conjure an image of comprehensive erudition, so Shigeo not only bought but also borrowed books to stock his shelves. By lending books from established shops, Iwanami helped his store achieve intellectual legitimacy, with the volumes' spines symbolizing the proprietor's knowledge of knowledge itself.[7] Further literary and cultural capital was gleaned through the sign of the shop, famously calligraphed by Natsume Sōseki (1867–1916), whose works played a key role in the transformation of Iwanami from used-book seller to nationally respected publishing imprint. On another sign hung above the register and written in the hand of Raphael von Koeber (1848–1923), professor of philosophy at Tokyo Imperial University, was an injunction attributed to Kant: "Du kannst denn du sollst" (Thou can, for thou shalt!). The quote was apparently the only line Shigeo remembered from philosophy class, but the aphorism's value came as much by dint of its display in German as much as by its content.[8]

In an announcement, Shigeo declared the store to be an endeavor imbued with "the hope of a life as an independent citizen free of falsehoods" (*dokuritsu shimin to shite itsuwari naki seikatsu o itashiki kibō ni sōrō*).[9] Written in the formal epistolary *sōrōbun* style, the tenor of the notice suggests an educated clientele rather than a general audience. Especially significant is the phrase "free of falsehood" (*itsuwari naki*); Iwanami Shoten was distinguished by a fixed-pricing scheme (*shōfuda hanbai*) in which all customers were given the same price, a phenomenon still relatively rare in a bookselling milieu in which collectors and traders often bartered and negotiated.[10] Shigeo's decision to sell at preassigned prices told customers that his bookstore aimed to function within a normalized commodity market rather than in an economy of antiquarian trade; he felt the public might purchase more if prices were clearly advertised. The shop was so committed to the policy that even Mori Ōgai (1862–1922) was scolded by a clerk when he asked for ten sen off a book's price; the clerk in question was subsequently scolded by Shigeo for shaming Ōgai.[11]

Shigeo doubled down on low-margin, high-frequency sales and sent out employees to confirm that Iwanami's prices were the lowest. One of the most revealing aspects of Iwanami's early business practices was a fundamental economic error made by Shigeo; as an accomplished teacher but novice merchant, Shigeo was at first unable to distinguish a book's market price from its philosophical and intellectual value. The story goes that a regular customer, a professor, inquired how much the shopkeeper had paid for certain tomes of German philosophy.[12] When he told the professor, Shigeo was chided for overpaying. Shigeo had been impressed with the erudite names of the authors and had based his prices on the philosophical value of the works rather than on the rarity of the particular editions. Shigeo's logic held that works by Kant should cost more than those of minor philosophers; he saw the books as objects imbued with the transcendental value of the knowledge contained therein. For young Shigeo, value was located in the content rather than in the form of the medium by which knowledge was sold, as he mistook the use value of the books for their exchange value. Disentangling these values via the economics lesson from the philosophy professor was crucial for Iwanami Shoten to succeed, though the company would later recombine them by imagining the transcendental value of knowledge through the manipulation of monetary value and the commodity form in the Bunko project.

Yet the best-selling volumes at the store were not works of German idealist philosophy but of modern vernacular Japanese translations of the Bible printed in cheap mass-market editions.[13] A substantial portion of Iwanami's early profits came from these Bibles, as well as from science textbooks, and the company played a role in popularizing the history and philosophy of science in Japan; an early best seller was Tanabe Hajime's (1885–1962) 1916 translation of Henri Poincaré's (1854–1912) *La valeur de la science* (1905). Iwanami would go on to publish both arcane works of hard science and popular works by the likes of Terada Torahiko (1878–1935), Ishiwara Jun (1881–1947), and Albert Einstein (1879–1955). Although Sōseki's *Kokoro* (1914) would be Iwanami's breakthrough book, it was preceded by a now obscure work on the philosophy of science, Ashino Keizaburō's *Uchū no Shinka* (The Evolution of the Universe, 1913).[14] The simultaneous publication of Sōseki and scientific studies gave Iwanami the cultural and monetary capital necessary for future projects. This commitment to science was a commitment to a comprehensive and totalizing vision of human knowledge that would inform Iwanami's programmatic approach to the massification of philosophy that followed. Poincaré's injunction would long resonate in Iwanami's mission: "The search for truth should be the goal of our activities; it is the sole end worthy of them."[15]

POPULARIZING PHILOSOPHY AND *BILDUNG* THROUGH READING

One of Iwanami Shoten's greatest innovations as a publisher was the construction of an ostensibly totalizing system of philosophical knowledge that could be sold as a recognizable, accessible, and affordable canon. Through a series of book and magazine publishing projects, Iwanami editors imagined a comprehensive genealogy of the evolution of modern thought. This began with the musings of a small clique of elite Ichikō graduates and culminated in a series of high-circulation publications and advertising campaigns to make the heritage of philosophy and social thought comprehensible to the reading masses of modern Japan. These projects included the coterie journal *Shichō*, the Tetsugaku Sōsho book series, the philosophy magazine *Shisō*, the Iwanami Kōza Sekai Shichō compendium, and above all the Iwanami Bunko pocket-paperback series. We can trace a trajectory in which a canon of world thought (and the heritage of German Idealism and Romanticism in particular) is transformed from the domain of highly educated Tokyo Imperial University alumni into a corpus of knowledge to be consumed by the general public. Thanks to the work of Iwanami's editors, "thought" (*shisō*) itself became a coherent category through the integration of these ideas into the print media market.

The first of these projects was the Tetsugaku Sōsho book series, which ran twelve volumes between 1915 and 1917. Published in hardcover (*tankōbon*) and organized around thematic problems such as "aesthetics" (*bigaku*) and "epistemology" (*ninshikiron*), the books were Japanese summaries of recent European scholarship that introduced key philosophical concepts to a domestic audience. The lack of accessible and affordable texts on such topics made the series popular among students, and it went through hundreds of pressings, selling seventy-five thousand copies in the following decade. Like Shigeo's shop, the Tetsugaku Sōsho books were predicated on a high-turnover, low-margin model; frequent Iwanami collaborator Abe Yoshishige recalled that the first pressing of the first book amounted to only a thousand copies, and that such success was "absolutely unthinkable." The series boasted an editorial board made up of Sōseki, philosopher-professors Nishida Kitarō (1870–1945) and Hatano Seiichi (1877–1950), and Shigeo's fellow Ichikō alumni Ueno Naoteru (1882–1973), Abe Jirō, and Abe Yoshishige, the last two of whom would play crucial roles in Iwanami's later editorial projects.[16] The short-lived Tetsugaku Sōsho project proved the marketability of metaphysics, established Iwanami's core editorial network, and built the framework for later endeavors.

In 1917, Iwanami Shoten sponsored another project exploring the problems of modern philosophy, the journal *Shichō*. *Shichō* was an unprofitable, low-circulation coterie magazine (*dōjin zasshi*) whose editors included Abe Jirō, Abe Yoshishige, and Watsuji Tetsurō, all of whom had attended Ichikō and Tokyo Imperial University.[17] The journal consisted primarily of articles on literary and philosophical topics domestic and European; pieces were penned by the editors and their friends for a limited readership that consisted of similarly educated peers. In the publisher's note that prefaces the first issue, the editorial note proclaims, "We must establish a broad base for the purpose of developing a full life and constructing a most excellent civilization [*suguretaru bunmei*] . . . to carry out this duty in full, we must first offer up all manner of knowledge to our readers."[18] The issues would go on to cover a broad range of themes, including European classical music, ancient and modern theater and drama, and the writings of Spinoza, Nietzsche, Kant, and the like. Raphael von Koeber, the revered philosophy teacher of many in the *Shichō* coterie, also contributed. The cover price was a reasonable thirty sen, but the potential audience remained limited.[19]

To the *Shichō* editors, the goal of achieving a "most excellent" level of civilization was based on understanding "the world as well as the nation, and the other as well as the self."[20] At the same time, the editors explicitly identified fervent nationalism as a pitfall for civilization, understood as broadly human rather than rooted in ethnos, occupying the registers of both the international and the deeply personal; it was the self-proclaimed task of the journal "to introduce to our country present trends in world thought, new and old [*sekai kokon no shichō*]." "Knowledge," to Abe Jirō, who wrote the journal's preface, is understood largely but not exclusively as the heritage of Greek and German philosophy and is not "simply that which has settled like dust upon the skin of our lives" but rather a force that "works within our lives [*seikatsu no naka ni hataraite*]."[21] In other words, to the *Shichō* group, an understanding of the Western canon of philosophical knowledge should be germane to the everyday life of modern subjects who see themselves as part of the global history of world civilization. The editors strove to connect the classical idealism of their scholarly curriculum to their new roles as budding public intellectuals: "Our purpose as members of this journal is, directly or indirectly, to somehow contribute to the form of life [*seikatsu keisei*] of our readers."[22] For these young thinkers, the goal of philosophy becomes the transformation of "everyday life" (*seikatsu*), and writing and publishing become means by which to carry out that transformation. *Shichō* aimed to propagate knowledge not through the direct translation of European texts but through summary and exegesis; the coterie mediated philosophical knowledge for its readers rather than making primary texts available in Japanese for analysis by others.

The *Shichō* coterie emphasized the self-conscious skills of reading and writing as it exported its methodologies for eager readers to follow their own paths to enlightenment. To that purpose, Abe Yoshishige, who would later become principal of Ichikō, then minister of education, penned a short column titled "Bonjin Bongo" (Common Words for Common People) at the end of the inaugural issue of *Shichō*. Abe muses that he "has been trying to write" but "doesn't seem to be able to . . . it's not that I can't write because I haven't read enough. Rather, I can't write without the desire for some meaningful development in my everyday life." For Abe, writing as the production of text has to be prefigured by a kind of arche-writing of the soul, the process of "engraving [*inkoku*] upon the pages [*kami*] of the heart [*kokoro*] . . . [and] putting the records [*kiroku*] of the heart into brushstrokes [*fude*]." The soul for Abe is both a surface to be written upon and a source of material worth writing about. In Abe's mixed metaphors of engraving and scripture, the individual soul becomes an ideal book, a scroll outside the mundane economy in which "business leads to the mechanization and hardening of everyday life."[23]

Writing for a limited audience of intellectual youths, Abe conjures the fantasy of writing outside the processes of commodification and reification that he associates with doing business. Instead, "in the words of Goethe," reading and writing "transform individual instants [*setsuna*] into eternity [*eien*]."[24] In Abe's model, these fleeting fragments of modern life can be made whole by educating and enlightening the self, or *kyōyō*, the translation of the German *bildung*. For Abe, reading as a part of everyday life conjures a sense of the infinite, total, and eternal. He closes his discussion with Nietzsche's theme of "thought as scraps of language [*danpengo*]"; according to Abe, the scrap occupies a central role in modern thought but begs the necessity of "systematic organization [*taikei*]."[25] Abe imagines the structure of thought as a kind of dialectical totality in which reading and writing allow the mind to move back and forth between the larger system and subject, assembling individual scraps to make sense of the self and the world.

ROMANCING THE PAST: JAPAN IN THE HORIZONS OF WORLD THOUGHT

The first advertisement in the first issue of *Shichō* is for coeditor Abe Jirō's *Santarō no Nikki* (Santarō's Diary, 1914), a record of intellectual investigations that would become a best seller and ad hoc life manual for bookish youth for decades. The ad copy for *Santarō no Nikki* beseeches the reader to behold "the resurrection of the teachings of the holy sages Christ, Shakyamuni, and Confucius and witness key movements of thought across world history reborn as new life in the bosom of one remarkable and extraordinary youth of modern Japan."[26] The rhetoric places the reader and the abstract concept of world thought into a dialectical relationship within which the heritage of philosophical knowledge is constitutive of the reader as a modern self, who in turn contributes to the ongoing evolution of trends in thought (*shichō*). The task for intellectual Japanese youths like Abe and his readers is thus nothing short of mediating the world history of philosophy, to allow that genealogy to be reborn in the soul of a living subject in the present.

Crucially, the advertisement locates the history of Japanese thought and culture on the horizon of a wider world, a perspective shared by the editors of *Shichō*, the first issue of which ran essays on Dante and ethics, a translation of Tolstoy, and an essay by Watsuji Tetsurō, "Nihon no Bunka ni tsuite" (On Japanese Culture). The magazine aligns these topics on a unified plane, where ideas from both "east" and "west" can be assayed within a comparative framework. Watsuji likewise understands the intellectual topography of contemporary Japan to be informed by the heritage of European thought. He opens his essay with the claim that modern Japanese subjects "typically do not notice, but we have been reared on the culture of the Greeks and Christianity. This goes for our feelings on beauty, our modes of thinking in our search for truth, and our moral consciousness. We are thus, by and large, of a different type than all previous generations of Japanese."[27] For Watsuji, the intellectual horizons of modern youth are inseparable from a system of ostensibly foreign knowledge and values that had become an inexorable part of domestic intellectual culture. To position himself in the history of ideas, Watsuji proposes a reversed, eastbound movement of Hegelian spirit in which Japan inherits world thought through the transmission of Chinese and Indian culture, which is in turn linked to ancient Greece, taken as the master sign for civilization as such.[28] Watsuji's notion of modern Japanese culture is interwoven with the amorphous entity of "world thought" on two levels—first through the currents of transcontinental cultural history connecting ancient Asia and the classical Mediterranean, and then through the modern movement of ideas following the Meiji-era institution of a Western-style educational regime. Watsuji's move is commensurate with a trend toward intellectual internationalism following the end of the Great War, when many Japanese authors and artists came to understand their work as contemporaneous with European trends. For the intellectual youth of this era, including Watsuji, Abe Jirō, and the other Iwanami editors, the ideas of Goethe, German Romanticism, naturalism, and natural science were always already a part of the experience of modern education.[29]

Given this worldview, the advertisement for *Santarō no Nikki*'s claim that the wisdom of Christ and Buddha had been reborn in Abe Jirō makes more sense. Abe and company's self-conscious discovery of "Japan" as a component in the system of world thought can be read as the rediscovery by modern youth of a purportedly long-lost heritage that is ultimately invented. The formal structure of this intellectual move reflects the influence of German Romanticism, which loomed large for these Tokyo Imperial University graduates. Watsuji's essay and later issues of *Shichō* abound with references to the lives and work of Goethe, Friedrich Schleiermacher (1768–1834), Friedrich Schiller (1759–1805), August Schlegel (1767–1845), and Friedrich Schlegel (1772–1829), who formed a coterie of spiritually minded youth engaged on a voyage of mythic self-discovery. The editors at Iwanami saw in those German thinkers a model for how intellectual youth might think about the world and change themselves through what Schiller called "the aesthetic education."[30]

In the fourth issue of *Shichō* in August 1918, Abe Yoshishige published "Schleiermacher and German Romanticism," in which he outlines a schematic history of German Romantic thought synthesized from Koeber's lectures. In crafting a comprehensive genealogy of Romanticism through Rousseau, Herder, and Goethe, Abe understands idealist philosophy as intellectual history rather than as isolated ideas. He investigates how Greek and French thought informed the history of German philosophy, which in turn constitutes the context of his own work in twentieth-century Japan. In contrast to earlier generations' reception of European philosophy, whereby works haphazardly entered the horizon of domestic thought, the *Shichō* coterie understood it as a system of knowledge constituted through complex conceptual and historical movements. This sense of thought as a coherent and constantly evolving totality, which Abe associates with Goethe's "progressive *Universalpoesie*" (*shinpoteki uchūteki bungaku*), would serve as the foundation for Iwanami's later projects, such as the Bunko library series and the Iwanami Lectures on Trends in World Thought compendium.[31]

Despite the conceptual work done by *Shichō*, the journal was ultimately seen as a financial sinkhole by Iwanami Shigeo. Although the transition from used-book seller to publishing house had gone smoothly thanks to the successes of Sōseki's *Kokoro*, the science texts, and the Tetsugaku Sōsho, Shigeo was not willing to write off projects that were not financially viable. The audience to which Iwanami appealed in *Shichō* was still limited and academic, and circulation remained in the low thousands. As a coterie magazine centered around a small number of contributors, *Shichō* followed the model of similar journals of that era. Eventually, Shigeo lost interest in bankrolling what he saw as Abe Jirō's personal, unprofitable project; he was interested in publishing such content but felt that *Shichō* had become little more than a "parasitic" red line in his company's budget.[32]

REGIONAL MAIL AND READING LISTS

Before, Iwanami Shigeo had been unable to distinguish between philosophical and economic understandings of value; now any experiments in thought had to be reconciled with the financial market, which *Shichō* never accomplished. The journal folded in January 1919 but helped expand the readership for literary and philosophical writing. Advertisements in *Shichō* reveal how the magazine functioned as a nexus through which readers could communicate via the book trade. Through mail sales, Iwanami laid the groundwork for an interregional network of consumers. An advertisement in the first issue of *Shichō* lists new and old books and journals available via regional sales (*chihō hanbai*) and able to be ordered by phone or postcard.[33] Each issue contained an ad on the back-inside cover iterating a table of fixed prices (*teika*) for new and used copies of available books. Some included a publisher's list price versus Iwanami's discount price, such as an abridged edition of Sōseki's *Bungakuron* (Theory of Literature, 1907) listed at 1.7 yen but offered from Iwanami for 1.3 yen plus shipping. Sending a book through the postal system reduces it to material weight, a further reckoning with the commodity character of the object without reference to content; the postal service cares not if a package contains Kant or comedy magazines. Iwanami Shoten also bought used books via mail from readers to be sold in the store or by mail to other *Shichō* subscribers, promising to ship "only the best books . . . both foreign and domestic as cheaply and securely as possible . . . at the greatest speed and convenience."

Shichō's used-book tables provide a fascinating picture of the reading list of a Taisho-era intellectual youth. Domestically, the works of Sōseki, Ueda Kazutoshi (1867–1937), Tanizaki Jun'ichirō (1886–1965), Chikamatsu Shūkō (1876–1944), Tokuda Shūsei (1871–1943), and Ikuta Chōkō (1882–1936) were all popular. The list of foreign books reveals how the curriculum of Western philosophy hewed ever closer to the canon as iterated in Europe or America, including Cervantes, D'Annunzio, Dumas, Shakespeare, Coleridge, Longfellow, Milton, Schiller, Nietzsche, Bergson, Darwin, and Dewey, in addition to less-salubrious fiction like that of Jules Verne.[34] Sales lists also include works in English about Japan, including volumes by Lafcadio Hearn (1850–1904), W. G. Aston's (1841–1911) *History of Japanese Literature* (1899), and Ernest Fenollosa's (1853–1908) *Epochs of Chinese and Japanese Art* (1912). The emergence of affordable books circulating between readers, publishers, and book dealers via a cheap and dependable postal network played an important role in the formation of both a national community of aspiring readers and the imagination of a canon of world writers.

MAKING SENSE OF A WORLD OVERRUN WITH SCRIPT

This trade was a site whereby a new concept of canon came into being through the work of Iwanami Shoten's editorial coterie. The scope of this ambition grew in the 1920s as the company attempted to synthesize nothing less than universal knowledge itself, making the concept of "world thought" (*sekai shichō*) into a coherent entity for analysis. Iwanami advocated an ideology of the eternal and universal, but the formation of those ostensibly transcendental values was mediated through shifting reading practices and the sales of books and magazines in the mass market. In 1921, a new magazine rose from the ashes of *Shichō* to become one of Iwanami's most successful endeavors—*Shisō* is still among the most prestigious places for popular and scholarly writings on philosophical topics. Unlike *Shichō*, *Shisō* was a business venture and began with a brief editorial manifesto credited to Iwanami Shoten. The vernacular (*arimasu* rather than *sōrō*) style of this inaugural editorial presents the journal as accessible to the lay reader and opens with a comment on the state of the publishing industry:

> There are far too many magazines in Japan today, and we, too, are at fault for publishing this magazine *Shisō*. There is no shortage of magazines that follow fashion and seize upon popular problems to catch the interest of readers. Even less so do we need any more specialist academic magazines [*senmon no gakujutsu zasshi*]. Yet, is there not a need that goes unfilled in Japan for a magazine that does not flirt with trends but attempts to bring matters of eternity [*eien no mondai*] closer to the general reader [*ippan no dokusha*]? To rectify this lack is precisely what we set out to do.[35]

By the early 1920s, it would have been nigh impossible for even avid readers to keep abreast of every periodical. The editors of *Shisō* acknowledge this excess in the ecology of print and ascribe value to their own endeavor by claiming transcendence over the very milieu from which they emerge.[36]

Shisō aimed to be profitable—the magazine cost eighty sen and was aimed at a broad audience of general consumers rather than of elite-university graduates. *Shisō* advocated a place beyond ideology, claiming that the magazine "does not advertise or propagate any one position but seeks to collect any worthy works that pursue truth, beauty, and the good, regardless of perspective, to contribute to the general education and cultivation [*ippan kyōyō*] of our nation's citizens."[37] Generality was marketability, and the magazine succeeded, spurring a boom of interest in Kant with a special issue in April 1924 following Iwanami's translations of *Critique of Pure Reason* (1921) and *Groundwork of the Metaphysics of Morals*.[38] The public could express its newfound interest in idealism by purchasing Iwanami's eighteen-volume *Collected Works of Kant* (*Kanto Chosakushū*,

1923–1926). *Shisō* and volumes of Kant were aspirational texts that often remained unread and served as status markers to perform intellectually oriented middle-class life. Readers and consumers responded to Iwanami's pitch that engaging with such ideas was fundamental to the development of self and society and the spirit of *kyōyō* (self-cultivation).[39]

Abe Yoshishige, who translated Kant's *Groundwork of the Metaphysics of Morals* (as *Dōtoku Tetsugaku Genron*, 1919–1924) for Iwanami, would later develop his personal "Theory of Reading" (Dokushoron) in a 1935 essay of that title. The essay is a discussion of Nietzsche's *Ecce Homo* (1908), wherein reading is described as "my means of recuperation; consequently part of that which rids me of myself."[40] To Abe, by contrast, reading is "both rest and work at the same time," a dive into the development of the self rather than a vacation from it. Abe notes that "in my laboratory of study are neither experimental machines, nor medicines, nor animals, nor plants, only books," which become the raw material for the production of ideas, the self, and more books. He argues that by reading, his own ideas emerge as he "organizes [*seiri*] the interior life of the everyday [*nichijō no seikatsu no kyūchū*]" and reassembles fragmented Nietzschean scraps of self and language into coherent forms.[41]

Abe laments that there are too many books and that "too much printed script [*katsuji*] peers down at our everyday lives." The organizational function of reading serves to solve this problem by structuring the reader's sense of self amid the tornado of text. Abe's solution to the anomie that arrives with mass-produced mechanized print is the close reading of the same, but he is not nostalgic for the past and contrasts his modern mode of reading with a youth spent listening to his father read Mencius and reciting the Confucian classics. Through his integration into the modern print regime, Abe's reading practice transitioned from "mechanical recitation" (*kikaiteki sudoku*) to a productive hermeneutic process for organizing the relationship between internal spirit and external world. Abe describes this process as a religious conversion, invoking the language of transubstantiation: "It is necessary for reading to both completely permeate into our whole soul and spirit [*zenshin zenrei*] and make it into our blood [*chi*] and flesh [*niku*]."[42] The spirit of the word is made flesh and then spirit again; the apparent contradiction highlights how for Abe the printed word mediates between the material and the immaterial, the immanent everyday and the transcendent, a dialectical literary communion wafer.

CUTE LITTLE BOOKS: THE BIRTH OF A FORMAT

Iwanami had firmly established itself as a significant entity in the Japanese publishing realm, but the mid-1920s was a period of crisis across the industry; the 1923 Great Kantō Earthquake devastated many firms, and Iwanami's offices were severely damaged by the quake.[43] The following years were financially challenging for Iwanami and many publishers, but in 1926 a revolution swept the industry as the company Kaizōsha released the *Gendai Nihon Bungaku Zenshū* (Collected Works of Contemporary Japanese Literature), a series of "one-yen volumes" (*enpon*) that became a sales phenomenon. Kaizōsha editor Kimura Ki (1894–1979) based the idea on the Harvard Classics series, with each volume costing one yen and containing the selected writings of one or two authors. Kaizōsha ran an expensive sales campaign organized by the advertising powerhouse Dentsū and sold more than half a million copies, making it the envy of the publishing world.[44]

Kaizōsha founder Yamamoto Sanehiko (1885–1952) pitched the anthology project as an altruistic gift to a public starved for books in the years following the quake and crafted an explicitly populist appeal to potential buyers:

> The vast majority of Tokyo's libraries had been burned, and the collection of books became an exceedingly difficult task, as there were many books that one could not get one's hands on, no matter how much one was willing to pay. The prices of the classics had skyrocketed, and it was the readers who suffered the most, as all the books soon found their way into the hands of those with money. The privileged classes came to be the monopolists [*dokusensha*] of knowledge, and no one else could get the books they wanted to read. Thus we had no choice but to publish the *enpon.*[45]

Yamamoto's rhetoric hinges on the general public's right of access to reading material and thus knowledge itself. This freedom to read is contrasted with the corporatist practices of the wealthy, "monopolists" withholding shared treasures from the masses; the implied duty of the publisher is to neutralize the nascent tendencies of the upper classes.[46]

Most Japanese publishers sought to duplicate Kaizōsha's success with their own anthologies, but Iwanami Shoten took another tack after ambitions to print an anthology of world literature were scuttled when rival house Shinchōsha preempted the plan with its own series. Iwanami responded by devising a new form of the book itself, the budget pocket paperback, or *bunkobon*. Unsurprisingly, the inspiration came from nineteenth-century Germany; the new series was modeled after books released by the Leipzig publisher Reclam Verlag. In 1867, Reclam began releasing cheap "cute little books" (*kawaiirashii kohon*) to the public for the low price of twenty *groschen*. The small, plain, yellow volumes made works of theater, philosophy, history, poetry, law, religion, and literature widely available, causing a panic in the German publishing world.[47] The series, which bore the Goethean title of *Universal-Bibliothek*, became favorite reading material both in Europe and among aspiring students like Iwanami Shigeo and his clique at Tokyo Imperial University.

Iwanami's plan to sell Reclam-style cheap paperbacks was risky. In the 1910s, publisher Akagi Sōsho had tried a similar strategy, offering works by Ibsen, Darwin, and Dostoevsky for ten sen apiece, but the series folded under low returns. Iwanami began the Bunko project by pressing runs of ten to twenty thousand copies per volume and charging twenty sen per hundred pages, about the cost of two cups of coffee or two plates of curry rice.[48] As late as the 1920s, despite a literacy rate of nearly 97 percent, the average Japanese reader regularly bought only newspapers or magazines, and books only rarely. Thousands of hardcover *tankōbon* books were released every year, but prices remained relatively high until Kaizōsha's *enpon* proved the viability of mass-market books. Before initiating the Bunko series, Shigeo consulted with his philosopher-contributors, including Nishida, Watsuji, and Abe Jirō. While Watsuji and Nishida readily approved the plan, Abe remained wary as he found the idea unsystematic and open to problems of profit and royalties.[49]

IMAGINING A NEW CANON

The first set of Iwanami Bunko paperbacks was released July 10, 1927, and included Sōseki's *Kokoro*, Kōda Rohan's (1867–1943) *Gojū no Tō* (The Five-Storied Tower, 1891–1892), Higuchi Ichiyō's (1872–1896) *Takekurabe* (Growing Up, 1895–1896), and collected writings of Kitamura Tōkoku (1868–1894) and Shimazaki Tōson (1872–1943), as well as volumes of Tolstoy, Chekhov, Plato, Poincaré, and others.[50] The Bunko series was conceptualized as both an economic maneuver and an act of philosophical significance, and

Iwanami employed a marketing strategy centered on the quality of the books and the positive repercussions of mass-produced print for the history of the human spirit. On July 9, the day before the first volumes were made available, the company took out an advertisement in the *Tōkyō Asahi Shinbun*, running a manifesto-like essay titled "Dokushoshi ni Yosu" (To the Readers) that extolled the virtues of thrift and availability embodied in the paperback. The manifesto, while officially credited to Iwanami Shigeo, was in fact written by Miki Kiyoshi, a young philosophy professor at Hōsei University and editor at Iwanami Shoten. The advertisement characterizes the series as follows:

> The Iwanami Bunko contains books of all types, including literature, philosophy, natural science, and social science. Each book is of a truly canonical value [*kotenteki kachi aru sho*] and absolutely necessary for all to read . . . This plan is more than a mere passing fancy of this mortal world; we have made great sacrifices to lend our meager powers to this enterprise of eternity [*eien no jigyō*]. We will continue to develop our plan so that we might complete our mission with no regrets.[51]

Reappropriating language from earlier projects, Iwanami's advertisement sold the Bunko as an ideal of universalist values of thought, knowledge, and self-cultivation that could transcend dimensions of time and money in the creation of spirit. In this logic, the history of philosophy is subsumed and released into the present, where publishing and editing practices forge an imagined future that transcends time and space. Bunko books allow for the conceptualization of a body of world thought to be made accessible through the purchase of paperback volumes. The series mission was to compile a canon of "the classics" (*tenseki*) of "new and old, east and west," in which Japanese literature could function as a part of the greater entity of world thought, a practical realization of Watsuji's earlier insight.

The Bunko series took on books deemed to possess canonical or "semi-canonical" (*junkoten*) value, and in 1930 Iwanami began using an easily recognizable color-coded system incorporating red, yellow, blue, green, and white, also inspired by the Reclam series and Goethe's theory of colors. Everything between the *Man'yōshū* (*Collection of Ten Thousand Leaves*, ca. 785) and Shikitei Sanba's (1776–1822) *Ukiyoburo* (Bathhouse of the Floating World, 1809–1813) became "national literature" (*kokubungaku*) and was marked yellow, while Meiji works and beyond were filed as modern literature and marked green.[52] Red was for foreign literature; blue for philosophy, religion, and the arts; and white for politics, law, and economics. The intellectual roots of the series's organization can be traced to earlier Iwanami publishing projects. In an article titled "National Literature and World Literature" (Kokubungaku to Sekai Bungaku) published in the first two issues of *Shisō*, Doi Mitsutomo traces the titular concept from Goethe through Adolf Bartels's (1862–1945) 1918 study *Weltliteratur*. To Doi, "world literature" (*sekaiteki bungaku*) is that which "overcomes national borders to enter into the mainstream of trends in thought [*shichō no chūryū*]." Only one volume of Japanese writing was included in Reclam's *Universal-Bibliothek* series; there were more from Bulgaria. By highlighting the French Enlightenment and German Romanticism as key moments for the development of world literature, Doi also makes visible the connection between mass-market publishing and the imagination of transcendental universalism. Both eighteenth-century France and nineteenth-century Germany saw major printing booms, and the authors and editors working at Iwanami were keenly aware of the historical parallels of these models.[53]

Doi believed that the inability of Japanese letters to enter the frame of world literature would not abide. In Japan's past, Doi writes, "there was precious little in our country's literature that might be linked to the content of world literature . . . but since Meiji, our literature has progressed through its affinity with world literature rather than its links to the narrow traditions of the past . . . to think of contemporary Japanese literature is to think of world literature." In other words, now that readers and writers in Japan were educated in the shared canon, it was possible to understand how Japanese writing might fit into that system. Doi argued that the task was to craft a genealogy (*taikei*) of Japanese literary history in the French or German model and find works of "universal interest" (*fuhenteki na kyōmi*) to enter the global pantheon. Doi identified the *Kojiki*, the *Man'yōshū*, *Genji Monogatari*, *Makura Sōshi*, *Tsurezuregusa*, and the works of Saigyō (1118–1190), Bashō (1644–1694), and Chikamatsu (1653–1725) as potential candidates for canonical status.[54]

One of the most sophisticated explications of the relationship between Japanese literary history and the heritage of world thought comes in Abe Jirō's 1928 essay "Sekai Shichō no Imi" (The Meaning of World Thought), the introductory essay to the Iwanami Kōza Sekai Shichō compendium.

Published from 1928 to 1929, it was the first in Iwanami's long-running "lecture" (*kōza*) series, wherein notable writers shared essays on academic subjects for popular consumption. The series was a montage of Japanese and foreign thinkers, with Rousseau adjacent to Kamo no Chōmei (1155–1216), Fukuzawa Yukichi (1835–1901) next to Leo Tolstoy, and Motoori Norinaga (1730–1801) sandwiched between Kant and Goethe. Like Doi, Abe sees the spirit of world history arriving in Japan via Meiji-era globalization but argues that it is only in 1928, once Japanese intellectual history had achieved a sense of synchronous contemporaneity with the West, that the question could be asked, what is world thought? For Abe, "it is not enough to treat Western and Eastern thought separately; rather, we must subdivide both and draw a necessarily large ring that encompasses their totality as they overlap like the rings on an old tree."[55] Abe's methodology is predicated on the ability to access that shared canon of texts via the publishing revolution. Here, the concept of "world thought" becomes thinkable through the marketing and selling of books in which those ideas appear. The transcendent value of knowledge emerges as works of literature and philosophy are made available for purchase to the general public. The forest of consumer choice in which Abe's tree of knowledge stands underwrites the discursively produced image of the book as a transcendent source of knowledge. The reader meets this tree not as a pillar of spirit but through the medium of pulped paper purchased as a book.

THE POLITICS OF THE PAPERBACK

The Iwanami Bunko paperback series was presented as a project encompassing a universalism of knowledge and values transcending temporal and monetary concerns to last for all eternity. This sense of the universal is imagined through the marketing and selling of the series to consumers eager to touch the transcendent corpus of texts by purchasing paperbacks. As such, the success of the Iwanami Bunko can be ascribed not just to the philosophical underpinnings of the series but also to the affordability and format of the books. The *bunkobon* pocket paperbacks were significantly smaller than *tankōbon* and *enpon* hardcovers, allowing eager readers to peruse them in far more places. With reading no longer limited to desks or tables in homes and offices, the circulation of Iwanami's books transformed growing swaths of space into sites for reading. A thin *bunkobon* could easily slip into a pocket and weighed almost nothing; Iwanami's Bunko manifesto accentuates this convenience: "Since we emphasize portability and affordability, the books' outer appearance is nothing worth giving a second look to, but we have made our best efforts to carry out the most stringent selection criteria in regard to the contents [*naiyō no gensen*]. Now more than ever, these books display the characteristics that you have come to expect from Iwanami products."[56] Previously, books as luxury goods predicated their appeal as commodities on their physical appearance. They were aesthetic objects and highlighted ornate features; Iwanami's first hardcover editions of Sōseki's works were famously designed by the artist Hashiguchi Goyō (1880–1921), and the editions are still considered paragons of modern book design.[57] By contrast, the Iwanami Bunko volumes wore only a thin beige paraffin sleeve.

Yet despite the advertisement's claim to eschew form for content, the Bunko project embodies extreme attention to form. The formalist focus on the text itself dovetails with Iwanami's rhetoric of a transcendent library in which sacred texts float through frictionless channels connecting the mind of the reader to world spirit. The mass public could now get their hands on otherwise unaffordable and inaccessible texts they had read about but not actually read. Almost all the texts released in Iwanami's Bunko series were already available in hardcover editions; Iwanami's innovation was to develop a new format and system of circulation with which those texts could be accessed.[58] Even more than the "stringent selection of content," Iwanami's true revolution lay in the radical formal experiment of the pocket paperback.

In an advertisement for the Iwanami Bunko printed in the October 18, 1927, edition of the *Ōsaka Mainichi Shinbun* newspaper, the copy reads, "The first duty of the truly popular edition [*fukyūban*] is the rigorous selection of contents. The second duty is affordability. But low prices must not come before the ability to make free selections of books."[59] This rhetoric of freedom constituted a crucial component of Iwanami's campaign and echoes the first advertisement for the series: "Truth is sought by all, and each seeks it for himself, just as art is loved by all and each loves it in his own way." The consumer's freedom of the spirit is explicitly linked to the freedom to purchase. One of the fundamental philosophical underpinnings and marketing strategies of the Bunko series was the ability for readers to "freely select whichever book they want, whenever they want . . . We conceived the

Iwanami Bunko to free readers from the fetters of the reservation system and to fully accomplish our mission of bringing out popular, accessible versions of the classics of east and west."[60] This freedom was explicitly posited against the restrictions and cost of the subscription-only one-yen-*enpon* anthologies like Kaizōsha's, whose expensive reservation systems limited their readership.

By encouraging the development of knowledge through consumer choice, the Bunko series helped establish the modern liberal reader-consumer; knowledge, art, and self-cultivation were constructed as necessities of modern life mediated through the act of reading. Yet there is more to the rhetoric of Iwanami Shoten than its role in structuring a middle-class intellectual sensibility. The Bunko advertising campaign was predicated on a politicized populism and often traded in rhetoric of class consciousness and revolutionary ideology: "Previously, art and truth were locked away under the eaves of palaces so as to keep the common people [*tami*] ignorant. Now there is the pressing desire for the people [*minshū*] to take back knowledge and art from the ruling classes [*tokken kaikyū*]. Iwanami Bunko was born from that desire."[61] In this ad, the author of the Bunko manifesto, the Marxist phenomenologist philosopher Miki Kiyoshi, appeals to "the people" as an active mass subject consummate with the reading populace, who are contrasted with a privileged class withholding the liberating forces of art and knowledge. In Miki's logic, the book becomes both the object of liberation and a tool by which that liberation can be achieved: "We must bring the people together to liberate these immortal books from studies and bookshelves; we must stand together to take those books out onto every corner of every street." At stake is nothing short of the transformation of consciousness itself; Bunko volumes become "materials necessary for the lives of all [*seikatsu kōjō no shiryō*]" that must be "released rapidly in the simplest form possible, so that they might contribute to the critique [*hihan*] of everyday life."[62] The book thus becomes both a bourgeois need and a medium through which to critique the very structure of that need. For Miki, the printed text possesses the potential to help the reading subject come to consciousness of the historicity and mutability of social life.

Iwanami Shoten was well aware of the appeal of their cheap volumes to a mass reading populace. Whereas the opening announcement of the Iwanami Shoten bookstore had been written in the epistolary *sōrōbun* style, newspaper advertisements heralding the Bunko were in standard colloquial language. Reading habits remained segregated along axes of gender, region, and class, and Iwanami's ads appealed to inclusive universalism, collapsing demographic striations into a single category of popular readership: "These paperbacks go out not only to the readers of the world but also to those who plow the fields, to those who hold hammers, to those who ride boats, to those who work in stores, to those who commute on trains, to those who pull horse carts, to soldiers, and to female students."[63] The intellectual interests of Iwanami's original editorial coterie were now available to all for a few sen.

Iwanami Shoten contrasted the company with *enpon*-anthology publishers, which it characterized as cynical businessmen deploying righteous but empty rhetoric. Advertisements for the Bunko series attacked other publishers, claiming that "those who seduce men so starved for knowledge by using cheap prices and savvy business methods do not follow the true path of 'publishing for the people' [*minshūban*]."[64] Competitors selling one-yen editions by subscription were singled out for scorn, and Iwanami readers sent in letters criticizing competing formats that revealed the class politics of mass readership:

> One volume for one yen! One thousand pages for one yen!
>
> They're nothing but goats covered in tigers' skins!. . . Do they think that those of us who aren't the prodigal sons of the rich have the space to line up all our money and our letters on our bookshelves? Our books are not for decoration, but they are what we need to live, and we want them just the same as the gruel-eating poor do. Our Iwanami Bunko! Our shining sun!!
>
> —A YOUTHFUL SUBJECT OF THE EMPIRE

> I recently received five volumes of your Iwanami Bunko in the post, and I would like to take this opportunity to praise your books. They are truly remarkable and are amazingly and refreshingly affordable . . . When I buy them at twenty sen a volume . . . it feels like I can hear the voices of the proletariat.
>
> —A WORKER AT SASEBO NAVAL HOSPITAL

> The arrival of an age in which one-yen volumes come tumbling one after the other has dazzled readers and made the proletarian classes seethe with envy . . . Even common peasants who can barely afford to live from day to day have sprouted the desire for knowledge of the world. We poor men [*binbō na oretachi*] are not the only ones who desire a Japanese series like the German Reclam volumes. We will support your valuable Bunko with our meager wallets.
>
> —A PEASANT OF TŌHOKU[65]

Miki's advertisement found its audience as the act of purchasing paperbacks came to represent not bourgeois intellectualism but an expression of proletarian solidarity and subjectivity. The success of the Bunko lay not only in Iwanami Shoten's formal innovations and skillful arrangement of content but also in the recognition of a mass market of readers unserved by existing forms of print media. Iwanami Shoten's affiliation of the company's name and progressive leftist intellectual culture would resonate for decades. Vanessa Ward has noted that during the American occupation authorities categorized Iwanami's magazines as "extreme left," an ideological linkage that remained tight through the postwar as conservative critics took Iwanami as a sign for intellectually bankrupt leftism.[66]

MIKI KIYOSHI AND LANGUAGE AS COMMODITY

Miki Kiyoshi, the man responsible for developing this political and philosophical pitch, was a recent graduate of the Kyoto Imperial University Faculty of Philosophy, where he studied with Nishida Kitarō and Hatano Seiichi.[67] Prior to joining the philosophy faculty at Hōsei University and the editorial staff at Iwanami Shoten, Miki spent several years studying in Germany with Nicolai Hartmann (1882–1950) and Martin Heidegger (1889–1976). In 1924, Miki sent an enlightening dispatch on German intellectual life that was published in *Shisō*, expressing his surprise that "free choice is permitted in choosing lectures and courses" in the German university system, in contrast to a fixed curriculum. There, libraries and archives are open for scholars to take books freely; as a result he "was able, for the first time, to systematically [*keitōteki*] peruse the books that he felt necessary for the development of [his] own research." Miki felt that this newfound freedom facilitated "not dilettantism" but rather the development of a "synthesizing spirit" (*sōgōteki seishin*) able to integrate and systematize philosophical knowledge. He argues that "only when the freely synthesizing function [*jiyū na sōgō sayō*] of scholarly consciousness is at work" can learning flourish.[68]

What made German academic culture appealing to Miki was not simply the ability "to visit a lot of schools and handle a lot of books." He describes an academic atmosphere facilitating the natural growth (*shizen seichō*) of scholarly consciousness (*gakumonteki ishiki*).[69] Miki is enamored with this social space, in which everyone can freely develop their ideas through contact with texts and like-minded individuals. He sees how the relationship between books and people can spur a sense of knowledge as a joint social project; it is easy to see the influence of this experience in Miki's work editing and advertising the Iwanami Bunko project. Whereas the earlier generation of Iwanami editors attempted to reproduce the Romantic coterie community, Miki sees modern German academic life as a contemporaneous inspiration. Miki's time in Germany provided a seed by which an education at once classical, systematic, free, and open might be sold to the Japanese masses as a purchasable commodity, the pocket paperback.

After returning, Miki published "Marukusushugi to Yuibutsuron" (Marxism and Materialism) in *Shisō* almost simultaneously with the initiation of the Iwanami Bunko series. The essay explicates an ontological relationship between language, commodity, and consciousness, drawing from Miki's phenomenological studies in Germany and his interest in Marxism as a philosophical system. Miki both critiques the reductive view of materialism as vulgar economic determinism and acknowledges the fetish power of the word "Marxism" itself, which he claims causes some who hear it "to scrunch their shoulders and make the sign of the cross." For Miki, "words work in magical ways" (*kotoba wa majutsuteki na hataraki o suru*), by which he means the near-mystical properties that Marx ascribes to the commodity form.[70] In Miki's schema, words can be commodities and commodities can be words, and the movement of both is what structures the deepest levels of human consciousness.

Miki seems to have become interested in the "strange entity" (*fushigi na sonzai*) of language (*kotoba*) while studying with Heidegger. For Miki, language is neither a set of "symbols representing thought [*shisō no fugō*]" nor a "transmission machine" (*dentatsuki*) but a system of feeling (*kanji*). Language to Miki is no mere vessel for the representation of sound or the expression of ideas as content but a force that possesses a distinct mediality innate to its own form. Referencing Wilhelm von Humboldt (1767–1835), Miki posits that "language [*kotoba*] is not something produced [*seisan sareta mono*] but production itself [*seisan de ari*]. It is not something made [*dekiagatta mono*] but activity itself [*katsudō de aru*]." Words, to Miki, are dynamic and productive forces as well as functions of "historical consciousness" (*rekishiteki ishiki*).[71] In other words, language both produces and is produced by social experience.

Miki outlines the related concept of the commodity form, which he claims is the deep material support of social life and which shares parallels in form and structure to his theory of language. The mass-produced commodity masks relationships "that play out in forms concealed from us," as "all social relations are buried and submerged . . . the commodity is what gives the material character to human relations and supports their ghostly objectivity." Miki acknowledges that his argument is in many ways a summary of the opening chapter of Marx's *Capital*:

> It is no coincidence that Marx began his greatest work [*Capital*] with an analysis of the commodity, which makes clear the totality of capitalist society and reveals its fundamental character. The reality is that modern society is a society of the mass-produced commodity. At this phase in the development of humanity, the commodity points toward the analysis of all problems, and their final mysteries lie in the construction of the commodity. The problem of the commodity is not a particular problem of the science of economics . . . but a problem of the totality of all capitalist society. The construction of the commodity is the model form of the object of existence . . . and as a result, consciousness is submerged away from real life [*genjitsu no seikatsu*]. The commodity is what supports the materialization of existence [*sonzai no busshitsuka*].[72]

Here, the commodity, much like language, produces the fundamental categories of perceived existence within which consciousness is both formed and sublated. Thus, the "magical" properties of words can be connected to the fetish character of commodities; social structures built upon language in the era of mass-market print are also built upon the commodity. Miki's innovation is to posit how the exchange of commodities and the associated movement of language serve to dictate social relations, form human consciousness, and constitute the bounds of experience. Addressing Marx's view that "there is nothing other than consciousness [*ishiki*, glossed as *das Bewusstsein*] and existence made conscious [*ishiki sareta sonzai*, glossed as *das bewusste Sein*]," Miki unpacks the construction of that consciousness, replacing "the absolute opposition of the spirit and the material" with a dialectical contradiction.[73]

In Miki's schema, the structures of social existence and human relationships are constituted by the dialectical exchange of language and commodities, although any consciousness of this process is always already submerged. Miki's solution is a plea for philosophical Marxism and practical materialism through which that consciousness of the movement of goods and words might be rectified.[74] Miki's essay is dated June 28, 1927, barely one week prior to the penning of the Iwanami Bunko manifesto. If the movement of words and commodities are fundamental to the evolution of social intercourse, then printed text as commodity might hold the key to transforming the material and ontological foundations of the social logos. Through his involvement as an editor at Iwanami Shoten and his work on the Bunko manifesto, Miki endeavored to bring the word to the people in the form that could best unravel the problem of the commodity—as commodity itself, as a pocket paperback book.

MARKETING MARX, CAPITALIZING ON *CAPITAL*

One volume included in the Iwanami Bunko series played a special role not only in Miki's thought but also in the development of the literary market—Marx's *Capital*. Since the Russian Revolution, socialist and communist themes could be encountered on bookshelves, at magazine stands, and in newspaper headlines, and book-length biographies of Lenin and translations of Trotsky and Lunacharsky sold well (a phenomenon I discuss in chapter 6). The moment in which explicitly revolutionary works became financially viable book ventures was precisely the point when the Japanese publishing industry achieved the phase that critic Nii Itaru (1888–1951) called "truly capitalistic capitalism" (*shihonshugi rashii shihonshugi*).[75] Ikuta Chōkō's introduction to his 1919 partial translation of *Capital* had declared Marx to be quite "the trendy person" (*ryūkōji*).[76] However, despite the public's familiarity with the name if not the ideas of Marx, there was still no complete and affordable translation of *Capital*. The earliest partial translation by Yasuda Yoshirō was released in 1907; Takabatake Motoyuki was the first to produce a complete translation of all three volumes, but the edition, published by Daitōkaku between 1920 and 1924, was prohibitively expensive. Iwanami recognized an open opportunity to market Marx to the masses and advertised translations of *Capital* (as *Shihonron*) and "Wage-Labor and Capital" (as "Chinrōdō to Shihon") in the upcoming Bunko library series. If Takabatake was right that "no one would mistake *Capital* to be pulp fiction for stockbrokers," there was money to be made from Marx.[77]

But Iwanami was not the only publisher to recognize the potential to capitalize on *Capital*; rival Kaizōsha also intended to make Marx into a flagship title. Both presses saw the publication of a popular edition of *Capital* as a significant social endeavor and an opportunity to win the format war between inexpensive hardcovers and budget paperbacks. Iwanami turned to Takabatake to contract his translation, only to find that he had already signed a contract with Kaizōsha to release a new popular edition.[78] Miki rushed to Kyoto to ask the socialist economist Kawakami Hajime (1879–1946) if he could quickly produce an alternative translation. Kawakami was a true believer who had quit a position in classical economics at Tokyo Imperial University to teach the poor; his reportage on the experience, *Binbō Monogatari* (Tales of Poverty, 1916–1917), proved phenomenally popular. Kawakami had since become a champion of the student movement in Kyoto and recognized the potential for "new editions of Marx in a cheap form that would reach as many readers as possible."[79]

Iwanami immediately began printing Kawakami's translation, attaching false covers to the galley plates to keep it a secret.[80] On September 23, 1927, Iwanami announced its new edition in a large advertisement in the *Tōkyō Asahi Shinbun* newspaper. The text of the ad, officially credited to Iwanami Shigeo, was likely penned by Miki and begins in a similar fashion to the "Marxism and Materialism" essay:

> The name of Marx is the name of a monster rampaging through the world. Some curse him as a devil and others praise him as a god. But he is neither a bringer of miracles nor a sorcerer. *Capital*, wellspring of mysterious power [*fushigi naru chikara*], is a simple scholarly work that can be understood, examined, and critiqued by anyone using the faculties of their own knowledge and reason . . . its study moves and shakes the world in a way like no work since Copernicus. *Capital* creates a new age and writes history. The appearance of this book in Japanese holds a special and immediate significance for the present situation of our country . . . its publication is an event in world history.[81]

Iwanami's ad copy brings together the dual dimensions of value in Iwanami's ideology—a book with the power to change the reader's life and the world itself, all for a low price. What Iwanami was selling was not just the content but also the possibility for readers to dispel the myths surrounding Marx by purchasing *Capital* in this cheap new format. The advertisement recognizes *Capital* as a commodity with that "mysterious power" of the fetish. In Miki's logic, the critique of social existence is based on the recognition of the material reality of the commodities that both form and sublate human consciousness. This is the process playing out in Iwanami's advertisement, where the masses are encouraged to engage their critical faculties with Marx's ideas. It is at once a practical application of Miki's philosophical ideas and a brilliant marketing strategy.

Kaizōsha responded with its own marketing campaign in October, publishing a full-page advertisement soliciting subscribers to buy Takabatake's complete translation in eight volumes for eight yen. The ad's tagline reads, "A new revised translation—the most affordable edition in the world—*Capital*, liberated unto the masses [*minshū ni kaihō suru*] for the first time!"[82] The main text of the ad reads,

> Marx's *Capital* is a masterpiece painstakingly produced through the scientific endeavors of man since the dawn of recorded history. Rare is the work that sixty years after its publication still sets aflame the soul of an age and turns the thought of our era on its axis. Sadly, the girth, profundity, and high cost of the book have kept it from being widely read, but Kaizōsha now brings you the world's most affordable edition of *Capital*, featuring a clear new translation based on rigorous scholarship of the original text, including explanatory footnotes. Now, for the first time, *Capital* is easy to buy and easy to read. We are elated to make such a contribution to the culture of our land, and we humbly await your support.[83]

Kaizōsha's promotional campaign imbues *Capital* with a double historicity, where the book's potential to change the world is located in its form as well as in its content. Both publishers' campaigns render *Capital* liberated and given over to the masses via the mechanisms of mass production. Kaizōsha and Iwanami alike had to convince the public that the text was not only financially accessible but also understandable to the average reader; in his introduction to the first volume, Kawakami assures his audience that he has "aspired to make the translation as vernacular [*tsūzoku*] as possible."[84]

Both editions went to press on October 1; Kaizōsha's was published on October 3, and Iwanami's on October 6. The translations are notably similar, although Takabatake's revised edition contains more detailed annotations than Kawakami's. In a preface, Kawakami calls *Capital* the key to "discovering the seeds of those contradictions of contemporary society";

Takabatake similarly muses, "It is impossible to develop a view of society without knowing Marx, and there is no better way to know Marx than to read *Capital*."[85] With these mass-market editions, Marx's work is transformed from a specialist work into a book necessary for modern subjects to understand their own lives. In promoting the massive *Complete Works of Marx and Engels* (*Marukusu Engerusu Zenshū*, 1928–1935) the following year, Kaizōsha reinforced this notion: "People of the present day are beset with the necessity [*hitsuyō*] to fully comprehend the truth of Marxism, which forms the basis of all social movements and is the root of modern thought . . . at present, the study of Marxism as the base for a worldview is a necessity."[86]

Iwanami and Kaizōsha marketed *Capital* by presenting the book as what Marx might call means of subsistence.[87] Both Kawakami and Takabatake translate the phrase as *seikatsu shiryō*, "material for everyday life"; Miki's manifesto for the Bunko advertisement uses a nearly identical phrase.[88] In Marx's words, the term indicates the fundamental abstraction of the commodity: "It does not matter here how the thing satisfies man's need, whether directly as a means of subsistence, i.e. an object of consumption, or indirectly as a means of production."[89] The mass production and mass marketing of *Capital* by Iwanami and Kaizōsha helped the paperback book to be reimagined as a necessity of modern life. As Miki points out, the book simultaneously becomes a new need and a medium to build a critique of the structure of needs, a critique crystallized in the act of publishing Marx's critique of capitalism. This referential self-consciousness of the book as commodity lends it the power to interrogate both its own nature and the larger cultural and economic systems through which it circulates.

THE INCOMMENSURABLE CONTRADICTIONS OF IWANAMI IDEOLOGY

As Miki's work highlights, mass-produced typographic text was seen as both a force for the liberation of the masses and a commodity inscribed into the same capitalist economy that it sought to critique and change. Although the dual nature of the *bunkobon* as commodity and medium of communication offered opportunities for thinkers like Miki to problematize how print structured the logos of social life, those same qualities put book production in a precarious position. Even Iwanami's books, despite their revolutionary aspirations, were still subject to the contingencies of modern Japan's consumer economy. In the case of the Iwanami Bunko edition of *Capital*, Kawakami Hajime soon found himself unable to translate Marx at the speed at which the books were scheduled to be released, and as Iwanami's desire to sell *Capital* outstripped Kawakami's ability to produce *Capital*, Shigeo broke ties with Kawakami and canceled the translation.[90]

Despite the success of the Bunko series, 1928 was a challenging year for Iwanami. In March, riding a tide of labor unrest sweeping the industry, dozens of Iwanami employees went on strike. Workers protested that the speed and scale of labor demanded to produce so many volumes so quickly and cheaply was untenable. On March 13, an ad hoc union organized by employees affiliated with the Japanese Communist Party occupied the shop and the next day delivered demands to Shigeo, including a 30 percent raise, paid medical care, a fixed raise schedule, autonomy to elect managers, and the firing of the editors Nagata Mikio (1906–1997) and Kobayashi Isamu (1903–1981). Nagata and Kobayashi were longtime Iwanami employees who oversaw the production of the Bunko series, but rank-and-file workers saw them as taskmasters. During the strike, Miki attempted to stand between the two sides and arbitrate a deal; the role was difficult but logical, as he was a high-ranking editor who also sympathized with the labor movement. Shigeo quickly agreed to the demands with the exception of the editorial firings; work resumed on March 17.[91]

The strike at Iwanami highlights the contradictions inherent in the idealistic logic of the publisher's projects. Regardless of the philosophical underpinnings, Iwanami needed to produce and sell the books; the intellectual aspirations of self-cultivation for the masses were revealed to be predicated on the exploitation of wage labor in the back of the house. For a brief moment, the mediating steps between a book's conception and its publication became a public problem, making visible oft-overlooked tasks like typesetting and proofreading. If the publication of the *bunkobon* edition of *Capital* marks the full commodification of books as cheap consumer goods in modern Japan, the subsequent strike proves both the penetrating power of Miki's critique and the difficulties of executing any action based on those ideas. Mass-produced typographic text was inscribed into the capitalist economy, regardless of revolutionary content.

The transcendental values endorsed by Iwanami's publications and marketing campaigns were ultimately inseparable from economic market value. Freedom as an ontological goal was inseparable from the freedom of consumer choice. While Miki negotiated between management and labor, Shigeo was advised during the strike by Koizumi Shinzō (1888–1966), an anti-Marxist liberal economist, as the Iwanami ideology was subsumed by market forces.[92] When Iwanami Shigeo first opened his bookstore, he mistook the transcendental for the monetary and was unable to separate the philosophical value of a volume from its market value. Once separated, these values were reunited via projects like the Tetsugaku Sōsho, the Iwanami Kōza Sekai Shichō, and the Iwanami Bunko, which introduced and made intellectualism and ontological concepts comprehensible and consumable. The mass circulation of these publications, apotheosized in the *bunkobon*, helped readers and writers envision an eternal, universal, and evolving corpus of world thought into which anyone could enter by buying a book. In the format war over *Capital* and subsequent strike, it became clear that the new need for popular philosophical knowledge remained lodged within existing structures of commodity production in a consumer economy. The selling of transcendental wisdom was still predicated on what Miki called the movement of words and commodities, themselves built upon the exploitation of wage labor. Miki was optimistic about the mass-produced book as a site to critique capitalism, but when that critique was confronted with its own commodity character, he and the workers at Iwanami were left in an impossible double bind.

Chapter Three

THE TOPOGRAPHY OF TYPOGRAPHY

Bibliophiles and Used Books in the Print City

In the 1924 short story "Machi no Soko" (The Depths of the Town) by the modernist author Yokomitsu Riichi (1895–1947), the nameless protagonist sits alone and impoverished in a tiny dilapidated room. He has just spent his last copper coin on a plate of food, but he finds the money to eke by another day in the form of a pile of used magazines in the corner of his room. "He knew that if he sold three magazines, he could get ten sen. With this in mind, he felt no fear; he sold the magazines, then set out with the coins tightly grasped in his hand."[1] The content of these magazines is irrelevant to Yokomitsu's protagonist; they are no longer useful as reading material, merely as goods to be exchanged for cash. Likewise, in an early scene in Natsume Sōseki's classic *Sanshirō* (1908), Tokyo Imperial University literature student and ne'er-do-well Yojirō helps Professor Hirota unpack his library and wonders aloud, "What does the Professor think he's going to do with all these useless books? He should sell them and buy stocks or something and really make some money. What's the use?"[2]

Magazines, books, and newspapers are made to be read but can also function in ways that have little to do with reading, objects imbued with economic and cultural value accrued as they circulate and are exchanged. Yojirō and Yokomitsu's laborer are aware that old books and magazines can be sold for coins then reread, pulped, or recycled. As scholars like Leah Price have noted, books are involved in any number of transactions that "stretch far beyond the literary or even the linguistic" and "accrue meaning not just at the moment of manufacture, but through their subsequent uses."[3] What, then, might tracing the circuits across which books and magazines are bought, sold, traded, collected, stored, and destroyed tell us about the diverse functions of print media in modern Japan? How might the circulation of books and magazines as material, monetary, and symbolic objects reveal uses for print beyond reading? In this chapter, I investigate the work of early twentieth-century booksellers, traders, and collectors in order to explore anxieties surrounding the commodification of books, as well as detail emerging discourses on the materiality of print media and the necessity of preserving typographic ephemera. We can thus examine the roles of bibliophiles and collectors, as well as authors and academics, in processes of canonization, the assignment of value to typographic media, and the possibilities of writing and archiving modern Japan's media history.

The chapter begins by detailing how Tokyo, as early modern Edo already a center for woodblock publishing, was transformed into a typographic print city starting in the late nineteenth century. The process began with a concentration of printers and publishers in the downtown Nihonbashi and Tsukiji neighborhoods that spread across the urban center via rivers, waterways, and the streetcar and train networks. Within a small radius of this nucleus were (and are) myriad places to print, bind, publish, buy, sell, read, trade, and store the millions of volumes printed each year. I briefly discuss modern Japan's most iconic bookstore, Maruzen, which served as a vector for the arrival of foreign goods and texts, then turn to the ideas of Maruzen's most famous employee, Uchida Roan (1868–1929), the pugnacious literary critic and bibliophile who wrote extensively about the uses and misuses of books. From there, the chapter follows the curve of the canal from the old downtown core to the used-book district of Jimbōchō to investigate how books were bought, sold, and bartered by the fanatical population of dealers and bibliophiles that still occupy the neighborhood today.

Some bibliophiles and booksellers published small-scale magazines that detailed the pleasures and pitfalls of the book trade. These writings, by nameless collectors and well-known literati alike, reveal insights about the symbolic significance of used and rare editions in an era of books as mass-produced commodities. Central to this trade were catalogs (*shomoku* or *mokuroku*) listing titles for sale; these indexes were compiled simultaneously with the building of the modern library system and the establishment of formal print archives, as bibliophiles worked with larger national institutions to preserve Japan's print heritage. The chapter closes with a discussion of the work of Miyatake Gaikotsu (1867–1955) and his apprentice Ebihara Hachirō (1907–1945?) and their efforts to establish modern Japan's largest periodical collection, the Meiji Shinbun Zasshi Bunko (Meiji Newspaper and Magazine Archive), which produced new possibilities for the writing of literary and media history. The chapter thus progresses spatially as much as temporally, beginning with early type printers and booksellers in Tsukiji and Nihonbashi, then following the expansion of the publishing industry along the canals to the used-book dealers and bibliophiles in Jimbōchō, and finally tracing the streetcar line up the hill to Hongō, where print periodicals found an archival home.

TOPOS OF TYPE

Around the turn of the eighteenth century, the gravity of the Japanese publishing industry first shifted to Edo from the Kamigata region of Kyoto and Osaka, where it had been centered since the woodblock-printing revolution of the seventeenth century. The concentration of political, economic, and cultural power in Edo during the early modern period, combined with the development of an efficient post-road network, facilitated the movement of materials into the capital and the flow of xylographic print media back across the regional domains. Within the capital, transportation networks were largely riverine; located at the edge of a bay and the mouths of multiple rivers, Edo was shot through with canals, waterways, and man-made channels that served as routes for moving people and goods into and around the city.[4] Many key sites for the publishing industry sprang up along these canals, especially in the Nihonbashi area. Following the Meiji Restoration and the renaming of Edo to Tokyo, the publishing industry became even more concentrated in the metropolis as modern transportation, communication, and infrastructure networks like railways, electric grids, shipping routes, and the postal system reinforced, expanded, and transformed early modern industries and institutions. The centralization of modern educational institutions in Tokyo in the late nineteenth century was also a crucial factor in consolidating the print and publishing industries in the city center, as schools, universities, publishers, and textbook makers were some of the first to require large-scale quantities of paper for printing.[5]

The first generation of typographic printers were clustered in the central neighborhoods of Tsukiji, Nihonbashi, and Kyōbashi at the heart of the old canal network. Nihonbashi had been a locus for print houses like Suharaya Mohei, which played a key role in the flowering of Edo's xylographic print culture since the Genroku period (1688–1704). This quadrant of Tokyo was thus a logical choice for the first imported typographic printing press set up in Tsukiji in 1869 by Japan's father of modern type, Motoki Shōzō. The Meiji government eventually worried that the print industry was too centralized and encouraged the establishment of presses in every prefecture, a goal achieved by 1877.[6] Yet, as Iwakiri Shin'ichirō has demonstrated, from the end of the Edo period through well into the twentieth century, a commanding portion of the Japanese publishing industry was clustered within a five-kilometer radius of Nihonbashi. During the early Meiji period, printing was as likely to be done via woodblock print as via typography, so it made sense for the craftsmen, carvers, and printers involved in the multistep process of making books to be situated in geographical proximity; any of these tradesmen could reach one another in about an hour's walk. Even after publishers shifted to industrial-type presses in the late 1870s and early 1880s, the topography of printing and publishing in Tokyo changed little, and in the early twentieth century the majority of printers and publishers were still headquartered in Kyōbashi and Tsukiji. From there, companies involved in the medial stages of publishing, marketing, selling, and distributing print media radiated outward across the city center to Kōjimachi, Kanda, and Ushigome, further northwest along the old canal system and well within the five-kilometer radius.[7]

The route of production of Japanese typographic print looked something like this: Timber was cut in the colonies of Korea and Sakhalin (Karafuto), then shipped to Tomakomai in Hokkaido, where the Ōji Paper Company maintained a huge plant for pulping. From Tomakomai, boats carried the pulp down the coast then up the Sumida River to the company's papermaking plant in Ōji in northern Tokyo. From there, paper was transported via canal or overland to either Kyōbashi, Kōjimachi, the large Shūeisha plant in Ushigome, or the Nihon Insatsu plant in Kanda for printing. Publishers were likewise located in Kōjimachi (newspapers like the *Tōkyō Mainichi* and *Hōchi Shinbun*), Nihonbashi (Hakubunkan and Shun'yōdō), Kanda (Iwanami Shoten), Ushigome (Shinchōsha), and other sites along the canal network. Once printed, books were sent to Kanda to be sold. This is the topos of Tokyo as print city in the early twentieth century, even after the fading of the canals as the primary transportation routes. But while printing and publishing remained concentrated in this geographic zone, the topography of readership spread across the country. The capital served as the central node of a distribution system whence books, magazines, and newspapers circulated outward via road, rail, and ship. Thanks to the portability of magazines and cheap pocket editions, reading could take place in public and private libraries, cafés, train cars, or almost anywhere. Likewise, traveling peddlers and temple fairs turned the city itself into a space to sell, buy, and read both typographic print and still-circulating early modern woodblock editions. As late as 1925, at the cusp of the cheap-book-format revolution, the number of book vendors working the streets of Honjō and Fukagawa still outnumbered brick-and-mortar stores in Kanda.[8]

MEDIA SPACE MARUZEN

At the vanguard of Japan's modern book trade was the iconic Nihonbashi shop Maruzen, which was founded in 1869 and remains one of the country's best-known bookstores. The shop's name is from a fictional proprietor, Maruya Zenpachi, an invention of founder Hayashi Yūteki (1837–1901). Hayashi was born to a wealthy doctor, and his interest in books grew from a belief that medical texts could improve public health. Maruzen at first resembled a dry goods shop, selling textiles and imported sundries and medicines as well as Western books. For Hayashi, who studied with enlightenment educator Fukuzawa Yukichi (1835–1901), modern Western books were specialized goods that could be used for physical, intellectual, and spiritual betterment.[9] At Maruzen, Western books were media that heralded new forms of knowledge, and the store's original stock consisted of reference texts like Noah Webster's *American Dictionary of the English Language* and other foreign textbooks and encyclopedias. The store's mission to bring Western knowledge to the Japanese public was evident in the shop's original name, Maruya, written with the character for "sphere" and chosen to evoke the globe and the wide world. Maruzen's mission to procure foreign literary and philosophical texts made the store a site for authors and intellectuals seeking new ideas from abroad; in addition to reading material, Maruzen also provided the necessary tools for writing modern literature, including imported European paper, ink, and pens.[10] Maruzen thus furnished both the possibility to consume modern literature and the media by which to produce it.

Maruzen's location adjacent to Ginza, the district synonymous with modern urbanism, was also crucial. Ginza boasted brick buildings, electric lights, cafés, department stores, bars, movie theaters, and other novel urban phenomena. Maruzen could be counted among these modern spaces; the store in its original incarnation sold Western books on tatami-mat floors and resembled an Edo-era dry goods store but was rebuilt into a modern brick-and-glass structure in 1910, resembling a department store filled with foreign commodities.[11] As a key location for encounters with new media for reading and writing, it is no surprise that Maruzen is a frequently occurring topos in the modern Japanese literary imagination. To literati—and presumably the general public as well—Maruzen was more than a place to shop for books. It was a place to seek immersion in a new media environment made up of strange and novel objects, and writings on Maruzen rarely mention something so mundane as purchasing a book; rather, the store is depicted as a strange and mysterious space that affects the psychological and physiological states of all who enter.

The essayist and scientist Terada Torahiko (1878–1935) recalls that "ever since I was twelve, the name Maruzen has always had a special ring to it, a certain suggestiveness." Terada describes climbing to the second floor to look at the books as its own enjoyment, even when he lacked the money to buy anything.[12] To Terada, Maruzen is more a site for the performance of urban consumerism than a bookstore: "The way the books are lined up on the shelves, one cannot help but feel that they are just like commodities [*shōhin*] in a typical department store [*futsū no depātomento sutoa*]." Shopping there is akin to taking a new drug; Terada feels excitement (*kōfun*) and stimulation (*shigeki*) as the objects surrounding him conjure a psychophysiological effect as he "looks up at the books and . . . becomes clearly aware of a tension that rises from his eyes and spreads across his face." He feels that his "head is of the old-fashioned type" (*kyūshiki*), at odds with the world of the books that surround him, commodities that can transform his old head into a modern mind: "Books [*shomotsu*] are the overcoat of the soul [*seishin no gaitō*], they are its necktie, its hairbrush, its toothpaste."[13] The Maruzen shopping experience serves as a technique for Terada to modulate his organism at both the psychospiritual (*seishin*) and physiosomatic (*shintai*) registers, embodying founder Hayashi's belief in books as vessels for the medicine of modern enlightenment.

Elsewhere, the store takes on more frightening dimensions. In Akutagawa Ryūnosuke's "Haguruma" (Spinning Gears, 1927) and "Aru Ahō no Isshō" (The Life of a Fool, 1927), Maruzen is a disorienting site of psychological breakdown. In "Aru Ahō no Isshō," the narrator begins, like Terada, as a young man climbing to the second floor to see the Western books at "a certain bookstore" with a strong resemblance to Maruzen. He is searching for new sensations as he scans volumes of Maupassant, Baudelaire, Ibsen, Tolstoy, Dostoevsky, Flaubert, and Nietzsche, and "eagerly reading the spines of books as dusk begins to fall . . . more than books, they seemed to become the fin de siècle itself." At first these books seem to offer the protagonist new ways of thinking and writing. But before long "the books sink into the shadows . . . and he feels somehow strange, climbing down the ladder and feeling the flame of the unshaded lightbulb."[14] The neatly shelved volumes overwhelm Akutagawa's narrator, overstimulating his body as he is unable to negotiate the excess of text and driven to the brink of madness. In "Haguruma," Maruzen is named explicitly; that protagonist opens a book only to discover "on the frontispiece [*sashie*] a row of mechanical gears with eyes and noses"; the content of the book is rendered irrelevant, replaced by the madness of the hallucinatory mechanical vision as the industrially reproduced book reflects back the psychological state of the mechanized modern subject and the inherent strangeness of consumerism for the author's old-fashioned head.[15]

Kajii Motojirō's depiction of Maruzen in "Remon" (Lemon, 1925) is remarkably similar. In this modernist short story, another young nameless protagonist wanders the city, destitute. "His favorite place to go is Maruzen," this time the Kyoto branch, where he wanders amid "the red and yellow eau de cologne in its colored cut glass and eau de quinine, the jade and amber bottles of perfume with raised patterns in an elegant rococo style, the tobacco pipes, knives, soap, and cigarettes," taking in the synesthetic stimulations of the store's commodities. The narrator barely mentions books at all, just that the store "tingles his nose" like the fruit at the greengrocer's. Kajii's protagonist is tempted to buy a pen but suddenly feels "oppressively heavy" when he imagines "specters of books, students, and bill collectors" before his eyes. If Akutagawa's Maruzen is a hallucinatory nightmare, Kajii's

FIGURE 3.1 Cover of *Gakutō* (The Light of Knowledge), Maruzen's advertising circular/bibliophile magazine, vol. 45, no. 5 (May 1941).

is an addictive trance, as "no matter where he walked, he always found himself standing back in front" of the store. Struck by a sense of mischief, the protagonist replaces one of the books with a lemon, turning it into "a glinting yellow bomb on the shelf of Maruzen" set to reduce the store to smithereens, the substitution reframing the book as a commodity with the potential to induce profound sensory and mental stimulation.[16]

LIGHT OF KNOWLEDGE, PILES OF BOOKS

Regardless of Maruzen's potential to incur insanity in its customers, the store presented itself as an institution committed to spreading the light of learning to the Japanese reading public. Beginning in 1897, the store began releasing *Gakutō* (The Light of Knowledge, 1903–present), a monthly magazine that served as an advertisement, a catalog of available books, and a quasi-intellectual journal. The magazine cast books and reading as literal lights akin to "arc illumination or fireflies" with the power to "light up the city streets" and "banish the dark" at a high wattage.[17] *Gakutō* presented the business of the bookstore as a mission to cultivate a love of learning, shedding light on subjects from philosophy and art to medicine and science.[18] After the Russo-Japanese War, editorial duties at *Gakutō* were designated to Uchida Roan, the literary critic who had taken a job as a Maruzen buyer.[19] Roan, who made his name penning satirical critiques of late nineteenth-century literati, turned his attention to bibliography and bibliophilia, and his writings reveal complex and conflicted images of the buying, selling, trading, collecting, and reading of books in modern Japan.

Uchida Roan was born in 1868 to a former samurai family and attended a Tokyo primary school that blended traditional Sinitic and modern Western methods of reading pedagogy. He recited Chinese Tang poetry and Edo-period primers and read the writings of Fukuzawa Yukichi and English reformers. He attended a Christian missionary school in Tsukiji, where he was introduced to the work of writers ranging from Yano Ryūkei (1850–1931) to Benjamin Disraeli (1804–1881). After briefly registering at Tōkyō Senmon Gakkō (later Waseda University), Roan ended his formal schooling but continued to read widely, from Edo *gesaku* fiction to Dickens, Tolstoy, and Wilde. Roan was of the same generation as Ozaki Kōyō (1867–1903) and Kōda Rohan (1867–1947) but used his columns in magazines like *Jogaku Zasshi* (Women's Learning, 1885–1904) and *Kokumin no Tomo* (The Nation's

Friend, 1887–1898) to critique his contemporaries, sometimes viciously.[20] Roan was also an active translator, producing the first Japanese editions of Dostoevsky's *Crime and Punishment* and Tolstoy's *Anna Karenina* (both from English translations), as well as those of Poe and others; lore has it that he joined the staff at Maruzen after scolding clerks, "I can't believe you bastards don't have *Anna Karenina* in stock."[21]

Yet Roan's relationship with reading culture was more complex than simple boosterism. Contra the ideology of his employer, Roan rejected the belief that the mere availability of literary texts could transform the public mind. Over a range of essays written in the 1910s and 1920s, Roan explored his skepticism of reading as a means for personal cultivation (*kyōyō*) and social achievement, which he called the "enlightenment theory of reading" (*keimōteki dokushosetsu*).[22] Instead, Roan argued for a view of relations between books and their owners that resisted instrumentalizing the medium as a tool for accumulating knowledge or achieving professional success. Roan was interested in a strategy for coping with an excess of books too great for any one individual. When books pile up unread, they exist as weighty objects taking up space rather than text; this is known as *tsundoku*, a playful portmanteau of *tsunde oku* (to stack up) and *doku* (to read). The neologism is generally credited to Tajiri Inejirō (1850–1923) but was popularized by Roan, who wrote frequently on the topic. In an essay called "Tsundoku Sensei Raisan" (In Praise of Mr. Tsundoku), Roan describes a "Tsundoku sensei" as someone who "lets books pile up without reading them," a category into which many bibliophiles (*aishoka*) inevitably fall. But, Roan asks rhetorically, "just what is so bad about *tsundoku*? Is letting books stack up without reading them really a practice that we can so easily deem scornful?" In the same scene in Sōseki's *Sanshirō* that opened this chapter, Mineko looks over Professor Hirota's library and marvels, "You have so many books," while a charmingly naive Sanshirō asks the Professor, "Have you read them all?" To which Hirota replies, "Hardly!"[23]

After clarifying that he does not refer to the odious practice of pretending to have read books one has in fact not read, Roan stages a defense of *tsundoku* in terms of the problem of processing an overwhelming quantity of material in a modern commodity economy: "There is a limit to how much one can actually read. No matter how fast a reader you are, there is only a certain amount possible to read in a day, even if you do nothing else but read from morning until night."[24] How, then, should the reader manage the sheer quantity of text produced in the age of mass-market print? What is to become of the huge surplus of material? Elsewhere, Roan claims that books are made precisely "for the purpose of being stacked up in unread piles" (*tsundoku no tame ni tsukurareta*). He notes that not everyone buys books to read them: "Are books for reading or for looking at? Since olden times, so-called *tsundoku sensei* who let books—considered things to be read—stack up have been scorned. But, since olden times, there have always been more people to whom books are things to look at or decorate with than to read."[25] It is also worth acknowledging that Roan's employer, Maruzen, had a financial interest in encouraging the public to buy more books than they could read. Roan argues that *tsundoku* is crucial to the preservation and transmission of culture: "If everyone believed that you shouldn't own books that you don't read, or that you have to read the books you own, then most books wouldn't end up being published in the first place. Even if they were, most would never see the light of day and would end up as insect nests in publishers' warehouses."[26] From Roan's point of view, it is consumption that drives the publishing market and allows knowledge to be passed on to future generations of readers. Roan goes so far as to argue that *tsundoku* is in fact "culture itself" (*sunawachi bunka de aru*), since the collection and preservation of books allows for the transmission of texts and ideas across space and time.[27]

USELESS READING AGAINST THE ENLIGHTENMENT

This relationship to books stands in contrast to what Roan sees as a debased obsession with "proper" reading techniques (*dokushohō*), a popular essay topic in the late nineteenth and early twentieth centuries. Roan calls this concern for righteous reading methodologies a remainder of neo-Confucian moralism repurposed for creating model citizens in the service of the state. Roan's goal is not to recommend a particular reading method but to encourage a relationship to books that allows the open-ended individuation of reading practices. In an essay published in *Gakutō* in 1916, "Keimōteki Dokushosetsu o Haisu" (Against an Enlightenment Theory of Reading), Roan critiques the instrumentalization of the book medium and attacks scholars who "make books into tools" (*shoseki o dōgu to suru*), arguing instead for their value as "useless" (*muyō*). When books are considered mere tools for reading, "the purpose of reading [*dokusho no mokuteki*] becomes simply the acquisition of knowledge," which is systematically reduced to information to be processed. Roan warns that such instrumental practices threaten to make reading "something akin to chemical or industrial engineering [*kagaku kōgei*] with books mere fabrication machines [*seizō kikai*] to be read as if they are industrial guides [*kōgyōsho*]."[28]

Roan links instrumentalized reading to the reproduction of government institutions, bureaucracy, and capitalist professionalization, lamenting, "If you visit the reading room at the Hibiya Library, everyone is studying for tests to advance to the next stage of their education, to enter the bureaucracy, to become a doctor or a lawyer." He fears that books might be reduced to means for achieving worldly success and points his finger at the education system, which he claims diminishes the vast possibilities for the uses of books to the simplistic shibboleth of self-cultivation (*shūyō*). Worse, so long as "reading is a mere auxiliary supplement to the education system," the public will "lose its desire to read" (*dokushoyoku*), and the opportunities opened by a literate public will be foreclosed at the precise moment when reading becomes universalized. Roan fears the newly literate masses will come to feel that "there is no necessity to read any books that won't help them make money."[29]

Roan aims to reclaim reading from instrumentalization by situating books as sensual material objects whose pleasures lie in their uselessness. To him "reading is an interest [*kyōmi*] like watching plays or listening to music" and a "hobby" (*shumi*) like indulging in liquor or tobacco—neither of which is to say that it does not have value (*kachi*).[30] Elsewhere, Roan declares that "reading is a cultural pleasure" (*dokusho wa bunkateki kyōraku*) and compares it to "baseball, billiards, photography, shooting, or gardening."[31] He argues that "reading is play" (*dokusho wa yūgi de aru*) and that readers are "neither philosophers or poets, nor moralists."[32] Roan's approach stands in opposition to that of publishers like Kōdansha, who saw mass-produced print as a means for the moral and monetary enrichment of individual and nation, and Iwanami Shoten, who aimed to cultivate philosophical knowledge in the public mind. Roan argues that rejecting reading as "a means for maximizing profit," "a method for moral training" or "worldly success" (*risshin shusse*) or "spiritual cultivation" (*seishinteki shūyō*) and placing it in the sphere of play paradoxically allows it to serve a salubrious role in producing modern culture.[33] In this framework, an anti-instrumentalist approach to reading allows for a "developed, enlightened, and universal" (*kaihatsuteki, keimōteki, fuhenteki*) future in which books retain medial properties beyond their function as vessels for the circulation and consumption of bureaucratically approved knowledge.

A useless, undirected, and excessive practice, Roan says, is the true meaning of popular reading as mass entertainment (*goraku*).[34] Rather than serve as grist for the mill of bureaucratic society, useless books allow for "solitude or reprieve for a few hours a week to be in a quiet place," a "refreshment" where new ideas might spring.[35] Roan sees mass publishing as precipitating a liberating loss of aura that allows books to shake off the last vestiges of their latent qualities as didactic religious objects: "With the development of printing technology, more and more malnutritious [*eiyō furyō*] books are published," by no means a bad thing.[36] In the age of mass production, "books are neither holy [*shinsei*] nor things of majesty [*songen*]" and thus no longer need to serve the ends of education or the Confucian "encouragement of good and punishment of evil [*kanzen chōaku*]." For Roan, since books are always more than a means to convey morals or knowledge, their value can never be reduced to the level of content. As a result, he maintains that "when it comes to classics . . . it is only through the original edition [*genpan*] that one can taste [*ajiwau*] the author's intentions . . . if we buy cheap editions, read only books borrowed from friends, and don't read the good books [*zenpon*] on our shelves, we will never fully appreciate the pleasures of reading."[37] To Roan the bibliophile, it is crucial to collect and own books oneself, and to read original editions, precisely because of the specificity of the experience of reading based in the materiality of a particular edition. Roan's attention to publication history and possession points us toward Japan's network of bibliophiles and used-book traders, in whose writings we can explore further meaning generated by the traffic in old books.

DOMAIN OF BIBLIOMANIA

The 1910s and 1920s saw the rise of an active community of bibliophiles, bibliomaniacs, and book dealers who built a robust trade in used books just as new books were being mass marketed. The expansion of the commercial book industry did not make old books irrelevant but rather lent them additional prestige, as a nexus of traders and collectors bought and sold all manner of preowned print ephemera. The bibliophiles' zone was (and still is) Kanda Jimbōchō, which became a bookselling district around the same time that the Japanese market for typographic print entered its high-circulation phase in the early 1890s. Prior, bookstores had been clustered near Nihonbashi, a remainder from the Edo system in which firms both published and sold books. In the early Meiji period, the Tokyo book trade was still organized around *shomotsu toiya nakama* and *shorin kumiai*, booksellers guilds and unions working in the model of the woodblock-print market.[38] Codes on the trade-in of used goods standardized sales practices and forced book dealers to operate in the same legal categories as other licensed businesses.[39] In the 1890s, Kanda-based booksellers like Tōkyōdō and Fuzanbō took over the commercial distribution of typographic books, facilitating the selling of books locally and nationwide.[40]

Jimbōchō was a physical space that buyers and sellers could visit but was also a logistical nexus for bureaucratic practices crucial to the expansion of book and magazine circulation, as the Tokyo Used-Book Sellers Union (Tōkyō Kosho Kumiai) and the Tokyo Book Dealers Union (Tōkyō Shosekishō Kumiai) set rules and restrictions for sales. It was forbidden for booksellers to do business without joining the unions, which controlled shipments from publishers and banned deliveries to nonunion locales. In turn, the unions worked to mitigate inflation, modulate paper demand, and negotiate prices for railway shipping, facilitating circulation on a national scale.[41]

Below, I discuss ideas that emerged in some of the dozens of bibliophile journals published starting in the 1910s. I use the term "bibliophile journals" to refer to periodicals ranging from reading-club circulars, to newspaper inserts, like the *Yomiuri Shinbun*'s monthly *Dokusho no Tomo* (The Reader's Friend, later *Dokusho Sekai* [Reader's World], 1912–1915), to bookstore trade magazines, to self-published coterie magazines, with a shared focus on books, book history, and the trade in antique books. These magazines had titles like *Hon Dōraku* (The Pleasures of Books, 1925–1940), *Hon'ya* (Bookstore, 1915–1922), *Furuhon'ya: Bibliographia Japonica Antiqua* (Used-Book Stores, 1927–1931), or simply *Hon* (Books, 1933) and featured articles by both nameless collectors and major authors and intellectuals, who occasionally contributed to the growing discourse surrounding the used-book trade. Attention to the bibliophilic perspective opens valences of meaning and value that used books took on when circulating on the edge of the mainstream consumer market.

BLIND BUGS AND MATERIAL OBSESSIONS

One of the core values of early twentieth-century Japan's bibliophile community was attention to the form and materiality of books. A conventional reader's attitude might mirror that of Tatsuno Yutaka (1888–1964), a scholar of French literature who felt that just "as any sake is good so long as it's drinkable [*nomereba yoshi*] . . . any book is good so long as it's readable [*hon wa yomereba yoshi*]."[42] The bibliophile's attitude is the opposite; books' content was of less interest than their typesetting, binding, printing, calligraphy, paper quality, and other formal and material characteristics as historical objects created at a particular place and time. The author Ibuse Masuji (1898–1993), who occasionally contributed to bibliophile magazines, claims in "Kami ya Hyōshi no Koto" (On Papers and Covers) that he likes "editions that are big and have some weight to them . . . there isn't much charm to books like the Bibles they give you in church, with their cheap paper and bindings that feel like cheaply made little toys." Ibuse's example of a Bible is telling, as he values the physical heft of an edition over its spiritual weightiness. Bibliophilic reading is an inherently sensory process; when the bibliophile holds a book, he thinks about "the relative merits of cotton paper, the way the light hits the page, how long it might last, how it feels in my hand . . . the smell of the leather binding."[43]

Similar sentiments are echoed by critic Chiba Kameo (1878–1935) in "Bookbinding and Authorial Sentiment" (Sōtei to Sakka no Kibun) in the bibliophile magazine *Shoshi* (Book History, 1927). Chiba is sensitive to the uses of books bound in the traditional Japanese versus Western styles: "If I write and publish a book with Western binding, I don't want it to end up on a bookshelf," he laments, but rather laid on its side like a Japanese book, which produces "a kind of unspeakable pleasure and stimulation" (*nantomo ienai kaikan to shigeki*). Japanese, Western, and Chinese books each necessitate a distinct set of reading practices via the binding, the color and quality of the paper, the sensation on the hands. Yet Chiba does not eschew the textual content (*naiyō*) of the book, which remains to him the ultimate "essence" (*honshitsu*); books are not just any object but "things meant to be read" (*yomu beki mono*). But even unread and left stacked up (*tsundoku*), unopened books generate pleasure via a "cleansing of the soul" (*tamashii*) and take on symbolic as well as sensual functions, from the blue covers of Conrad's seafaring tales to the "feeling of the embossing" on a volume of Chekhov.[44] In addition to Chiba, the list of literati frequently spotted in Jimbōchō or who contributed to bibliophile magazines included Akutagawa Ryūnosuke, Yokomitsu Riichi, Kitahara Hakushū (1885–1942), Hori Tatsuo (1904–1953), and Nagai Kafū (1879–1959), among others.[45] These bibliophiles would have agreed with Jean-Luc Nancy's more recent claim that "typography and page layout, printing, stitching, or binding, packaging, window-, shelf-, or table-display are what make up entry into the commerce of thinking."[46]

For bibliophilic readers and collectors, the value of a book is inseparable from its form. The bibliophile apprehends the medium first, which affects what and how she or he reads. Close reading to a bibliophile is less the careful parsing of prose than a dive into the surfaces and textures of the book as an object in order to understand the historical circumstances of the book's life. This goes not just for the production but also for the destruction of books, which can break, be ripped apart, burned to ash, or chewed up by bugs. The book-eating bug is an apt metaphor for the obsessive consumer, and there is no better example of the bibliophilic desire to wriggle into a book than Uchida Roan's satirical "Shimi no Jiden" (Autobiography of a Silverfish, 1924). Roan writes from the perspective of an insect that lives in old books and eats pages; as a literal consumer of books, Roan's bug develops a sharp critique of human readers. The silverfish narrator—the term is slang for one who reads without understanding—rhapsodizes how it "eats up the classics of Occident and Orient alike as if they were so much bread" and delights in "the sweet scent of old ink." To the silverfish, taste is not metaphorical but literal; the bugs are blind and illiterate and thus navigate the world of paper entirely via the senses of taste, smell, and touch. Without an ability to process content, tactility to Roan's silverfish becomes the primary sense with which to understand books and their history, as the bug becomes the bibliophile par excellence. The silverfish's knowledge of the bindings, covers, and glues used to make books becomes "material [*shiryō*] to understand and study book history [*shomotsushi*] and printing history [*insatsushi*]" and gain historical perspective on the objects that constitute their world. As with humans, there are "fancy bourgeois silverfish who eat only books by Saikaku and self-published rare old editions" and a silverfish proletariat who settle for cheap print editions. Younger generations of silverfish eat up the Western binding on new books but eschew smelly traditionally bound books.[47] The narrator is aware that its ilk may be "cursed by bibliophiles who disdain them as the enemies of books," but

Roan's bugs see themselves as population control—"there's no need to feel too guilty since rich humans will never read their big book collections anyway" and "rare books become prized precisely because we eat them."[48] Through the blind bug's eye, Roan parodies modern Japan's book trade. The present is positioned within the scope of a longer book history and printing history via obsessive attention to the physical constitution of books as objects to be consumed in the most literal sense. In the words of Nancy again, "in the bookstore . . . the consumption of merchandise—the devouring of the book—remain[s] inseparable from a penetration into its intimacy . . . back to the gesture that gave birth to the book."[49]

A similar mechanism is at work in the anonymous "Wagahai wa Shomotsu de Aru" (I Am a Book), a parody of Natsume Sōseki's *Wagahai wa Neko de Aru* (*I Am a Cat*, 1905–1906). Here, the pseudonymous author Kosho Chijin (Maniac for Old Books) takes as narrator a book itself as it describes its birth and life cycle. It begins as a sheaf of pages, is "bound up with unforgettable pain" at the bindery, sent from the production factory to the publishers' warehouse without seeing the light of day, and sentenced to "life in prison." The narrator leaves the warehouse to find itself bouncing in the belly of "that great land-born monster of the twentieth century," the delivery truck. Whereas Roan's silverfish focused on materiality, Chijin's *shomotsu* highlights the means by which books are bought and sold. Eventually the narrator finds itself sitting on a bookstore shelf when a gentleman and his paramour come browsing. The gentleman is drawn in by the book's title, *The Searcher* (*Tankyūsha*), convinced it must possess some kind of "deep philosophical thought."[50] Noticing the customer's interest, the clerk lies that the book is about to go out of print and will soon cost many times the cover price. The narrator notes that many friends have been sold through such strategies and soon finds itself on the shelf of a well-appointed bourgeois home. Once the narrator settles onto the bookshelf, it meets its neighbors, who establish a social order based on market value. There are old books, cheap books, expensive books, Western books that speak a little English, and a volume by Ihara Saikaku (1642–1693), the seventeenth-century author whose original editions commanded some of the highest prices among prewar bibliophiles. The latter results in bickering as to what the book might be about to make it so expensive; the book-narrator knows itself as an object and understands how it is made, marketed, and sold, but its awareness does not extend to content.

COLLECTOR SCUM CRITICS AND BOOK-BURNING BIBLIOFREAKS

This consternation over the rising prices of rare volumes points toward a burgeoning trade in antique books in the 1920s. As new books were being mass-produced for a broad readership, the trade in old and used books expanded exponentially, spurred both by serious collectors and by a general public with a fresh interest in bibliophilia. A generation earlier, digging up an original copy of a woodblock Edo edition or a recently out-of-print book might have been the only way to read a rare text. But by the 1920s, anthologies, collected works, reprints, and popular editions made such texts far more accessible, shifting the interest in used books away from content and toward the materiality of old volumes lost in contemporary mass-market pressings. Beginning in the 1880s, reprint series generated interest in domestic classics and early modern works, peaking with the "Saikaku boom" of the late nineteenth and early twentieth centuries. The renewal of literary interest in Saikaku and his repositioning as a forefather of modern prose led to a dramatic jump in the value of older editions; in 1919, original copies of *Kōshoku Ichidai Otoko* (*The Life of an Amorous Man*, 1682) and *Kōshoku Ichidai Onna* (*The Life of an Amorous Woman*, 1686) sold for about four hundred twenty yen each, the equivalent of about one million yen in today's money.[51] By 1924, the price had jumped to about eleven hundred yen, or more than one thousand times the cost of a new book.

Interest in Edo fiction helped drive the used-book trade, as woodblock-printed, string-bound *wahon* were distinct from cheap mass-market editions, and illustrated early modern genres like *kibyōshi* could not easily be reproduced through typography alone. The novelist Ozaki Kazuo (1899–1983) recalls daily trips to used-book stores in the 1910s and 1920s to scoop up treasures like *Nise Murasaki Inaka Genji* (A Fraudulent Murasaki's Bumpkin *Genji*, 1829–1842) and *Shunshoku Umegoyomi* (The Spring-Colored Plum Calendar, 1833).[52] This used-book-buying boom led to gnashing of teeth by bibliophiles, who bristled at the "antiquitization" (*kottōka*) of old books and the accompanying price bubble.[53] Among bibliophiles, "antiquitization" served as shorthand for anxieties over the integration of old books into a general market of commodities for profit. The pseudonymous collector Tokushū Yūshō noted that new books were "advertised the same as any medicine . . . with big ads in the newspapers" and feared that used books might end up sold the same way as more people saw them as a means to make money. Tanmachi Shigeo (1901–1991), a dealer renowned for trading museum-quality rarities, wrote a polemic to disabuse the notion of the used-book trade as a get-rich-quick scheme. He worried that "the same myths heard over and over again" about rare finds turned into big money threaten to transform the practice of *horidashi* (digging up old books) into prospecting for profit. Thanks to the price bubble, "people have the idea that you can make a lot of money in the used-book trade, that it's good business," but the reality, he chides, is that book dealers "have some of the lowest standards of living of any job . . . far from the so-called bourgeois consumer lifestyle."[54]

The critic Kobayashi Hideo (1902–1983) identifies a similar dynamic in a brief essay on antique ceramics, where he acknowledges the relationship between the sensuality of the fetishized object and the desire for possession contrapositioned with the act of detached reflection: "Antiques are things to touch and play with [*ijiru*], and art is something to appreciate [*kanshō*] . . . Collectors say that it is impossible to understand antiques without buying them."[55] For Kobayashi, the modern antique trade is inseparable from the bourgeois need to possess (*shoyū*); the antique is an auratic object that belongs to the collector rather than one iteration of a master copy that can be endlessly reproduced, as is the case with a commodity. This obsessive need for possession is the mark of a bibliophile; the desire to say, in the words of Gustave Flaubert (1821–1880), "This book is mine! And to hold it in [one's] two hands . . . to fondle it . . . to take in all its fragrance" as the book collector is beset by a madness to own the object at the expense of all else.[56]

Perhaps the most famous bibliomaniac is the nineteenth-century fictional Spanish monk Don Vicente, said to have committed murderous arson for a rare edition; his tale was retold in a fourteen-year-old Flaubert's early novella *Bibliomanie*.[57] Flaubert's protagonist, Giacomo, was "one of those men with a pale face, dull and sunken eyes, one of those satanic and bizarre beings such as Hoffmann dug up in his dreams . . . people rarely saw him in the streets, except on the days when they sold rare and curious books at auction . . . he passed for a strange and infernal man, for a savant or sorcerer. Yet he scarcely knew how to read . . . he did not think, he did not dream, he did not see anything but books."[58] The collector, whose relationship to the book is primarily sensual—in the case of the illiterate Giacomo divorced entirely from content—is bewitched by the dark magic of the fetish. Yet this fetishism is subtly distinct from that related to the mass-produced commodity; in his own retelling of the Don Vicente story, Uchida Roan clarifies that bibliophiles are "not interested in books that are commodities [*shōhin*]," only the rare and unusual.[59] To the bibliomaniac, books at once bewitch and, in their talismanic materiality, become the only objects capable of dispelling the very magic that they cast; per Roan, "for bibliomaniacs books are not for reading—it is as if they are a kind of charm for warding off evil [*mayoke no gofu*]."[60]

The image of the bibliomaniac (*shochi*) or bibliofreak (*shokyū*) emerges in tandem with the development of the commercial publishing industry in Japan, as was the case in Flaubert's France or among the bibliomaniacs of early nineteenth-century England beset by "black-letter mania."[61] Although the professionalization of the book trade created anxiety among Japanese bibliophiles, the integration of antique books into the consumer market also produced new possibilities for scholarship and thought. Increased communication between collectors facilitated analysis, as information regarding publishing, printing, binding, and the like could be compared and cataloged.[62] Used-book shops and bibliophile magazines served as sites to investigate and collate book histories, especially of the Edo period. Collected editions and reprints of Meiji works made out-of-print texts widely available, and the circulation of old journals provided prismatic pictures of the development of modern Japanese literature.[63] Scholars like the philologist Yamada Yoshio and the linguist Ueda Kazutoshi used antique-book catalogs to accumulate texts for crafting new histories of the Japanese language. By the late 1920s, the used-book trade helped situate the literature of the recently passed Meiji and Taisho periods as an object of historical study.

In a critical reassessment of the bibliophiles of early nineteenth-century England, John Klancher identifies the role of obsessives in precipitating a more robust "history of books" as a field made possible through interest in writing, printing, typography, bookmaking, and binding. In early twentieth-century Japan, the collector impulse played a role in evolving what Klancher calls "a bibliographical self-consciousness" that would lead to new possibilities of research in book history.[64] Ichishima Kenkichi (1860–1944), the first head of Waseda University's library, described the bibliophile fantasy of digging up obscurities in musty storerooms to produce a revelation of forgotten history akin to the archaeological discoveries at the Dunhuang caves.[65] The dissemination of old editions through the book trade also played an important role in preserving texts and materials for future generations; when fires reduced much of Jimbōchō to ash after the Great Kantō Earthquake of 1923, even more books would have been lost but for the thousands of volumes already in the hands of collectors across the country and thus saved from the flames.[66]

Uchida Roan and other bibliophiles saw used-book stores as the ultimate receptacle of public knowledge. Roan asks rhetorically, "Through whose power have books become universalized [*fukyū*] and appreciated? Authors? Critics? Or the general public?" His answer is none of the above but rather through bookstores, circulatory forces that promote the development of discourse as "books tossed aside end up in the used-book shops" from where they "return to life and rise like phoenixes from the ashes to be found by trash diggers."[67] In the words of an anonymous collector writing under the name Tamagawa Rōjin, "the advancement of publishing technology has made human life [*ningen no seikatsu*] all the more scriptural [*mojiteki*] . . . there is almost nothing in the totality of modern life that cannot be expressed by script . . . as a result, everything ends up as the content of used-book stores."[68] As all manner of knowledge was reconciled into mass-produced typographic print, the used-book trade became a kind of cosmos in which the detritus of modern mass culture could be accumulated into an archive for the historical analysis of future generations.

THE INDEXICAL IMAGINARY

The central functionaries of the used-book trade were catalogs known as *shomoku* or *mokuroku*, which listed available titles, bibliographic details, and prices and were used for placing orders via telegram, telephone, and postcard. These indexes structured the trade in old books and were inseparable from bibliophile journals and publications in both form and content.[69] Many of the bibliophile magazines were themselves glorified *mokuroku*, lists of titles for order with a few articles attached; other journals evolved from catalogs to become full-fledged magazines. The long-running Kyoto-based magazine *Hon'ya* (Bookseller, 1915–1936) was founded "out of a reading society's need for a catalog index" as an organizational strategy to track and sort the rapidly growing market for used books.[70] *Shomoku* or *mokuroku* were thus another technique for managing the overwhelming quantity of printed text that flooded Japan in the early twentieth century. Some of these magazines and catalogs were oriented toward readers and collectors, while others, like *Hon'ya*, were essentially trade magazines.

The renowned bookseller Saito Shōzō (1887–1961) identified *mokuroku* as the core medium for the trade; the format and organizational strategies of *mokuroku* were crucial to their utility since "a simple list of names and titles would be of no interest whatsoever . . . as there is no need to know just the names of books."[71] The true value of the *mokuroku* and trade magazines lay in the metaorganization of information—the ways in which they sorted books by publishing information, age, format, and edition, as well as more subjective, conceptual, and thematic categories such as dictionaries, poetry, theater, diaries, and so on. *Mokuroku* magazines such as *Hon'ya* also included accompanying articles by dealers, collectors, authors, and scholars to generate interest in the catalogs among potential buyers. *Mokuroku*, as metatextual books about books, were themselves objects of fascination since they gestured toward infinite accumulation while cataloguing their objects in minute detail, thus suggesting the sensual materiality of actual books beyond the page.

According to Uchida Roan, "Used-book catalogs are like beautiful women floating through the demimonde of the red-light district in a port town . . . you can see their faces, and with enough money any of them could be yours."[72] This erotic metaphor casts books as courtesans on display, fetish objects conjuring fantasies of a sensual world of print, a Borgesian illusion of the universe as book collection waiting to be explored—for a price. Roan compares skimming a catalog to a traveler's gaze across a map; articles and artwork in these *mokuroku* magazines likewise locate modern Japan's print boom in the context of a domestic history of reading and situate Japan's print tradition in the scope of world book history alongside France's bouquinistes, Goethe's Germany, and the scribes of Tang China. Essays in these bibliophile magazines belie a robust understanding of global print history, from European illuminated manuscripts, through the incunabula and Renaissance printing, to the present, locating Japan's transition from xylography to typography in comparative historical context.

The need to move beyond individual catalogs toward a systematic approach to archiving was underscored by periodic fires resulting in the loss of thousands of volumes, including the burning of the Maruzen bookstore in 1908, multiple Jimbōchō blazes, and the conflagrations following the

Great Kantō Earthquake of 1923.[73] To Roan, the loss of so many books was especially devastating since he saw Japan as a "storehouse in which what had been lost elsewhere in Asia" could still be found. Roan feared for the future of civilization; the books lost in the flames transcended any measure of monetary value, with knowledge transubstantiated into smoke. He dubbed the greatest losses the catalogs and archival manifests that served as the "compasses" (*rashinban*) of bookstores and the "lives of the library" (*toshokan no seimei*).[74] Without those catalog records, it was nigh impossible to even know what had burned.

CATALOGING A NATIONAL HERITAGE

The used-book trade surpassed the status of hobbyism to generate a shared sense of Japanese national culture through the preservation of old texts. The incorporation of bibliophilic knowledge in the service of cultural history is apparent in the short-lived journal *Tenseki* (The Classics, May–November 1915), which was privately published by the Kosho Hozonkai (Society for the Preservation of Used Books). Members of the society included disciplinary pioneers like the linguist Ueda Kazutoshi (1867–1937), the ethnographer Yanagita Kunio (1875–1962), the historian Mikami Sanji (1865–1939), the publisher Tokutomi Sohō (1863–1957), the literary historian Haga Yaichi (1867–1927), the philologist Yamada Yoshio (1873–1958), and the dictionarist Ōtsuki Fumihiko (1847–1928). It is easy to see the appeal of systematic textual preservation for scholars with interests in the study of Japanese linguistic, literary, and cultural history, who worked to preserve and present the heritage of the past and create a distinctly Japanese book history: "It has been less than thirty years since the development of printing and publishing technology and the universalization [*fukyū*] of typography [*katsuji*] in the mid-Meiji period; the special techniques of woodblock printing have become rare, and we want to preserve those collections for our country [*wagakuni*]."[75] These scholars acknowledged that the rise of type had endangered the domestic print tradition but also saw in the booming book economy a chance to preserve, reprint, and popularize old books as shared heritage. Ōtsuki explained, "There is a need to reprint [*fukuhon*] rare books [*chinsho*] . . . we can leverage new printing technology to create a new archive, with photographic reproduction [*shashin satsuei*] and metal-plate technology" allowing the reprinting of woodblock or script editions in their full visual splendor, rather than simply transferring the textual content into type and losing the specificity of their format.[76]

Yanagita argued that reprinting and preservation must "be carried out systematically, not just preserving a few things here and there."[77] He hoped for the involvement of the Home Ministry to hold reproduction to the highest bibliographic standard, maintaining formatting and reducing illegibility. The metaorganization of old books in modern Japan was carried out gradually, through the efforts and activities of collector groups. Book dealers explored local libraries and temples, listing extant editions to create an archive of archives. This initiative culminated in 1928 with the publication of the *Koshoseki Zaiko Mokuroku Nihon Shihen* (Index of Old Books in Japanese Collections, referred to as the *Nihon Shihen*), the largest *mokuroku* at the time, with more than a thousand pages collating data from used-book stores and collections across the empire, including Karafuto (Sakhalin), Ryukyu (Okinawa), and Chōsen (Korea).[78]

Significantly, the *Nihon Shihen* was compiled concurrently with the one-yen-book boom and the rise of pocket paperbacks. But rather than make old books cheaper, mass-market editions spurred a run in prices on rare volumes: "Recently, a veritable deluge of one-yen books has spread across the country, with daily advertisements in the newspaper . . . you would expect that you would be able to read old books for cheap prices, but actually just the opposite is true . . . the market prices of used books has been ceaselessly exploding upward thanks to nouveau riche collectors [*zōsho narikin*]."[79] The *Nihon Shihen* was not a catalog for ordering books but an attempt to create an exhaustive list of what was extant. The introduction was written by Yanagita, who expresses the hope that the *Nihon Shihen*, and *mokuroku* more generally, might expand the circulation of old books beyond Tokyo and facilitate the systematic organization of regional and local archives, thus increasing access to otherwise forgotten texts.[80] The *Nihon Shihen* was organized by topic, beginning with the imperial house (*Kōshitsu*) and emperor (*tennō*), then moving through categories such as religion, education, literature and the arts, military, economics, business, trade, and society, each of which was divided into any number of subgroups; "society" (*shakai*) includes subsections on labor, poverty, agriculture, and the like, while "literature and the arts" (*bungei*) is broken down into literary history, publishing, libraries, theater, poetry, song, and so forth. In these attempts to create a schema for the categorization of all knowledge, modern *mokuroku* like the *Nihon Shihen* served to schematically organize ideas and spur new forms of academic discourse and disciplinary knowledge.

AT THE LIBRARY

The relationship between bibliophilic collector impulses and the nationalist project to popularize the history of Japanese reading and writing culture was most explicitly manifest in a series of public exhibitions of rare books as cultural properties. Archiving of bibliographic rarities began in earnest after the Sino-Japanese War and increased in intensity in the first decade of the twentieth century, with exhibitions displaying rare books to the public. The first of these exhibitions was the Monbusho Bijutsu Tenrankai (Ministry of Education Art Exhibition) in 1899. Curators selected unusual items, borrowing or purchasing them from individual collectors to elevate rare editions to the level of shared cultural property in museums and exhibitions.[81] The goal of these exhibitions at public venues like the Tokyo Imperial University Library was to show volumes "whose value was well beyond that of normal books" (*kachi haruka ni futsūbon no ue*) and thus cultivate a "consciousness of books more generally" (*ippan tosho ni kansuru gainen*) and an appreciation for Japanese book culture.[82] Selected works included old editions of Chinese classics like Confucius's *Analects*, Buddhist sutras, works in Sino-Japanese *kanbun*, mythical histories like the *Kojiki* and *Nihon Shoki*, illustrated scrolls (*emaki*), script copies (*shahon*) of medieval tale literature, Edo-period ukiyo-e prints, and letters of Tokugawa Ieyasu. Further exhibitions were held nearly biannually throughout the Meiji and Taishō periods; later exhibitions placed increasing emphasis on a nativist literary tradition at the expense of Chinese texts. The books on display could not be "read" by visitors, just witnessed as museum pieces attesting to an august history of Japanese writing and printing.

Simultaneously, the state was developing an extensive domestic library system, which proved to be immediately and immensely popular, with new regional branches so crowded that patrons would often queue up to enter. The first modern Japanese library was built in Tokyo in 1872 and the Library Code (Toshokanryō) was promulgated in 1899, after which the government organized the national library system. In the following years, small town libraries sprang up in every prefecture, with holdings between ten thousand and a hundred thousand volumes. By 1912 there were approximately 3.6

million library users, and by 1926, nearly 21 million, further testament to the emergence of a mass reading public in the early twentieth century.[83] In contrast to the privately held scroll and book collections or roving lenders of the Edo period, the form and function of modern Japanese libraries were linked to the Western model, with modern concrete buildings and open-stack systems. Branches functioned as loci within a national bureaucracy and circulatory network whereby books were bound in Tokyo then sent out to regional branches. Scholar Ōsawa Satoshi describes early twentieth-century libraries as spaces for "general self-cultivation" (*ippanteki kyōyō*) through broad reading as a practice of modern everyday life.[84]

The socialist activist Katayama Sen (1859–1933) declared libraries to be "the center of civilization" (*bunmei no chūshin*), having been impressed by how open stacks in the United States allowed free access to knowledge.[85] Late nineteenth-century libraries, such as the Tokyo Shosekikan government archive, architecturally resembled Chinese temples, but by the twentieth century libraries were akin to cutting-edge new media spaces built in modernist concrete styles influenced by De Stijl, Bauhaus, and Le Corbusier, such as Waseda University's Central Library, drafted by Imai Kenji (1895–1987) and completed in 1925.[86] But even reinforced concrete can crumble, and the Tokyo Imperial University Library was destroyed in the Great Kanto Earthquake.[87] However, the subsequent rebuilding of the collection constituted an important turning point in the history of Japanese bibliographic archiving. In the final section of this chapter, we move from the bookstore district up the streetcar line to the Hongō campus of Tokyo Imperial University to witness the opening of a new era of media history in modern Japan.

MIYATAKE GAIKOTSU'S ARCHIVAL IMPULSE AND CRITIQUE OF PRINT CAPITALISM

The destruction of seven hundred sixty thousand volumes in the Tokyo Imperial University Library collection by fire in 1923 was catastrophic. The collection held not just Japanese volumes but also rare Chinese and Korean books, as well as irreplaceable documents in Central Asian languages excavated from the caves at Dunhuang.[88] If the early twentieth century saw the incorporation of Japanese print history into the scope of a global history of print, then Japan's position within that frame appears to have been mutually recognized. The Rockefeller Foundation acknowledged the devastation of the library as a blow to world cultural heritage and contributed the sum of four million yen to the rebuilding of the library and the restoration of the collection. But the destruction of the collection and its *mokuroku* also provided a chance to reimagine cataloging and preservation techniques, what Roan called "an opportunity to advance reading culture as a public undertaking [*kōkyō jigyō*]," rather than simply fill the hole left by the fire.[89]

The most compelling expansion of Hongō's archives was not the rebuilding of the Central Library but the creation of the Meiji Shinbun Zasshi Bunko (Meiji Newspaper and Magazine Archive), a first-of-its-kind attempt to encyclopedically collect periodicals and the ephemera of modern popular print culture.[90] The archive was the labor of love of the Meiji Bunka Kenkyūkai (Society for the Study of Meiji Culture), which was led by the idiosyncratic and iconoclastic satirist and publisher Miyatake Gaikotsu (1867–1955) and included the political journalist Yoshino Sakuzō (1878–1933), the literary scholar Yanagida Izumi (1894–1969), and the editor Kimura Ki (1894–1979), all bibliophiles interested in preserving the heritage of modern literature, culture, and thought through the archiving of magazines and newspapers.[91] Although the law library had kept runs of major newspapers, until that point there had been no complete archive or record of all newspapers and magazines anywhere in Japan, meaning that periodicals, typically consumed and summarily thrown away, were especially susceptible to loss.

Yoshino, a political journalist, maintained a personal newspaper collection for his research, and Gaikotsu had amassed back issues of rare broadsheets and illustrated newspapers from the early Meiji period. The capital funding to transform the Meiji Bunka Kenkyūkai's private collections into a public research archive came from the advertising industry. In 1925, Hakuhōdō, one of Japan's leading advertising firms and a major newspaper distributor, offered Gaikotsu a sum of one hundred fifty thousand yen to organize and house the archive at Tokyo Imperial University. According to Hakuhōdō founder Seki Hironao (1852–1939), "as an advertiser and distributor for newspapers and magazines, there could be nothing more beneficial for our company" than "to leave these cultural works [*bunka jigyō*] in perpetuity for future generations."[92] At a time when the preservation and study of newspapers and magazines were yet to be taken seriously, it took a corporate insider searching for a way to increase his firm's cultural capital to see the value in systematically cataloging periodical print ephemera. Ironically, this put Gaikotsu, a lifelong contrarian with a vehement anticorporate streak—in 1927 he released a single-issue spoof journal ironically titled *Sōban Haikan Zasshi* (The Going Out of Print Sooner or Later Magazine)—in the position of accepting cash from one of Japan's most powerful modern media corporations, a contradiction he happily embraced for a budget to build his collection.

Gaikotsu began his career around the turn of the twentieth century, releasing short-lived magazines on antique collecting while working as a proofreader in Osaka before earning wider renown with the *Kokkei Shinbun* (1908–1910) newspaper, whose biting satire sometimes overstepped the limits of the printable, resulting in censorship and stints in jail. Over the following decades, Gaikotsu released a flurry of short-lived personal projects under a dizzying variety of pen names on topics ranging from early modern eroticism to the history of oratory. The shared sensibility of all of Gaikotsu's projects was a resolute opposition to commercialism and the commodification of print. In 1928, concurrently with his work on the Meiji Newspaper and Magazine Archive, Gaikotsu published a pamphlet titled *The Poisonous Trend of One-Yen Books and Its Dark Side* (*Ichienpon Ryūkō no Dokugai to Sono Uramen*), in which he denounced cheap books as a "social problem" (*shakai mondai*) that could lead to "the complete collapse and eradication [*zenmetsu*] of the publishing industry." Warning of negative repercussions ranging from low royalties to the quality of bookbinding to the overloading of boats to the debilitation of taste among the uneducated masses, Gaikotsu sees the commodification of books as precipitating "a generalized economic crisis [*ippan zaikai no fukeiki*]. Yet he hails this disaster for "revealing the workings of mass production and the damage done by paper money" and laying bare the inner workings of commercial print capitalism.[93] He ends his tirade with a hilarious list of parody titles for as-yet-unreleased one-yen anthologies, the titles of which make the contours of his critique abundantly clear:

Goji Goyaku Zenshū (Anthology of Misprints and Mistranslations)
Shinbunsha Ōmōke Zenshū (The Newspapers Make a Killing Anthology)
Yoyakusha Kōkai Zenshū (Anthology of Subscriber Regret)
Furuhon Kōzui Zenshū (The Flood of Old Books Anthology)
Yosō Uragiri Zenshū (Anthology of Betrayed Expectations)
Kamiya Fumitaoshi Zenshū (The Paper Companies Take a Beating Anthology)
Nihon Guhitsu Zenshū (Anthology of Poor Japanese Prose)

Dabora Senden Zenshū (Anthology of Advertisers' Tall Tales)
Shūgu Raidō Zenshū (Anthology of the Masses Following Blindly)
Sōzei Ranzō Zenshū (Anthology of Mass-Produced Inferior Goods)
Fudoku Tsundoku Zenshū (Anthology of Unread Books)[94]

Gaikotsu labored to craft an alternative vision of print culture, implicitly critiquing mass-market publications through his own idiosyncratic means of production. In 1925, as he was negotiating the terms of the newspaper archive, Gaikotsu, working with Yoshino Sakuzō and the Meiji Bunka Kenkyūkai collection, released six volumes of a limited-run journal called *Meiji Kibun* (Weird Tales of Meiji, 1925–1926). The magazine was printed with woodblocks and string bound on uncut Japanese paper in the traditional style, made to be virtually indistinguishable from books printed in the late-Edo or early-Meiji period prior to the rise of typography. The journal, which exhibited the form as well as content of an era of publishing history rapidly fading into the past, was a miscellany of assorted news finds based on "our hobby [*shumi*] of collecting magazines and newspapers from the early years of Meiji."[95] *Meiji Kibun* was an alternative vision of how the history and letters of the recent past might be reconstituted into the mind of the present, implicitly contrasted with contemporary anthology projects. By aligning the format of his magazine with the original sources he analyzed, Gaikotsu provided a counterfactual vision of modern media history, as if the modern typographic publishing industry had never developed.[96]

The goal of this quixotic endeavor was to show the birth of Japanese modern media in its contingency by revealing a strangeness that had since been normalized. Gaikotsu encourages his readers to "turn around and look at ourselves" and recognize that "at present our people and nation are spiritually lost [*seishinteki na mayoi*]." At the same time, he rejects any explicit purpose for the magazine, preferring its contents "to be read and found interesting, to be heard and found funny." Like Roan, Gaikotsu rejects the instrumentalization of print media, instead encouraging his readers to revel in the confusion inherent in its contents.[97] In its string-bound pages, *Meiji Kibun* presents an archaeology of strange crimes and unexplained incidents that fascinated the first generation of modern Japanese citizens, from disembodied limbs discovered on crowded streets, to deformed children born between humans and animals, to the weirdness of modern technologies and neologisms before they were normalized.

Gaikotsu ran notices in *Meiji Kibun* asking readers to send in rare old periodicals; the appeal was part of a strategy by the Meiji Bunka Kenkyūkai to scour Japan and unearth forgotten pieces of print. With funding from Hakuhōdō, Gaikotsu and his assistants traveled across Tokyo to the older districts east of the Sumida River, knocking on doors at homes, shops, and flophouses, looking to gather the detritus of modern print culture. They then spread out across the country, taking buying trips, placing ads in local newspapers, and even searching paper-recycling businesses (*kamikuzu toiya*), where trashed newspapers were pulped, to rescue old issues. Nishida Taketoshi (1899–1989), one of Gaikotsu's assistants, recalls working with the used-book-seller networks and collector clubs to use the *mokuroku* indexes to expand their collection. Further funds for finding rare materials came from the *Ōsaka Mainichi* and *Tōkyō Nichinichi* newspapers, who recognized the value of writing themselves into print history at a moment in which, according to Nishida, "research on newspapers [*shinbun no kenkyū*] was not

FIGURE 3.2 First of six issues of *Meiji Kibun* (Weird Tales of Meiji), produced and published by Miyatake Gaikotsu in 1925 using woodblock printing and traditional *wahon* string binding.

yet considered to be appropriate for serious scholarship [*gakumon toshite tekitō de wa nai*]."[98]

LOST HORIZONS OF MEDIA HISTORY

This was the paradigm that Gaikotsu, Yoshino, and their colleagues set out to shift by building the newspaper and magazine archive at Hongō. These collectors saw potential in their collection and endeavored to expand it for future scholars. Yoshino, who had worked as a newspaper-delivery boy as a student, used the collection to compile materials for his writings on modern Japanese politics; he called the newspapers fundamental materials (*konpon shiryō*) necessary to "discuss the true state of affairs of politics in the Meiji period."[99] He also labored to compile detailed indexes of works that might be of use to himself and others as "objects of academic research [*gakumonteki kenkyū no taishō*]."[100] The archive held occasional exhibitions of its holdings to display the evolution of print from the late Edo period into the Shōwa era. Yanagida Izumi drew heavily on the archive for his writings on Meiji literature and culture and later when compiling the postwar *Meiji Bungaku Zenshū* (Anthology of Meiji Literature, 1965–1983).[101] The apotheosis of the Meiji Bunka Kenkyūkai's impetus was the eponymous *Meiji Bunka Zenshū* (Anthology of Meiji Culture, 1927–1930); edited by Yoshino, it aimed to provide a kaleidoscopic view of the beginnings of modern Japanese culture by means of the materials found during the collation of the periodical archive.

Gaikotsu's assistant Nishida makes the important point that this new type of archive did not simply make more content available but also opened new forms of discourse by reframing modern Japanese history in a context of media analysis.[102] The 1920s marked the moment in which modern Japanese print media itself became an object of study, as print capitalism precipitated a need to understand the contemporary media landscape as a historical phenomenon. The first work in this vein was perhaps Meiij Bunka Kenkyūkai member Ono Hideo's (1885–1977) *Nihon Shinbun Hattatsushi* (History of the Development of Newspapers in Japan, 1922), and Ono would found the newspaper research office that served as a key site for the academic study of mass communication and journalism in Japan and later became the Tokyo University Institute for Socio-Information Studies. But the most prescient work of early media history was *Meiji Bungaku Zakki*

(Assorted Notes on Meiji Literature, 1935), by another of Gaikotsu's archival assistants, the nearly forgotten Ebihara Hachirō (1907–1945?).[103] Ebihara's work is perhaps the first in Japan to narrate modern literary history explicitly from the perspective of print media, demonstrating how attention to the material specificity of periodicals can provide a panoramic view of the mutual evolution of print and written expression.

Ebihara, who had no higher academic training, was employed at Maruzen when Gaikotsu recruited him to catalog the periodical archive; he devised the filing system that systematically indexed information on each magazine. The task of sorting Japan's largest collection of newspapers and magazines gave Ebihara an unparalleled panoramic view of the functions of publishing and journals in the unfolding of modern literary history. He was the only person with that level of access to the full runs of all Meiji magazines; the book positions the ebb and flow of literary schools and authors' works in the context of their associated magazines, journals, and publishing practices. Ebihara explicitly links commercial newspapers and magazines to "the rise of modern Japanese literature [*kindai Nihon bungaku*] over the past decades," beginning with Narushima Ryūhoku's writings in the *Marumaru Chinbun* (1877–1907) and Kanagaki Robun's *Robun Chinpō* journal (1877–1882), and moving through what he calls the great age of literary magazines starting in the mid-1880s.[104]

Ebihara had a clear sense of the shifting valences of the concept of literature across his period of analysis: "At that time [the early Meiji period], the term *bungaku* held a different meaning from today; it was rather closer to *mongaku*, scholarship in the Chinese sense."[105] Ebihara identifies the beginning of *bungaku* as modern belles lettres with Ozaki Kōyō's *Garakuta Bunko* (Library of Odds and Ends, 1886–1888) magazine and locates the beginning of literary magazines as a commodity around the Sino-Japanese War, with *Miyako no Hana* and *Kokumin no Tomo* setting the stage for Hakubunkan's *Bungei Kurabu*. Ebihara's complete access to the archive allows his eye to rove perceptively, and he traces the evolution of literary expression through early coterie magazines, the reception of Zola, the rise of detective fiction, turn-of-the-century newspaper serials, and beyond, crafting a literary-historical narrative that resonates with far more recent scholarship. Ebihara was also aware of the pitfalls in his methodology; lacking any formal literary education or involvement in the literary scene, he acknowledges that his relationship to his subject is essentially objective. He sees his research as a kind of "science" (*kagaku*) and "technique" (*gijitsu*); he is interested in books and magazines "less for their artistic value" (*geijutsuteki kachi*) than for their interest as a "social phenomenon" (*shakai genshō*). Nonetheless, Ebihara makes the point that "it is impossible to ignore literary magazines if one wants to understand Meiji literature."[106] Ebihara's prescient work would itself essentially disappear from history, much like Ebihara himself. After writing *Meiji Bungaku Zakki* and leaving the Hongō archive, Ebihara moved on to Dalian to take a job with the Manchurian Railway Company. He was taken prisoner by the Soviet Army in August 1945 and never heard from again.[107]

This chapter began with a single pile of scrap magazines traded for cash, then moved through the city of Tokyo along the route of circulation of used books and print goods to probe the economics of the used-book trade and paint a picture of how the exchange of books generated meaning and value in bibliophilic discourse. In this trade, reading was often secondary or even incidental, as bibliophiles focused on the material aspects of the volumes they bartered and collected. Uchida Roan argued that the "uselessness" of excess volumes both challenged the instrumental logic of modern capitalism and provided for the transmission of culture. The bibliophilic impulse toward collecting and indexing was appropriated for the cataloging and exhibiting of books as part of the national imaginary as trade journals and collector circles became important actors in the creation of modern libraries and archives. This was the moment in which the published output of modern Japan since the Meiji period was itself integrated into the horizons of the Japanese and global histories of print culture. The used-book trade and the bibliophilic discourses surrounding it were thus indispensable for the possibility of writing modern Japanese literary and media history as we know it.

PART II

Prose, Language, and Politics in the Type Era

Chapter Four

NEW AGE SENSATIONS

Yokomitsu Riichi and the Contours of Literary Discourse

Part 1 of *The Typographic Imagination* detailed how magazines and books became part of everyday life for modern Japanese readers and constituted a new era of literary discourse and cultural production in the early twentieth century. Part 2 travels across another roughly synchronous set of axes to explore how prose, language, and political action were remade in the age of mass-market typographic print via discussions of experimental literature, orthographic script reform, and the links between the proletarian movement and the publishing industry. What we see shared both within and across these discursive fields is a dialectical consciousness of printed language as a material quantity—a medium both subject to sociohistorical forces and possessing the potential to affect not only the future of writing but also the course of history and the structure of society.

In *The Gutenberg Galaxy*, Marshall McLuhan argues that in the print era the sensory and perceptual apparatus of human bodies is transformed by writing as a mass-produced commodity. When we encounter new media, according to McLuhan, "no longer do our eyes and ears and other senses remain the same."[1] This chapter explores how authors born into this new media ecology of mass-produced typographic text reimagined the possibilities for prose as a means to transform the human sensorium. Yokomitsu Riichi (1898–1947) and the coterie of ambitious young writers involved with the journal *Bungei Jidai* (Literary Age, 1924–1927) negotiated the economic realities of literary critical discourse and pushed the boundaries of legitimate style and syntax in writings that investigated the relationships between the human body's perceptual apparatus and capacity for language. Yokomitsu and his compatriots developed a materialist concept of writing in which units of script (*moji*) were understood as material objects (*buttai*) able to interrogate the transformations of human sensibility. Chapter 1 of this book detailed how mass-produced print in Japan was predicated on the integration of nontypographic media such as photography and oral performance; Yokomitsu and his circle, known as the Shinkankaku-ha (Neo-Sensationists or Neo-Perceptionists), belonged to the first generation to come of age in this era of mass-produced print, and experimented with the new possibilities for expression nascent in a publishing regime made possible by that synthesis of visual and auditory media. The *Bungei Jidai* authors implicitly understood both writing and reading as sensory, embodied, physiological processes.

Close readings of Yokomitsu's fiction as well as his theoretical writings reveal specific iterations and operations of how, in the words of McLuhan decades later, "sense ratios change when any one sense or bodily or mental function is externalized in technological form" and how "when sense rations change, men change" through encounters with different forms of language in print.[2] For Yokomitsu and the Shinkankaku-ha, these encounters did not take place in isolation but within an economic system in which literary writing was bought and sold on an open market. Regardless of whether we believe McLuhan's claim that typography is "the first uniformly repeatable commodity, the first assembly-line," these authors understood type as a mass-produced medium that provided "instructions for the making . . . of muscular movements" and participated in the individuation of the reader into a capitalist socioeconomic order.[3] For Yokomitsu and his colleagues, literary production was closely bound to the consumer market, but no less powerful for it; they used their writings to investigate how the circulation of money and commodities—including printed text—fragmented and reconstructed the human body and human consciousness as technologized sensoria integrated into modern economic, transportation, and communication networks.

The *Bungei Jidai* group considered themselves to be the vanguard of a new literary age. They heralded their work as an attempt to overthrow ossified Japanese prose and the established literary realm, akin to a capitalist revolution against a feudal domain. At the same time, these authors were mindful of their own position inside that establishment and its associated economies of publishing. As such, *Bungei Jidai* provides a fascinating perspective on how authors were able to establish themselves and work within the market to transform literary writing at precisely the moment in which the production of prose became fully integrated into Japan's consumer economy. Ōsawa Satoshi calls this the transition from guild (*girudo*) to market (*shijō*) and the commodification of discourse (*genron no shōhinka*) via the selling of manuscripts to magazines.[4] For this would-be vanguard, commercial considerations, the strategic manipulation of critical discourse, and the dialectic of avant-garde and advertising were never distant. We can thus examine this coterie as a case study of how new literary movements can negotiate economic, discursive, grammatical, and stylistic boundaries in an era when typographic print for sale occupies a constitutive place in the structure of everyday life.

The chapter begins with a discussion of the founding of the journal *Bungei Jidai* by the publisher Kinseidō as a loss leader to lend itself belletristic credibility while it made its money elsewhere. The Shinkankaku-ha savvily wielded their new moniker to carve out a unique position within the crowded space of critical discourse and to theorize the changing relations between the human body, the material world, and the literary text. Treatises like Yokomitsu's "Kankaku Katsudō" (Sensory Activity, 1925) advanced an understanding of human sensation and perception as necessarily mediated rather than direct and immediate and argued for the importance of literary expression, experimental prose, and formalist grammatical techniques in those processes. The middle section of the chapter turns to the practice of these ideas via close readings of Yokomitsu's early short stories, characterized by a tension between straightforward literary style and experimental formal techniques; works of both types probe the relationship between the movement of human bodies and the legibility of language. In the late 1920s, Yokomitsu developed a theory of writing in which script is a physical object and advocated for literary formalism in heated public debates against Marxist critics over the rights to claim the mantle of properly materialist literary practice.

The Formalist Debate (Keishikishugi Ronsō) of 1928 to 1930 was on its surface a squabble about the primacy of "form" (as per Yokomitsu) or "content" (as per proletarian critics) and the "proper" relationship between aesthetics and politics in Japanese literature. But a close reading of the debate reveals a mutual understanding by both parties of the literary text as a dialectical, material artifice possessing creative and critical power. The chapter concludes with a reading of the critic Kobayashi Hideo's (1902–1983) seminal essay "Samazamanaru Ishō" (Myriad Designs, 1929), in which he castigates both Marxist and modernist concepts of materialism as empty ideology divorced from lived experience and ignorant as to the role of the commodity form in the making of modern literature, life, and consciousness. It is no coincidence that the problem of form (*keishiki mondai*) became a key site for negotiating the politics of aesthetics at the exact moment in which the publishing industry entered a new phase characterized by new formats of books as commodities, including paperbacks, one-yen anthologies, and million-seller magazines.

PILGRIMAGE INTO AN UNKNOWN WORLD: THE FOUNDING OF *BUNGEI JIDAI*

The short-lived but influential journal *Bungei Jidai* was the primary publication venue for a group of young authors aiming to make their mark on the modern Japanese literary scene, including Yokomitsu Riichi, Kawabata Yasunari (1899–1972), and Kataoka Teppei (1894–1944). The *Bungei Jidai* authors were a new wave of writers who worked to expand the boundaries of the literary establishment while working within it. Although they were keenly conscious of European avant-garde movements such as Dada and surrealism, these authors were by no means set on tearing down the belletristic establishment. Rather, their self-conscious play with grammatical form and critiques of established authors were ultimately internal to the literary realm. By the early 1920s, most Japanese fiction authors made their livings by selling manuscripts at per-page rates to magazines, rather than subsisting on salaried stipends from newspapers or enjoying the patronage of established authors, as in the Meiji period. Under this economic system, writers marketed their work to publishers via personal connections with editors and critics who played important roles in approving manuscripts. Yokomitsu and the *Bungei Jidai* clique found their entrée through the new general interest magazine *Bungei Shunjū* (Literary Chronicle, 1923–present) and its editor, the author and literary businessman extraordinaire Kikuchi Kan (1888–1948), whose magazine quickly accrued substantial critical and commercial power.[5] Yokomitsu attracted attention with the publication of the story "Hae" (The Fly, 1923) in the magazine, and Kikuchi took him and other promising young writers under his wing to teach them the business of producing literature. Yokomitsu, Kawabata, and company soon organized a journal of their own, sending shock waves through literati circles with the rumor that they had incurred Kikuchi's wrath by challenging *Bungei Shunjū* with their upstart *Bungei Jidai*.[6] Kawabata visited Kikuchi to assuage concerns about competition, and in the inaugural issue, Yokomitsu, who had been on the dole from Kikuchi, penned a piece titled "*Bungei Jidai* to Gokai" (Misunderstandings about *Bungei Jidai*), clarifying, "All manner of nasty speculative rumors may come on the heels of this magazine's publication . . . but I have received no small amount of favor from *Bungei Shunjū* and have no reason to attack it."[7]

The new magazine was independent but very much a part of the literary realm's existing economies of money and discourse alike. The magazine's publisher, Kinseidō, was founded in 1919 by Fukuoka Masuo (1894–1969), who had ambitions to become a mainstream publisher of literary fiction but had trouble competing with powerful established houses like Shinchōsha that could offer higher page rates, distribution, and prestige. In the early 1920s, Kinseidō was peddling pieces by second-rate writers and cast-off minor works by major authors like Tanizaki Jun'ichirō (1886–1965) and Tayama Katai (1872–1930) in low circulation. To compete, Kinseidō solicited the work of young up-and-coming authors for a new magazine to produce an image of the company as a force to be reckoned with in the literary world—*Bungei Jidai*. Editors Iida Toyoji (b. 1898) and Nakagawa Yoichi (1897–1994) entreated Yokomitsu and Kawabata to join in founding this new journal, and Kinseidō published the first issue of *Bungei Jidai* in October 1924.[8]

Bungei Jidai was part of a savvy marketing strategy by Kinseidō that aimed to draw attention to itself in a competitive economy. For the new generation of authors associated with the magazine, their goal was less to overthrow the old guard than to delimit their own position contrapuntal to the constitutive other of the category of "established writers" (*kisei sakka*). In an editorial introduction to the first issue, Kawabata observes that his generation of "emerging authors" (*shinshin sakka*) are characterized by critics as "challenging established authors and starting a movement to destroy the literary realm [*bundan*]."[9] He mocks those established authors as "legless dancers" but concedes that his cohort's goal is ultimately "not to throw stones at them." Rather, the sign of "established author" served as a straw man against which Kawabata's new wave could define themselves.[10] Critics, however, saw the goal of the *Bungei Jidai* project in less-circumscribed terms. Chiba Kameo (1878–1935), who would coin the name Shinkankakuha that would be ascribed to Kawabata, Yokomitsu, and their compatriots, saw in *Bungei Jidai* a schismatic move, "a complete rejection of the established authors" and a "pilgrimage into an unknown world."[11] This tension between *Bungei Jidai* and the literary establishment constituted a self-conscious frame within which Yokomitsu, Kawabata, and their cohort could situate themselves as simultaneously inside and outside the accepted realm of practice and discourse. The gambit worked, and the new journal's editors were bold enough to claim that "people everywhere are talking about *Bungei Jidai*" before the inaugural issue hit the shelves.[12]

THE END OF LITERARY FEUDALISM?

In the founding issue, Yokomitsu writes that the new magazine "should by no means be taken as a bivouac against the literary establishment . . . Kinseidō pays for our manuscripts, so I can make no such claim."[13] Yokomitsu's acknowledgment of financial considerations underwriting his journal is revealing; while *Bungei Jidai* authors argued for a new discursive territory apart from the establishment, it was revenue generated by Kinseidō's sales of books by successful writers like Tayama Katai that kept the magazine afloat. Katai provided Kinseidō publisher Fukuoka with editing advice, layout tips, and permission to publish his works, which gave Kinseidō the wherewithal to publish *Bungei Jidai* as a loss-leading literary experiment.[14] It was thus precisely the continued literary production and circulation of those "established authors" against which Yokomitsu and Kawabata railed that allowed their cohort to push prose forward.

Kinseidō's other major moneymakers were books on leftist topics, which sold briskly in the years after the Russian Revolution, and harmonica sheet music. Although Kinseidō crafted an image as an upstart avant-garde publisher of literary fiction, the booming trade in harmonica songbooks was what kept the company in the black while it lost money on *Bungei Jidai*. By economic metrics, the magazine was anything but a success; the plan was to pay authors three yen a page for fiction, one yen a page for essays, and

FIGURE 4.1 Pamphlet of harmonica sheet music of the kind sold by Kinseidō during the harmonica boom of the mid-1920s; this example was published by Tosen Rakufu in 1924.

sell five thousand copies a month at thirty sen a piece, which would allow the magazine to break even with no profit and no loss to the bottom line.[15] Literary historian Itō Sei (1905–1969) estimated that the company lost as much as a thousand yen per month publishing *Bungei Jidai*.[16] Kawabata later claimed that it was by explaining the magazine as a money-losing indulgence rather than a financial venture that the group convinced Kikuchi Kan that they would pose no competition to his *Bungei Shunjū*.[17] *Bungei Jidai* was simultaneously an important literary magazine and a loss-leading advertisement produced to affix the sign of literary value to Kinseidō's mantle and advertise the company's new publications.

In a seminal essay that gave the *Bungei Jidai* group the moniker Shinkankaku-ha, with which they would be remembered to literary history, critic Chiba Kameo sketches a new methodology of literary writing in terms of the shifting ground of mass-market print capitalism: "Perhaps it is the ability to print more freely [*insatsuryoku no jiyū*] that has made possible a large number of personal magazines [*kojin zasshi*] and coterie magazines [*dōjin zasshi*] . . . The position of the established authors has stagnated . . . up-and-coming authors hold strong convictions about art . . . and [intend to] advance the literary realm [*bundan*] a step forward." Chiba singles out *Bungei Jidai* from a new crop of magazines "struggling for literary hegemony": "For those paying attention to the vicissitudes of the literary realm, it is impossible to ignore the rise of coterie journals as a force for expression. Many of these magazines bubble up only to fade away, but some shunt aside the flow of the mainstream to themselves become great rivers of thought . . . *Bungei Jidai* is unique among the magazines in how it has used that weapon called the advertisement."[18] As Chiba sees it, in a literary market flooded with new magazines, it is not merely the prose that appears in a journal that allows it to stand out but also the savviness with which a magazine's editors are able to advertise themselves and position their writing within the limits of critical discourse and commercial viability.

At the discursive level, Kawabata posits his compatriots' writing as heralding the collapse of a feudalistic "kingdom of letters" (*bungei no ōkoku*) unable to sustain its closed structure in the age of mass-market print capitalism. In an essay called "Atarashiki Seikatsu to Atarashiki Bungei" (New Life and New Literature), Kawabata claims that the world's "religious age" (*shūkyō jidai*) has been replaced by a "literary age" (*bungei jidai*) and the birth of a "new spirit" (*atarashii seishin*), "new values" (*atarashii kachi*), and "new sensibility" (*atarashii kanjō*) in which literature is embedded in everyday life and vice versa. He continues that there cannot but be "mutual interaction between the lives of authors and artists and their art [*geijutsu*]"; for Kawabata, the integration of new experiences of modern life allows young authors to "break down the gates" and occupy the once-feudal literary kingdom.[19] Here, the reading and writing of literature are ineluctably interior to modern everyday life, and the cultivation of self-consciousness toward that reality bequeaths literature the ability to investigate the material world and create new notions of spirit and sensibility.

MEDIATING SENSATION, PERCEPTION, AND REPUTATION

As reading and writing became naturalized practices in the age of mass-produced typographic print, the sensory and perceptual aspects of experience emerged as critical themes for literary writing. Sensation and perception were central problematics for Yokomitsu, Kawabata, and the *Bungei Jidai* writers, who came to be known, following Chiba's nomenclature, as the Shinkankaku-ha school. In "Shinkankaku-ha no Tanjō" (The Birth of the Shinkankaku-ha), Chiba argues that the *kankaku* of the *Bungei Jidai* group is distinct from that of earlier writers of modern literature.[20] The valences of meaning of the term *kankaku* were ambiguously complex at the time and have been debated across literary historiography, with the name varyingly translated as "Neo-Sensationists," "Neo-Perceptionists," "Neo-Sensualists," "New Sensationalists," and "Neo-Impressionists"; I have elected to leave the term untranslated to leave open the interlocking dimensions of meaning surrounding the term at the time of its coinage and circulation. Chiba writes,

> We might call ours the "age of *shinkankaku*." Those authors stand and revel from atop a special visual field, looking out with a gaze that pierces through all hidden aspects of life . . . they allow us to peer through little holes at interior life in its totality of existence and meaning . . . Why, in their expression of life, must they open these little holes? Because they use the instantaneous sensations of extreme stimulations and small external forms and shapes to symbolize the vastness of interior life.[21]

Chiba's concept of *shinkankaku* embodies both sensation and perception, as the stimulations of the sensory register precipitate perceptual shifts that make visible new contours of experience. The agglomeration of sensation structures both interior life and its expression, as sensory experience delimits changes in perception, with internal and external aspects conjuring a dialectical totality; the literary text stands at the point where sensation and perception are mutually constituted.

Chiba's term stuck to the *Bungei Jidai* group with tenacity, and the coterie seized upon it as a way to formulate a distinct identity in the literary marketplace.[22] The power of Chiba's moniker lay not only in the central concept of *kankaku* but also in the prefix *shin-* and its appeal to the "new" in an age of mass commercialism. Seeking to distinguish his generation from its predecessors, Kawabata dubbed "newness" (*atarashisa*) the "passport" to the realm of modern literature and the major problem of the moment, which he in turn described as a "new age" (*shinjidai*) wherein "new literature" (*atarashii bungei*) was predicated upon "new expression" (*atarashii hyōgen*) and "new content" (*atarashii naiyō*), both of which form "new sensibility" (*atarashii kankaku*).[23] As for *kankaku*, it mediates between sensation, perception, and sensibility, an ambiguous yet powerful floating signifier that could act as a site for theorizing the relations between the literary text, the material experience of modern life, and the transformation of the human sensorium. Again, it is helpful to think of the Shinkankaku-ha project together with McLuhan's ideas about the adoption of new media: "Those who experience the first onset of a new technology . . . respond most emphatically because the new sense ratios set up at once by the technological dilation of eye or ear present men with a surprising new world . . . But the initial shock gradually dissipates as the entire community absorbs the new habit of perception into all of its areas of work and association. But the real revolution is in this later and prolonged phase of 'adjustment' of all personal and social life to the new model of perception set up by the new technology."[24]

The *Bungei Jidai* group negotiated this dialectic of shock and normalization via the concept of *kankaku*; in 1926, the editors published *Bungei Shingo Jiten* (A Dictionary of New Literary Terms), a compendium aimed at introducing popular concepts; therein, *kankaku* is defined as "an exterior stimulus that passes through the five senses and creates a psychological phenomenon [*seishin genshō*] in the brain. Sight, sound, taste, smell, and touch are the five senses. 'Sensory depiction' [*kankaku byōsha*] is the identification and discovery of what is specific to each sense and the depiction thereof. In the literary world, there has recently emerged a group of authors that make use of such techniques."[25] Here, *kankaku* is linked to perceptions processed via the sense organs of the human body as a physical, biological capacity. This physiological body figures centrally for Shinkankaku-ha authors like Kataoka Teppei, who locates "nerves, sensations . . . and flesh itself [*nikutai koso*]" as the basis of modern life and argues that literature is likewise built upon the sensory register of material experience: "People in our works of literature are human flesh furnished with nerves and senses [*shinkei to kankaku*]—only the human body can be recognized by modern readers."[26] Kataoka conceives of the human body as a bundle of sensory nerves that mediate existence inside and outside the literary text. Kawabata identifies sensation and perception as an "epistemological problem" (*ninshiki no mondai*), whereby *shinkankaku* is "not merely the discovery of sensation or perception but also a different way of thinking about the functions that sensation and perception occupy in human life."[27] Literature is in turn a medium by which to understand this recombination of sensation and perception; it follows that, to the *Bungei Jidai* authors, the relationship between reader and text was understood in materialist terms.

Yokomitsu's most sustained theoretical investigation of the relationship between literature and *kankaku* appears in the 1925 essay "Kankaku Katsudō" (Sensory Activity), which explicates the linked machinations of sensation, perception, and sensibility. In Yokomitsu's figuration, *kankaku* refers to the commonsense understanding of sensation and perception as "the transformation of the object of stimulation [*shokuhatsu taishō*] from an objective form [*kyakkanteki keishiki*] to a subjective form [*shukanteki keishiki*]." *Shinkankaku* exceeds the simple function of the sense organs (*kannō*) in which an external stimulant is transmitted to the internal realm of perception and is necessarily tied to symbolization and representation, and thus literary art:

> For the Shinkankaku-ha, the concept of sensation—that is to say, sensory symbolization [*kankakuteki hyōchō*]—is the directly sensed stimulus [*chokkanteki shokuhatsubutsu*], the outward appearance of which is suspended as the subject [*shukan*] leaps into the thing-in-itself [*mono jittai*] . . . The subject is that which has the capability for understanding [*ninshiki*] the object [*kyakutai*] as the thing-in-itself. This understanding is the synthesis [*sōgōtai*] of intellect [*gosei*] and sensibility [*kansei*].[28]

Yokomitsu's explication draws on neo-Kantian philosophy, which enjoyed intense popularity in the mid-1920s thanks to the translations published by Iwanami Shoten, and his terms here, such as *mono jittai* (*Ding an sich*), *gosei* (*Verstand*), and *kansei* (*Sinnlichkeit*) are adopted from Kantian epistemology, albeit used idiosyncratically. Essentially, Yokomitsu's concept of *kankaku* transcends the simple movement from sensed object to sensing subject as a process through which sensory data is mediated via the faculty of the intellect in the subject's construction of the world.

Crucially, this operation is inseparable from the process of representation: "Sensation [*kankaku*] is the representation [*hyōshō*] of the operation of representational capability [*hyōshō nōryoku*] of the exterior object and transcendental object [*junsui kyakkan*], rather than the object [*kyakutai*] in contrast to the subject . . . Sensation is the symbolization [*hyōchō*] of the matter [*shitsuryō*] of sensible knowledge [*kanseiteki ninshiki*] that arises from stimulation by the transcendental object."[29] For Yokomitsu, new sensations and perceptions are themselves mediated representations rather than the immediate transmission of stimulus from object to subject. *Kankaku* is always already mediated by epistemological activity (*ninshikiteki katsudō*), which is contrasted with pure sensory activity (*kankaku katsudō*) as unmediated physical stimulus, which he relegates to the realm of the merely animalistic rather than human. By contrast, Yokomitsu posits that the material experience of modern life should be understood through the internal faculties of the subject with consideration of the mediating processes of representation, including the writing and reading of literature: "For the Shinkanku-ha writers, objects that trigger *kankaku* arise from the vocabulary, poetry, and rhythm of writing . . . from the inflected perspective of the narrative. . . . from the jumps between the silent lines of text, and from the reversals, repetitions, and speed of the plot's progress."[30] It is thus prose technique, narrative construction, and other literary devices that Yokomitsu argues offer possibilities for investigating materiality, sensation, and perception. His examples include literary writing that disrupts concepts of time, narrative, and form via the "disturbance and arrangement of tone [*jōchō hairetsu*] and the fragmentation, assemblage, and synthesis of parts [*pāto*]."[31] Here, literary form is not just expression but also a key function in the constitution and recombination of sensation and perception. For Yokomitsu, the reconfiguration of grammatical and narrative structure is central to the formation of consciousness in the modern world.

A FLY IN THE TEXT: SOUNDING OUT *SHINKANKAKU* STYLE

So, whither Yokomitsu's prose itself? Yokomitsu's fictional practice may not be as avant-garde as his theory, but he employs strategies at the levels of both form and content to investigate the relationships between language, writing technique, the materiality of the human body, and the shifting positions of reading and writing subjects. Despite Yokomitsu's insistence that the historical avant-garde of "futurism, cubism, expressionism, Dada, symbolism, constructivism, and realism" were all innate to the *Bungei Jidai* project, the magazine was ultimately internal to mainstream commercial literary production.[32] By contrast, any number of other experimental authors, poets, and artists, including Takahashi Shinkichi (1901–1987), Hirato Renkichi (1893–1922), and journals like *MAVO* (1924–1925) and *Shi to Shiron* (Poetry and Poetics, 1928–1931), engaged in more explicitly avant-garde poetic practice that problematized "the self-criticism of art in bourgeois society" and worked toward the "negation of the autonomy of art" as per Peter Bürger's definition.[33]

Yokomitsu's fiction may not have problematized the boundaries of literature itself, but at the level of form he engaged in expressionistic techniques of unconventional personification, onomatopoeia, and distorted, fragmented grammar to defamiliarize the literary text; at the level of content, his work investigates the materiality of print media, the circulation of commodities, the reimagination of the human body, and the contingencies of communication. Yokomitsu's early fiction often reads quite conventionally, but he introduces subtle yet significant innovations in writing and grammar that urge the reader to reassess their position vis-à-vis the literary text. These works decenter the singular coherent human subject and unified body and call attention to the ways in which printed language serves to structure consciousness and the experience of modern life. Significantly, these stories are set in the interstitial spaces between the country and the city during a time of rapid but uneven urbanization and explore in various capacities the distortions of seemingly linear language and movement, as well as the relationships between textual and infrastructural systems.

Yokomitsu's breakthrough story was "Hae," published in *Bungei Shunjū* in May 1923, in which a group of country folk await the departure of a horse-drawn cart heading into the city, an event long delayed by the driver's wait for breakfast dumplings. When the buggy begins moving, the driver falls asleep at the reins, and the cart careens over a cliff. All the passengers perish and only a fly survives, alighting at the last minute. Throughout the story's ten short sections, Yokomitsu plays with the passage of time, language, and narrative framing to distort the experience of reading. In the first half of "Hae," the rushed passengers wait for the hungry driver; a farmwoman, eager to get into town and see her sick son after receiving a telegram, pleads, "It takes three hours to town, three full hours. My son's dying, help me make it!" The story's narrative time and diegetic time initially extend in tandem as both the passengers' and readers' waits expand; but, at the start of the seventh section, the problem of duration is shifted as an unidentified narrator, rather than one of the diegetic peasants, wonders aloud, "When would the carriage depart? The sweat of the people gathered in the station had dried. But when will the carriage leave? No one knows. The only ones that might know were the dumplings swelling inside the shop's pot." This narrative voice is explicitly literary in style—"when would the carriage depart?" (*deru no de arō*) in contrast to the accented dialect of the characters' "still ain't leaving?" (*mada jarō*).[34] The narrator's voice frames the vernacular inflections of the characters' language and shifts the experience of duration to the reader, who is likewise forced to wait. The narrative voice seems to confess that the matter of the cart—and thus the plot—is outside its control and at the mercy of external factors beyond the text's diegesis.

In the following brief section, Yokomitsu's narrative synthesizes the divergent durations of the marked time of the clock with the immeasurable yet constitutive time of the boiling dumplings and produces an array of auditory sensations: "The carriage station's clock struck ten. Steam whistled out of the dumpling shop's cauldron. *Zaku, zaku, zaku.* The hunchbacked driver cut some hay for the horse. The horse lapped up some water beside the driver. *Zaku, zaku, zaku.*"[35] The striking of the clock and whistling of the pot are conventionally narrated, but the onomatopoeic *zaku zaku zaku* of the driver cutting hay transforms the reading process. The reader is told of the sounds of the clock and cauldron but "hears" the hay being cut as the onomatopoetic device internalizes the reader into the diegetic space, as if able to perceive the sound from within the world of the story. This onomatopoeisis may seem pedestrian but at the time was an experimental technique without much precedent in modern Japanese prose. Despite the long history of *giongo* and *giseigo* (onomatopoeic words) and *gitaigo* (mimetic words) in classical poetry and premodern literature, in modern Japanese prose these almost always take on an adverbial function to describe a verb, such as the *shikejike* with which Bunzō gazes at Osei or the *jirori* with which she rolls her eyes back at him in Futabatei Shimei's (1864–1909) *Ukigumo* (*The Drifting Cloud*, 1887–1889).[36] There, the onomatopoetic phrase does not gesture toward the generation of sound as such but characterizes the quality of the action, in contrast to Yokomitsu's *zaku zaku zaku*, in which the printed word is understood to be producing sound as sound. *Zaku zaku zaku* does not describe the cutting of the hay but creates an aural sensation that bifurcates the reader's perspective across the inside and outside of the text.

Although I focus here on Yokomitsu's manipulation of duration and audition in his *shinkankaku* writing practice, numerous critics have detailed Yokomitsu's textual innovation and experimentation in regard to the visual register in "Hae." Kuritsubo Yoshiki and Yura Hiromi have read the fly's compound eye as a lens, the "objectification of the position of the solitary fly that has internalized the eye as a device," and Komori Yōichi has explicated the cinematic quality of the fly's eye as a screen projection that sees and is seen by the reader, who recognizes himself projected into the text as the cart careens off the cliff.[37] In "Hae," Yokomitsu pulls the reader across the inside and outside of the text via the manipulation of sight, sound, and time, devising subtle yet effective ways for the reader to experience the sensations of the diegetic space even while made aware of how those sensations are generated by the distortion of narrative, grammar, and prose. As in Yokomitsu's theory of *kankaku*, sensation forms the constitutive base of perception, as apprehended through its own representation and symbolization.

SEVERED LIMBS IN THE NOVELISTIC IMAGINATION

If "Hae" explores the contingencies nascent in the movement of bodies between the country and the city through formalist experimentation, another early short story, "Onmi" (My Beloved), examines similar themes at the level of content. Published in 1924, "Onmi" was the title story of Yokomitsu's first solo collection and a representative work of the countervailing naturalist tendencies in his prose. In contrast to early experimental works, most of the stories collected in *Onmi* are straightforward tales of country life penned in the style of Shiga Naoya (1883–1971), of whom

Yokomitsu quipped that he was so "hopelessly influenced by that whatever I write tastes like bad dumplings."[38] In "Onmi," a young student, Matsuo, travels from Tokyo to the countryside to visit his sister's new baby, Yukiko. Matsuo dotes on his niece and revels in her affection until the girl is rendered ill by a vaccine. Despite the absence of any of the formalist techniques that characterize "Hae" or Yokomitsu's other *shinkankaku* works, "Onmi" constitutes an investigation into how different types of textual media can structure and distort the human body, both real and imagined.

"Onmi" opens with an act of reading; Matsuo is glancing through a book as his mother tells him his sister is about to give birth. When Matsuo arrives in the village to meet his niece, he has difficulty distinguishing between the reality before him and how modern fiction has trained him to imagine village life:

> He snapped awake from a dream of a baby crying somewhere far away. To his side, the baby was crying and thrashing her hands to free herself from a thread that had become tangled around her.
>
> "Wah, wah, wah, waah." That's how the baby cried. He recalled the depiction [*byōsha*] of a baby crying in just the same way before it died in a sketchlike work of fiction [*shaseiteki na shōsetsu*] by a famous author that he had once read.[39]

Matsuo first apprehends the new life before him in terms structured by his reading of literature; he cannot but see the baby through his imagination informed by novelistic realism. When he returns to Tokyo, he likewise thinks of his niece as she might appear in a work of fiction: "He remembered a scene in a story called 'The Umbilical Cord,' in which a baby dies after blood seeps out of its navel, and grew uneasy."[40] Ultimately, there proves to be no cause for worry, as Matsuo's interpretation of reality informed by fiction has no material effect on Yukiko's health, and her body remains distinct from Matsuo's imagination of it.

It is not Matsuo's internalized understanding of fiction but another form of print that ultimately fractures Yukiko's body, as the arrival of an official notice summoning the baby for vaccination precipitates a shattering of her physical well-being: "The day before Matsuo returned to Tokyo, a printed notice [*insatsubutsu*] announcing the date of vaccination for babies born that year was delivered . . . Two weeks later, Matsuo received a letter from his sister in which she wrote that Yukiko grew weak with a fever five days after being vaccinated . . . the way that his sister wrote the letter put no limits on Matsuo's troubled imagination." In Matsuo's mind, disease and damage come to Yukiko's body in tandem with the print notice. This fragmentation is underscored by his sister's awkward phrasing and inability to write smoothly as another letter arrives from Matsuo's sister: "Coarsely written and crossed out in places, it said, 'The vaccine has given Yukiko an infection. Her arm was taken but her life was spared.'" Reading the letter, Matsuo is no longer able to imagine his niece's body as a coherent whole as "the image of Yukiko with her arm severed, rolling around like a broken toy" manifests in his mind. This image renders Matsuo unable to write himself as he "breaks down crying, powerless to dip his pen into the inkpot."[41]

Matsuo associates the image of Yukiko's shattered body less with the printed notice that heralded its fragmentation than with the illegibility of his sister's handwritten letter and her poor prose; he criticizes his sister for her coarse writing as if it were somehow her messy handwriting and crossed-out words that erased Yukiko's arm. Eventually, further letters arrive, reassuring Matsuo that his sister had been prematurely worried and that Yukiko was healthy again. These calmly written letters thus restore to whole the image of Yukiko's body in Matsuo's mind, even while her physical body had never been broken. Through the series of notices, telegrams, and epistles passing back and forth between the city and the country, Yukiko's body is broken and put back together again in Matsuo's imagination. As these different forms of writing come into argumentation and negotiation, Yokomitsu subtly explores how the materiality of the body is mediated through the reading of literary texts, printed documents, and handwritten letters.

READING ALONG THE LINES: DISRUPTED TRAINS AND DISTORTED GRAMMAR

The relationships between literacy, language, and linear movement also structure two of Yokomitsu's other early short stories, the naturalistic "Teki" (The Enemy, 1924) and the more experimental "Atama Narabi ni Hara" (Heads and Bellies, 1924). Taken together, these two stories exemplify a concern for the contingency, mutability, and functionality of modern language explicated alongside the development of modern transportation infrastructure. "Teki" tells the story of Kitagawa Manji, an illiterate man who works as a rural station attendant; the titular "enemy" is Goichi, a friend turned rival who is able to advance his station in life by dint of having completed his schooling, while Manji had dropped out. Manji spends his life plotting against Goichi, but when their paths finally cross, he is unable to take any action. The crux of the narrative is an utterance by Goichi that prevents Manji from tracking any movement away from his original position on the line:

> When Manji was twenty-three years old, he and Goichi were both set to be promoted to the next level of employment . . . But Goichi moved up and left Manji behind. Goichi had finished primary school. Manji had quit halfway through second grade. When word got around that Manji and Goichi would be promoted to the same rank, Goichi sneakily approached the stationmaster about Manji's lack of schooling. "You know, Kitagawa never passed the second grade. Just try asking him to write a sentence. That man doesn't know a single character."[42]

Here, literacy is tied to both social progression and smooth linear movement. Reading is conflated with steady, mechanical movement, and the inability to read leaves Manji languishing in the margins. When, at age thirty-six, Manji begins learning characters from a school primer, he is finally able to move away from his countryside station. For Yokomitsu, whose father's career as a train track laborer moved the family back and forth across the country, the legible iteration of letters is linked to the movement of not only vehicles and passengers but also all those who take part in the construct and operate the transportation network, as the schism between the lives of those who can read and those who cannot are made incommensurable.

If "Teki" demonstrates the necessity of literacy for social and topographical movement, "Atama Narabi ni Hara," published the same year, questions any assumption of the immediacy of language and problematizes the expectation of grammatical legibility. Upon publication, the story was read as a challenge to accepted standards of modern Japanese prose; it drew attention to the artifice of language and instigated a discursive incident. Like "Hae" and "Teki," "Atama Narabi ni Hara" is built around movement and stoppage along transportation networks and describes a momentary panic in a crowd of train passengers when an express train comes to a sudden halt. With little explanation given beyond "a problem on the line between stations H and K," the passengers are left confused and disoriented until a replacement train arrives; the only figure who remains on the original train is a disturbed young man whose nonsensical singing continues throughout the duration.[43] It was the opening line that caused such scandal in the literary establishment: "High noon. The crowded express train ran at full speed. The small stations along the tracks were ignored like stones."[44] To the modern reader, the sentence seems innocuous. In a subsequent issue of *Bungei Jidai*, Yokomitsu's colleague Kataoka Teppei notes, "In the opinion of a certain established author, this is a very bad sentence. The implication is that the expression needlessly goes out of its way to be strange, or perhaps it is that there is no new content in this so-called 'sensory' [*kankakuteki*] writing deemed to be the herald of a new era on the basis of its eccentric grammar." At issue is the personification of inanimate objects as the train takes on a subjective aspect to "ignore" the stations as if they were stones. Kataoka contrasts Yokomitsu's construction with how established authors might have styled the same sentence, including, "The train ran at full speed without stopping at the small stations"; "The train did not stop at the small stations, but continued on," and so forth. To some, such techniques were attempts to meaninglessly subvert accepted norms of prose style without providing any new literary interest. Kataoka critiques them as "unable to escape a naturalistic [*shizenshugi*] mode of writing; that is to say, the typical style of Japanese realists [*Nihon no riarisuto*] working in naturalist modes based upon realist practices [*shajitsushugi*] concerned with the five sensory organs of the scientist."[45] Like Yokomitsu in "Kankaku Katsudō," Kataoka distinguishes a "sensory" textual practice engaged with grammatical structure and the mediating properties of the written word from a simplistic conception of sensation produced via an objective reality outside of and a priori to the text.

As the train passes, a string of ambiguous vocalizations are generated inside:

> Among the packed-in passengers was a lazy-looking boy. He sat respectably and began twirling his kerchief into a headband. He then started pounding on the window with both hands and singing in a loud voice.
>
> "Oh my wife is so lucky
> Lucky

Yoi yoi
Lucky, lucky
Oh so lucky
Yoi yoi"

Yokomitsu implies that the mentally ill boy's meaningless fragments of language extend beyond the boundaries of the narrative so long as the train remains in the interstitial space between its points of departure and arrival: "He shook his head. His voice grew louder and louder . . . it seemed as if he would continue singing every song he knew until the train arrived at its destination. The songs continued to flow from his mouth, constantly changing."[46] The story concludes with another string of nonsensical singing as the boy remains long after all other passengers have alighted.

If in "Teki" the movement between stations is associated with literacy and legibility, then in "Atama Narabi ni Hara," the same intermediary space is characterized by the continual generation of nonsensical language not easily reconciled into normative expectations of grammar. Likewise, as in "Hae," humans lose their subjectivity and are reduced to mere bodies as their ability to communicate erodes. "The train comes to a sudden halt . . . the passengers are set silent before they begin chattering again . . . Everything becomes unclear" as the passengers cry out and find themselves unable to understand the events that have led to their present impasse. They become nothing more than the story's eponymous organs, "heads wrapped up in fat bellies," mere agglomerations of body parts caught by the contingencies of communication and transportation and the distortion of language.[47]

In addition to the diegetic vocalizations of the passengers, the train in "Atama Narabi ni Hara" produced discursive chatter among the literati. As Kataoka alludes, the train's act of "silently ignoring" the stations generated a clamor of voices debating the legitimacy of Yokomitsu's prose as the stones ignored in the story became objects of intense critical attention; Kataoka observes, "The term 'silently ignore' [*mokusatsu*] conveys the feeling of psychological violence; put differently, a fever of the mind. This violence, this fever, conveys a sense of pressure. The term 'silently ignore' pushes upon [*semaru*] the reader with this pressure . . . the result is an internal musical effect [*naimenteki na ongakuteki kōka*] that sensorially stimulates us."[48] Through the representation of sound in and outside the train and the text, and via Yokomitsu's grammatical inversion that produces "silence," "Atama Narabi ni Hara" thrusts the reader into a new relationship with the text, much like the formalist techniques of "Hae." Kataoka describes the process as such: "The reader's sensations [*kankaku*]—ideally the sensations of their whole body—are, along with the writer, given a life force [*seimei*] at once deep within, below, and beyond a given object. Then it is the reader who writes."[49] Here, the literary text, understood as a fragmented collection of stylistic devices and individual words, can mediate between author and reader, sensation and perception, subject and object. Sensations, while material, are not immediately located in the physical world but are understood as phenomena instigated through particular forms of literary practice. In Yokomitsu's and Kataoka's understanding, the production of the text is transferred from the writer to the reader as reading becomes a productive act in which sensations, mediated from printed word to reader's body, produce a new perception of world and text alike.

DIALECTICAL VISION IN THE LOWER DEPTHS

Across Yokomitsu's theoretical work, experimental stories like "Hae," and naturalistic works like "Onmi," we see a sensibility in which the human body is imagined and produced through the circulation of literary text between the city and the periphery. Later in the 1920s, Yokomitsu's work moved to the metropolitan center to explore how the circulation of people, commodities, and print structures the experience of modern urban space. In this period, Yokomitsu penned numerous works concerned with life in modern cities, including "Nanakai no Undō" (Seven Floors of Movement, 1927), about a department-store scion who imagines an ideal woman constructed from the body parts of multiple shop girls, and the long novel *Shanhai* (Shanghai, 1928–1932), with its montages of people, products, and bodies in that semicolonial city. *Shanhai* has rightly been the subject of extensive critical attention, but Yokomitsu's concerns with how circulating bodies and commodities allowed readers to reimagine themselves and their city preceded his visit to China.[50]

The previous chapter on the used-book trade began with a brief reference to a scene in the 1924 short story "Machi no Soko" (The Depths of the Town), in which a destitute worker decides to trade a stack of used magazines for a ten-sen coin so that he can live another day. There, I took the nameless laborer's magazines as a starting point to explore the shifting meanings and uses of print beyond reading. Here, a closer reading of "Machi no Soko" reveals how, in Yokomitsu's vision, this dog-eared pile of print exchanged for a single copper coin sits at the crux of one man's reimagination of the modern metropolis and the urban experience in the age of consumer capitalism. The story opens not with the anonymous protagonist but by iterating the contours of the physical and economic landscape in which that subject is situated:

> There was a shoe store on the street corner. A girl languished amid the black shoes stuffed like heavy doors from wall to wall. Next door was a clock shop, with thickets of clocks laid out in patterns. Next door to that was an egg shop, where a hunched old man sat wiping his brow amid the froth of eggs. Next door to that was a china shop . . . Next door to that was a flower shop from which a foolish-looking boy emerged and where a girl even filthier than the flowers sat.
>
> Next door to that was a clothing shop . . . Next door to that a bookshop with a gaping maw like a plate of armor . . .

The nameless protagonist passes silently by the shops, row after row of goods and commodities described in a mélange of mixed metaphors, objects from amid which people only occasionally appear. Those not ensconced amid their wares are represented as flows of an endlessly moving faceless crowd: "Colorful waves of schoolgirls that go streaming out of the gate at three in the afternoon" and "throngs of black-and-blue workmen avalanching out of the factory gates like a weary wind." The anonymous laborer threads through these ceaselessly circulating masses, then "climbs to the top of the green hill behind the street" to seek a parallax vision whereby "objects [*kyakkanbutsu*] compete for attention in his two fields of vision [*shiya*]" and he can perceive the structure of the city in its totality.[51]

These two fields of vision correspond to two contrasting images of the city as a social topos akin to David Harvey's description of the city as "the high point of human achievement . . . [and] the site of squalid human failure":

> To the north, the manors of the gentry spread out across a high plateau. There, wind and light flowed freely . . . He thought nothing at all. He looked down onto the city to the south, sitting at the bottom of a narrow ravine. Carbonic gases made the air

thick. Dust, typhus, and smoke from the military factories blowing on the east wind were the only things that moved. There were no plants. The only things gathered below were tiles, bacteria, empty pots, goods left unsold in the market, laborers, prostitutes, and rats.[52]

From this vantage point, the protagonist sees the inverse images of the grime of the lower depths below and the bright free space of the upper city. In this first panoramic viewing, these two pictures of the city appear distinct rather than dialectically linked in their contradiction. But the deeper structure of urban space begins to emerge as Yokomitsu's narrative descends from the hill back into the slum and the depths of the protagonist's mind: "He wanted money, ten sen. With that much, he could live for a day without thinking about anything. If he didn't think, he would feel better. When he moved, he got hungry. If he got hungry, ten sen would no longer be enough. He sat in the grass on the hill all day with his pale green face like an insect's camouflage. When the sun sank low, he descended from the hill and entered the city streets."[53] To Yokomitsu's protagonist, a single copper coin can cease the cycle of thinking, moving, and eating that constitutes his experience of everyday life. Money orders the sequence of his actions; with it, he can maintain his existence in the limited realm of the lower city, and without it he can climb the hill to gaze at the bifurcated vision of the metropolis. These two sides of the city and two modes of experience, visual and sensory, are mediated via the coin in his pocket.

The deeper dialectical structure of the urban landscape then comes into focus for the protagonist. He passes through a marketplace gleaming with acetylene lamps and shiny objects for sale and reimagines the city as an abstract form structured by coin:

He peered affectionately at the mountain of copper coins piled on the mat. He felt a strange sense of refinement emerging from the masses of lumpy copper clinging to one another, as if the pile of coins was a mysterious tower [*kikai na tō*]. He saw the dynamic volume of the copper coins settled at the bottom of the city as if they formed a pin single-handedly supporting the sloping line of the giant cone of the city, radiating out from the coins at the center.[54]

The man grasps the internal dialectic at work in the glinting lump of metal on the vegetable merchant's mat; the coins are momentarily at rest, but their movement and circulation determine the contours of his life. The stack of money is simultaneously a familiar brown lump and an enchanted tower that represents the underlying structural topography of the city. "I've got to pull out the pin!" he exclaims as his earlier illusion of the city is shattered: "The illusion [*gensō*] of the city lying on its side, cracked into pieces, hovered before him; he felt satisfied and reentered the crowd, where amid the stench of human bodies he stopped, overwhelmed with sudden sadness."[55] With the vision of the city as contiguous totality stripped away, the experience of urban space becomes little more than the jostling of smelly bodies.

Seiji Lippit has argued that "the protagonist's capacity for a rational comprehension of sensory phenomena collapses in the face of this fragmentation"; I would say that the protagonist's movement within the city and his grasp of the exchange relationship imbued in the money form produce a more ordered vision of the city that allows the high city and the low city to be grasped as a totality beyond this apparent fragmentation.[56] The copper coin mediates the protagonist's ability to perceive the city, in part because it is exchangeable for other commodities, including, crucially, commercial print. Once he returns home, the man considers how he can live for another day: "If he sold three magazines, he could get ten sen. With this in mind, he felt no fear. One day, he sold the three magazines and set out with the money he had made."[57] The internalization of the principle of exchange between commodities, language, and money is what ultimately structures the protagonist's consciousness and existence. The content of the magazines is less important than their form as mass-market commodities that can be resold for money for daily necessities. In the end, the protagonist takes pity on an old beggar, is again left penurious, and sets off for the hill once again. This time, Yokomitsu omits any vision of the city, and the worker returns to the slum's streets, where "his head aches" as "the city spreads out with him at its center." The story closes with a repetition of the opening frame of the array of shops in the slum; having passed through the dialectical motions of the story's core, the reader can now see the street and its denizens as part of the deeper structure of the city as a mass of ceaselessly moving money and goods as the protagonist finds himself again amid the circulating crowds, watching "waves of girls peacefully flow by him like flowers swaying in a garden."[58]

AN ATOMISTIC IMAGE OF SCRIPT

In the late 1920s, Yokomitsu continued to develop his theory of text as a means to mediate sensation and perception, whereby the literary work was an agglomeration of atomistic units of script. Here, printed script, as a material quantity, could enter into relations of exchange with physical, spatial, and social structures, all understood as fractured totalities, via the recombination of constituent parts. In this line of thought, once units of script have been arranged as components into larger units of text, story, or magazine, those objects become estranged from the writer and free to circulate among readers in the literary marketplace. In a 1929 theoretical treatise originally titled "Keishiki to Mekanizumu ni tsuite" (On Form and Mechanism) and later retitled "Moji ni tsuite" (On Script), Yokomitsu argues how literature and consciousness are constructed through the rearrangement of units of script: "Script is a material thing [*moji wa buttai de aru*] manufactured by humans [*ningen ga seizō shita*] . . . The works [*sakubutsu*] that we make, works of literature as the enumeration of script [*moji no raretsu naru bungaku sakuhin*], are material objects iterated as forms [*keishiki*] completely independent from the reader or writer."[59]

In Yokomitsu's thought of this period, the literary work is an independent material quantity that comes into existence as a product alienated from its author; units of script as individual physical objects—pieces of typographic text—make up the form of the literary work. His approach is akin to analysis in the chemical sense, in which the substance of a complex body is divided into small parts in order to comprehend the inner workings of the object. In this conceptualization, units of script are the atomlike quantities containing their own internal mechanisms and constituting the structure of the completed work as apprehended by the reader: "The fundamental element [*yōso*] of literature as literature [*bungaku to shite*] lies in an understanding of letters as material objects [*buttai*] . . . consciousness itself is a physical [*butsuriteki*] quantity." As scholars like Komori Yōichi, Yamamoto Ryōsuke, and Gregory Golley have noted, Yokomitsu's ideas were influenced by contemporary popular discourse on atomic science and quantum mechanics and the work of the physicist Ishiwara Jun (1881–1947) in particular. Yokomitsu returns to this materialist and scientific concept of writing again and again, experimenting with ideas of the internal mechanisms of script.[60]

Yokomitsu's model, in which individual characters are aggregated into increasingly complex units, mirrors the making of typographic text, in which an iteration of individually set letters are arranged on the printing press to form first sentences, then full texts, then books to be bought and sold: "First the letters that are the initial form are gathered together to become the form known as a word [*kotoba*]; those take the form of sentences [*ku*]; the combination of those sentences takes the form of 'parts' (*pāto*); the combination of those parts constitutes structure [*keisei*]; then, for the first time, the totalized form of the literary work [*bungaku sakuhin to shite no zentaiteki keishiki*] is born."[61] What emerges is form (*keishiki*) as a central problem of literature. As Toeda Hirokazu and Komori Yōichi have argued, "form" to Yokomitsu is writing as the rhythmic iteration of script for the transmission of meaning. Rather than understand writing as the unmediated representation of speech or thought, Yokomitsu advocates an approach in which authors should "write as one writes" (*kaku yō ni kaku*).[62] Yokomitsu and his Shinkankaku-ha compatriots' interest in formalist techniques was also informed by an interest in and involvement with cinema, notably Kawabata's involvement with the production of the 1926 expressionist film *Kurutta Ichipēji* (A Page of Madness).[63] It is at just this moment, the late 1920s, as technological visual media gained increasing popularity and the publishing industry entered a new phase characterized by commodities such as Iwanami's paperbacks, million-seller magazines, and one-yen anthologies, that "the problem of form" (*keishiki mondai*) becomes a key site for negotiating the politics of aesthetics in modern Japanese literature.

FORMALIST ANTAGONISTS

In the late 1920s, Yokomitsu argued for an approach to literature that was explicitly formalist (*keishikishugi*), a term that circulated as an overdetermined signifier in Japanese literary discourse. The constitutive other against which Yokomitsu and his allies positioned themselves was the proletarian literary movement, which by 1928 had ascended to a position of relative power in the critical realm. As labor disputes, social unrest, and discontent over social inequalities rose with the rapid industrialization and urbanization of Japanese society, the leftist movement grew in size and strength. So, too, did the breadth of approaches to the publishing of political literature as a means to realize a new model of social organization. From roughly 1928 to 1930, a series of exchanges known as the formalist debates (*keishikishugi ronsō*) were carried out between Yokomitsu, other former *Bungei Jidai* writers, authors of the Japanese proletarian literary movement, and an array of critics. The debate, which played out in mainstream magazines and newspapers, positioned form and formalism as central problematics for the Japanese literary establishment. Standard literary historiography understands Yokomitsu and the proletarian writers in fundamentally opposed positions, a schism between aesthetic and political avant-gardes, Marxism and modernism. However, it is more productive to take the debates as a moment in Japanese literary history in which a shared understanding of form and materialism emerges as a means to mediate the relations between literature and social activity.[64]

By 1928, as socialist, communist, and Marxist thought came to constitute a major force in modern Japanese literary discourse, a fractious array of artists and writers unions formed and split over theoretical disputes in regard to the direction of the movement. Two of the most influential movement thinkers were Hirabayashi Hatsunosuke (1892–1931), who served as editor of the mainstream magazine *Taiyō*, and Kurahara Korehito (1902–1991), the central theorist of the Zen-Nihon Musansha Geijutsu Renmei (All-Japan League of Proletarian Artists, or NAPF, following its Esperanto name, Nippona Artista Proleta Federacio) and its associated literary journal *Senki* (Battleflag, 1928–1931). In November 1928, Yokomitsu lowered a scathing critique at Hirabayashi, Kurahara, and the rest of Japan's Marxist literary critics, accusing them of the belief that "form is determined by content [*naiyō*]," which Yokomitsu argues is consummate with allowing "subject to determine object [*shukan ga kyakkan o kettei suru*]." Yokomitsu claims that allowing "content to determine form" places the Marxists squarely in the camp of not materialism but "idealism" (*yuishinron*) and leaves them with an ironically "anti-Marxist theory of literature."[65]

Kurahara's response, titled "Keishiki no Mondai" (The Problem of Form), opens by questioning the binaries upon which Yokomitsu structures his accusation: "Is the form of art really its 'object' [*kyakkan*] and is its content really its 'subject' [*shukan*]? Put another way, is the form of art really 'matter' [*busshitsu*], while its content is 'spirit' [*seishin*]?"[66] Kurahara applies a dialectical approach to the logic of Yokomitsu's argument, in which form and content are distinct from each other, with one in a necessarily dependent relationship to the other:

> Form and content are both important elements [*yōso*] in art, and we cannot say that one should be above or below the other . . . in art there is an inseparable unity of form and content . . . Formalists say that "content arises from form," but Marxists do not say that "form arises from content." In regard to form and content, to paraphrase Hegel, "they arise reciprocally" [*sōgo ni hassei shiau*] . . . Art is not born naturally [*shizen hasseiteki*], but is made by man.[67]

For Kurahara, literature is a historical, material creation. He continued to develop his concern for the functions of form and formalism in works such as the book-length treatise *Puroretaria Geijutsu to Keishiki* (Proletarian Art and Form, 1930) and an essay "Puroretaria Geijutsu no Naiyō to Keishiki" (Form and Content in Proletarian Literature), published in *Senki* in February 1929: "The content of art is certainly not, as the formalists say, determined by its form but rather just the opposite, in that the social [*shakaiteki*] and class [*kaikyūteki*] content determine the artistic form that is set within the limits of formal possibility [*keishiteki kanō no han'inai*], which are remade through the production process [*seisan katei*] that determines form."[68] Kurahara's concept of form and content is not ultimately deterministic, although it may first appear so; content may come first, but it emerges through historically specific production processes, including literary writing, the limits of formal possibility of which take on an enframing function. To him, literature is first and foremost artifice rather than unmediated expression, and as such, modes of writing change across history. Kurahara is best known for his seminal "Puroretaria Rearizumu e no Michi" (The Road to Proletarian Realism, 1928), but his notion of realism is distinct from socialist realism (itself not Soviet doctrine until 1934); he understood "realism" itself as a historically contingent mode rather than the immediate depiction of an independent objective reality.[69]

These opening salvos by Yokomitsu and Kurahara were followed by months of squabbling over which came first, form or content, by writers from the opposing camps, such as former *Bungei Jidai* author Nakagawa Yoichi and proletarian critic Katsumoto Seiichirō (1899–1967). But the debate's true import lies in its own condition of possibility—namely, a shared understanding by those on both sides of the literary work as a dialectical artifice made up of form and content, regardless of the "proper" relationship between the two. Not many years earlier, in the Content-Value Debate (Naiyōteki Kachi no Ronsō) of 1922 between Satomi Ton (1888–1983) and Kikuchi Kan, "content" (*naiyō*) was understood as an unmediated, independent value able to be separated from form, whereas by 1928 Yokomitsu and his interlocutors take it as given that the two terms must be interdependent.[70] Unsurprisingly, then, the debating parties were in fact far from diametrically opposed; recall that Yokomitsu did not initially accuse Kurahara of being too Marxist but rather of not properly grasping the materialism at the core of Marx's philosophy.

Chiming in was Nakagawa Yoichi, who had begun his career as a painter and scholar of avant-garde art interested in futurism, expressionism, and the creation of visual effects in literary works. While critical of socialist doctrine, he was one of the most well-read critics in Japan on the subject of Russian formalism, familiar with the work of Anatoly Lunacharsky (1875–1933), Georgy Plekhanov (1856–1918), and contemporaneous Soviet theoretical debates. In his 1930 treatise *Keishikishugi Geijutsuron* (On Formalist Art), he writes, "Literature is an art [*geijutsu*] based on script [*moji*] . . . if script is a medial form [*baitaiteki keishiki*] that induces thoughts [*shisō*] and feelings [*kanjō*], then literature is an art based on form . . . Form is not style. It is a physical thing with shape. It is structure [*kōsei*]. It is concrete [*gutai*]." Nakagawa claims that the antithesis of this concept of form as a physiological force is realism based on socialist ideology; he also hubristically compares the state of formalist literary theory in Japan favorably to the work of Viktor Shklovsky (1893–1984), whom he claims is "behind the times."[71] His complaint, though, is less based in the content of Marxist politics than in what he sees as a lack of commitment to writing techniques such as literary formalism, which he dubs "the best path to materialism."[72] Elsewhere, Yokomitsu argues that Marx's own written grammar produced a material understanding of history, claiming that his inventive use of descriptive language in *Capital* exemplifies "how adjectives can be used effectively in the service of materialism" since they show "how two things cannot exist in the same space at the same time"; literature is likewise a "thing [*buttai*] that expresses through script the individual movements of things."[73]

By reading Marx as a rhetorician, Yokomitsu implies that a particular form of language and argument makes it possible to historicize the rise of the commodity economy. Implicitly contrasted is the approach of Japanese Marxists, whom he accuses of blindness to the reification of their own work, which he writes off as commercialized criticism ignorant of language and dependent on Marx's name as an empty signifier used to stimulate sales.

Yokomitsu is thus less troubled by the "content" of proletarian ideology than by the way in which Marx's name becomes the sole arbiter of meaning as critics ascribe "the value of a product [*seisanbutsu*]" to the presence or absence of his name as ideological signifier. He warns his opponents, "Marx himself remained vigilant against the commercialization of Marxism, which leads to the forgetting of Marxist theory by those writing under his name."[74] Yokomitsu was not alone in his anxiety over the commodification of Marxist ideology—the commercialization of communist thought was an ongoing concern for the Japanese socialist movement from its nascent moments, as discussed in the final chapter of this book. Ultimately, Yokomitsu is concerned less with the eradication of Marxism than with the reification of Marxism as a one-dimensional sign for value, wherein the name occludes how the form of printed language can mediate a critique of consciousness.

WORDS AS WEAPONS FOR THINKING

By pulling back the frame of analysis of the formalist debate, it is possible to see the Shinkankaku-ha and proletarian theories of literature as contrasting manifestations of a shared understanding of the literary text as a material artifice made up of dialectically interlinked form and content. The literary critic Kobayashi Hideo, however, had a less-positive assay of the terms of debate and the parties' approach to literary writing, accusing both sides of having succumbed to the logic of reification and abstraction. Kobayashi's seminal 1929 essay "Samazamanaru Ishō" and the following year's "Ashiru to Kame no Ko" (Achilles and the Tortoise) served to collapse the terms of the formalist debate. Kobayashi accuses Marxists and modernists alike of eschewing the literary materialism upon which both their positions are ostensibly based; to him, both sides have eagerly adopted abstract theoretical designs detached from reality and the writing process as a lived experience.[75] He accuses Yokomitsu of an empty formalism that has forsaken all connection to the textual experimentation and symbolism of Baudelaire and Mallarmé, leaving little more than "the weakness of their own ideas," pointing out that the idea of art as a material substance (*busshitsu*) has precedent going back at least as far as Poe.[76]

Kobayashi singles out Nakagawa's *Keishikishugi Geijutsuron*, claiming that any attempt to schematically diagram the dialectics of form and content can be "correct only so long as they remain diagrams . . . but a diagram is mere style [*share*] . . . and has no meaning other than as a diagram . . . ultimately, Nakagawa does nothing but loquaciously reiterate the idea that 'form is important' [*keishiki wa taisetsu da zo*]."[77] For Kobayashi, equating form with materiality cannot make a formalist theory of literature into a materialist one by fiat. On the contrary, treating "form" as a point in a conceptual sketch rather than as a writing practice serves only to abstract, reify, and render the idea of form meaningless. Kobayashi has equally harsh words for the Marxist critics, whom, like Yokomitsu, he claims have been blinded by the fetishistic qualities of Marx's name in the literary market and thus by the very object that they set out to critique:

> Those who argue for the inseparability of the consciousness of modern man [*gendaijin no ishiki*] and Marxist materialism are doing little more than following their metaphysical whims. What controls [*shihai*] modernity [*gendai*] is not the "thing" [*mono*] of Marxist historical materialism but, as Marx clearly points out himself, the particular thing called the commodity [*shōhin to iu mono*] . . . Isn't it so that in the minds of the Marxist literary critics of today, Marxist ideology [*Marukusu kannengaku*] has turned into something that is neither praxis based on theory, nor theory based on praxis? It is merely an instance of the particular figure of the commodity, and it wields the magic of the commodity [*shōhin no majutsu*]. Marxism says that commodities rule the world [*shōhin wa yo o shihai suru*], but the design [*ishō*] of Marxism is a design spread wide through the minds of people, and it itself is a marvelous commodity. This transformation thus possesses the power to make people forget the simple fact that commodities control the world.[78]

Present in Kobayashi's analysis but a lacuna in the approach of those he critiques is an understanding of literary writing and criticism itself as a commodity and thus a component of the economies of money and language that structure the experience of social life. Kobayashi is suspicious of approaches to criticism based on a prescriptive set of abstract analytical rules rather than on a critique of the role of the commodity and its fetish power as a key constituent of modernity. As such, for Kobayashi, the failure of Marxist literary criticism in Japan lay in its inability to develop a robust theory and practice of language and expression. Similar to Miki Kiyoshi, Kobayashi links the commodity economy to the use and exchange of language, itself the bearer of near mystical power: "Words [*kotoba*], bestowed unto humans along with consciousness, are our sole weapon [*buki*] for thinking [*shisaku*] and continue to work their magic, as in ancient times."[79] It follows that for Kobayashi, true literary materialism as a means for critique can be found in the embodied experience of reading and writing of language rather than in abstract concepts of materialism as either formalist or Marxist ideology.

Kobayashi's critique at once makes apparent the limits of theoretical ambitions like Yokomitsu's and points toward other strands of discourse where we might look for deeper engagement with problems of language, materialism, and social action. Although prewar Japan's leftist movements may not have fashioned the level of linguistic thought of which Kobayashi opined, there was a robust strain of socialist and communist criticism concerned with the commercialization of radical thought. Kobayashi derides the proletarian critics for their failure to recognize their own output as internal to the commodity market, but as I detail in the final chapter, the confluence between the proletarian movement and the business side of the publishing industry was structural from the first. Likewise, at the level of linguistic thought, the same period saw extended debates over orthographic reform and Romanization conventions and a burgeoning movement in support of the international auxiliary language of Esperanto. The vicissitudes of these arguments are the subject of the next chapter.

Chapter Five

BRAVE NEW WORDS

Orthographic Reform, Romanization, and Esperantism

With the ubiquity of a media ecology and social logos predicated on mass-produced typographic print, the fundamental shape and function of written Japanese emerged as a problem. This chapter explores the rethinking of language under this print regime by exploring three roughly coterminous concerns: the controversy over historical versus phonetic kana orthography, debates on conventions for writing Japanese in roman script (*rōmaji*), and the rise of the international auxiliary language Esperanto. The first decades of the twentieth century may seem to be a phase of linguistic fixity in contrast to the debates over vernacular prose (*genbun itchi*) in the 1880s, but in fact we can observe the appearance of a new set of questions revolving around the material and ontological nature of printed language; the relationship between script, history, and social organization; and the role of language in mediating Japan's place in the modern global order. For or against phonetics, Japanese script, or roman letters, whether aligned with conservative nationalism or progressive internationalism, a wide range of critics understood script in the typographic era as a fundamental, atomistic building block of consciousness and a tool to be wielded for political purposes.

Orthographic and phonetic conventions of kana script arose as an issue in the first years of the twentieth century, in tandem with the promotion of *hyōjungo* (standard Japanese) by the linguist Ueda Kazutoshi (1867–1937) and the institution of the national education curriculum. In 1902, the Committee on National Language Inquiry (Kokugo Chōsa Iinkai) was convened by the Ministry of Education to investigate kana usage for the implementation of the national textbook (*kokutei kyōkasho*) system. Writers, bureaucrats, and critics debated the merits of a so-called historical orthography (*rekishiteki kanazukai*) versus an ostensibly phonetic orthography (*hyōonshiki kanazukai*), culminating in a controversy over the ministry's Proposal for Orthographic Reform (Kanazukai Kaitei-an) in 1924. Figures like the poet Yosano Hiroshi (1873–1935), the philologist Yamada Yoshio (1873–1958), and the authors Akutagawa Ryūnosuke (1892–1927) and Kawabata Yasunari (1899–1972) imbued individual kana with atomistic, elemental qualities from which words, expressions, and discourse could be constructed. These proposed reforms revealed deep anxieties over the ontological status of writing.

A similar argument unfolded in regard to the writing of Japanese in the roman alphabet as the so-called *Nihon-shiki* (Japanese-style) romanization movement challenged the model developed by the American James Curtis Hepburn (1815–1911) prior to the Meiji Restoration. Like historical kana orthography, the *Nihon-shiki* convention follows the written Japanese syllabary without concessions for English transliteration and pronunciation. Many *Nihon-shiki* advocates were scientists who experimented with language as a measurable physical quantity; to them, the system was rational and efficient and allowed for Japan's participation in the international production of knowledge. Later, the *Nihon-shiki* system became imbued with ethnonational autonomy in tandem with the expansion of empire and a global wave of romanization movements. A countervailing vision of linguistic internationalism was apparent in the movement for Esperanto, the artificial auxiliary *Lingwe uniwersala* created by Ludwik Zamenhof (1859–1917), which exploded in popularity after its introduction to Japan in 1906. A utopian planned language built to transcend national boundaries, Esperanto offered an opportunity to imagine the speaking subject beyond citizenship. The new language was infused from the first with political significance and adopted by the Japanese proletarian socialist movement as a means to commune with a brotherhood of workers across the world as linguistic thought became linked to Marxian materialism.

At issue in the discourse on these reforms were less the questions of national solidarity and educated citizenry that were central in the 1880s and early 1890s than concerns about the capabilities of printed language for individual and social expression, the place of Japan and Japanese in the international global order, and the material qualities of mass-produced printed type. Intellectuals considered how sound and symbol work together in the making of meaning and how different phonetic systems could mediate the evolution of expression. The diverse range of thinkers and authors discussed here wrote from a variety of positions in regard to kana, *rōmaji*, and Esperanto, but their ideas demonstrate shared interests in the transformations of sensation, perception, consciousness, communication, and social organization through and with the mechanical reproduction of typographic text at a mass scale. What we see emerge is a sense of script as a historically contingent and materially fungible artifice and agent of change.

SPEAK AND SPELL: KANA ORTHOGRAPHY AS A NATIONAL CONCERN

Shortly after the establishment of the modern Japanese nation-state, the simplification and rationalization of writing styles, orthographic approaches, and regional pronunciations was a key aim as reformers sought to craft a language appropriate for mass education, literary writing, and social discourse.[1] The form of the Japanese language was subject to near-constant debate in the late nineteenth century, from calls in the 1870s by Mori Arinori (1847–1889) and Nishi Amane (1829–1897) for the abolition of Japanese and debates over vernacular prose (*genbun itchi*) in the 1880s through the later consensus of Japanese as "national language" (*kokugo*) and linguist Ueda Kazutoshi's (1867–1937) standard language (*hyōjungo*) initiative. Intellectuals in the 1870s and 1880s agreed on the necessity of a standardized writing pedagogy distinct from Edo primers and Sinitic recitation but could not decide on a specific form of the written Japanese language. Even once Japanese as *kokugo* took root as national linguistic ideology, there was little agreement as to how standardization might be practically achieved. In the wake of language reforms to engender imperial subjectivity in the model of European nationalist projects, it was necessary to install a national school curriculum based on standardized forms and conventions of written language. Ueda's response to the need for standardized linguistic pedagogy was *hyōjungo*, a convention based on a modified form of Tokyo vernacular speech.[2] Ueda was one of the first to train in Western academic linguistics and a leading advocate for the "phonetic" (*hyōonshugi* or *hatsuonshugi*) kana system, and in 1900 the Ministry of Education fixed the kana syllabary as per his recommendations, severing the educational curriculum from the Chinese pedagogical paradigm.[3] Ueda learned linguistics from Basil Hall Chamberlain (1850–1935) at Tokyo Imperial University, then studied in Berlin, Leipzig, and Paris, where he adhered to a classical philology curriculum with courses in folklore, Sanskrit, English, Greek, German, Romanticism, and phonetics.[4] Ueda and his disciples like Hoshina Kōichi (1872–1955) later outlined genealogies tracing the history of domestic linguistic thought (*kokugogakushi*) from Fujiwara no Teika (1162–1241) through Edo nativist scholars like Ogyū Sorai (1666–1728) and Motoori Norinaga (1730–1801), but the structure of their approach was based in modern European academic disciplines. Despite Ueda's claims to the incommensurability of Western linguistics with the particularities of Japanese grammar, the epistemological reframing of Japanese as a linguistic system like any other was a necessary prerequisite to the construction of these nativist genealogies. Ueda's approach, based on a scientific (*kagakuteki*) methodology for the study of language (*gengogaku no hōhō*), circulated through the Imperial University Department of Linguistics and beyond.[5]

By the turn of the twentieth century, the combination of kanji and kana as a shared script system had reached a point of practical entrenchment in government policy, mass media, and popular usage, and Ueda's push for linguistic standardization made orthography a newly important problem. Throughout most of the Meiji period, a fifty-syllable convention based on the so-called historical orthography (*rekishiteki kanazukai*) derived from the monk Keichū's (1640–1701) treatise *Waji Shōranshō* (Notes on Correcting the Disorder of Japanese Script, 1693) was widely used, but actual practice remained in flux. *Rekishiteki kanazukai* was not so much a unified system as a spectrum of similar styles, and teaching primers varied in spelling conventions. The 1880s and early 1890s saw pushback against "historical" conventions as writers like Futabatei Shimei (1864–1909) moved away from the older script system to adopt "phonetic" vernacular writing practices, including some borrowed from *rakugo* theater. This period of ambiguity had come to a close by the mid-1890s, whence the continued use of kanji and kana settled in as a national norm. The same moment saw attempts to standardize and simplify *kanazukai* via government sponsorship of primers and reference tools.[6]

In 1891, Ōtsuki Fumihiko (1847–1928) completed the publication of his comprehensive thirty-nine-thousand-word *Genkai* (Sea of Words, 1889–1891), the first modern dictionary made by a Japanese scholar for a Japanese audience. Ōtsuki's project was supported by Itō Hirobumi (1841–1909) and Fukuzawa Yukichi (1835–1901), who saw it as a necessary enterprise for the nation; the Marxist thinker Fukumoto Kazuo (1894–1983) would later call its release the final phase of the Japanese enlightenment. *Genkai* was described by its author as a "dictionary of the common Japanese language [*Nihon futsūgo no jisho*]" and was patterned after the English alphabetic model, aligned in kana syllabary (*aiueo*) order rather than following the *iroha* order of the almanac-like Edo period *jisho*.[7] The book aimed to synthesize a vision of the modern Japanese language as a totalized whole, including "old words, new words, the elegant [*ga*] and the vulgar [*zoku*], dialect, Chinese words [*kango*], and foreign words" collated from scores of books and periodicals, all organized on equal status as per the kana syllabary. The book was a success, and *Genkai* was loved by authors, reissued in cheap editions, and given as a graduation gift to students for generations.[8]

Nonetheless, orthography remained erratic. In 1902, the Ministry of Education convened the Committee on National Language Inquiry, which was chaired by Katō Hiroyuki (1836–1916), former head of Tokyo Imperial University, with Ōtsuki as acting director.[9] The committee included Meiji bureaucrats and politicians, led by Saionji Kinmochi (1849–1940), as well as journalists and scholars, including Tokutomi Sohō (1863–1957), Miyake Setsurei (1860–1945), Haga Yaichi (1867–1927), Inoue Tetsujirō (1855–1944), and Mori Ōgai (1862–1922). The group, which would remain in session until 1917, was charged with investigating dialect and pronunciation, developing a standardized language, exploring characters, grammar, and foreign words, reducing kanji, and proposing a preferred kana orthography. In 1904, the committee released the first Proposal for Orthographic Reform, which recommended a transition from the so-called historical orthography to an ostensibly phonetic orthography, much to the chagrin of many Meiji literati, who preferred the former convention. Proposed changes included the adoption of the *bōbiki* mark for long vowels, the use of the kana *e* え for the particle *he* へ, *wa* わ for the particle *ha* は, and the elimination of *dzu* づ and *dzi* ぢ from the *t* line of the syllabary. The phonetically based orthography was adopted as textbook policy, but by the end of the decade the reform would be rolled back in favor of historical conventions.[10] The committee published its investigations in massive volumes like *Gimon Kanazukai* (Problems in Orthography, 1912–1916) and *Kōgohō* (Colloquial Grammar), edited by Ōtsuki. In 1915, Ueda released his widely used *Nihon Kokuji Daijiten* dictionary; Haga praised the editors for "finding and organizing [*seiri*] old words [*kogo*] and new words [*shingo*] in hundreds of thousands of books and volumes" to create an effective synthesis of the modern Japanese language, calling it "the basis of the national spirit [*kokumin seishin no kiso*]."[11]

SCRIPT CONTESTED AND REFORMED

Debates over kana orthography reached a pitch following the convening of a second Temporary Committee on National Language (Rinji Kokugo Chōsakai) in 1921, which revived the phonetic option. In this later phase, the publishing industry was far from neutral, thanks to the guidance of Prime Minister Hara Takashi (1856–1921), previously president of the *Ōsaka Mainichi Shinbun* newspaper. For decades, Hara had campaigned for the reduction of kanji, a position shared by earlier publishers, including Fukuzawa Yukichi and Maejima Hisoka (1835–1919), first postmaster general of Japan and founder of the *Hōchi Shinbun* (Postal News, 1872–1949) newspaper. For Maejima and Hara alike, orthographic and kanji reform could facilitate the proliferation of mass-market print and thus a literate public; conversely, the cooperation of newspapers and magazines was indispensable to achieve this goal. Hara's proreform sentiment was shared by newspaper editors, as limiting characters saved time and money at the printing press. In 1921, sixteen newspapers petitioned the government for a kanji reduction, and the following year a larger conglomerate of periodical publishers and printers announced a new list of twenty-one hundred *jōyō* kanji for standard usage.[12] Hara's committee of proreform publishers carried on his mission after he was felled by an assassin's bullet, but the committee also included many literati who did not share Hara's view. The group was chaired by Mori Ōgai (1862–1922) and included the authors Shimazaki Tōson (1872–1943), Arishima Takeo (1878–1923), and Abe Jirō (1883–1959), as well as the critics Chiba Kameo (1878–1935) and Hasegawa Tenkei (1876–1940). Ōgai was a supporter of historical orthography and aimed to assure that it remained "proper" (*seisoku*) and "correct" (*tadashii*), but his position was more than simply reactionary.[13] In a short piece written for the previous committee, he posits that writing is based on speech, but both have changed across history; *rekishiteki kanazukai* is not so much writing that is old as writing subject to historical forces. Orthography for Ōgai is imbued with material character, a thing that possesses "firm existence" (*hakkiri sonzai shiteiru mono*) and a "sense of reality" (*hontō no sonzaikan*). In contrast to spoken language (*kōgo*), which transforms "naturally" (*shizen ni*), written language (*bungo*) is for him a "thing imbued with artifice" (*jinkō ga kuwawatta mono*), and it is only "once language becomes writing that it is truly complete."[14] But Ōgai died in 1922, and his replacement by Ueda assured the committee's favor for a phonetic system, which it announced on December 24, 1924.[15] The key elements of the plan were the use of small *ya* ゃ, *yu* ゅ, *yo* ょ for vowel combinations, such as *shou* しょう in place of *seu* せう, or *kyou* きょう in place of *kefu* けふ; the exclusive use of small *tsu* っ for agglutinated double consonants; the *a*-line kana *a* あ, *i* い, *u* う for elongating *a*, *i*, and *u* sounds; the kana *u* う rather than *fu* ふ to elongate *o* sounds; the standardization of all grammatical particles to ostensibly phonetic sounds with the exception of *ha* は, *he* へ, and *wo* を; the elimination of *w*-line *wi* ゐ, *we* ゑ, and *wo* を in favor of *i* い, *e* え, *o* お; and the elimination of the *t*-line *dzi* ぢ and *dzu* づ in favor of the *s*-line *ji* じ and *zu* ず.[16]

AGAINST AN IDEOLOGY OF EFFICIENCY

Trenchant attacks on the committee's plan ran in the poetry journal *Myōjō* (Bright Star, 1900–1908, 1921–1927) in February 1925: "Monbushō no Kanazukai Kaitei-an o Ronzu" (On the Ministry of Education's Proposal for Orthographic Reform), penned by the philologist Yamada Yoshio, and "Kanazukai Kaitei-an Kōgi" (An Objection to the Proposed Orthographic Reforms), cosigned by the journal's editors Yosano Hiroshi, Yosano Akiko, and several minor poets. Yamada's and the Yosano's pieces problematize the lacunae of an ostensibly phonetic script and find fault with the committee's turn toward communicative rationality and convenience. Yamada was an accomplished linguist whose publications included *Nihon Bunpōron* (On Japanese Grammar, 1902–1909) and *Nihon Bunpō Kōgi* (Lectures on Japanese Grammar, 1922).[17] A self-taught schoolteacher, he attempted to synthesize a complete grammar by merging the methodological approach of German philology with the linguistic work of Edo-period *kokugaku* (national learning) scholars like Motoori Norinaga (1730–1801) and Kamo no Mabuchi (1697–1769). Yamada felt that a grammar of Japanese should immanently emerge from domestic language study, substituting concepts from Edo nativist scholarship and premodern poetics for parts of speech, such as the dialogic aspects of linked-verse *renga* poetry, which he saw as a rich font for the "codes and principles" (*shikumoku sahō*) of a systematic grammar.[18]

Yamada and Yosano charged the reform faction with misunderstanding the relationship between everyday language usage and changes in linguistic form. Both argued that the proposed orthography would destabilize the balance of sight, sound, and meaning embedded in the written Japanese language. Their critique of script reform is summarized in Yamada's declaration that "the script [*moji*] commonly used by the people [*minzoku jōyō*] is not something that should be reorganized [*kaihai*] via the power of legal ordinances and bureaucratic government."[19] For Yamada, language is rooted in the mutual activity of the masses and evolves over time in a sphere of everyday action beyond the ken of law or policy. Yosano's essay makes a similar point: "This thing called language is very much like a plant [*shokubutsu*]—it develops naturally amid the climate and customs [*fūdo shūkan*] of a country." For Yosano, language grows gradually through the unconscious actions of its users, and he anoints "script" (*moji*) as the "highest expression of the lives of the Japanese people."[20] Yamada likewise links language to a vaguely abstract "spirit of the nation's people" (*kokumin no seishin*), but for him language is by no means a transcendental phenomenon beyond history. Although he evokes tropes like "two thousand years of Japanese culture since the time of Shōtoku Taishi," Yamada is explicit in identifying scriptural form as "a social and historical product" (*shakaiteki rekishiteki no sanbutsu*).[21] Although Yamada would later serve as a chief linguistic ideologue for the wartime imperial polity, at this moment his primary concern is the fate of language in the modern age rather than the purity of its ancient forms.

In Yosano's view, the proposed orthographic reform is sullied by an instrumentalist attitude whereby language is reduced to a mere tool:

> The goal of the practical use [*jitsuyō*] of language by the people at large [*ippan shomin*] for their immediate convenience [*mokuzen no benri*] . . . is the road that is

easiest to walk . . . This is one of the sicknesses of our nation in the present age . . . you can see it in the types of clothes the people wear, and in their manners. Even at our nation's first-rate theaters, like the Imperial Theater, it's a disorderly state of affairs, with people wearing loose-fitting kimonos as if at a country lodging house, students watching the performance with their caps on, and the theater door opening and closing.

Yosano's curmudgeonly analogy places language in the realm of contemporary urban life, where it is subject to the same pressures that transform other modern human behaviors. He fears an "ideology of efficiency" (*nōritsushugi*) whereby reformers and publishers interested in the profitability of the newspaper business foist unwanted rationalization and standardization upon the public. Yosano believes that the power to change language lies with the people but rejects the reduction of language to exclusively practical use: "It is not enough for script [*moji*] to be used only for everyday purposes [*nichijō no yōji*]."[22] Rather, art and knowledge have evolved in tandem with orthographic forms and should not be forced into a relationship whereby kana is merely the representation of phonemes. Yamada is more explicit still: "This reorganization is not merely the interchanging of script [*moji no chikan*] but something that will influence all aspects of language . . . the reform of language and script [*mojigengo*] is akin to a type of social revolution [*shakai kakumei*]."[23] For these critics of reform, if the logos of the written word is always already inscribed in the sphere of the social, it follows that the restructuring of script might reorder the life world at large.

FEAR OF A MACHINE FOR SIGNS AND SOUNDS

At the core of the antireform position are the specific relationships between the oral, visual, and semantic dimensions of language vis-à-vis an insurmountable gap between phonetic sound and printed script. Yamada argues, "To the degree that we are working with actually usable script [*moji*], 'the unification of spoken and written language' [*genbun itchi*] will never be achieved . . . since time immemorial the kana used daily by the people have never strictly represented voiced sound [*onsei*]."[24] Both authors acknowledge the fundamental artifice of written language—the fact that sign symbols remain ultimately arbitrary, as even in the most ostensibly "phonetic" system, there is nothing inherent in a particular grapheme to indicate the representation of a particular phoneme. Yosano sees the incommensurability of the sign-sound relationship as a universal truth: "There is no country where letters are pronounced just as they are written . . . writing as PHONETIQUE . . . has never since antiquity been practiced in any land."[25] The goal then is not the impossible unification of speech and writing but a strategy to manage the internally bifurcated nature of language as both phonetic sound and written sign.

Fascinatingly, Yamada's position immediately prefigures the translation of Ferdinand de Saussure's (1857–1913) *Cours de linguistique générale* (1916) into Japanese in 1928.[26] Yet the semiotic approach was not without precedent; in 1910, the reformer Hoshina Kōichi described a phonocentric view of language in which speech (*gengo*) is deemed "the represented" (*hidaihyōsha*) and "script" (*moji*) labeled "the representer" (*daihyōsha*); spoken language is a "material object" (*jittai*), and letters "code" (*fuchō*).[27] Implicit in both Hoshina's prophonetic argument and Yamada's critique thereof is an implicit understanding that orthography can influence and not just shadow speech patterns.

For opponents of reform like Yamada and Yosano, the relationship between the auditory and visual components of language produced a problem whereby spoken language transforms more rapidly and varies more widely than more fixed printed script:

> Letters are a solid form [*kokeiteki no mono*]. Voiced sound [*seion*] is a fluid [*ryūdōteki*] form; that is to say, voiced sound is something that changes from one moment to the next. As characters are a solid form, they momentarily become affixed to these sounds, and from that point on their forms do not change . . . even if at that initial moment the sound and the letter are entirely unified, with the passage of time the sound changes and takes on an aspect quite different from its original form [*katachi*].[28]

The gap between the speed of change of the sonic and that of the visual registers forms the core of the phonetic problem, but Yamada ascribes material qualities to both speech and writing, as if they were the same element in different states of matter; one solid and one liquid. He argues that since no orthographic system has the capability to represent all possible sounds, true phoneticization would require a complex iteration of visual signs on the order of millions. A written language with such an impossibly large number of signs could not retain any semantic usage:

> If one truly wants the unification of speech and writing [*genbun no itchi*], one would not rely on the characters commonly used but rather on abstractly devised mechanical signs [*kikaiteki kigō*] to represent the voice. These signs would not be used for language [*gengo*] but simply as signs for sounds . . . Mechanically generated signs are made into phonetic symbols . . . We would have shared worldwide [*sekai kyōtsū*] sound signs [*onsei kigō*], but how could such signs ever be used for everyday purposes by ordinary people?

Only a machine would be capable of generating and processing visual representations of all possible phonetic sounds, a nightmarish mechanical representation of pure sound. Yamada's fear is that the committee's *kanazukai* skews toward "the extreme mechanical realism of sound [*oto no kikaiteki shajitsu*] without reflecting on how it might destroy the national language," turning the written word into little more than a phonetic widget.[29] By pushing phonetic orthography to its most extreme limit, Yamada aims to expose the lacuna of abstraction inherent at the core of the reform plan. The antireformers' concerns belie an ontological anxiety that even a subtle shift in orthography could disrupt the internal balance of meaning, sound, and signification in Japanese script. But implicit in their argument is an understanding that "historical" orthography, too, is only one particular relationship between sound and symbol. The committee and its critics thus ultimately agreed—not dissimilarly to the arguing parties in the contemporaneous formalist debate—that written language is a historical phenomenon that changes across time, though they disagreed in how those changes should transpire. The poet and the philologist favored an evolutionary model, while government and press reformers took an interventionist approach.

THE WAGES OF NEW WORDS: LITERARY RESPONSES TO KANA REFORM

Yamada's and Yosano's skepticism toward the proposed orthographic reform found sympathy elsewhere in the literary realm. Honma Hisao (1886–1981) agreed that the proposal would "damage the public good . . . and as our tradition of words and letters are like our flesh and blood, we would destroy ourselves."[30] Akutagawa Ryūnosuke published a commentary in the magazine *Kaizō* (Reconstruction, 1919–1955) in which he labeled himself "a mere fly stuck to the tail of Yamada's donkey" in opposition to the new policy. Writing in an atypically ornate classical style as a gesture of resistance to the simplification of language, Akutagawa posits that phonetic orthography sullies written literary language:

> [The plan] fails to reflect upon the degradation of the Japanese language [*Nihongo*] and ignores the dignity of reason . . . it is a blow from an unsheathed sword directed at the spiritual life of our people [*waga kokumin no seishinteki seimei*], a sin unforgivable under heaven and upon earth . . . This is a serious affront to our forebears Kōyō, Rohan, Ichiyō, Bimyō, Sohō, Chogyū, Shiki, Sōseki, Ōgai, and Shōyō. Moreover, it is a great affront to the frivolous work of all us hacks under heaven who have followed in their footsteps.

The Meiji authors Akutagawa names all experimented with forms of literary writing, and he fears that the new policy will produce a schism between the present and the diversity of past prose styles. Echoing Ōgai, Akutagawa argues that the complexity of the relationship between written and spoken Japanese produces literary art, which he fears will be eschewed in favor of an instrumental understanding of language as a means for practical communication. Like Yamada, Akutagawa sees the disruption of the syllabary as an affront to the cultural heritage of Japan and warns of the "danger of casting the Yamato language [*shikishima no Yamato kotoba*] into disarray," invoking an ancient poetic epithet amid a thicket of florid neoclassical grammar to prove his point.[31] For Akutagawa, like Ōgai, Yamada, and Yosano, the distinctive nature of literary expression cannot be reconciled with writing as mere mimesis of the voice.

This negative view of orthographic reform was by no means the only opinion among literati, as some writers saw the proposed script system as a new form of language that opened up aesthetic possibilities. In support of the policy was Kawabata Yasunari, who exhorted, "I have one hope for the people of the literary establishment: that they quickly adopt the 'new orthography' [*shinkanazukai*]."[32] For Kawabata, the reformed orthography promised new forms and modes of literary expression, an opinion ironically shared by Yamada, who agreed that the proposed changes would produce previously unknown permutations of signs and sounds, giving rise to "new forms [*shinkeishiki*] never seen before."[33] Interestingly, the modernist Kawabata does not highlight stylistic experimentation but praises the phonetic system as a means to engender clear communication: "There should be no problems writing as one pronounces [*hatsuondōri*]. It will be easy to write [*kakiyasuku*] and easy to read [*yomiyasuku*]."[34] Kawabata locates the transmission of meaning in the auditory sense of language, elsewhere naming the ideal sentence one "in which meaning can be understood by listening only with the ears, not reading letters with the eyes."[35]

But Kawabata's auditory model of semantic transmission stems from a secondary, rather than primary, orality, and the result is an evocation of spoken language produced by a specific system of print artifice rather than the unmediated representation of speech. Kawabata appears to eschew the printed letter in favor of communicative rationality, but the semantic register of writing remains rooted in the reproduction of the auditory imagination via the printed word. If Kawabata saw aesthetic possibilities in the proposed reform, the poet Satō Ichiei (1899–1979) saw political potential. Satō, a translator of Edgar Allan Poe (1809–1849), posits that the proposal might provoke the self-destruction of the bourgeois literary realm and dispel the specter of mystification from literary language:

> In our present age, bourgeois organizations and bourgeois culture are heading toward collapse . . . Language [*gengo*] should already belong to the people [*minshū*]. Literature will go out to pasture and the language of the people [*minshūgo*] must become literary language . . . we have the limitation of kanji, the orthographic-reform plan, proletarian literature, expressionism . . . It is unthinkable that scholars of national learning or literary men might create a literature and language of the people. The only thing they can do is make their language, their literature, and themselves go extinct.

Satō advocates a radical vernacularism in which a new language rises from below to overthrow the old, grouping the proposed orthography with emergent movements to revolutionize literature; this new vernacular is contrasted to the "aesthetic feudalism" (*shinbiteki hōken*) of Yamada and Yosano.[36] Yet the structure of Satō's argument again mirrors the antireform faction, with which he likewise shares an understanding of language as a historical and material quantity that emerges through mass activity—Satō simply sees the *kanazukai* proposal as a way to throw language back to the citizens rather than wrest it from them. Pro- and anti reform factions ultimately shared a belief that the new orthography would precipitate literary and social effects extending far beyond the strokes to write a given syllable.

TIMES FOR A NEW *RŌMAJI*

Kana was not the only Japanese orthographic system subject to change and suffused with sociohistoric significance in the age of mass-market print media. The form and function of roman script (*rōmaji*) also grew increasingly important as the Japanese empire expanded and integrated into the global economic and political hierarchy of the early twentieth century. Roman script has a long history in Japan, dating back to its use in transliterated texts and translation tools printed by Portuguese mercenaries and Dutch traders in the late sixteenth century, including editions of the *Heike Monogatari* (*Tales of the Heike*) and *Aesop's Fables* (as *Isoho Monogatari*). These early examples of Japanese in roman script, later dubbed Christian editions (*kirishitan-ban*) or Christian script (*kirishitan moji*), encompassed a range of orthographic schema and experiments and played an important role in mediating so-called Dutch learning (*Rangaku*) in the early modern period but never constituted a significant challenge to mainstream Japanese and Sinitic script conventions.[37] But the expansion of foreign intercourse in the second half of the nineteenth century made a romanization system necessary for international communication and trade. The most widely adopted convention was devised by the American James Curtis Hepburn in conjunction with his assistant Kishida Ginkō (1833–1905). Hepburn was an eye doctor practicing in Japan who also knew Chinese and devised a twenty-thousand-word Japanese-English dictionary, the *Wa-Eigo Rinshūsei* (Japanese-English Dictionary), which was completed in 1866 and published in 1867.[38] The Tokugawa shogunate ordered three hundred copies made, but printing the dictionary proved to be no easy task, as none of the rudimentary presses in Japan were able to handle the book's extreme degree of precision in character cutting and typesetting; ultimately, the manuscript was taken to Shanghai's more developed typographic printing industry.[39] Following modification, Hepburn's convention, which was devised to match Anglo-American English spelling and pronunciation, would ultimately occupy the mainstream of modern Japanese romanization, but not before decades of debate.

Some early-Meiji politicians and intellectuals, such as Mori Arinori and Nishi Amane, saw in *rōmaji* an alternative to kana as a primary script system for the national language.[40] The Rōmaji-kai society was formed in 1885 and worked to promote and codify an orthography based on Hepburn's model, but by the turn of the century, it had become clear that Japanese would continue to be written using kanji and kana. Interest in *rōmaji* was renewed around the time of the Russo-Japanese War (1904–1905) as the growing empire sought to stake its position on the world stage. In 1908, the powerful politician Saionji Kinmochi established a new Rōmaji Hiromekwai (Society for the Promotion of Roman Script), and debates over *rōmaji* spelling conventions ramped up in tempo with the contemporaneous controversies over kana orthography.[41] Critics of the Hepburn system made a case for replacing it with the *Nihon-shiki* convention, which differed slightly but significantly on points of pronunciation, phonetics, and spelling. As in the kana debates, a close reading of the discourse surrounding *Nihon-shiki rōmaji* provides a picture of the shifting status of printed language in the early twentieth century.

THE SCIENCE OF THE ALPHABET

Many early proponents of the *Nihon-shiki* system were not linguists or literati but scientists who treated script as a substance subject to modern experimental methods, including the physicist Tamaru Takurō (1872–1932), who lent the orthography its name following a schema designed by the mathematician and astronomer Terao Hisashi (1855–1923). The term *Nihon-shiki* was at first used as a catchall for a range of systems whose conventions did not align with the Hepburn model and more rigidly followed the arrangement of the kana syllabary without deviation to accommodate English pronunciation.[42] *Nihon-shiki* proponent Kikuzawa Sueo (b. 1900) later drafted a genealogy of a native romanization schema beginning with the *Rangaku* scholar Aoki Sukekiyo (dates unknown), whose *Waran Moji Ryakkō* (Abbreviated Thoughts on Japanese and Dutch Script, 1746) he identifies as the first roman script orthography to be devised by a Japanese person for Japanese use.[43] In the polemic *Rōmaji Kokujiron* (For Roman Script as National Script, 1914) and the follow-up study *Rōmajibun no*

Kenkyū (Research on Roman Script, 1920), Tamaru makes the case for *Nihon-shiki* as a practical model based on domestic writing conventions of the early twentieth century. Like Yamada Yoshio in regard to kana, Tamaru is critical of any ostensibly phonetic system, especially one based on the pronunciation of foreigners.[44] Tamaru argues that "*Nihon-shiki rōmaji* is not based on the pronunciation of humanity as a whole [*ningen zentai*] but on that of the Japanese language [*Nihongo*] . . . our purpose is not simply to transcribe sound [*oto o utsusu*] but to achieve a method of writing able to

	ア a	イ i	ウ u	エ e	オ o	拗			音
						-ya	-yu	-yo	-wa
k	カ ka	キ ki	ク ku	ケ ke	コ ko	キャ kya	キュ kyu	キョ kyo	クワ kwa
g	ガ ga	ギ gi	グ gu	ゲ ge	ゴ go	ギャ gya	ギュ gyu	ギョ gyo	グワ gwa
s	サ sa	シ si	ス su	セ se	ソ so	シャ sya	シュ syu	ショ syo	—
z	ザ za	ジ zi	ズ zu	ゼ ze	ゾ zo	ジャ zya	ジュ zyu	ジョ zyo	—
t	タ ta	チ ti	ツ tu	テ te	ト to	チャ tya	チュ tyu	チョ tyo	—
d	ダ da	ヂ di	ヅ du	デ de	ド do	ヂャ dya	ヂュ dyu	ヂョ dyo	—
n	ナ na	ニ ni	ヌ nu	ネ ne	ノ no	ニャ nya	ニュ nyu	ニョ nyo	—
h	ハ ha	ヒ hi	フ hu	ヘ he	ホ ho	ヒャ hya	ヒュ hyu	ヒョ hyo	—
p	パ pa	ピ pi	プ pu	ペ pe	ポ po	ピャ pya	ピュ pyu	ピョ pyo	—
b	バ ba	ビ bi	ブ bu	ベ be	ボ bo	ビャ bya	ビュ byu	ビョ byo	—
m	マ ma	ミ mi	ム mu	メ me	モ mo	ミャ mya	ミュ myu	ミョ myo	—
y	ヤ ya	(イ i)	ユ yu	(エ e)	ヨ yo	—	—	—	—
r	ラ ra	リ ri	ル ru	レ re	ロ ro	リャ rya	リュ ryu	リョ ryo	—
w	ワ wa	ヰ wi	(ウ u)	ヱ we	ヲ wo	—	—	—	—

FIGURE 5.1 Syllable chart of Tamaru Takurō's version of *Nihon-shiki rōmaji* (Japanese-style roman script), as it appears in *Rōmajibun no Kenkyū* (Research on Roman Script, 1920).

grammatically express meaningful thought in Japanese [*shisō o kakiarawasu*] . . . the *Nihon-shiki* system duly matches the properties of Japanese [*Nihongo no seishitsu*] and is the most scientific [*kagakuteki*] way to express ideas in Japanese."[45] The goal of Tamaru's *Nihon-shiki* convention is not a phonetic ideal in which spelling matches pronunciation but the promulgation of an orthographic system suited for writing modern Japanese as a semantically rich language.

Tamaru's invocation of "science" (*kagaku*) as a rationale is significant, as *Nihon-shiki* developer Terao was a mathematician and astronomer, Tamaru himself was a physicist, and early proponent Tanakadate Aikitsu (1856–1952) was a polymathic pioneer in geophysics and aeronautics. Terao, Tamaru, and Tanakadate were first and foremost scientists who dabbled in language reform, and their approach to romanization demonstrates how scientific principles and experimental practices informed the reimagination of script and language understood as a measurable quantity. Tanakadate felt that submitting script to scientific rationalization would facilitate the integration of Japanese scholars into the community of global scientific knowledge. His first essay on the subject was "My Opinion on the Usage of Roman Script and the Case for Publishing *Rigaku Kyōkai Zasshi* in Roman Script" (*Rigaku Kyōkai Zasshi* o Rōmaji nite Hatsuda suru no Hatsugi oyobi Rōmaji yōhō iken), published in 1885 by the eponymous *Rigaku Kyōkai Zasshi* (Journal of the Association of Physical Science). In it, Tanakadate argues that since Japanese scientists were reading Western publications written in roman script, "it would be difficult to read and express our opinions using translated mixed kana script [*kanamajiri yakubun*]." If an effective romanization schema facilitated the consumption of knowledge, Tanakadate also saw it as crucial to the production of the same, and he argued that *rōmaji* would allow Japanese scientists to participate in the global scientific community without hindrance, to "spread our ideas into the world without being misunderstood, since kanji are a pain [*mendō*] and kana are confusing to use [*magirawashi*]."[46]

Tanakadate undertakes his analysis as if script were a physical substance on which to experiment, operationally defining "kana as a symbol [*kigō*] that represents a phoneme [*on'in*]," with the corollary that roman script used for writing Japanese is structured similarly. To Tanakadate, it made sense that the basic system of phonetic symbols used in Japan should match that used in the West—as "the standard script [*futsū no moji*] of enlightened nations [*bunmeikoku*]," roman letters also functioned as a shared notation system used for mathematical computation, scientific charts, and telegraphy. By this logic, kana was simply a domestic phonetic system, but the roman alphabet had achieved the status of a global master script utilized for nonlinguistic communication and calculation. As such, Tanakadate analyzes the utility of his fifty-syllable proto–*Nihon-shiki* system in comparison with phonetic models like Hepburn's, calculating to several decimal points the amount of page space saved and devising a complex mathematical formula for why nonphonetic romanization is more efficient.[47]

Tanakadate's approach to spoken language is similarly scientific. In a follow-up essay, "Hatsuonkō" (Thoughts on Pronunciation), he conceptualizes speech as a physiological mechanism, beginning with the voice as "a tool for making sounds [*oto o hassuru dōgu*] . . . This pronunciation tool is based in the organization of the flesh and tendons in a person's throat, the form and shape of their mouth, nose, and tongue, the capacity of their lungs," and the production of vocal sounds "is affected by their race, gender, age, and occupation, as well as their clothing and even what they have eaten." Tanakadate's model of language is rooted in the material circumstances through which a body acts under particular experimental conditions. From there, he moves to the physics of sound waves, declaring that "human pronunciation is nothing other than waves produced by the lungs then expelled via the mouth" and speech organs to produce vocal forms. Language is conceptualized via an atomic model whereby "pronounced sounds are joined together to make words [*kotoba*]; these words are then combined to make speech [*hanashi*]."[48] For Tanakadate, Tamaru, and their followers, the *Nihon-shiki* convention was the most systematic way to represent language as conceived in purely physiological terms. Unlike the Hepburn model, which was crafted with foreign pronunciation in mind, the *Nihon-shiki* system was based on an appeal to scientific rationality.[49] Despite Tanakadate's research in phonetics and audiology, *Nihon-shiki rōmaji*, like "historical" kana orthography, rejected the ideal of script as the immediate representation of sound and instead was structured to retain a separation between written and spoken Japanese, even when using roman letters.

Tanakadate crusaded for the *Nihon-shiki* system at home and abroad, writing and publishing in *rōmaji* and delivering lectures overseas. In an English lecture presented to the Japan Society of London in 1920, he criticized the Hepburn model as "chiefly meant for foreigners," comparing roman letters to "ready-made suits, which are elastic enough to work for anybody but fit nobody exactly."[50] Like the kana reformers working at the same time, Tanakadate argued that orthography was ultimately a practical problem and that the twentieth century was "no longer the age of theory [*giron no zidai*] but the age of practice [*zikko no zidai*]."[51] *Nihon-shiki rōmaji* was, he claimed, the ideal linguistic technology for the age of industrial culture and electric communications like radio and wireless telegraphy; he surmised that roman script in Japan would eventually be naturalized over time, just as had other technologies of industrial modernity.[52]

With the goal of popular practice in mind, Tanakadate and Tamaru worked with the literary historian Haga Yaichi to release a self-study manual for their orthography, *Rōmaji Hitorigeiko* (Rōmaji Self-Instruction, 1909). The book begins with the working definition of "script as symbols to represent words [*kotoba o arawasu*]" and crafts a teleological schema in which "phonetic script [*otomoji*] is more evolved than kana or kanji."[53] Privileging *rōmaji* also served to symbolically shift modern Japanese away from Sinitic writing systems and toward the West.[54] The superiority of alphabetic script is justified on the grounds of efficiency, since it uses a few dozen letters versus thousands of kanji; Tanakadate and his compatriots argued that although kanji and kana may seem more "convenient" (*benri*) at the moment, they are ultimately "uneconomic for education . . . Japan's transformation into a country that uses roman script will benefit the development of individual and nation alike [*kojin oyobi kokka*]."[55] As such, the choice of romanization convention was considered to have repercussions at the level of national subjectivity as Japan sought to negotiate its status in the world:

> French people [use roman script] in a French way, Germans in a German way, and British and Americans in an English way. Just as how Germans and French use roman script as they see fit, so should Japan, rather than be bound to English . . . There may be those who critique the *Nihon-shiki* orthography with regard to pronunciation problems, but the system was made not for the purpose of pronunciation but rather to be an everyday instrument [*nichiyō yōgu*] for the expression of ideas.[56]

Nihon-shiki advocates denigrated Hepburn as a limited model developed at an earlier historical moment and claimed it no longer suited the needs of a twentieth-century industrial empire. In this logic, it follows that if the roman alphabet is an abstract universal script, there is no reason why Japan should not claim autonomy to devise its own schema rather than submit to the pronunciation needs of another linguistic realm.

FOREIGN LETTERS, NATIVIST IDEAS

The implicit nationalism of the *Nihon-shiki* faction's position would become more explicit over time. A treatise published by the Teikoku Rōmaji Kurabu (Imperial *Rōmaji* Club) in 1907 and reprinted for decades gives a revealingly encyclopedic list of rationales behind the use of roman script in the twentieth century, a sample of which are excerpted here:

- It is the shared script of the civilized world [*bunmei sekai*]; it requires few characters, its form [*katachi*] is simple, it is easy to propagate, and is aesthetic [*bijutsuteki*].
- It is easy to learn, easy to read, and easy to write.
- It will advance the development of the Japanese language [*Yamato kotoba*].
- It will eliminate differences in language between social classes.
- It will make foreign languages more Japanese [*Nihonka*].
- It will allow for the spread of Japanese into China, Taiwan, and Korea.
- It will make Japan more global [*sekaiteki*].
- It will allow Japanese brands to become more global and will dramatically increase the number of people coming from abroad as well as the number of Japanese going abroad.
- It will make printing easier by reducing redundancies in kana and kanji.
- It will allow the further development of the Japanese language and Japanese literature.[57]

Roman script is seen as a necessary medium for Japan's integration into international registers of time, space, language, money, culture, and communication at a moment when the nation was renegotiating its place on the world stage. *Rōmaji* is presented as a modern and efficient technology, "a machine [*kikai*] for writing the national language [*kokugo*]" to facilitate internationalism as a two-way street, whereby Japan can participate in global business and shape world politics in its own image.[58] Interestingly, *rōmaji*

FIGURE 5.2 *Rōmaji* edition of the twelfth-century *Konjaku Monogatari* (*Tales of Times Now Past*), published by the Rōmaji Hiromekwai organization in 1914.

advocates saw no apparent contradiction between the use of roman script and nativist language ideology. In their thinking, *rōmaji* does not act as a foreign element sullying the spirit and character of ethnonational language but as a vector for linguistic imperialism into colonies elsewhere in Asia.[59] The authors of the pamphlet explicitly aim to dispel the myth that "because roman script is a foreign product [*gaikokusei*] it damages the national polity [*kokutai*] and denigrates the national character [*kokuminsei*]."

Rōmaji advocates aimed to prove the commensurability of roman script with the Japanese language by publishing *rōmaji* editions of canonical works such as the *Konjaku Monogatari* (*Tales of Times Now Past*, ca. 1120) and the *Kojiki* (*Record of Ancient Matters*, 712). At the same time, modern authors began playing with possibilities for literary expression by writing Japanese in roman script. The poet Kitahara Hakushū (1885–1942) experimented with *rōmaji* and, most famously, Ishikawa Takuboku (1885–1912) kept several months of *rōmaji* entries in his diary during 1909, later published as *Romazi Nikki*.[60] The unfixed conventions of *rōmaji* orthography are apparent in Takuboku's writing; he begins by following the *Nihon-shiki* system but later shifts to a style resembling the Hepburn model.[61] Takuboku, who was working as a corrections editor for the *Tōkyō Asahi Shinbun* newspaper, writes that his rationale behind using *rōmaji* was, "I love my wife, so I don't want her to read my diary. But that's a lie. I do love her and I don't want her to read it, but the two aren't related." Kuwabara Takeo and others have argued that Takuboku's use of an unfixed and not-yet-universalized script allows Takuboku a freedom of self-expression as he describes both his personal sexual awakening and the fault lines of late Meiji literature. Takuboku logs his readings of works by authors like Yano Ryūkei (1850–1931) and Futabatei Shimei, who were themselves involved in an earlier wave of literary experimentation. He describes reading Futabatei's translations of Turgenev, which were so important in developing a modern literary vernacular, as well as criticizes recent fiction "for being little more than just a new type of literary sketching [*syaseibun*]."[62] The use of roman script serves as a metalevel writing practice for Takuboku, a stylistic experiment that lends him distance and perspective on the historical artifice inherent in the ostensibly vernacular fiction of his own moment.

A MOST CIVILIZED SCRIPT: JAPAN, ROMANIZATION, AND THE WORLD

Competition between the *Nihon-shiki* and Hepburn systems was protracted, but by the late 1920s critics on both sides had agreed to support the *Nihon-shiki* orthography, a decision ratified by the Ministry of Education's Temporary Committee on Roman Script (Rinji Rōmaji Chōsakai).[63] This change in convention took place at the level of practice as well as policy, and major newspapers such as the *Tōkyō Asahi Shinbun*, *Nichinichi Shinbun*, and *Hōchi Shinbun* adopted the *Nihon-shiki* orthography.[64] By the early 1930s, the rise of academic philology and phonetics and the influence of foreign linguistic thinkers like Otto Jespersen (1860–1943) and Edward Sapir (1884–1939) lent credence to the *Nihon-shiki* model. Tamaru's pupil Kikuzawa Sueo cites the work of Ferdinand de Saussure, whose ideas on language as a sign system became increasingly influential following his translation into Japanese in 1928.[65] According to Tanakadate, those who had once denounced his work as "eccentric" and "heretical" at last came to recognize his system as "philologically ideal."[66]

To its supporters, the *rōmaji* cause in the early twentieth century was not merely linguistic but also a cultural movement (*bunka undō*) with the potential to change both the Japanese language and the Japanese state. *Rōmaji* was understood as a "necessary tool [*yōgu*] for carrying out everyday life [*nichijō seikatsu*]" in the industrial age, a "new national language and new national script [*shinkokugo shinkokuji*]" befitting a "new society" (*shinshakai*): "We must demand a new script [*atarashii moji*] for the new words [*atarashii kotoba*] necessary for this new world [*atarashii yo no naka*].[67] An effective romanization scheme was seen as a necessity for Japan to function in a modern global network structured by international post, telegrams, telegraphs, bank transfers, rail and shipping tables, the metric system, and other aspects of the world economic market.[68] *Nihon-shiki* romanization was ultimately chosen as the best orthography for Japan to fully exert its national subjectivity as an imperial power within that system. As Japan began its incursion into China in the 1930s, critics imagined a future in which Japan was at last able to detach itself from the Sinitic writing system that Tanakadate derided as a "waste of the youthful vigor and intellect of the Japanese nation."[69]

The *Nihon-shiki* advocates aimed to use roman script to distinguish Japanese writing from both Chinese and Anglo-American hegemony, which meant jettisoning the Hepburn model. Tamaru argues that "Japan is not a colony [*shokuminchi*] of either England or America" and casts his orthography as the means for Japanese writing to at last escape a semicolonial status.[70] In *Nihon-shiki rōmaji*, alphabetic script—the marker of a fully civilized nation—is an abstract symbolic system over which Japan claims its own right, and Japan's romanization drive was contemporaneous with a global wave of linguistic nationalisms seeking self-determination via script reform and the adoption of the roman alphabet. Japanese scholars were well aware of movements for ethnolinguistic autonomy via script reform in China, Mongolia, Turkey, and the Central Asian Soviet republics.[71] In the Japanese case, this turn toward linguistic nationalism included the reframing of discourse on *rōmaji* orthography as a matter pertaining to national ideology. Writing in 1931, Tanakadate argues that the adoption of the *Nihon-shiki* convention is tantamount to the awakening of "ethnic spirit" (*minzoku seishin*); his pupil Kikuzawa Sueo sees it "as a necessity for Japan to become 'a first-rate country.'"[72] Even Yamada Yoshio, a vehement critic of romanization given his support for historical kana orthography, finds common cause, declaring the *Nihon-shiki* system to "duly respect the principles and grammar of the Japanese language . . . even though I am unable to agree that *rōmaji* should be made the script of Greater Japan."[73] Yamada's support for *Nihon-shiki* romanization is less surprising than it may seem, since it parallels historical kana orthography in rejecting the possibility of a fully phonetic script and favoring a system reserved for written expression rather than beholden to the representation of speech. Kikuzawa sums up this perspective: "The writing of language [*kotoba*] in script [*moji*] follows the principle of 'writing as one writes' [*kaku tōri ni kake*] rather than 'writing as one speaks.' This is only natural from the standpoint of script as a means for the exchange of ideas."[74]

ESPERANTO AS ARTIFICIAL LINGUISTIC TECHNOLOGY

Romanization was by no means the only linguistic movement that aspired to negotiate Japan's place in the global political hierarchy. If *Nihon-shiki rōmaji* became imbued with ethnonationalist ideology, then the Japanese Esperanto movement constituted an alternative vision of script's ability to advance transnational solidarity. Esperanto, an international auxiliary planned language, was developed by Zamenhof in the 1880s as a utopian linguistic project built to transcend race and nation for the sake of global human brotherhood. Zamenhof was born to a Jewish family in late nineteenth-century Białystok, Poland, and grew up in a multiethnic, multilingual milieu where Russian, Polish, German, and Yiddish identities and speech practices coexisted in a conflicted mix. Zamenhof was confronted with the impossibility of reconciling a single national language with his linguistic reality and undertook the creation of his *Lingwe uniwersala* as a solution to the "Jewish Question" that occupied a Europe beset by discrimination and pogroms. The language, which was crafted as a mélange of Romance, Germanic, and Slavic vocabulary and grammar, is fundamentally agglutinative, in which prefixes, suffixes, conjunctions, and particles can be added to transform meaning and parts of speech and produce new vocabulary through a process of word building. According to Esperanto scholar Esther Schor, Zamenhof envisioned Esperanto as a modern tool and essentially political undertaking rooted in "reason, efficiency, and pragmatism" through which humanity could envision a transnational "shared future."[75]

Zamenhof's first guide to his new language, *Lingvo Internacia*, was published in 1887, and its popularity spread quickly as it proved itself the most effective attempt yet to realize the dream of a universal language. Beginning in 1905, Esperantists began holding annual conferences across Europe, and by the 1920s the new language had begun to be encouraged by organizations like the International Postal Union.[76] Esperanto was introduced to Japan immediately after the Russo-Japanese War, in the same interval in which kana orthography and *rōmaji* conventions were debated, and would find a more enthusiastic reception there than anywhere else outside Europe.[77] Upon its introduction, Esperanto boomed in popularity; that initial excitement waned, but Esperanto usage climbed to new levels in tandem with the rise of the proletarian political movement to which it was closely linked in the late 1910s and 1920s. In the late 1920s, the Japana Esperanto-Instituto (Nihon Esuperanto Kyōkai, known as JEI) boasted an official membership of nearly seven thousand, although there were many thousands more unregistered practitioners spread across the country.[78] In the 1920s, major magazines such as *Kaizō* took to writing their names in Esperanto, and radio stations launched Esperanto-language broadcasts;

Esperanto clubs sprang up at institutes of higher learning like Waseda, Keio, and Tokyo Imperial Universities, and chapters were established in every prefecture of Japan, as well as in the colonies of Taiwan, Korea, and Karafuto (Sakhalin).[79]

We can examine Esperanto as a kind of synthetic linguistic technology that presented an alternative role for Japan in the world system and engendered a rigidly materialist conception of language through its adoption by the proletarian movement. Interest in Esperanto was ideologically diverse, and figures ranging from the writer Futabatei Shimei, to the pioneering ethnographer Yanagita Kunio (1875–1962), the rightist reformer Kita Ikki (1883–1937), the Christian moralist philosopher Nitobe Inazō (1862–1933), the anarchist Ōsugi Sakae (1885–1923), the poet Kitahara Hakushū, the liberal journalist Yoshino Sakuzō (1878–1933), the children's author Miyazawa Kenji (1896–1933), and the leftist dramaturge Akita Ujaku (1883–1962) were all involved in the movement to various degrees. As with the contemporaneous orthographic reforms, Japanese discourse on Esperanto was often imbued with utopian, world-historical social significance. Esperanto's status as a synthetic supranational "world language" (*sekaigo*) was appealing to Japanese intellectuals at a moment when Japan was renegotiating its place on the global stage. At the same time, communist, anarchist, and socialist activists experimented with possibilities for political intercourse beyond the borders of the empire, and Esperantists considered it what Sho Konishi calls "a language without culture or civilization" able to facilitate "the horizontal flow of knowledge at a grassroots level" and achieve the dream of world culture structured through the shared subjectivity of common people (*heimin*).[80]

Esperanto was a new answer to the persistent problem of "gaining freedom from the shackles of the difficult Japanese language." According to Esperantist Ishiguro Yoshimi (1899–1980), part of the language's appeal lay in its use of roman script and "ideal pronunciation, in which one letter makes one sound [*ichiji ichion*]." Since roman script was "already a global script [*kokusaigo no moji*] universalized [*fukyū*] throughout the world," Esperanto could evolve "completely new forms [*atarashii keishiki*] of thought." In this utopian drive—the word "esperanto" is derived from the Spanish *espero*, "hope"—Esperantists saw as their spiritual predecessor the fantasy of universal language conceptualized by Gottfried Wilhelm Leibniz (1646–1716) and its dream of transcending disciplinary categories of knowledge.[81] Via the medium of Esperanto, the Japanese experience of modernity could be made commensurable with the spirit of world history.

A frequently used term to describe Esperanto in Japanese was "shared artificial language" (*jinzōteki kyōtsūgo*). In the wake of Ueda Kazutoshi's work to propagate *hyōjungo* as a shared Japanese national language, Esperanto was cast as a parallel project on a global scale, a linguistic standard to unite speakers of different world languages: "Esperanto is not merely an artificial language [*jinzōgo*] but a language [*gengo*] to organize [*seiri*] the various national languages of the world. In other words, it is as if each national language is one dialect [*hōgen*], and Esperanto is the standard language [*hyōjungo*] of the world." Esperantists were keenly aware of the medial quality of their newly minted artificial language, frequently described as a *chūritsugo*, "neutral language," but more literally a language standing between nations. According to Schor, this mediality was essential to Esperanto as the integration of translation into everyday life and international commerce—its power lay in its invented nature and its neutrality. The artificiality implicit in kana reform and *hyōjungo* was explicit in Esperanto; as such, its advocates claimed that "its theoretical structure cultivates an improved understanding of the true nature [*honshitsu*] of language [*gengo*] as such."[82] The new language also tested the phonetic limits of Japan's extant kana and *rōmaji* scripts, neither of which could encompass the full range of Esperanto sounds. The phonetics and pronunciation of Esperanto required textbook authors to create new uses for existing syllabaries and dispatch unconventional combinations of hiragana, katakana, and diacritical marks to explain the pronunciation of the twenty-eight letters of the Esperanto alphabet.

THE PRACTICAL VALUE OF A POSTNATIONAL SCRIPT

Esperantists also saw the possibility of "literary value" (*bungakujō no kachi*) and "greater stylistic freedom" (*buntai no jiyū*) in their modern language.[83] Existing works of modern Japanese literature were translated into Esperanto, including stories by Arishima Takeo (1878–1923), Shiga Naoya (1883–1971), and Natsume Sōseki (1867–1916).[84] The person who brought Esperanto to Japan was none other than Futabatei Shimei, whose vernacular literary experiments in the 1880s played a key role in shaping the form of modern Japanese prose. Returning from an assignment in Russia for the *Asahi Shinbun* newspaper, Futabatei met a group of Esperantists in Vladivostok who knew of his work translating Russian and asked him to help transmit Esperanto to Japan.[85] In 1906, shortly after the end of the Russo-Japanese War, Futabatei released a primer titled *Sekaigo* (World Language) and a translation of one of Zamenhof's exercise books, *Sekaigo Dokuhon* (Reader in World Language) with the goal of introducing a new vernacular suited to the internationalism of the twentieth century.[86] Futabatei's opinions on Esperanto were less informed by the utopian humanism of Zamenhof than by its practical application for the Japanese nation's success in global business and politics: "As the intercourse between people [*ningen no kōtsū*] develops in an ever more complex manner, we feel the need for a global vernacular [*sekai tsūyōgo*]."[87] Futabatei introduced Esperanto schematically and pragmatically, but he never became proficient himself and soon lost interest in the movement. His utilitarian approach focused on the possibility of the language as an "official and commercial dialect that would yield economies of time and money," the countervailing tendency to the international movement's utopian impulse.[88]

This practical rather than spiritual or political approach to Esperanto was shared by another of Japan's best-known Esperantists, the ethnographer Yanagita Kunio. Yanagita's interest in Esperanto was spurred by his experience as a delegate to the League of Nations in Geneva in 1921 and 1922.[89] Yanagita's trip to Switzerland was linguistically traumatic, as he found himself barely able to read English and almost entirely unable to communicate via speech: "I needed to know what was going on in the world, but even reading a newspaper or two would take up half the day . . . I had been given an important task but was totally unable to express myself on the matter as I might be able to in Japan." Esperanto emerged as a solution to Yanagita's communication frustration: "At just that moment, a proposal on recognizing Esperanto was submitted. I became extremely interested in the language; my motives were simple . . . [Esperanto] could be important for delegates from small countries . . . Even if [Esperanto] did not rise to the level of French or English, its use might allow us greater freedom."[90] Yanagita also surmises that Esperanto might "possess the power to save the world from suffering," an opinion shared by Japan's lead delegate to the league, the Christian moralist Nitobe Inazō, who saw the potential "to make various peoples [*minzoku*] with their own different histories, nationhood, and skin color into brethren" and dreamed that "should Esperanto come to be widely used, it will abet the moral unification [*dōtokuteki tōitsu*] of the world."[91] Nitobe acknowledged the prospects of the language "for meeting the demands of science and commerce" but also saw a higher purpose in it. The spiritual aspect of Nitobe's view echoes Zamenhof's original intentions, and Esperanto's reception in Japan was also linked to the work of Baha'i missionaries, who proselytized a religion of global unification.[92]

While in Geneva, Yanagita sent a postcard to the storyteller Sasaki Kizen (1886–1933): "Europeans know little about Japan. I thus believe in the necessity of the Esperanto movement."[93] Like *Nihon-shiki rōmaji*, which Yanagita supported, Esperanto was seen as a project to make the movement of knowledge between Japan and the West into a two-way street; the new language was an opportunity for Japanese scholars to participate in the production of a shared global future.[94] After his return from Geneva, Yanagita participated in Esperanto organizations, serving as chairperson to the Japanese Esperantist convention in 1926, proclaiming the "importance of campaigning for its universalization [*fukyū*]" and dreaming of a plan to catalog all the Esperanto documents in the world. At his peak of participation in the late 1920s, Yanagita insisted that Esperanto was "by no means an idle fantasy" but a next step in the evolution of the Japanese language.[95]

INSTRUCTION AND REVOLUTION IN A *LINGVO INTERNACIA*

Regardless of ideological orientation, all Esperantists shared a goal of the implementation of the language at the world scale. Esperantists understood the present as an intermediary "age of actual use" (*jitsuyō no jidai*) that would lead to the utopian "age of universalization" (*fukyū no jidai*); they devised practical self-study manuals to make the language into a part of everyday life.[96] Esperanto textbooks presented the language as a simple modern communication tool that "one could grasp with a mere thirty minutes of study" and hone through daily practice.[97] This sense of language learning as a form of praxis is most apparent in the politically inclined manuals released in solidarity with Japan's proletarian movement. Despite Futabatei's and Yanagita's utilitarian approach to the language, from the first the Esperanto movement in Japan was closely linked to leftist political action. From Zamenhof's time onward the language was built for human ideals beyond national boundaries, and, following the Russian revolution, leftist movements looked to Esperanto as a means to unite subaltern subjects across borders. Socialist, communist, and anarchist currents were likewise nascent in the Japanese Esperanto movement from its earliest years; the anarchist Ōsugi Sakae, who learned the language while in prison, set up the first Esperanto school in Japan upon his release, which served as a meeting place for the fomenting anarchist movement.[98]

The leftist approach to Esperanto instruction is explicated in textbooks and teaching pamphlets such as *Mohan Esuperanto Dokushū (Memlernanto de Esperanto)*, which was published by Akita Ujaku and Osaka Kenji in 1923 and went through dozens of pressings. The authors argue that "to be an Esperantist is not simply to be one who uses Esperanto" but also "one who has moved from the age of theory [*riron*] into the age of praxis [*jikkō*]."[99] Ujaku and Osaka call Esperanto a mode of being whose "spirit" (*Esuperanto seishin*, glossed as *Esperantismo*) has long been "buried in the bosom of humanity" (*jinrui no mune*) ready to emerge as a guiding flame for the unification of the human race.[100] Paraphrasing Romain Rolland (1866–1944), the authors declare that through "countless hands upon hands the Esperantist searches for still more hands," with Esperanto acting as the medium to structure a massive worldwide community of language practitioners. Ujaku, who led the Japan Proletarian Esperanto League (Nihon Puroretaria Esuperanto Dōmei), continued to develop his thinking on Esperanto as a materialist praxis throughout the 1920s. After studying English at Waseda University, where he attended lectures by leftist thinkers like Abe Isoo (1865–1949), Kōtoku Shūsui (1871–1911), and Sakai Toshihiko (1879–1933), Ujaku made a name for himself as a poet, editor, and dramatist, as well as contributing to the early proletarian journal *Tane Maku Hito* (The Sower, 1921–1923).[101]

Ujaku's interest in Esperanto was stoked by the blind Russian anarchist Vasilii Eroshenko (1890–1952), whose salons at the Nakamura-ya curry shop in Shinjuku introduced the language in a context of European modernism and the international anti-imperialist movement.[102] Ujaku tutored his daughter in Esperanto and took a trip to the Soviet Union, where he heard Esperanto sung on the Trans-Siberian Railway, delivered several radio addresses in it, and saw how the language created access to the international labor movement.[103] Ujaku was struck that "in Soviet Russia, unlike in other countries, the Esperanto movement is not just for scholars and academics but also is a deep part of the activities of spiritual and material life [*seishinteki oyobi busshiteki katsudō*]."[104] As for Eroshenko, he was soon deported from Japan and continued his mission in Republican China, where he fomented interest in Esperanto with the writer Lu Xun (1881–1936) and the education reformer Cai Yuanpei (1868–1940).[105]

Ujaku and Osaka's manual begins by instilling in the reader a self-consciousness of the human body, its movements, and its organs before moving on to more complex social concepts. The primer includes detailed diagrams of how the aspiring Esperantist should position their mouth, lips, and teeth to aspirate and move their throat muscles and jawbones when speaking. It encourages readers to awaken to the physicality of their own bodies as a first step toward understanding the production of language as a historical, material process. From this embodied physiological base, the text transitions from Japanese to Esperanto and introduces concepts like "mutual aid" (*kyōdō sagyō*) and "self-generated production" (*jihatsuteki sōzō*) along with the poetry of Heine and Lessing. Esperanto, the artificial language, is made akin to the electric light that heralds a new enlightenment and a new type of humanity: "The new human race [*atarashii jinrui*] has opened its eyes, like Michelangelo's Adam," an awakening that begins with the self-conscious movement of a single body's throat muscles to spread across the world and structure a global community.[106]

The apotheosis of proletarian Esperanto theory is the *Puroretaria Esuperanto Kōza* (*Proleta Kurso de Esperanto*, Lectures in Proletarian Esperanto, 1930–1931), a six-volume compendium produced by the Proletarian Science Research Institute, which teaches Esperanto grammar in tandem with the tenets of Marxist materialist philosophy. The book sets out a daily course of study linking speech, pronunciation, script, and writing practice to the reconstruction of the reader as a new subject in a socialist society. The compendium begins with the operational definition of Esperanto as a technological thing, drawing a parallel between it, man-made energy sources like fire and electricity, and the construction of the Soviet Union. The textbook is a user's manual for this linguistic tool, a grasp of which is consummate with an understanding of modern social structure, and vice versa: "Without proper knowledge of human social life [*shakai seikatsu*], it is impossible to fully comprehend the principles of this linguistic technology [*gengo no gijutsu no hōsoku*]." The book begins, like the kana and *rōmaji* reformers, with the assumption of language as a historical phenomenon, asking, "Where does it come from, what can it do, and how does it change?" The primer presents language as intimately interwoven with the category of human experience and argues that "language [*kotoba*] moves throughout all aspects of our lives [*seikatsu*] . . . yet do we ever really think about just what language is?"[107] This advocacy for Esperanto aims to defamiliarize speech and script from their positions as unconscious aspects of everyday life and show how language, like all tools, evolves in tandem with the forces of human labor.

The primer contends that this self-conscious relationship between language and social structure allows the Esperantist to recognize how the ruling classes use the language to organize society for their own benefit; it is ultimately "language [*kotoba*] that rules [*shihai*] the world," and language is dialectically structured by collective material activity. The corollary of this logic is that in the modern era, language and power are inseparable from the mass production of print as a commodity; its converse is that the popularization of a new language like Esperanto might bring about new forms of "shared group social life" (*kyōdō no shūdan seikatsu*).[108] Again, this revolutionary project is traced from an origin in the physiology of the human body toward the rebirth of the very idea of the human. The textbook's first lesson is the Esperanto word *mamo*, "breast," placed next to a drawing of a baby suckling its mother, followed by a series of diagrams showing how readers should wield their throat muscles to pronounce their first words in the new language. The lesson thus creates a circuit between baby, mother, breast, and the primordial word to evoke a symbolic rebirth of the reader as a new socialist human. To the proletarian Esperantist, "speech [*gengo*] is labor [*rōdō*], is a tool [*dōgu*]," and "language [*kotoba*] is a medium constituted through the physical [*nikutaiteki*] mechanism [*hataraki*] of the throat and the brain [*zunō*] and the spiritual mechanisms [*seishinteki hataraki*] of the will [*ishi*]. Speech is thus the tool that links physical mechanisms and the workings of the mind."[109] That is to say, language to the proletarian Esperantist acts as a mediating force that dialectically modulates the relationship between physical and intellectual labor and spiritual and material life. This approach to language is deeply rooted in Esperantist thought, as Zamenhof and his followers were influenced by Wilhelm von Humboldt's (1767–1835) theory of language as the mediating function between cognition, the empirical world, and human experience.[110] Esperanto, then, is to the proletarian not only a means by which to communicate with comrades but also a tool and technique for understanding and transforming the multimediated process by which human bodies labor to build a new society via thought and action.

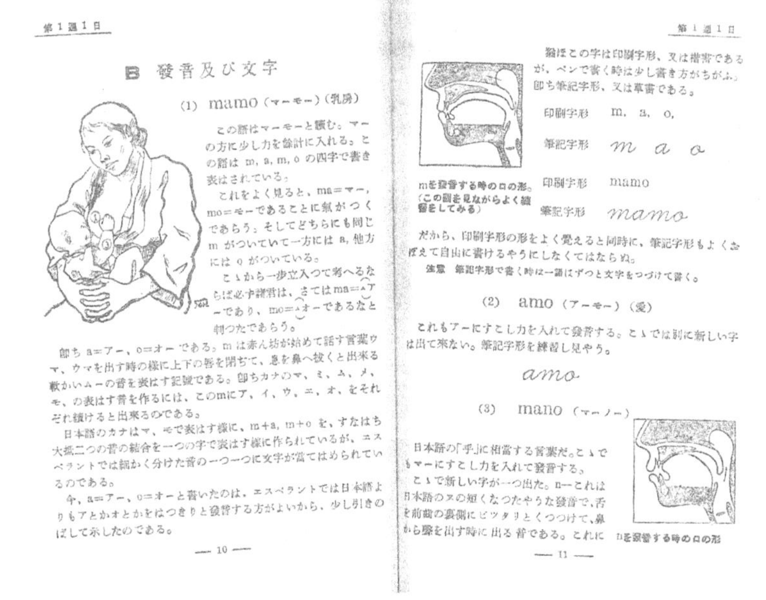

第1週1日

B 發音及び文字

(1) mamo (マーモー) (乳房)

この語はマーモーと讀む。マーの方に少し力を餘計に入れる。この語は m, a, m, o の四字で書き表はされている。

これをよく見ると、ma＝マー, mo＝モーであることに氣がつくであらう。そしてどちらにも同じ m がついていて一方には a, 他方には o がついている。

こゝから一歩立入つて考へるならば必ず諸君は、さては ma＝ムアーであり、mo＝ムオーであるなと判つたであらう。

即ち a＝アー、o＝オーである。m は赤ん坊が始めて話す言葉ウマ、ウマを出す時の樣に上下の唇を閉ぢて、息を鼻へ拔くと出來る軟かいムーの音を表はす記號である。即ちカナのマ、ミ、ム、メ、モ、の表はす音を作るには、このmにア、イ、ウ、エ、オ、をそれぞれ續けると出來るのである。

日本語のカナはマ、モで表はす樣に、m+a, m+o を、すなはち大抵二つの音の結合を一つの字で表はす樣に作られているが、エスペラントでは細かく分けた音の一つ一つに文字が當てはめられているのである。

今、a＝アー、o＝オーと書いたのは、エスペラントでは日本語よりもアとかオとかをはつきりと發音する方がよいから、少し引きのばして示したのである。

— 10 —

第1週1日

猶ほこの字は印刷字形、又は楷書であるが、ペンで書く時は少し書き方がちがふ。即ち筆記字形、又は草書である。

印刷字形 m, a, o,

筆記字形 m a o

印刷字形 mamo

筆記字形 mamo

mを發音する時の口の形。(この圖を見ながらよく練習をしてみる)

だから、印刷字形の形をよく覺えると同時に、筆記字形もよくおぼえて自由に書けるやうにしなくてはならぬ。

注意 筆記字形で書く時は一語はずつと文字をつゞけて書く。

(2) amo (アーモー) (愛)

これもアーにすこし力を入れて發音する。こゝでは別に新しい字は出て來ない。筆記字形を練習し見やう。

amo

(3) mano (マーノー)

日本語の「手」に相當する言葉だ。こゝでもマーにすこし力を入れて發音する。

こゝで新しい字が一つ出た。n—これは日本語のヌの短くなつたやうな發音で、舌を前齒の裏側にピツタリとくつつけて、鼻から聲を出す時に出る音である。これに

nを發音する時の口の形

— 11 —

FIGURE 5.3 Diagrams from the first volume of *Puroretaria Esuperanto Kōza (Proleta Kurso de Esperanto)* (Lectures in Proletarian Esperanto, 1930), displaying the circuit of infant and breast and instructing readers how to properly use their mouth and throat muscles to form sounds in Esperanto and thus be reborn as an Esperantist and proletarian subject.

Ujaku edited a monthly magazine, *La Kamarado* (The Comrade, 1931–?), which was the official organ of the Proletarian Esperanto League, a handwritten, mimeographed (*gariban*) journal whose mission was the "universalization of the study of proletarian Esperanto." The magazine advertised itself as "la Kamarado estas Traktoro de l'Pro-esp-movado" (the tractor of the proletarian Esperanto movement). For Esperantists, reading bilingual journals like *La Kamarado* or *La Revuo Orienta* (1920–present) was its own form of praxis, requiring constant code switching between national and international languages. The contents of a typical issue of *La Kamarado* included Esperanto translations of writings by the likes of Henri Barbusse (1873–1945) and Romain Rolland as well as of stories by domestic leftist authors like Tokunaga Sunao (1899–1958), political essays and critiques of capitalism, Esperanto vocabularies for activists, handwriting lessons, songs, and calls for union contributions. The editors of *La Kamarado* were aware of the role of the magazine in unifying a geographically diverse community, and the magazine also regularly ran reports from local chapters across Japan, addresses for international correspondence, letter and telegram writing tutorials, advertisements, strategies for communicating with comrades in prison, directions for forming factory activity "circles" (*sākuru* or *rondo*), and other methods for maintaining an Esperantist community. *La Kamarado* was at once a magazine and an activist handbook, an agitprop pamphlet and a language textbook, as readers were encouraged to work with comrades to activate an alternative vision of an internationalist mass culture built upon the artifice of this experimental language.

CODA: TOP-SECRET FILES ON THE DANGERS OF ESPERANTO

Today, Esperanto is sometimes derided as a failed experiment, a linguistic also-ran outmoded by the rise of global English. In Japan in the 1930s, however, Esperanto was taken seriously as a political force. The "threat" of the proletarian Esperanto movement is evident in a now-declassified top-secret file prepared for the Ministry of Justice in 1939 on the dangers of the language as an internationalist movement inimical to the aims of the Japanese empire. The report, submitted to the ministry's Division of Criminal Investigation (Keijikyoku) was prepared by Takeuchi Jirō (dates unknown), an Esperantist turned informant accredited as a "special thought researcher" (*tokubetsu shisō kenkyūin*). The two-hundred-plus-page report serves as both a chilling coda to the movement and an impressively encyclopedic record of Esperanto in prewar Japan. It appears that the breadth of government spies' knowledge of the movement extended to essentially every activist and author, every associated publication large or small, and even the details of evening Esperantist meetings in girls' schools, warehouses, and ateliers, as well as the contents of private letters and communications, serving as a frightening reminder of just how complete was official surveillance of the publishing world.

Takeuchi, who appears to have been an active member of the proletarian Esperanto movement, demonstrates an impressive knowledge of the contours of modern linguistic thought in Japan as informed by the work of Otto Jespersen and Ferdinand de Saussure, whose brother René (1868–1943) was a noted Esperantist. In the report, Esperanto is positioned within a genealogy of universal-language projects tracing back to Leibniz and

Descartes; its innovation lies in its use of "language [*gengo*] as a technology [*gijutsu*] . . . [and] a means for human social correspondence." At the same time, Takeuchi calls leftists' trust in the power of Esperanto a mystical "form of idolatry" (*gūzō sūhai*) in which the new language was "worshipped as if it were a holy object [*shinsei naru mono*]" and critiques the belief in materialist science at the core of the communist movement. From Takeuchi's perspective, the Esperanto movement's aspiration toward utopian socialism was in direct conflict with the ethnically oriented internationalism of the Japanese empire: "Esperanto continues to develop as an international language [*kokusaigo*] bound to mass [*taishūteki*] organizational [*soshikiteki*] social life [*seikatsu*] . . . that can be used as a powerful weapon [*bukki*] of the international union of the masses." Esperanto is cast as one aspect of the popular front movement (*jinmin sensen*) and thus fundamentally at odds with the ideology of the wartime government.[111] Globally, Esperanto was considered suspect as a "cosmopolitan subversive movement inimical to nationalism and tainted by its Jewish origins" and could not be reconciled with the Japanese language as the medium for the expansion of the Greater East Asia Co-Prosperity Sphere. The government's fear was that "growth of the movement in Japan, China, and the East together with its development in the West would constitute a worldwide movement of formidable power." This concern was not entirely misguided, as activist Japanese Esperantists based in occupied Korea and China in fact wielded the language as a weapon in anticolonial struggles.[112] But, like the rest of the proletarian movement in the late 1930s and early 1940s, left-wing Esperantists had little choice but to recant or disavow their positions lest they face the power of the wartime police state.

Rather than be resolved by the long war and its aftermath, kana orthography, romanization, and Esperanto all remained unsettled areas of inquiry through the end of the twentieth century and in some ways right up through to the present. Debates over historical versus phonetic *kanazukai* continued to simmer throughout the postwar period, the Hepburn system saw a return to prominence, and the Japanese Esperanto community remains one of the most active in the world.[113] The true significance of the debates discussed in this chapter, however, lies not only in the way that they set the groundwork for language usage across the twentieth century but in what they reveal about the changing status and political implications of language as a material quantity in the age of mass-produced typographic print.

Chapter Six

THE MEDIUM IS THE MASSES

Print Capitalism and the Prewar Leftist Movement

In July 1923 the union organizer and aspiring author Hayama Yoshiki (1894–1945) sat in Nagoya's Chikusa Prison, jailed under the Police Law for Public Order (Chian Keisatsu Hō) for fomenting labor unrest. Hayama had dropped out of Waseda University for a life in the leftist movement and spent time as a deckhand, dockworker, factory worker, reporter, and socialist bookseller. This stint in prison would not be the end of Hayama's career in the proletarian literary movement but rather its beginning. Early in his sentence, Hayama received permission to read and write, musing in his diary, "How necessary is volume 1 of *Das Kapital* to pass the time in this quiet, unobstructed cell," and revising drafts of what would become his most important works of fiction, "Inbaifu" (The Prostitute, 1925) and *Umi ni Ikiru Hitobito* (Those Who Live on the Sea, 1926).[1] He would later recall, "When I was thrown in prison, I was not permitted to receive the manuscript pages I had previously written, so I rewrote the work with a form and inspiration entirely different from those I had written before."[2] Hayama entered what he called "the little prison inside the heedlessly large prison without walls" a laborer and emerged an author shaped by a scene of writing where censorship was an everyday occurrence and items, ideas, texts, and money circulated precariously between his cell and the outside world.[3]

Hayama's case vividly exemplifies a dialectic of publishing economics deeply structural to the prewar Japanese leftist movement. Authors, critics, and publishers committed to socialist, communist, and anarchist political ideals expressed and advertised their ideas by mediating between the dynamics of mass-produced print capitalism on the one hand and the threat of state suppression on the other, a balance crystallized in Hayama's experience. Hayama could receive pens, paper, and volumes of Marx but was unable to make any money to provide for his wife and children via forced prison labor. Hayama passed his manuscripts to his wife; outside the prison walls, revolution writing could be transformed into an exchangeable commodity. In the end, Hayama's manuscripts did not sell during his sentence, but his literary debut came the next year through a reworking of his prison writing via an edited version of his diary under the title "Rōgoku no Hannichi" (Half a Day in Prison, 1924), which was published in the proletarian literary journal *Bungei Sensen* (Literary Frontline, 1924–1930).[4] The text self-consciously cites Hayama's time in prison, as would the published version of "Inbaifu," which opens with a note acknowledging the goodwill of his warden and drawing the reader's attention to the dialectical dance between state suppression and the economics of literary production nascent in the making of a politically radical mass culture in modern Japan.[5]

Like the literary modernism and linguistic materialism discussed in the previous chapters, the rise of the leftist movement in Japan was coterminous with the expansion of the publishing industry. Yet a schema whereby a politically pure movement is diametrically opposed to the powerful forces of consumer capitalism cannot accurately describe the dynamics of proletarian publishing. The conjunctions between them were far more complex, as politically motivated writers and publishers managed a multifarious set of relations between activism, agitprop, censorship, and commodification. Socialist, anarchist, communist, or otherwise, Japanese leftist movements aimed to become mass movements that appealed (at least in theory) to a broad public. Leftist critics understood the necessity of work within the mainstream print media complex as crucial to spreading their messages. This chapter traces the popularization of leftist political discourse from small journals into large magazines, through debates over print capitalism and revolutionary popular culture, and finally into the material stratum of the printing press itself, where labor struggles propagated an internal critique of paper-based mass media. From the work of small underground publications where workers controlled the means of textual production, to activists working as commercial literary agents and advertising editors, the proletarian political mission was deeply intertwined with the contours of the publishing industry. Likewise, the rapid expansion of the publishing industry cannot be separated from the rise of leftist movements beginning at the turn of the twentieth century as labor struggles and proletarian thought generated huge amounts of popular interest in new forms of print media. From the early days of Christian-inflected Meiji socialism through the struggles of the late 1920s and early 1930s, leftist writing and mass media mutually inscribed each other's possibilities as well as limits.

PEACE, LOVE, AND SOCIALISM IN LATE MEIJI JAPAN

The first wave of socialist thought in Japan was closely linked to the universalist and humanist impulses of fin de siècle Christian idealism and mystically inflected Tolstoyan utopianism. Thinkers like Uchimura Kanzō (1861–1930), Kinoshita Naoe (1869–1937), and Ishikawa Sanshirō (1876–1956) advocated for a just society in which all humanity could dwell with equanimity, whereby the kingdom of Christ was interpreted as a liberal workers' paradise. This same milieu was instrumental in forming Japan's first socialist party, the Shakai Minshutō in 1901, and the intellectual genealogy of Japanese Christian socialism included the politician Abe Isoo (1865–1949), the Marxist economist Kawakami Hajime (1879–1946), Katayama Sen (1859–1933), who would later cofound the American Communist Party, and the anarchist Kōtoku Shūsui (1871–1911), who would later disavow Christianity in the strongest terms.[6] As scholars like Umemori Naoyuki have noted, this liberation-minded intellectual foment was as much an interpretive paradigm as an organized political movement. Early socialism in Japan was internationally oriented and predicated upon an understanding of Japan's place in the changing world system of turn-of-the-century globalization, wherein the present and future of Japanese society was apprehended through the lens of humanity writ large. Linked to this utopian vision was a structural understanding of global capitalism and modern imperialism informed by Japan's victory over Qing China in 1895, its emergence as a colonial power, and the specter of war with Russia.[7]

FIGURE 6.1 Inaugural issue (November 1905) of the pioneering Christian socialist magazine *Shinkigen* (New Era, 1905–1906).

Since little leftist social thought had been translated into Japanese, foreign-language skills were a necessity for participating in radical discourse; the task of early socialist intellectuals was to mediate these ideas into the Japanese language and local discursive paradigm. To that effect, the organized socialist movement in Japan emerged from mainstream journalism. In 1903, Kōtoku and Sakai Toshihiko (1870–1933), reporters at the centrist *Yorozu Chōhō* (Morning Report, 1892–1914) newspaper broke with the paper over their opposition to the coming war with Russia to found the Heiminsha company and start the *Heimin Shinbun* (The Commoner's News, 1903–1905, 1907). The *Heimin Shinbun* was Japan's first regular socialist periodical, published first weekly then later daily and monthly.[8] Advocating "freedom [*jiyū*], equality [*byōdō*], and philanthropy [*hakuai*] . . . and advocating for socialism [*shakaishugi*] in the service of equal welfare for all humanity [*jinrui*]," the paper took a militant antiwar (*hisenron*) editorial line contra the fervor for the Russo-Japanese War shared by nearly all mainstream publications.[9] Although its circulation was only about four thousand, Sakai and Kōtoku, exiles from another paper's editorial room, saw their paper as a nascent mass medium in theory if not yet in practice.

The *Heimin Shinbun* was created for a theoretical population of common global subjects and aspired to internationalism by running articles in English as well as Japanese and publishing antiwar essays by figures like Tolstoy.[10] While politically radical, the paper was by no means anticommercial, and the short-lived 1907 daily edition regularly ran ads for commodities like dictionaries, department-store goods, tea sets, cooking oil, and even military uniforms. Like other popular periodicals of the era, the daily *Heimin Shinbun* encouraged the formation of "tea and chatting" reading circles (*chabanashikai*) and discussion groups (*kenkyūkai*), albeit on topics like workers strikes at the Ashio Copper Mine and the Mitsubishi factory in Nagasaki.[11] However, the newspaper's ability to raise revenue and circulation was hampered by periodic censorship, such as a canceled first anniversary issue in 1904 featuring a translation of Marx's *Communist Manifesto*.[12] Heiminsha, like any other firm found to be publishing material deemed by the Publication Law (Shuppanhō) to be "damaging to peace and order or injurious to public morals" (*antei chitsujo o hōgai shi mata wa kairan suru mono*) faced severe hardship from fines and the confiscation of printing material.[13] The *Heimin Shinbun* may have functioned on the principles of the new mass-media complex and been made by alumni of the same, but its theme of liberation of the commoner class proved too controversial to organize a true mass readership.

AN ASSASSINATION PLOT AND A LITERARY AGENCY

It was one of Heiminsha's cofounders, Sakai Toshihiko, who would help usher socialist publishing and the organized leftist movement into a new stage. A journalist, critic, and cofounder of the Japanese Communist Party, Sakai's trajectory was intimately interwoven with the dialectic of print commodification and repression. Sakai counted himself as a Meiji literary youth who read fiction by Ozaki Kōyō (1867–1903) and criticism by Tsubouchi Shōyō (1859–1935) and later translated socially conscious works by Émile Zola (1840–1902), George Bernard Shaw (1856–1950), and Jack London (1876–1916).[14] Born in Fukuoka in 1871, Sakai contributed fiction to Hakubunkan's popular children's magazine *Shōnen Sekai* (Boys' World, 1895–1933) prior to becoming a reporter at the *Yorozu Chōhō* newspaper. He was keenly conscious of the functions of literary form and prose style in building a mass political movement in modern Japan; he began his career using the epistolary *bungotai* style but shifted toward the vernacular *kōgōbun* mode and was deeply committed to the *genbun itchi* movement, which he advocated via his children's stories, newspaper journalism, and two writing primers, *Genbun Itchi: Futsūbun* (Vernacular Style: Standard Script) in 1901 and *Bunshō Sokutatsuhō* (How to Write Quickly) in 1915.

Sakai favored the ostensible objectivity of the vernacular as well suited to conveying ideas to the widest possible audience and subscribed to an ideology of efficiency whereby modern prose acted as a technology to transmit messages to a mass public.[15] In *Genbun Itchi*, Sakai calls vernacular style "the most important reform that can be made for the strengthening of society" and cites the movements to revise national script via kana orthography, *rōmaji*, and kanji reform as crucial to modern life. He deems newspapers the "mirror of society [*shakai no kagami*] and reflection of human hearts [*jinshin no han'ei*]," the medium through which to promulgate and achieve the goal of vernacular writing.[16] Sakai's opinion that print media was crucial for building an organized political movement was shared by other socialists. His comrade Katayama Sen was a fierce advocate of libraries as public spaces with the potential to raise consciousness, sites to provide intellectual resources for democratic education outside the national education curriculum, as well as meeting spaces for study groups, workers' clubs (*rōdō kurabu*) and commoners' clubs (*heimin kurabu*). In Katayama's vision, libraries in regional towns could serve as "Heimin milk halls," cafélike spaces where activist circles could meet, read radical publications, and discuss organizing strategies.[17]

Sakai's, Katayama's, and Kōtoku's ambitions to build a mass movement meant intense political pressure, including strict censorship and jail sentences. In 1908, Sakai was jailed for involvement in the Akahata Jiken (Red Flag Incident), which may have saved his life, since he was incarcerated and could not be implicated in the alleged plot against the emperor in the Great Treason Incident (Taigyaku Jiken) of 1910 and 1911, which resulted in the execution of Kōtoku and a dozen others. Sakai's prison sentence also marked a turning point in his relationship with the commercial publishing industry. While behind bars, Sakai faced a situation parallel to that later encountered by Hayama, who was born in the same village in Kyushu a generation later.[18] While jailed, Sakai was granted permission to receive books and read European tomes on socialism, Zola's *Vérité*, the New Testament, Emerson, Tolstoy, Marx, Upton Sinclair, and Feuerbach. Like Hayama, he used the time to consider how writing and publishing could support his family and the movement—how to turn the pen into bread, an image that would become the logo of the firm founded upon his release, Baibunsha (The Script-Selling Company).

When Sakai founded Baibunsha in 1910, Japan's literary economy was transitioning from a model of salaried newspaper employ to a new mode in which writers sold manuscripts by the page. Sakai's strategy was to broker the production and sale of all manner of texts for Japan's expanding print market; Kuroiwa Hisako calls Baibunsha the forerunner of the modern Japanese literary agency. Upon his release, Sakai ran an advertisement in the New Year's Eve edition of the *Tōkyō Asahi Shinbun* advertising services for literary editing, indexing, copywriting, translation, transcription, document revision, business letters, personal letters, copyediting, or any other task germane to the production and circulation of text. Baibunsha charged fifty sen for twenty lines of text, monetizing type regardless of content, and solicited capital investors, including the pharmaceutical tycoon Hoshi Hajime (1873–1951).[19] But Baibunsha was by no means a cynical sellout; Sakai used it as an employment agency for a stable of leftist comrades, allowing them to survive financially while continuing their activist work. Among Baibunsha's employees were the anarchist Ōsugi Sakae (1885–1923), leading socialist thinker and future Japanese Communist Party cofounder Yamakawa Hitoshi (1880–1958), and translator of *Das Kapital* Takabatake Motoyuki (1886–1928).

In the early 1910s, the leftist cause was reeling from the Great Treason Incident and undergoing retrenchment to sustain the movement and appeal to a broader public. The trial and execution of Kōtoku and his comrades was a major media event and an object of interest for literati, inspiring writings by Nagai Kafū (1879–1959), Tokutomi Roka (1868–1927), and Ishikawa Takuboku (1885–1912), but the incident was far from the cause célèbre of the Dreyfus affair in France.[20] Kafū, who claimed to have seen the prison wagons pass on the day of the trial, would later reflect that "I must not remain silent on matters of thought [*shisō mondai*] above and beyond the ken of literati. Zola cried out for justice in the Dreyfus affair and went into exile. But along with the other literati, I did nothing. I could not stand the suffering of my conscience. I felt a great shame toward all things literary [*bungakushataru koto*]."[21] Prior to the widespread commercial interest in socialist themes spurred by the Russian Revolution of 1917, leftwing discourse in the 1910s was not yet economically self-sustaining. Rather, as Sakai's case demonstrates, the spread of revolutionary ideas was underwritten by the commodification of writing as radicals sustained themselves by churning out the gray snow of advertising copy. This state of affairs would change dramatically in the coming years as political and commercial concerns drew closer together and the leftist movement developed savvy media strategies.

KAIZŌ AND THE RECONSTRUCTION OF THE SOCIAL REALM

In the early 1910s, leftism in Japan remained a threatening foreign ideology external to the mass mind, despite the efforts of journals like Ōsugi's *Kindai Shisō* (Modern Thought, 1912–1916) to proselytize and agitate. But the impacts of World War I, the Russian Revolution, and the growth of Japanese industrial society reframed labor and class struggles as issues internal to the experience of the mass public. The representative magazine of this period was *Kaizō* (Reconstruction, 1919–1955), which was launched after the end of the Great War by the journalist and entrepreneur Yamamoto

Sanehiko (1885–1952). *Kaizō* was founded as an ambitious general-interest magazine on the model of *Chūō Kōron* (The Central Review, 1899–present) or *Taiyō* before it, a thick mainstream periodical that aimed to synthesize all manner of social, cultural, political, and literary discourse for popular consumption. *Kaizō* opened a discursive space wherein diverse viewpoints could engage the mass public in debates about the functions of literature and government in modern life.

The organizing ideological grounding of *Kaizō* was the flexible concept of "reconstruction" that gave the magazine its title. The term was already circulating in Japan but reached a new level of popularity with the translation of Bertrand Russell's (1872–1970) *Principles of Social Reconstruction* (as *Shakai Kaizō no Genri*, 1916) into Japanese. The phrase gained further credence with the translation of John Dewey's (1859–1952) *Reconstruction in Philosophy* (1920) (as *Tetsugaku no Kaizō*, in 1921), and Yamamoto would enlist both Russell and Dewey as regular contributors to the magazine; their articles "caused an uproar so great as to turn the Japanese intellectual world nearly on its head."[22] Russell expressed optimism for socialist political action in the reconstruction of labor, education, marriage, and religion, so long as ideology did not impinge on the freedom of human instinct:

> We cannot limit the recourses to power of our countries, and we cannot rid ourselves of the evils of private property. We cannot as yet bring about a new life through only educational circles. Accordingly, we can recognize these problems, but it is not possible to quickly remedy these problems by utilizing only conventional political means . . . to see the changes to the world that we firmly desire, we must first straighten our hearts and minds and live a life in which we think positively.[23]

For Russell, this transformation of all aspects of social life was grounded in an idea of the self, spirit, and individual experience as both subjects and objects of "reconstruction," a term linked to the aftermath of the Great War. Japan's military involvement in the war was peripheral, but formal participation in the Allied effort, the Treaty of Versailles, and inclusion as a charter member of the League of Nations served to mint Japan's status as a world power and produce a sense of global simultaneity. Japanese intellectuals of all ideologies could see their work as contemporaneous with international discursive currents as they participated in a shared "postwar" (*sengo*), a term now associated with the period after 1945 but that appeared frequently in magazines beginning in 1919. *Kaizō* embraced this sense of internationalism and ran articles by cosmopolitan thinkers like Albert Einstein (1879–1955) and Rabindranath Tagore (1861–1941), whom the magazine hosted for visits to Japan, where they were heralded as intellectual celebrities.[24]

Kaizō's inaugural issue in April 1919 begins with an incantation to "the great spirit of reconstruction" (*kaizō no dairei*) by the poet Doi Bansui (1871–1952), paying homage to Jean-Jacques Rousseau (1712–1778), whose *Social Contract* would be given a popular retranslation that same year: "Inscribed on the grave of Rousseau beneath the Paris Panthéon is a great arm rising out from a casket and waving a pine torch."[25] Japanese critics traced genealogies of reconstructionist thought from Rousseau's guiding flame through guild socialism, Karl Marx, and Peter Kropotkin (1842–1921) to their present. "Reconstruction" moved from the abstract discursive level into the realm of praxis as the authors and activists writing for *Kaizō* argued for practical solutions to reform social spheres such as education, labor, economics, women's rights, and theater. In the words of the pioneering literary theorist and dramaturge Tsubouchi Shōyō (1859–1935):

> Now is a time of unprecedented great social reconstruction. The world must be lifted up and reconstructed from its roots. This reconstruction concerns all aspects of society. Politics, economics, industry, the production of goods, the system we live in, cultural production, manners, customs, and not a little bit more will be reconstructed in a manner for which there is no precedent. Our own lives must be reconstructed from the bottom up. Thoughts, feelings, tastes, fashions, beliefs, and all our ideas must be totally reconstructed.[26]

Reconstructionist thought was a mutable and inclusive framework that would provide a conceptual underpinning for a wide variety of theoretical and practical goals, ranging from the left-wing feminism of Yamada Waka (1879–1957) to the rightist social engineering of Kita Ikki (1883–1937).[27] Although *Kaizō* itself did not start from an inherently radical position, its work in popularizing discourse on social reconstruction helped set the stage for the popularization of socialist politics in the modern Japanese mainstream.

RECONSTRUCTIONIST THOUGHT AND RADICAL POLITICS

Despite the gravitas implied by large-scale social reconstruction, the magazine *Kaizō* remained a private business venture of its founder Yamamoto's, a former owner of the *Tōkyō Mainichi Shinbun* newspaper. At first, sales floundered, with 60 percent of the twenty thousand copies of the first issue returned unsold. The second and third issues performed equally poorly. What saved the magazine was a full turn into controversial labor politics, a strategy that both drew new attention to the magazine and admitted socialist concerns of class struggle into the mainstream media sphere. Yamamoto turned over editing duties to Yokoseki Aizō (1887–1969), a politically radical young editor who ran a special feature on the state of socialism and labor disputes (*rōdō mondai shakaishugi hihan-gō*) in July 1919; all thirty thousand copies quickly flew off the shelves.[28] The October Revolution of 1917 had generated intense public interest in all things socialist, turning books and magazines on the subject—including writings by Lenin and Trotsky—into unexpected best sellers.[29] Yokoseki and his editors seized on this strategy and made the August, September, and October issues into specials on labor and radical politics, proving that socialism could now sell to a much wider audience. Sakai, Yamakawa, Katayama, and their comrades were called up from their limited-run journals to contribute to the magazine.[30]

Along with increased interest in socialist themes came suspicion and stricture from the state censorship apparatus. The Home Ministry Police Bureau Publication Section (Naimushō Keihokyoku Toshoka) enforced the Publication Law of 1893 and the Press Code (Shinbunshi Jōrei) of 1909, which restricted the publication and dissemination of any works "injurious to public order and morals." All publications were to be submitted for approval to the Home Ministry, which prevented the distribution and circulation of any text violating state standards. Publications in violation could be banned, confiscated, or redacted. Publishers and authors were heavily fined and quickly learned to self-censor through the use of omitted characters (*fuseji*) and strategic deletions in anticipation of the process. The purpose of this censorship was punitive, but it also produced a new kind of advertising strategy wherein the public was drawn to socialist scandal. The September 1919 labor-themed issue of *Kaizō* was banned from sale or distribution (*hatsubai hanpu kinshi*) because of an offending article by

Yamakawa Hitoshi on sabotage, and its censorship helped *Kaizō* earn renown as a magazine on the political vanguard; circulation climbed from thirty thousand to more than two hundred thousand in a little more than a year, even while severe financial penalties hung like a Damoclean sword.[31]

In January 1920, *Kaizō* published the first installment of the Christian socialist Kagawa Toyohiko's (1888–1960) *Shisen o Koete* (Beyond the Brink of Death), a work of literary reportage on life in a Kobe slum. The magazine's editors were concerned that Kagawa's prose was too pedestrian (*tsūzoku*) to befit the magazine's aspiring intellectual readership; Yokoseki would recall, "I thought the writing was terrible."[32] At the time, general interest magazines (*sōgō zasshi*) were often called high-class magazines (*kōkyū zasshi*), and despite its coverage of class struggle, *Kaizō* was more likely to be read by the middle class than by laborers, who favored newspapers and popular magazines from Kōdansha.[33] *Shisen o Koete* would change that. After grudgingly agreeing to its publication, Yokoseki discovered that "the boys in the binding factory were reading it as they bound it and were eagerly awaiting the second and third installments."[34] Those print-shop workers thus instigated the release of Kagawa's socially committed work, which would become a great best seller. This unexpected success via the favor of print-factory laborers marked an important change in the demographics of the book-reading public as the working classes were integrated into the sales audience for socialist writing. The ability to imagine a coherent phenomenon of the masses emerged as working men became both subject and object in the act of reading. Kurokawa Iori has made the important point that legal socialist-leaning media such as *Kaizō* helped establish the conditions of possibility for the founding of the illegal first Japanese Communist Party (Nihon Kyōsantō) in 1922.[35] The converse was also true, as support for the labor movement generated sales for magazines like *Kaizō*, which in turn expanded the reach and visibility of left-wing discourse into the 1920s.

CENSORSHIP, COMMERCE, AND SMALL PUBLISHERS

As leftist criticism entered the mainstream, smaller vanguard journals concerned with advancing theory and practice continued to sprout up. Perhaps the most important of these was *Tane Maku Hito* (The Sower, 1921), which was founded by a coterie in rural Akita prefecture before moving to the metropole. *Tane Maku Hito* took its name from Jean-François Millet's (1814–1875) painting (which also served as the logo for Iwanami Shoten), and its editor, Komaki Ōmi (1894–1978), was strongly influenced by the writings of the first generation of Japanese socialist writers and by the pacifist thought of Henri Barbusse (1873–1935).[36] Despite its origins as a small regional journal, *Tane Maku Hito*'s editors situated it from the first in an international context, dubbing it a Japanese version of Barbusse's magazine *Clarté* and printing the title in Esperanto (*La Semanto*), billing their project as one manifestation of a global project for peace and socialism. As with the *Heimin Shinbun* a generation before, the international situation of the Japanese empire lent a unity of purpose; where the *Heimin Shinbun* had decried the Russo-Japanese War, the *Tane Maku Hito* group opposed the Siberian Intervention (Shiberia Shuppei), in which the Japanese military was dispatched to fight against the Bolsheviks in the Russian Civil War, claiming supranational solidarity against counterrevolution. Subtitled *Critique and Action* (*Hihan to Kōdō*), the journal remained resolutely international, running coverage on topics like the Sacco and Vanzetti trial while laboring to instigate a domestic proletarian arts movement.

Tane Maku Hito would launch the careers of many prominent figures in Japan's proletarian movement, including the critics Aono Suekichi (1890–1961) and Hirabayashi Hatsunosuke (1892–1931) and the authors Maedakō Kōichirō (1888–1957) and Kaneko Yōbun (1894–1985); this group would transform *Tane Maku Hito* into the important proletarian journal *Bungei Sensen* (Literary Front Line, 1924–1930). At first glance, *Tane Maku Hito* appears to be in no way a commercial product, beginning as an eighteen-page pamphlet in rural Akita and peaking at a circulation of three thousand copies. But it might make more sense to think of *Tane Maku Hito* as a magazine for the masses unable to find a mass audience. The editors had few qualms about running commercial advertisements for larger publishers and the Mitsukoshi Department Store, which advertised in multiple other far-left publications. *Tane Maku Hito* likewise faced the pressures of government censorship; proletarian fiction writer Imano Kenzō (1893–1969) recalls warnings that it would be too difficult to anticipate censors' criticisms and thus too dangerous to publish.[37] The concluding paragraph of the editors' opening manifesto reads, "Take a look. We fight for modern truth [*gendai no shinri*]. We are the masters of our own lives. Those who seek to deny us those lives are not modern men. We advocate the truth of revolution [*kakumei no shinri*]. The sowers [*tane maku hito*] will rise up with our comrades [*dōshi*] around the world!"[38] The first Tokyo issue, which was ultimately banned, includes the text in full, the second through fourth issues use circles to censor the word "revolution" (*kakumei*), and beginning with the fifth issue, the whole text is struck but for the final phrase; with the ninth issue, the manifesto appears in Esperanto translation with the problematic phrase unevenly and visibly scratched out. The first Tokyo issue was banned with the reason given that "in the opinion of the government it is on the whole unacceptable [*zentai ga ki ni kuwanai*]."[39] But as with *Kaizō*, censorship became a badge of honor—the following issue was released wrapped with a bright red band across the cover stating, "Second Issue: Inaugural Issue Censored" in large black type, and the issue sold out immediately.

Core to the mission of *Tane Maku Hito* and the proletarian magazines that followed was the concept of a universal, international mass movement. This vision of a proletarian popular culture as an alternative to mainstream consumer society would continue to develop across the 1920s and early 1930s in magazines like *Bungei Sensen* and the more staunchly Leninist *Senki* (Battle Flag, 1928–1931). *Bungei Sensen* acted as the organ (*kikanshi*) of the social democratic Rōnō-ha (Workers and Farmers Faction) group, and *Senki* served as the organ of the Nippona Artista Proleta Federacio (NAPF) union, which was aligned with the reorganized Japanese Communist Party and the Third International. I discuss the theoretical delineations between the

NIA DEKLARO

Iam antaŭe homoj kreis diojn. Sed homoj nun estas ilin mortigintaj. La destino de l'kreitaĵoj estas facile divenebla.

Nuntempe ne sintrovas dioj. Tamen ĉie aliformigaĵoj de dioj estas plenaj. Dioj devas esti mortigataj. Kiuj ilin mortigas, estas ni; kaj kiuj ilin aprobas, estas la malamikoj. Du kampadejoj kontraŭstaras unu la alian. Dum ĉitiu stato daŭradas, homoj estas malamikoj de homoj. Neniam estas inter ili la vojo de kompromiso; tie nur estas „jes" aŭ „ne," „vero" aŭ „malvero."

Vero estas absoluta. Ni do diras pri la Vero, kiun aliuloj ne diras. Homoj estas lupoj kontraŭ homoj. Landoj aŭ rasoj estas en nenia rilato por ili. Sub la lumo de Vero okazas unuiĝo kaj apartiĝo.

[illegible] —kune kun la kamaradoj el la tuta mondo!

La Semanto. (*TANEMAKIŜA*)

FIGURE 6.2 Editors' manifesto in *Tane Maku Hito* (The Sower) as it appears in the March 1923 issue. Printed in Esperanto, the final phrases about worldwide revolution are visibly scratched out and censored.

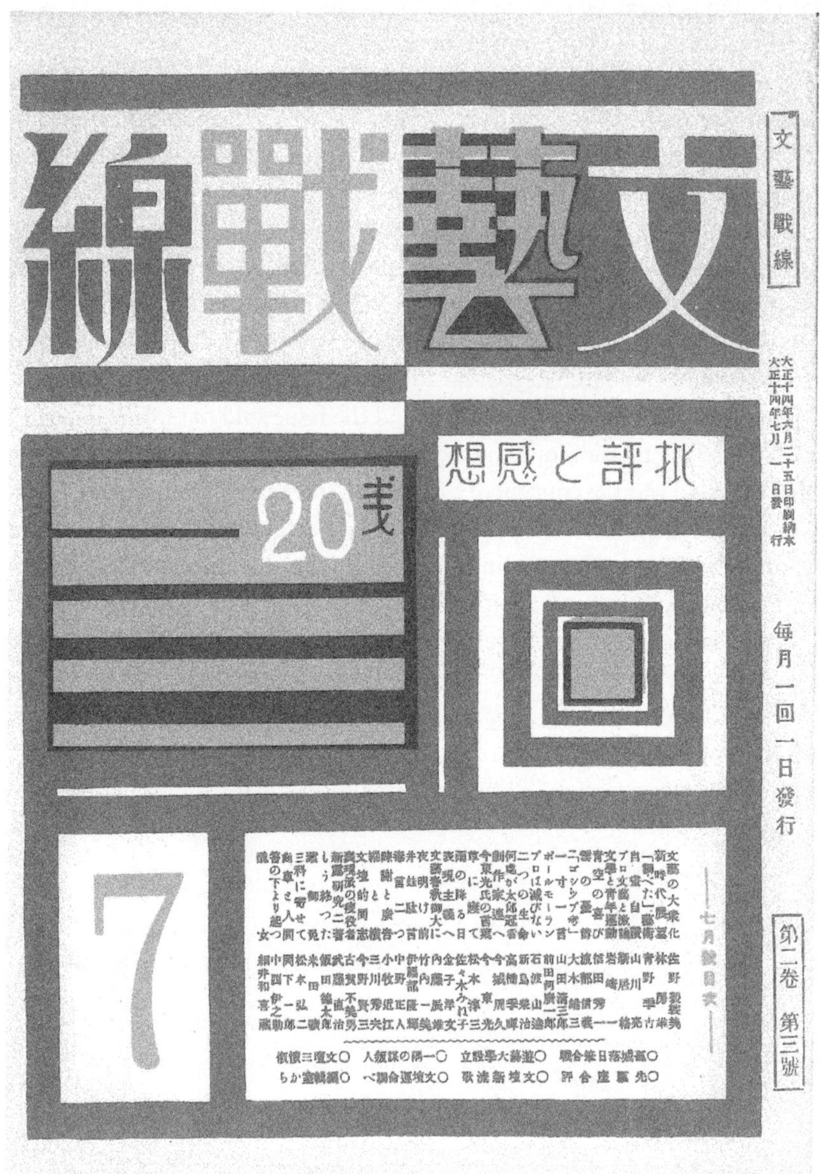

FIGURE 6.3 Cover of the July 1925 issue of *Bungei Sensen* (Literary Front Line), the successor of *Tane Maku Hito* and one of the most important proletarian literary journals of the mid-1920s.

two groups later, but here I want to highlight how both publications continued to negotiate the balance between censorship and commercialism. *Bungei Sensen* faced run-ins with censors, including in July 1926, when it was declared that "the entire magazine is unacceptable" (*zenshi warui*).[40] *Senki* met still heavier suppression following the infamous crackdown and mass arrest of leftists of March 15, 1928. Ko Youngran has described *Senki* as a kind of "catalogue of illegal commodities" whose editors were able to successfully commodify the very notion of suppression in order to increase media attention and circulation, tripling print runs to more than twenty-two thousand copies per month despite, or perhaps because of, eight banned issues. As with *Kaizō* and *Tane Maku Hito*, bans attracted publicity as eager readers hurried to bookstores to snap up issues before they were confiscated; it is also important to note, as Ko does, that for barely legal magazines like *Senki*, low circulation numbers belie a readership that was likely much higher, as each copy was shared among multiple readers, sometimes in organized clubs.[41] This precarious situation encouraged the production of an alternative system of distribution apart from bourgeois channels subject to confiscation, resulting in a direct if dangerous network of circulation that extended across the metropolis, the nation, and the empire.[42]

PROLETARIAN CULTURE AS POPULAR CULTURE

By the late 1920s, the proletarian movement had risen to a position in popular discourse well beyond the rarefied world of leftist circles, though the latter remained the locus for negotiating theory and practice. The Leninist NAPF organ *Senki* envisioned a politicized mass culture that constituted a revolutionary alternative to the extant bourgeois culture industry, including the development of proletarian children's magazines, women's magazines, graphic arts, film, and theater, seeking to parallel but not imitate media and genres already in place. Committed authors such as Kataoka Teppei (1894–1944), Miyamoto Yuriko (1899–1951), Kobayashi Takiji (1903–1933), Sata Ineko (1904–1998), and Hayashi Fusao (1903–1975) wrote politically inflected short stories aimed at instilling radical attitudes in young children. *Shōnen Senki* (Boys' Battle Flag, 1929–1931) was a pamphlet for kids that aspired to emulate the format of mainstream popular children's magazines and featured May Day photo pictorials, Esperanto lessons, fairy tales,

FIGURE 6.4 Cover of the October 1930 issue of *Senki* (Battle Flag), the most influential communist literary journal of the late 1920s.

and essays by figures such as Akita Ujaku (1883–1962) and Murayama Tomoyoshi (1901–1977), who were directly involved in radical youth education. Like its parent magazine, it often faced sales bans and censorship.[43] Likewise, *Fujin Senki* (Housewives' Battle Flag, 1930–1931) was a radical alternative to women's magazines and ran poetry, fiction, and criticism marketed to so-called working wives (*hataraku fujin*) circles. The proletarian movement also took graphic design seriously, borrowing techniques from the advertising industry to create appealing agitprop. Murayama contributed art, writing, and theater work to the movement while working as a commercially successful advertising artist, and Yanase Masamu (1900–1945), of the *Yomiuri Shinbun* newspaper, designed covers and incidental art for both *Bungei Sensen* and *Senki*, as well as for political posters influenced by artists like George Grosz (1893–1959) and contemporary graphic design.[44] There was likewise a robust proletarian film movement and an active theater movement that included productions like *Das Kapital: The Play* (*Gikyoku Shihonron*, 1931).

The circulation of proletarian magazines may have been low, but they aspired to do nothing less than replace capitalist mass culture itself. The

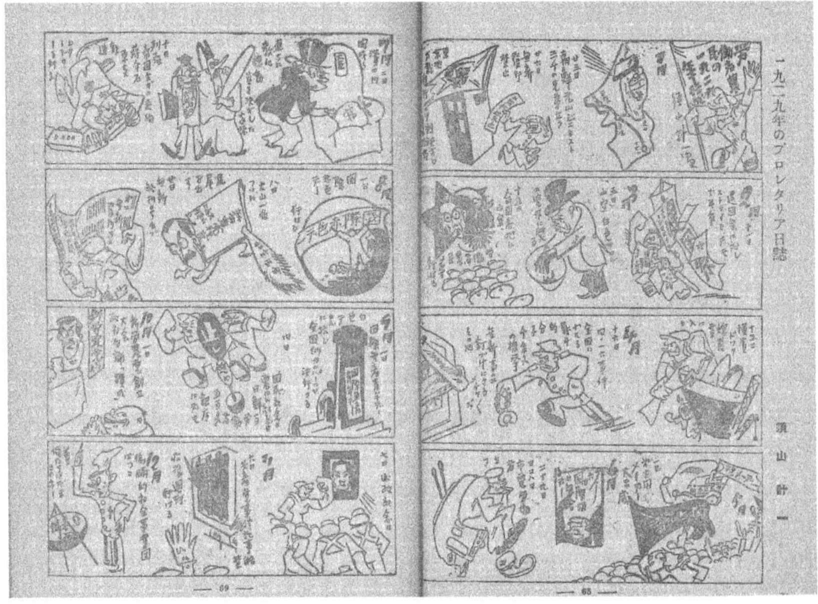

FIGURE 6.5 Caricature manga feature of "A Proletarian Diary of 1929" in *Senki*.

problem remained, however, of just how to convert the working masses to the proletarian political and cultural program. The question of audience and appeal was central to the proletarian movement in the late 1920s and early 1930s. Competing answers to the conundrum would lead to one of the most ripping schisms of the movement. In the so-called massification debate (*taishūka ronsō*) of 1928, leading Marxist critic Kurahara Korehito (1902–1991) sparred over the popularization of proletarian literature against Nakano Shigeharu (1902–1979) and Kaji Wataru (1903–1982), who were disciples of the Leninist theorist Fukumoto Kazuo (1893–1984); the latter's vanguardist approach dictated that revolutionary culture could arise only after the destruction of all tenets of bourgeois society. Kurahara took a more moderate line in which extant forms of bourgeois culture could be adapted to revolutionary aims to transform the social order. The debate took place at a fraught moment in which the proletarian movement simultaneously faced conceptual attack from literary formalists, the brunt of police force and mass arrests, and direct criticism from the Comintern. In the 1927 Theses on the Japan Problem, Moscow had criticized both factions of the Japanese communist movement and advocated for a two-step revolution in Japan, implying that Japan was still beset by "feudal remnants" and had not yet achieved a bourgeois state to be supplanted by proletarian revolution.[45] This evaluation spurred the unfolding of the Debate on Japanese Capitalism (Nihon Shihonshugi Ronsō), in which Yamakawa Hitoshi's Rōnō-ha and critics like Aono Suekichi and Sakai Toshihiko sparred with Noro Eitarō (1930–1934), Hattori Shisō (1901–1956), and the Kōza-ha (Lecture Faction) over the question of to what degree Japanese capitalism was internally generated versus externally stimulated and what stage it had achieved, questions with profound effects on the advancement of revolutionary theory and praxis. In the simultaneous massification debate, Nakano (following Fukumoto) sought to build a radically new model of proletarian culture, while Kurahara argued for the proletarianization of popular culture.[46] Regardless of the order of operations, the precondition for such a debate, however, is an implicit belief that the masses are constituted in part through the consumption of a shared body of writing produced by the expansion of print capital, and thus could be restructured through the promulgation of literature and other forms of mass culture.

REIMAGINING THE MASSES

The massification debate thus marks the proletarian literary movement's confrontation with its own ambitions to become a popular genre, and in fact so-called mass literature or popular literature (*taishū bungaku*) emerged as a discursive concept simultaneously with the rise of proletarian literature. *Taishū bungaku* consisted of swashbuckling samurai tales, detective stories, romantic melodramas, and other forms of genre fiction written for popular consumption. The discursive signifier *taishū bungaku* took hold in the 1920s as new weekly magazines inspired by the American *Saturday Evening Post* (1897–1969), such as *Shūkan Asahi* (Weekly *Asahi*, 1922–present) and *Sandē Mainichi* (Sunday *Mainichi*, 1922–present) allowed readers to indulge in exciting stories.[47] Popular magazines like Kōdansha's *Kingu* (King, 1924–1957) filled their pages with genre fiction, publishers like Shun'yōdō promoted what they called light reading (*yomimono*), and the work of authors like Nakazato Kaizan (1885–1944), Shirai Kyōji (1889–1980), Edogawa Rampo (1894–1965), and Naoki Sanjūgo (1894–1934) helped cement the idea of mass literature in the mass mind.

The question facing leftist critics was how to recognize their own literary and critical output within rather than external to the commodity market. In an essay titled "Shōhin to shite no Kindai Shōsetsu" (Modern Fiction as a Commodity), the critic Hirabayashi Hatsunosuke (who edited the magazine *Taiyō* and himself penned detective fiction) writes, "For popular literature [*taishū bungaku*], selling well—that is to say commercial value [*shōgyōteki kachi*]—is the first priority . . . this holds true for not just popular literature but also all modern fiction . . . All fiction is becoming popular literature . . . and this means the commodification [*shōhinka*] of the literary work [*bungaku sakuhin*]."[48] Recognizing economic value as a function that supersedes questions of genre, Hirabayashi lays the groundwork to think about proletarian literature as internal to mass culture and deftly pivots his analysis to the level of the literary market: "The popularity of a literary work is more than an essential [*honshitsuteki*] problem of literature [*bungaku*]; it is a problem tied to commercialism [*shōgyōshugi*] . . . I truly believe that the essential element of a work's popularity lies in the power of the commercial publishing industry [*shuppan shōgyō no chikara*]." This analytical rubric situates literary work within the economic and social circumstances under which it is produced and consumed, as Hirabayashi places the production of political literature firmly within the economic sphere. He argues that any attempt to write proletarian popular literature must recognize how literature as a mass phenomenon informs the valences of artistic, political, and economic value it seeks to create:

> As long as one looks at the literary work as a commodity, the only value that is problematized is economic value . . . Of course, I am not saying that the problem of the popularity of literature [*bungaku no taishūsei*] has nothing to do with form [*forumu*]. In regard to the problem of proletarian popular literature [*puroretaria taishū bungaku*], it is distributed for the purposes of propaganda [*senden'yō*] in addition to being sold as a commodity, so we might not choose to emphasize the commercial value. But even so, in this capitalist nation [*shihonshugi-koku*], proletarian popular literature cannot take the matter of economic value lightly . . . form itself is an element simultaneously composing artistic value and commercial value.[49]

Here, "form" (*forumu*, rather than *keishiki*) is the term that links artistic value to commercial value and captures the dual nature of the literary work as both aesthetic and economic object, a multivalent concept that simultaneously evokes both literary form and the commodity form. Hirabayashi's essay points toward a tendency in late 1920s proletarian criticism that skirted internecine theoretical debates to address the politics of the literary economy. Figures like Takabatake Motoyuki, who translated Marx's *Capital*, and anarchist social critic Nii Itaru (1888–1951) chose instead to investigate the role of the publishing industry in the making of the masses. In a 1927 essay titled "Shuppan Shihonshugi to Chojutsuka" (Print Capitalism and the Author), Nii describes the Japanese publishing industry in the following terms: "Truly capitalistic capitalism [*shihonshugi rashii shihonshugi*] has at last been established in the Japanese publishing industry [*shuppankai*] . . . the late-coming publishing industry has reached the point of fully matured capitalism . . . it has entered the age of mass production [*tairyō seisan jidai*]." Nii goes on to note that "publishers are now expanding the targets of their publishing endeavors [*shuppan taishō*] from the so-called 'reading classes' [*dokusha kaikyū*] to the whole of society [*zenshakai*]," as the universalization of reading allows the imagination of a social totality that both includes and transcends class divisions.[50] Nii imagines the masses as readers and equates publishing with social totality; in this schema, commercial capitalism, the consumption of print media, and the structure of society are seen as consummate and mutually mediating forces as the circulation of the medium comes to constitute the masses. In other words, it is at the precise moment when consumption of print reached a point of practical ubiquity that the idea of "the masses" (*taishū*) emerged as a key trope in social discourse.

MASS MEDIA, MASS POLITICS

In April 1928, Takabatake penned an essay, "Taishūshugi to Shihonshugi" (Massism and Capitalism), tracing the popularization of discourse on *taishū*, where he notes that the term reached a near universal prevalence in the early 1920s. Takabatake claims that the popularization of the idea of "the masses" heralds the arrival of a new social age, but that the concept remains ambiguous: "What are the masses [*taishū wa nan de aru ka*]? The masses are the masses [*taishū wa taishū de aru*] . . . their identity is entirely unclear . . . there are as many interpretations of the semantic content [*imi naiyō*] of the masses as there are people, with each employing their own logic as a justification to validate their view's legitimacy."[51] The concept of the masses served as a sliding signifier and site of struggle over the mobilization of varying visions of modern social life, as evidenced by the venue of Takabatake's essay, the centrist general-interest magazine *Chūō Kōron*, which ran a special feature in April 1928 on the theme of *taishū*. The feature included commentary by the political journalist Hasegawa Nyozekan (1875–1969), the liberal politician Tsurumi Yūsuke (1885–1973), the editor Kimura Ki (1894–1979), and the Marxist critic Aono Suekichi.

Hasegawa identifies the masses as a concept (*gainen*) that emerged in opposition to the ruling classes and remained necessary for achieving democracy at scale: "The masses do not control production [*seisan*] or distribution [*bunpai*] but possess the power to produce; a crowd [*mure*] of these producers [*seisansha*] have now entered the mechanisms of politics."[52] Aono interprets *taishū* more discursively, as a category that evolved from earlier and similar terms such as *minshū* (the people) or *tsūzoku* (the popular). Aono sees the potential for social organization through discourse surrounding the term *taishū* but warns of the dangers of reification should the word become overused, fetishized, and separated from its political valence: "Today, everyone talks about the masses [*taishū*]. They call upon the masses.

They appeal to the masses. They risk not looking progressive [*shinpoteki*] if they do not. The idea of 'the masses' has thus been bestowed with a kind of magic [*majutsusei*] . . . but what is left when we sweep away that magic? It is the working masses [*rōdō taishū*] and the salaried masses [*kinrō taishū*]. They are the true masses."[53]

In 1928, it was possible to imagine the masses as either mobilized workers or bourgeois national subjects. Per Takabatake, "According to proletarian critics, the masses are another name for the proletariat itself, but bourgeois critics . . . use the term in a vague sense referring to a large number of people as national subjects [*kokumin*]." Takabatake himself takes an essentially quantitative definition of "the unchosen many" (*erabarazaru tasū*) in contrast to "the chosen few" (*erabaretaru shōsū*); that "many" comes into being through the universalization of mass production:

> Today's world is a capitalist world [*shihonshugi no yo*] . . . an era of big business dependent on big capital. Put another way, a capitalist world means an era of mass production [*tairyō seisan*]. If we take our present age to be one of mass production, then the only applicable business principle is selling at high volume for low margins. The object [*taishō*] of these high-turnover low-profit [*hakuri tabai*] sales is precisely "the masses" [*taishū*] . . . They say that the masses have become self-aware [*jikaku*]. This may be true. But the masses most certainly have not become self-aware autonomously [*shudōteki*]. They were made self-aware by an outside force.

Takabatake argues that the masses are constituted through the circulation of goods, emerging via consumer sales practices. Print capital plays a key role in constituting the self-consciousness of these masses, especially the newspaper, which is the model of a product constantly reproduced, circulated, and sold at high speed, low price, and high volume. Takabatake critiques the newspaper industry as "corporations dependent on mass production . . . that skillfully seize upon the psychology of the masses [*taishū no shinri*] and never forget business profits" but nonetheless acknowledges that the industry serves an important purpose in mediating an awareness of the masses' subjective existence. Takabatake eschews any attention to the content of newspapers, books, or magazines and focuses solely on modern print's formal qualities, claiming that print possesses the potential to encourage democratic tendencies by "resisting state power . . . as an ally of the proletariat," even while singing "a siren song of sympathy that rids [the people] of what is in their pockets."[54]

A COMMON COMPANY: HEIBONSHA, REVOLUTIONARY PUBLISHING, AND PUBLISHING REVOLUTION

The critic Ōya Sōichi (1900–1970) described the expansion and transformation of the Japanese print market in the 1920s as nothing less than a "publishing revolution" (*shuppan kakumei*): "With the rapid rise in circulation numbers of popular magazines and the surprising success of one-yen volumes, the publishing world has undergone a complete industrial revolution [*sangyō kakumei*]."[55] But would this be a bourgeois revolution or a proletarian one? The line between the two blurred as socialist themes went mainstream, as in Takabatake's description of the publisher Kaizōsha:

> The company has a left-wing image [*sakei kanban*], but Kaizōsha does not necessarily make its money off left-wing books. Books of left-wing literature and thought do not sell particularly well . . . other than [my translation of *Capital*], Marxist works don't sell well either . . . But modern society is moved by stimulus [*shigeki*] and tempo, so intense stimulations are necessary to win people's attention. In this respect, Kaizōsha's left-wing image has great effect.[56]

Takabatake raises the proverbial red flag to show how politically conscious writing can be reified into a sophisticated form of advertising wherein Marxist thought becomes just another type of appealing content. Nonetheless, these proletarian critics acknowledge that mass-produced print remained the best means for radical currents in social thought to become a constitutive part of mass culture.

The publishing house best exemplifying this dynamic was Heibonsha, which was at once a premier publisher of leftist writing and literary entertainment. The firm simultaneously published Japan's first comprehensive anthologies of proletarian and popular literature, parallel canons of two distinct but linked visions of mass culture. In 1927, Heibonsha released the *Gendai Taishū Bungaku Zenshū* (Anthology of Contemporary Popular Literature), a massive multivolume compendium of Japanese and foreign fiction, which quickly proved a huge success, clearing three hundred thirty thousand copies in sales. The anthology aspired to be "passionately received by members of all classes [*arayuru kaikyū*]," according to a two-page advertisement in the *Tōkyō Asahi Shinbun*. Heibonsha solicited words of support from figures across the ideological spectrum, ranging from socialist politician Abe Isoo to the nationalist critic Miyake Setsurei (1860–1945), as well as Takabatake and *Bungei Shunjū* editor Kikuchi Kan. Readers eagerly signed up for the series, marveling in happy letters to the company, "I can't believe all this can be had for a single yen."[57]

Concurrently with the publication of the *Gendai Taishū Bungaku Zenshū*, Heibonsha instigated more political projects. Company founder Shimonaka Yasaburō (1878–1961) helped teachers' unions organize Japan's first May Day protest in 1920 and maintained close ties to anarchist factions, and in 1928 the company released the *Shinkō Bungaku Zenshū* (Anthology of Emergent Literature), the first attempt to systematically catalog, canonize, and anthologize leftist literature in Japan. By creating a totalizing anthology, Shimonaka sought to overcome the deepening factional schisms and synthesize political writings ranging from anarchist to social democrat to communist. Nii Itaru, Hirabayashi Hatsunosuke, and Aono Suekichi worked as editors, and the twenty-four-volume series included both Japanese writings and translations of foreign texts by the likes of Maxim Gorky (1868–1936), Sinclair Lewis (1885–1951), Eugene O'Neill (1888–1953), Aldous Huxley (1894–1963), Jack London, and Upton Sinclair. A partner compendium, the 1928 *Shakai Shisō Zenshū* (Anthology of Social Thought), sketched a genealogy of utopian and socialist thought that followed from Thomas More's *Utopia* through Fourier, Marx, Kropotkin, and Lenin to twentieth-century Japan.

Like Heibonsha's popular literature anthology, these political compendia were heralded with full-page ads in the *Tōkyō Asahi Shinbun* and public lectures at Yomiuri Hall and Waseda University. Shimonaka's attempt to ameliorate infighting between leftist groups was perhaps overambitious; the release party devolved into an all-out drunken brawl between political factions. Even if sales numbers never approached the three-hundred-thousand-plus mark of the *Gendai Taishū Bungaku Zenshū*, the *Shinkō Bungaku Zenshū* and *Shakai Shisō Zenshū* are evidence of how far socialist and communist discourse had been integrated into the mass mind; in breathless ad copy, Heibonsha announced its new compendium:

> It is impossible to discuss the present without speaking the names of Marx and Lenin. It is impossible to discuss social thought [*shakai shisō*] without knowing Kropotkin and Proudhon. It is impossible to grasp modern social science [*shakai kagaku*] without going back to Saint-Simon and Fourier. Trends are fleeting. Thought is forever [*shisō wa eien de aru*]. The age in which we can deal with social problems via shouts rising from the scraps of knowledge in newspapers and magazines and excerpts of ideas appearing in advertising pamphlets is over . . . the disorderly scraps of thought must be put into order [*seiri*] at once. They must be organized [*soshiki*] . . . then social thought can become the bread of life of modern man.[58]

Heibonsha advertised its books as commodities with the unique ability to organize a broad range of ideas into a coherent understanding of the present in historical context, not unlike in Iwanami's Bunko project. Under a print regime dominated by periodicals, where words and ideas are unable to be preserved or collated, "social thought" remained a fragmented entity. Through the new anthology medium, Heibonsha's editors posit, social thought can be imagined for the first time in its totality. In the rhetoric of the advertisement, the possibility of mass organization emerges only with the new medium itself.

Heibonsha's promotional copy reproduces in miniature Marx's narrative of society's passage into capitalism, in which a coherent whole is separated into alien fragments that must be organized into a new totality. The movement from alienated individual to social organization in Heibonsha's ad suggests that changes in the production, circulation, and consumption of print media underwrite the coherency of social thought, with the book functioning as a tool for social revolution. The output of Heibonsha in the late 1920s thus embodies the apparent dialectical contradiction of popular and political images of the masses, understood as the market for publisher's advertising campaigns. This tension demonstrates how the radicalization of the masses and the popularization of social thought were not merely problems internal to the realm of proletarian discourse but also issues embedded within the changing state of Japanese print media itself.

READING WHILE TYPESETTING

Despite the growing power and prestige of leftist cultural discourse in the late 1920s, the task of producing a corpus of literature that unified the popular and the political remained a challenge. One of the few works able to encompass both valences of literature for the masses was Tokunaga Sunao's (1899–1958) 1929 novel *Taiyō no Nai Machi* (Streets Without Sun), which sold tens of thousands of copies in book form following its serialization in *Senki*.[59] Nakano Shigeharu hailed it as the long-awaited solution to the massification debate, and the work received kudos from authors across the ideological spectrum. *Taiyō no Nai Machi* was advertised in mainstream magazines such as *Chūō Kōron*, and Kawabata Yasunari (1899–1972) heaped praise upon it:

> I am happy to name this story as the one that has raised my spirits most out of the dozens I have read this month. It is not just because of the plot. I heard that laborers were enjoying the work, so I decided to give it a look. I was impressed with the clarity of crisp expression and the healthy power springing naturally from the work as a whole. The organization of the material, the freshness of the plot development, and a certain level of sentiment and impact—such things do not only please laborers . . . It should be praised as a model example of literature that the masses [*taishū*] can approach with ease.[60]

Despite its subject matter (a labor strike), and serialization venue (an explicitly communist magazine), *Taiyō no Nai Machi* was received first and foremost as a work of literature rather than a polemic. Part of the excitement over Tokunaga's work was the result of his origin as an organic intellectual who made the transition from laborer to writer. Tokunaga worked as a typesetter whose process of learning to read was intimately tied to his labor deep within the most material strata of print capitalism. We can trace Tokunaga's formational experiences as a reader, strike organizer, and writer to gain a unique perspective on the process by which a worker in the publishing industry developed an internal critique of exploited labor in the system of Japanese print capitalism, wherein the publishing industry is both a factory for the reproduction of bourgeois consumer culture and a site for the fomenting of revolution.

Tokunaga was born in 1899 and belonged to the first generation of Japanese authors to come of age as readers in the milieu of mass-market typographic media, although he was poor and dropped out of school to find work as a typesetter while still a teen.[61] Tokunaga grew up reading not literary fiction but popular *kōdan* magazines that he borrowed from a traveling book lender. Even once he had expanded his literary horizons, his low salary at the printing press did not provide the wherewithal to pursue his reading interests:

Right around the time when I started working at the Nakajima printing factory in Kumamoto, I first discovered new fiction . . . I could just barely buy dog-eared editions at the used bookstore, since there was no way I could afford new magazines . . . I read serials in old newspapers posted to walls, I got my hands on ratty copies of women's magazines, I read whatever I could . . . Even if I worked every day, there was no way I could afford a fifteen- or twenty-sen magazine.[62]

Tokunaga's struggle underscores the reality that as late as the 1910s, books and magazines, while widely circulating, remained far from universally available to the reading public. Tokunaga may have self-identified as a reader, but the monetary value of his labor was not high enough to be exchanged for the same print commodities that he produced as a typesetter. At the same time, Tokunaga discovered that his ideas about reading were sharply at odds with those of his fellow workers:

My first printing factory job was a letdown. I had chosen the printing industry since I figured I would have the chance to read words and books [*ji ga yome hon ga yomeru*], but most of the other working boys were essentially illiterate, even though they could read script [*moji*]. As tradesmen, they had learned how to read typeset characters [*katsuji*] in mirror image but had no inclination to learn them through study. For printing-press workers like us, manuscripts were completely separate from the tens of thousands of type characters we used every day.[63]

At the printing press, the opposition between the two different kinds of reading came into clear distinction for Tokunaga. Working with script as blocks of metal type used to set and print newspapers and magazines, Tokunaga was confronted with a contradiction in which his sense of the literary text as a thing to be read could not be reconciled with his experience arranging characters as nonsemantic objects on a machine tray. Though he first hoped he might be able to read as he worked arranging type into texts, Tokunaga was made painfully aware of the contrast between his sense of reading and that of his fellow factory boys, who merely recognized reversed pieces of type as symbols to be set. Tokunaga's experience stands in contrast to the bookbinding boys that read the galleys of Kagawa Toyohiko's *Shisen o Koete* in 1920; the typesetters worked with individual units of metal script in reverse and thus could not read the text as a coherent object, while bookbinders saw printed pages in full and could follow the text.

At the printing press, Tokunaga witnessed at the most material level the stages of mediation of the assembly of the literary text, as handwritten manuscript was translated to an array of mirror-image metal script units that were then transformed into a final product fit to be sold and read. Standing at the type tray, Tokunaga was confronted with the reality that his yearned-for books, newspapers, and magazines were produced by alienated workers like himself. Tokunaga would later address this antinomy of his dual existence as both literary youth and alienated laborer by transforming himself into a writer who critiqued the publishing industry through fiction while working within it. Eventually, while working as a printer for the *Kyūshū Nichinichi Shinbun* newspaper, Tokunaga learned to read Sino-Japanese poetry (*kanshi*) and prose. After "handling manuscripts for the first time while standing in front of the type case," Tokunaga eventually tried penning a play and embracing a dual sense of the production of text through both writing and typesetting.[64]

Around the same time, Tokunaga became politically radicalized. He took part in labor-union activism; read Gorky, Kropotkin, Dostoevsky, and Marx; attended speeches by Japanese Communist Party cofounder Sano Manabu (1902–1953); met with the socialist leader Yamakawa Hitoshi; and cultivated friendships with leftist writers while searching for a new job in the metropolitan printing industry. Tokunaga continued writing and impressed the critic Aono Suekichi, but his manuscripts never went to press. The position of writers in the proletarian labor movement was no less fraught; authors were initially considered part of the Publishing Employee's Union (Shuppan Jūgyōin Kumiai) as "working writers" (*bunpitsu gyōsha*) but were eventually kicked out as the intellectual labor of writing was separated by the union from the manual labor of printing. Tokunaga himself encountered a reticent "scorn for literature" (*bungaku keibetsu*) among publishing-shop workers and was forced to formally submit a self-critique stating, "I shall hereafter never again dabble in literature" (*issai bungaku nado wa yarimasen*) when his foreman caught him working on a story.[65] Tokunaga's literary and activist ambitions seemed to be mutually exclusive, and he put his writerly plans on hold to focus on labor organization once he joined the communist-leaning union at Hakubunkan Printing in 1922.

THE WAGES OF LITERARY LABOR

The plant at which Tokunaga worked was the printing arm of the mass-media conglomerate Hakubunkan Shihon, which had expanded to become a fully integrated capital interest firm and the largest contract producer of print media in East Asia. In late 1925, the printing division of Hakubunkan absorbed the Seibidō firm and the Nihon Shoseki textbook concern, renaming itself Kyōdō Printing (Kyōdō Insatsu).[66] Labor unrest had been stewing at the company for years, with the HP Kurabu union leading a successful strike over working hours and minimum wage in 1924. When the Nihon Rōdō Kumiai Hyōgikai (Japan Labor Union Council) took over worker organization after the Kyōdō merger, the plant boasted twenty-five hundred unionized workers. Following a reduction of working hours announced in December 1925, the workers struck in January 1926, shutting down the factory. After months of work stoppage, violence, negotiations, and arbitrations, the strike would eventually end in mass firings, blacklistings, and a crushed union.[67]

Publishing-industry unions played an important role in the radical labor movement. In 1919, the Kakushinkai newspaper-printers union initiated a strike resulting in the stoppage of nearly all major newspapers in Tokyo; for four days, the sixteen largest newspapers in Tokyo released no editions, an unprecedented event. The same year saw the first major strike at Hakubunkan, in which more than a thousand people threatened to stage a mass suicide to protest working conditions and low wages. More strikes at major papers followed in 1920, the year of Japan's first May Day rally, where printing unions worked with the Keimeikai educators' union, led by Heibonsha founder Shimonaka Yasaburō, to form the backbone of the protest.[68] The popularization and mass production of cheap high-circulation magazines and affordable books was a boon for consumers but put pressure on printing, publishing, and binding laborers as they struggled to meet large orders as quickly and cheaply as possible. Strikes at major printing firms like Toppan continued through the early 1920s, leading up to the watershed Kyōdō strike of 1926; demands typically included higher wages, an eight-hour workday, equal pay for women, reduced overtime, fixed vacation allowances, hygienic working conditions, and protection from political firings.

As a union leader in the Kyōdō plant, Tokunaga was deeply involved in organizing the strike, and after its end set out to put the story in writing. *Taiyō no Nai Machi*'s Daidō Printing is modeled after Kyōdō, and the first book edition contains an endnote apologizing to union members for using real names but changing the facts. In an essay detailing his experience writing the novel, Tokunaga describes his process as closer to reportage than fiction: "There was a long period in which my life and my literature were totally unrelated . . . Even when I bought *Kaizō* or *Chūō Kōron* I didn't even look at the creative writing section. I had nothing but scorn. . . . So my motive when I first began writing *Taiyō no Nai Machi* was certainly not fiction or any thought of the literary establishment [*bundan*]."[69] Whereas Tokunaga had once attempted to maintain the dual valences of reading and writing innate to his work at the printing press, by the late 1920s the two had become separate.

It was through transforming the story of the strike into a literary narrative that Tokunaga was able to reconcile this contradiction and become a "literary worker" of the type that had been expelled from the printer's union. Ironically, he did so by approaching the writing of the manuscript as if it were a type of factory labor:

> Every day for about three years, I walked across the campus of Kyōdō Printing, doing my best to piece together still raw memories of the old battlefield while commuting to the local factory . . . I sat down at 8 a.m. and wrote until 2 p.m. Perhaps because I wasn't used to this kind of labor, I found it harder than factory work . . . I lived on the second floor of a small factory, so I arranged a work space, writing in the rooms of friends who were off at the factory and posting up a notice on the door stating, "At work, no visitors." I felt it was necessary to take care of everything just as one keeps one's work tools [*shigoto dōgu*] at the factory in good shape.[70]

By reproducing yet reversing the factory labor process, Tokunaga is finally able to synthesize the dissonance of his dual existence as a worker and a writer, a literary youth and a typesetter, producing a manuscript of his own to be set in type and not merely arranging the text of others. In doing so, he is able to de-alienate his work and represent the contradictions of labor and print capital in narrative form.

THE KYŌDŌ STRUGGLE AND THE LIMITS OF ACTION

Rather than a straightforward narrative of events focused on a single protagonist, *Taiyō no Nai Machi* presents a multifaceted montage of the Kyōdō strike. Tokunaga's novel follows a variety of figures, ranging from female laborers and their families to city councilmen and company owners as they participate in and observe the strike. The novel opens with the strike already under way and is unconcerned with the particulars of labor at the publisher, but Tokunaga by no means ignores the specificity of the printing factory as the topos of the strike. His novel opens a critique of print media's role in structuring social space as the novel's diverse characters are unified by the strike via a sudden rupture in the circulation of media commodities. The first section of the novel, "The Handbill" (Bira), opens with a stoppage in the movement of people in the city streets:

> The train stopped. The car stopped.— The bicycle, the truck, and the motorcycle with the sidecar barreling forward at full tilt twisted to a halt one after the other.
> —What happened?
> —What is this, what's going on?
> The crowd's simple stark faces crudely stuck out amid the terrible dust beneath the yellow October sun.
> Throngs of people pushed forward, wriggling as if they were a school of tadpoles in a puddle of water.
> —His Majesty is passing by—it's His Majesty Prince XX's royal procession!
> In an instant, whispers at the front of the crowd spread to the back. The cars stopped their blaring horns and people took off their caps . . .[71]

The Crown Prince himself does not appear as the masses' attention turns toward a detective chasing a man through the crowd:

> —Thief!
> The throngs fell into a state of mayhem . . .
> —Pickpocket!
> —No it's not, it's a socialist!
> Uniformed and plainclothes police officers jumped into the crowed, lurching after the criminal. But the man in the half-length coat had slipped away and was nowhere to be found.
> —Did you get one of the handbills? He was passing them out . . .

Tokunaga then reproduces the handbill in full, a manifesto beseeching the public to support the strike, which hails it as "the front line of the proletarian class across Japan." The handbill is boxed off and separated from the main text, reproduced in the form of a flyer across two pages of the original edition. The police examine it and give up their search as the narrator remarks, "What an unreasonable amount of commotion for a single handbill."[72] The actual handbills distributed during the historical strike, some printed in type, some mimeographed (*gariban*), appeal to the general public to "rise up and join the workers at Kyōdō, who have been flung into a state of extreme precarity [*seikatsu fuan*]—join the great class struggle [*kaikyū tōsō*]."[73] Flyers called on workers from across the country to assist their comrades against the capitalist classes. The Kyōdō laborers refused to produce commercial print for publishers' profit and instead autonomously produced and circulated their own forms of print to direct attention to their cause. Tokunaga's novel can be read similarly as a narrative intervention directing readers toward a socialist critique of the economics of publishing. In another early section, Tokunaga advocates for defamiliarizing the strike's representation in mass media and replacing it with a new picture of the production process of print by citing an unnamed, thinly fictionalized newspaper article:

> The strike [*sōgi*] at Daidō Publishing Company in Koishikawa-ku Hisakata-chō has reached unprecedented size, and there is no hope of a settlement in sight. The factory has been shuttered for fifty days and three thousand strikers hold firm in their resolution. The national Hyōgikai labor union is contributing funds from across the country . . . After the first round of negotiations were scuttled, the company has shifted its tactics, steeling its reserve and aiming for the total elimination of leftist unionists . . . The *Tōkyō Nichinichi*, the *Asahi*, the *Hōchi*, the *Tōkai*, and other Tokyo newspapers ran similar articles on the strike. But the citizens [*shimin*] are busy. News of this unprecedented strike appeared in large print script [*ōkina katsuji*] right before their eyes every few days, but it didn't stick in their brains . . . Maybe the good people of Tokyo had been struck with amnesia, or maybe they'd gone crazy. Luckily for them, the major events spiraling around them were mostly forgotten as if they were newspapers left inside the trains running on that clear autumn morning.[74]

Like Takabatake, Tokunaga sees the newspaper as a medium that begets a fragmentary understanding of current events easily forgotten and never synthesized into a systemic worldview. Yet he understands that print remains the only medium through which to reach a broad audience and incite them to action. In striking, Tokunaga and the print-shop workers at Kyōdō recognized their role in the production of print media as a commodity whose circulation structures the communication networks of modern Japan; stopping the presses disrupted the distribution of books and magazines that had become necessities of modern life.

The ultimate resolution of the historical Kyōdō strike brings us full circle to the same actors with which this book began—Hakubunkan and Kōdansha. The latter was one of the biggest clients of the former, now known as Kyōdō. When the strike shut down plant operations, Kōdansha was forced to turn over printing duties to rival firms Toppan and Shūeisha, which faced their own labor struggles; the strikers then turned to Kōdansha president Noma Seiji (1878–1938) to arbitrate the dispute and mediate between labor and capital.[75] A similar scene appears in *Taiyō no Nai Machi*, where workers visit Noma analogue Kunio, head of "Yamato Kōdan Shuppan" and "total master of the global publishing kingdom . . . who wields absolute power over his client Daidō" from his luxury estate replete with menageries of rare animals and menservants in judo uniforms.[76] In novel and history alike the arbitration fails, but the appeal to Noma/Kunio indicates an important shift in consciousness for the striking workers, who are themselves avid readers of Kōdansha's magazines. They are now able to recognize Kōdansha as a capital firm rather than metonym for mass entertainment and thus leverage their dual position as both producers and consumers of mass-market print media.

The final strategy of the striking workers was the unsuccessful call for a nationwide boycott of all products printed at Kyōdō, including all the most popular Kōdansha magazines. Flyers and handbills were produced and distributed to the general public, calling on consumers to "boycott all Kyōdō products! Laborers, farmers, salaried workers, and students: force the capitalist Ōhashi Shintarō [head of Kyōdō] to submit to the power of a boycott."[77] By threatening to stop the production of print media at the largest printing press in Asia, the attempted boycott would have drawn attention to the exploitation of manual labor implicit in the creation of printed text as a modern mass need. In taking the means of production of industrial typographic text as a site of both struggle and representation, Tokunaga laid bare how the consumption of literature and the possibility of popular critical discourse were underwritten by the capitalist exploitation of labor.

APPEALS TO THE PEOPLE AND FORECLOSED AMBITIONS

The Kyōdō strike did not succeed and the Hyōgikai union was crushed in 1928 under the Police Law for Public Order. But the strike of 1926 instigated a new era of activism across all sectors of the publishing industry, including papermaking, typesetting, printing, bookbinding, and bookselling. Following the Kyōdō strike, the printing and publishing labor movement became increasingly radicalized, militant, and explicitly antifascist. This period of unrest is, not coincidentally, almost exactly consummate with a new phase in the commoditization of print media in modern Japan. The same interval saw the rise of one-yen anthologies, cheap pocket paperbacks, and high-circulation magazines like Kōdansha's *Kingu*. Even publishers ostensibly committed to leftist thought and social movements were subject to unrest as workers took issue with the brutal work regimes established to ensure the rapid mass production of book series, regardless of ideological content. In addition to the strike at Iwanami discussed in the second chapter of this book, there were strikes at printers and booksellers like Sanseidō and Yūrindō in 1925 and a major struggle at Heibonsha in 1929; workers cited the lagging sales of the left-wing *Shakai Shisō Zenshū* and *Shinkō Bungaku Zenshū* compendia as causes for cost cutting leading to grinding overwork on other anthologies.[78] Strikers at Heibonsha explicitly called out Shimonaka, who had organized Japan's first May Day protest, for betraying the workers' cause and exploiting labor for capital profit on the very anthologies that purported to promote the leftist movement. One of the darkest secrets of popular left-wing publication, then, is that it, like all publishing in Japan's age of mass-market print, was made possible by the exploitation of industrial labor in creating high-volume low-cost commodities.[79]

Unions increasingly appealed to the reading masses in their struggle with print capital; many flyers begin with an address "to the citizens" (*shimin e*) and called for consumer boycotts. Handbills from a strike at the *Tōkyō Nichinichi Shinbun* in 1930 beseech consumers in large-point script, "Refuse to take the *Tōkyō Nichinichi* until the strike is resolved" and urge, "Don't read it [*yomu na*]! Don't support it! Cut off your subscription!" until fired workers are reinstated and wages are raised. During strike periods, workers at the *Nichinichi* and elsewhere created their own small-scale media ecosystems, using *gariban* mimeography to produce and distribute hand-scratched "daily strike news bulletins" (*sōgi nippō nyūsu*) to circulate among union members and supporters. *Gariban* mimeography had been adopted as a strategy for creating political and discursive communities outside mass media since at least the 1907 Ashio Copper Mine strike and was used broadly throughout the proletarian movement, including among Esperantists working in Japan's colonies. As mimeographed editions, these small-scale nontypographic papers could be produced by individual activist cells and were easier to distribute without the fear of censorship of print editions, as when the Shuppan Rōdō Kumiai newsletter was confiscated by the police in January 1926 prior to binding or censorial review.[80] Strikers also used direct mail, designed posters featuring modernist socialist art, and utilized all available surfaces to circulate their message.

Synchronization of struggle between the different industries involved in the publication process provided industry workers with a deep and comprehensive view of the entire system of print capital all the way up the supply chain, from typesetting to printing to binding to selling, a process invisible to the consumers who purchased the finished commodities. But the publishing-industry workers and proletarian critics were not the only ones with access to this totalized perspective of print capitalism and its discontents. The state, as manifest in the censorship apparatus of the Home Ministry, was the most comprehensive consumer of mass media in prewar Japan, able to receive and read essentially every last work of potentially problematic political publications. In early 1928, just prior to the infamous crackdown and mass arrests of March 15, workers at the government's own Ministry of the Cabinet Printing Bureau (Naikaku Insatsukyoku) struggled for fifty days, threatening the government's own ability to print necessary documents for the running of the state.[81] Ultimately, however, the state as überreader worked to foreclose the precarious balance of popularization and political suppression that constituted the central dynamic of the leftist movement in prewar Japan. Declassified secret files reveal the ministry as a frighteningly omniscient reader with comprehensive knowledge of nearly every scrap of published material on leftist topics. The ministry's Police Division's *Shuppan Keisatsu Gaikan* (Overview Report of the Publishing Police), released semiregularly from 1926 to 1931, lists every manner of book and journal large and small from every sect and faction, down to high school student essays, collating all possible political positions at the exact moment when the proletarian movement itself was beset by internal ideological schism.[82] It was this terrifyingly comprehensive state reader that would write the future of the dark years to come. Yet despite the brutal fates faced by so many associated with Japan's prewar proletarian movement, it behooves us to recall the complex dynamics of these decades in which radical political action danced close with popular print culture.

CONCLUSION

Ends, Echoes, and Inversions

I have chosen the early 1930s as an admittedly jagged edge upon which to close this study. The normalization, naturalization, and massification of typographic media that began in the 1890s were, by the early 1930s, if not complete then advanced to the point that those media were no longer "new." The forms of print popularized in this period, including the million-selling magazine, the pocket paperback, and the hardcover compendium, would continue to define the contours of Japanese publishing for decades. Around the same time, a phalanx of new media, including radio (first public broadcast 1925) and sound film (first "talkie" 1929), captured the attention of the masses. The ending of this era of print in Japan contains both a positive and a negative aspect—the positive aspect being typographic print's success in achieving a status as ubiquitous medium for social discourse; the negative aspect being how the suppressive tendency in the state's relationship with the publishing industry came to outweigh the countervailing productive tendency.

To begin with the negative—the negotiation of implicit and explicit forms of censorship was an ever-present condition of writing in modern Japan, and the excision of text, the banning of books, and the fining and jailing of authors and publishers were always in the realm of the possible. But by the late 1920s, the suppression of works and ideas considered politically seditious became increasingly frequent, blatant, and forceful. The mass arrests and regular roundups of proletarian authors and activists beginning in March 1928, the stringent enforcement of the Public Security Preservation Law (Chian Ijihō) by the Special Higher Police, the torture and murder by police of Kobayashi Takiji in 1933, the infiltration and surveillance of organizations, and the threat of imprisonment for leftists not willing to commit apostasy (*tenkō*) foreclosed the possibilities for political discourse in the mass media.[1] As Japan's involvement in the "China Incident" deepened, those darker currents thrumming at the edges of empire shifted from subtext to text; in a nation at war, the public expression of political dissent became a serious crime. Writers and editors avoided sensitive issues, fell silent, or recanted their beliefs and denounced their former comrades. Of the leftist authors discussed in this book, the only ones to avoid such fates were those who died of illness, like Sakai Toshihiko (in 1933) and Hirabayashi Hatsunosuke (in 1931). As for the others: Miki Kiyoshi was imprisoned and died in jail in 1945; Kurahara Korehito served a long sentence and paused his pen; Nakano Shigeharu committed apostasy in prison and was prohibited from publishing until the postwar; Tokunaga Sunao requested *Taiyō no Nai Machi* be withdrawn from publication; Hayama Yoshiki joined the war effort as a reporter in colonial Manchuria and never returned. As the fantasy of a proletarian mass culture faded, a competing vision of ultranationalist mass culture won out.

Yet despite the narrowing horizons of political discourse, the 1930s were by no means a moment of silence. Magazine circulations were high and publishers were powerful cultural forces, and the decade saw robust critical debates over literature, aesthetics, and popular culture. By the 1930s, cheap and accessible books and magazines—and the reading processes and discursive paradigms that accompanied them—had become constitutive parts of everyday life; this is the "positive" aspect of the end of the era. Formats and genres like general interest magazines, anthology series, paperbacks, and illustrated magazines came to function as a kind of intellectual and cultural infrastructure and ceased, in their success, to be discussed as new forms of media. With the notable exception of the popular paperback nonfiction *shinsho* (new book) in 1938, there were few innovations in terms of format until the publishing boom of the early postwar period.[2]

When typographic print is ubiquitous, it is in one sense hypervisible as it saturates the experience of everyday life and structures the social realm. Yet in another sense it is increasingly invisible as it becomes ready-to-hand

and used without conscious thought. In their instrumentality (which critics like Uchida Roan raged against), the mediality and materiality of these so recently new forms receded. Books and magazines become "content" that could be considered without regard to form. The infrastructural ubiquity of typographic print also bequeathed these media with enormous ideological power, and it would be the imperial state and wartime government that would most effectively harness this potential. During the late 1930s and early 1940s, as the war deepened, popular print culture and ultranationalist ideology would become increasingly indistinguishable as the negative aspect of politically limited publishing and the positive aspect of commercial print's ubiquity together constituted a powerful dialectical expression of totalitarian mass media and total war. Publishers like Kōdansha actively centered their enterprises around imperialist propaganda, realizing the nascent ambition in founder Noma Seiji's vision of magazine culture as a powerful means for mobilizing devoted nationalist subjects.

In the early 1940s, once Japan had mobilized for total war, paper restrictions (*kami seigen*), rigid press codes, and censorship practices made publication difficult. In late 1942, dozens of journalists and publishers deemed to be in violation of the Newspaper Law (Shinbunshihō) were arrested in the Yokohama Incident, and by mid-1944 general interest magazines like *Kaizō* and *Chūō Kōron* were forced to halt publication.[3] Following the end of the war in August 1945, the Japanese public was hungry to read, and the comparative easing of practical and ideological restrictions led to a rapid resurgence in publishing, even as some firms, notably Kōdansha, were identified as "war-criminal publishers" (*senpan shuppansha*). Censorship under GHQ/SCAP occupation was robust and extensive but nonetheless far more permissive than under the wartime regime.[4] During the early years of the occupation, readers were eager for the intellectual and cultural stimulation they had been denied during the war, as memorialized in the famous photograph of people sleeping on the streets to reserve copies of the collected works of philosopher Nishida Kitarō (1870–1945).[5] The decades that followed would see another publishing boom, beginning with thin, short-lived "sake-lees magazines" (*kasutori zasshi*) and leading to a new golden age of middlebrow print culture spanning from entertainment magazines like Heibonsha's *Heibon* (The Commoner, 1945–present) to accessible intellectual magazines like Iwanami's *Sekai* (The World, 1945–present) that would set the tenor for postwar publishing as big business once again.

Many of the problems of language, literature, and politics debated during the prewar period were left unresolved and indeed continued to be contested in the postwar. The Japanese Communist Party reemerged as a political force, and leftist authors who had ceased writing picked up their pens to revive the proletarian project under the mantle of "democratic literature" (*minshushugi bungaku*). Critics found themselves again at odds over questions of aesthetics, politics, and how literature might serve as a social force. The problem of war responsibility (*sensō sekinin*) hung heavy over the future of Japanese literary writing, and many of the authors associated with *Bungei Jidai*, including Yokomitsu Riichi and Nakagawa Yoichi, were branded as collaborators. Likewise unresolved was the problem of the national language; for a brief moment the elimination of Japanese script was again considered, new committees on kanji and kana usage were formed, and guidelines for contemporary orthography (*gendai kanazukai*) were promulgated in 1946.[6] The historical orthography promoted by Yamada Yoshio, who had risen to the position of chief wartime linguistic ideologue, was deemed feudal and dangerous. The form and function of Japanese script were again conflated with the political future of the nation, and struggles over kana usage continued vigorously for decades. The question asked in regard to the relationship between print and the public by Takabatake Motoyuki in 1928 as "what are the masses?" (*taishū to wa nani ka*) would be rephrased for the postwar era as "who are the people?" (*minshū to wa tare ka*).[7]

THE (IM)MATERIALITY OF NEW MEDIA, THEN AND NOW

This book opened with the image of a teenager coming home and flopping down on the tatami mats to read a book after finishing his farm chores, then rushing out to flip through the latest magazines. Today, such a tableau seems to belong to another era—what would a parallel scene look like now, more than a hundred years later? Nearly every aspect would be different, from the medium used to read, to the material quality of its surface, to the positioning of the reader's body, to say nothing of the processes by which that text had been produced, edited, packaged, and distributed to reach that reader, let alone the content of the text. Perhaps today's reader would leave her part-time job at a convenience store and pull a *bunkobon* out of her bag and read it with one hand on the train ride home. Or maybe she would tap open her smartphone screen, load up an app or e-book to read a bit of fiction, or just scroll through articles on the web or social media sites. For years, books and magazines of the kind birthed in the early twentieth-century typographic revolution seemed to maintain their stubborn presence in Japan, even as much of the rest of the world tended toward digital devices. But each time I returned to Japan while researching *The Typographic Imagination*, the number of books and magazines in the hands of train commuters seemed to decrease as paperbacks and manga volumes were replaced by the familiar pose of neck craned over phone, fingers scrolling and tapping.

For the moment, typographic print does not seem to be in danger of disappearing as such. These forms of print media will likely continue to be coeval with the regular usage of postprint digital devices, just as xylographically printed books continued to be read and traded for decades after the typographic shift. The Japanese population was largely literate by the turn of the twentieth century, but it took several decades before books became objects bought and read on a regular basis by the average citizen. Today, we are perhaps at a similar interstitial point in regard to the ubiquitization and naturalization of reading and writing via digital means. Consumer computer technology has been available for decades, but it is relatively recently that the expansion of online networks and popularization of handheld devices have made digital text a truly inexorable part of our everyday lives as we live in a mixed-media ecology of type and postprint books. We seem to be on the cusp of an era in which this new set of staple media become our primary means for both popular discourse and private communication.[8] With the hindsight of history, the core of the typographic era in Japan, seen as so epochal upon its arrival, may end up having lasted little more than a century.

Japan's early twentieth-century typographic revolution thus constitutes a fascinating comparative context through which to consider how our own imaginations are in the process of being reshaped by the daily usage of digital media for reading. The parallels abound, and it is easy to find corollaries between the contents of this book and the state of affairs at the turn of the third decade of the twenty-first century. Chapter 1 considered the reorientation of the relationship between text and image and the role of audiovisual media in the popularization of new media for mass communication. In Meiji Japan, this was the rise of illustrated magazines, photo

FIGURE 7.1 From Jillian Tamaki, *SuperMutant Magic Academy* (Montreal: Drawn and Quarterly, 2015). Image courtesy Drawn and Quarterly.

gazetteers, and the adaptation of oral entertainment to the printed page; today we could think about images as text and text as image on the pixelated screen, online reading saturated with embedded photos, hypertext links, videos, sounds, and advertisements, as well as the rise of serial, born-digital narrative media. Chapter 2 was concerned with the opening of access to an expansive range of content via new forms of cheap, user-friendly commercial media framed by utopian ideals of freedom of choice. Iwanami Shoten made philosophical texts accessible to the masses in affordable, portable formats imbued with political and transcendental significance, and the canon was transformed. Today, online ordering, e-books, and digital downloads make all manner of text more accessible and portable than ever. When Steve Jobs unveiled the iPad, he called it "a truly magical and revolutionary new product"—a phrase that we might find in an advertisement for paperback books in Japan in 1927. Chapter 3 examined archival impulses and the organization of previously unknown quantities of text, allowing for the rewriting of the past and the opening of future possibilities for writing while producing anxieties surrounding an unmanageable sea of text. Today, sites like Google Books advertise universal accessibility to an infinite expanse of seemingly disembodied knowledge. A shifting array of content sources presented through a constantly updating social media feed makes the management of information a pressing task for individual readers and social organizations alike.

Chapter 4 explored young writers who grew up in a new media ecology always already saturated with cheap, ubiquitous text. They began writing in a new era of commerce and experimented with styles that were alternately criticized and praised for pushing the boundaries of legitimate syntax and orthography. This characterization of Yokomitsu Riichi and his clique might readily be applied to "digital native" contemporary authors writing in unconventional styles, publishing in born-digital formats, and drawing from programming language and symbol usage outside the phonetic alphabet. Chapter 5 probed debates over spelling, the usage of orthographic symbols, and the necessity of making language legible in an international context. In early twentieth-century Japan, the matters at hand were kana usage, romanization, and Esperanto. Today the grammar of text messaging, emoji characters, and the usage of automated machine translation are all in play as we negotiate the legibility of discourse in an era of constant online global interconnection. Chapter 6 asked, given the economic realities of publishing, what are the possibilities and pitfalls for using a new mass medium for radical social change? How might that medium be wielded to recruit for political causes, and how might the dangers of reification and the reduction to commodity status be avoided in a mission to move the masses? I raise the question in regards to Japanese proletarian publishing, but the same might be asked in regard to the revolutionary or reactionary potentials of platforms like Twitter and the fraught roles of social media and online journalism in contemporary politics. I cannot pretend to have easy answers to any of these questions, but I do believe that a materialist analysis of the present in historical context might make us aware of what is at stake in our changing ideas and practices of reading and writing vis-à-vis the universalization of a new set of staple media.

In comparing early twentieth-century Japan and the present, we find not only echoing parallels but also inversions, as the specific patterns of production, circulation, and consumption of postprint text and technology in the digital era are distinct from those of the typographic, just as the typographic were distinct from the xylographic.[9] The new constellation of postprint media differs from print in terms of the material qualities of the surface of inscription, the means of inscription, the channels through which it circulates to reach the reader, and the ways in which it is read, in every sense. Print books are made by industrial workers and machines setting type to ink and paper; digital text is made of malleable electronic charges arranged via computer code. Paper books are sold in stores or by mail; digital text is stored in databases, downloaded or streamed via networked telecommunications channels, and accessed through individually calibrated screens and interfaces. Depending on how a text is produced, the structure of the database in which it is hosted, and the channels by which a reader accesses it, the exchange of text for money may or may not happen. Digital books might be sold as discrete units like paper books, but piracy might make that book available for free, or different parts of a book may travel via different channels; monetization can take place through subscription services, fee-based access limitations, or advertising. John B. Thompson calls this as much a "revolution in the process" as a "revolution in the product" as "the book itself has been reconstituted as a digital file . . . a file of information that has been manipulated, coded, and tagged in certain ways."[10] The practical and physiological relationships between reader and text transform as well. In mid-nineteenth-century Japan, a book was printed with wood, bound with string, and borrowed from a lender; reading often occurred aloud. By the 1920s, a book was an industrially produced piece of typographic text to be bought as such and read silently and independently. In the present paradigm, texts can be accessed electronically on a computer, phone, tablet, or other device and read nearly anywhere. Patterns of readers' movement both within a text and between texts are reconstructed as well, as hyperlinking, scanning, and other electronic paratextual behaviors and systems replace the flipping of pages, indexing, and other strategies for moving amid a sea of words.[11]

One of the central arguments of part 2 of this book is that Japan's typographic shift precipitated an understanding of printed text as a material quantity able to affect the perceptual apparatus of the reader and restructure the organization of society. We saw in the writings of the Shinkankaku-ha, socialists, Esperantists, and others a corollary conceptualization of the reader as an irreducibly physical body, an agglomeration of nerves and sensory organs able to be remade via the reading process in an engagement with text as an equally physical artifice. In the postprint era, critics like N. Katherine Hayles have identified an inverse tendency in which human bodies and language are dissociated from the sense of embodiment innate to an earlier media regime and disembodied data is detached from the material stratum. Hayles argues that in the cybernetic era, information "loses its body," leading to a logic of virtuality whereby when "bodies are constituted as information, they can be not only sold but fundamentally reconstituted in response to market pressures," with profound social repercussions.[12] The body in the digital paradigm is imagined as a biological supercomputer interfacing with data-processing devices, and new anxieties arise about the effects of electronic media on the genetic formation of the human body itself. Philosopher Bernard Stiegler discusses how human usage of different tools for reading and seeing may transform the process of synaptogenesis to produce divergent arrangements of brain neurons; he also argues that postprint methods of learning create fundamentally distinct human subjects from those constructed via book reading in the Enlightenment mode championed by Kant and promoted in Japan by Iwanami Shoten.[13] Although the science is still unsettled as to the relationship between brain and digital circuitry, Stiegler's suggestion that the techniques and technologies we use to read, learn, and think mediate our very understanding of what it means to be human is both a prescient warning for our present and an idea with antecedent in the discourse on books as new media in early twentieth-century Japan.

There is a tendency in contemporary discourse to use metaphors of immateriality and intangibility when discussing digital text and the internet. We zap files to the cloud, conjure up sites, surf on a sea of data, zip through virtual realms, and navigate near-infinite flows of information. John Durham Peters points out the religious character of our thinking when it comes to Google, likened to God in its ability to transubstantiate universal knowledge: "Google is the text that contains the universe," like "Hegel's absolute *Geist* coming to self-consciousness in algorithms"; Peters has also detailed how the fantasy of frictionless channels for communication is as old as writing itself.[14] Yet the possibility of this fantasy, this ability to imagine the universal library of instantly accessible knowledge, is ultimately not only built upon strings of code but also powered by and housed in a massive, complex network of hard infrastructural systems. All of this is, in the end, made possible through huge quantities of metals and minerals and human labor, in addition to the work of symbolic processes. This material strata of work and workers is often occluded or ignored in our conversations about the fantastical capabilities of the internet or the latest networked communication device, program, or tool. This forgetting is facilitated by the very language that we use to discuss our staple media, often without regard to the physical infrastructure that underwrites the metaphorically infrastructural role that those media play in our modern lives. However we choose to think or talk about the internet, it functions by dint of server towers, power factories, hardware banks, massive data centers in the desert, and countless cables running beneath the oceans and underground across continents. As Tung-Hui Hu has recently argued, the emergence of "the cloud," as both a metaphor for expansive computer networks and the construction of those networks' physical infrastructure, has been a historical process inseparable from a politics of "sovereign power within the realm of data."[15]

From the mining of mineral resources, to the construction of hardware, to the maintenance of server farms, to the laying of cable, to the writing of code, to the selling of software, it can be easy to ignore the myriad intermedial processes necessary for us to conjure up any text of our choosing at the click of a button. Yet sometimes the medium itself manifests reminders of the countless human bodies that have worked to make our access possible, such as in what Kenneth Goldsmith calls the "Artful Accidents of Google Books," when some of the legion of workers responsible for scanning books into the database end up with their hands scanned onto the digital images of the page.[16] The final chapter of this book ended with Tokunaga Sunao, who learned to read and write while standing at a typesetters' tray, developing a dual consciousness as both a producer and a consumer of mass media as infrastructure for modern life. What might the Tokunagas of today look like and write like? How might their work help us understand the deep material structures that work together with the symbolic and immaterial movements with which our daily staple of digital text circulates? *The Typographic Imagination* is a study of how interstitial actors in a new media ecology produced not only new ways to read and write but also new senses of self and society—a century from now, how will historians see our own moment?

NOTES

INTRODUCTION

1. I. A. Richards, *Principles of Literary Criticism* (London: Routledge, 2001), vii. First published in 1924; the preface cited here is dated 1928 by Richards.
2. Ōya Sōichi, *Chūgakusei Nikki 1*, in *Ōya Sōichi Zenshū*, vol. 29 (Tokyo: Sōyōsha, 1982), 9, 14, 31, 51–52.
3. See Maeda Ai, *Kindai Dokusha no Seiritsu* (Tokyo: Yūseidō, 1973), 132–67.
4. Ōya, *Chūgakusei Nikki* 1, 24–25.
5. Friedrich A. Kittler, *Gramophone, Film, Typewriter*, trans. Geoffrey Winthrop-Young and Michael Wutz (Stanford, Calif.: Stanford University Press, 1999), 8.
6. Uchida Roan, *Bungakusha to Naru Hō* (Tokyo: Tosho Shinbun, 1995), 48–49, 62.
7. Robert Darnton, "What Is the History of Books?" *Daedalus* 111, no. 3 (Summer 1982); Nicholas Barker and Thomas R. Adams, "A New Model for the Study of the Book," in *A Potencie of Life: Books in Society*, ed. Nicholas Barker (London: British Library, 1993). See also Darnton, "What Is the History of Books? Revisited," *Modern Intellectual History* 4, no. 3 (2007): 495–508.
8. Alexander John Watson, introduction to *The Bias of Communication*, by Harold A. Innis (Toronto: University of Toronto Press, 2008), xiii–xvi.
9. Innis, *The Bias of Communication*, 3.
10. Marshall McLuhan, *The Gutenberg Galaxy: The Making of Typographic Man* (Toronto: University of Toronto Press, 1962), 198–99.
11. Elizabeth L. Eisenstein, *The Printing Revolution in Early Modern Europe* (Cambridge: Cambridge University Press, 2005), 50.
12. Adrian Johns, *The Nature of the Book: Print and Knowledge in the Making* (Chicago: University of Chicago Press, 1998), 3.

13. Fujimoto Yukio, "Chōsenchō no Kinzoku Katsuji Bunka to Nihon e no Sono Eikyō," in *Edo Jidai no Insatsu Bunka*, ed. Insatsu Hakubutsukan (Toppan Insatsu, 2000), 58–62.
14. Roger Chartier, *The Order of Books* (Stanford, Calif.: Stanford University Press, 1992), 3, 8.
15. Innis, *The Bias of Communication*, 8, 23–24.
16. Laurel Brake, "Trepidation of the Spheres: Serials and Books in the Nineteenth Century," in *Print in Transition, 1850–1910: Studies in Media and Book History*, ed. Laurel Brake (London: Palgrave Macmillan, 2001), 3–5, 14–16.
17. Kenneth C. Davis, *Two-Bit Culture: The Paperbacking of America* (Boston: Houghton Mifflin, 1984); Cynthia Brokaw, *Commerce in Culture: The Sibao Book Trade in the Qing and Republican Periods* (Cambridge, Mass.: Harvard University Asia Center, 2007), 1–32, 535–70.
18. Lynne Tatlock, "Introduction: The Book Trade and "Reading Nation" in the Long Nineteenth Century," in *Publishing Culture and the "Reading Nation": German Book History in the Long Nineteenth Century* (Rochester, N.Y.: Camden House, 2010), 1–6; Katrin Völkner, "*Bildung* for Sale," in Tatlock, *Publishing Culture*, 251.
19. James L. Huffman, *Creating a Public: People and Press in Meiji Japan* (Honolulu: University of Hawai`i Press, 1997), 53–58.
20. See Ōji Seishi, *Ōji Seishi Shashi* (Tokyo: Ōji Seishi, 2001) and *Ōji Seishi Sanrin Jigyōshi* (Tokyo: Ōji Seishi, 1976).
21. Huffman, *Creating a Public*, 50–58, 60; Yamamoto Taketoshi, *Shinbun to Minshū: Nihongata Shinbun no Keisei Katei* (Tokyo: Kinokuniya Shoten, 1973), 57–64, 86–91; Jay Rubin, *Injurious to Public Morals: Writers and the Meiji State* (Seattle: University of Washington Press, 1984), 15–16, 27.
22. See Haruo Shirane, *Early Modern Japanese Literature: An Anthology, 1600–1900* (New York: Columbia University Press, 2002); Mary Elizabeth Berry, *Japan in Print: Information and Nation in the Early Modern Period* (Berkeley: University of California Press, 2006).
23. Konta Yōzō, *Edo no Hon'yasan: Kinsei Bunkashi no Sokumen* (Tokyo: Heibonsha, 2009), 29–34; Shimizu Bunkichi, *Hon wa Nagareru: Shuppan Ryūtsū Kikō no Seiritsushi* (Tokyo: Nihon Editā Sukūru Shuppanbu, 1991), 3; Peter Kornicki, *The Book in Japan: A Cultural History from the Beginnings to the Nineteenth Century* (Honolulu: University of Hawai`i Press, 2000), 132–35.
24. Konta, *Edo no Hon'yasan*, 81.
25. See Shirane, *Early Modern Japanese Literature*; Berry, *Japan in Print*, 27–35; Kornicki, *The Book in Japan*, 187–93, 199–204; as well as Edward Mack, *Manufacturing Modern Japanese Literature: Publishing, Prizes, and the Ascription of Literary Value* (Durham, N.C.: Duke University Press, 2010), 31–36. On illustrated books, see Jun Suzuki and Ellis Tinios, eds., *Understanding Japanese Woodblock-Printed Illustrated Books: A Short Introduction to Their History, Bibliography and Format* (Leiden: Brill, 2013), 15–46.
26. Shimizu, *Hon wa Nagareru*, 4; Kornicki, *The Book in Japan*, 179; Fujizane Kumiko, "Santo no Hon'ya Nakama," in *Shuppan to Ryūtsū*, ed. Yokota Fuyuhiko (Tokyo: Heibonsha, 2016), 36, 42.

27. Konta, *Edo no Hon'yasan*, 181; Shimizu, *Hon wa Nagareru*, 14. Michael Emmerich, *The Tale of Genji: Translation, Canonization, and World Literature* (New York: Columbia University Press, 2013), 47.
28. Konta, *Edo no Hon'yasan*, 184–85, 192.
29. Kōso Toshiaki, "Seiyōshiki Katsuji Insatsujutsu no Nihon Denrai to Kirishitan-ban," in Insatsu Hakubutsukan, *Edo Jidai no Insatsu Bunka*, 42–43.
30. Fujimoto, "Chōsenchō no Kinzoku Katsuji Bunka," 58–62.
31. Ogata Hiromu, "Ieyasu no Shuppan Jigyō o Sasaeta Futatsu no Yōso," in Insatsu Hakubutsukan, *Edo Jidai no Insatsu Bunka*, 10–13; Momose Hiroshi, "Suruga-ban Dōkatsuji e no Michi," in Insatsu Hakubutsukan, *Edo Jidai no Insatsu Bunka*, 86–90.
32. On early typographic experiments, see Mack, *Manufacturing Modern Japanese Literature*, 23–27.
33. Itakura Masanobu, *Motoki Shōzō to Nihon no Kindai Katsuji* (Osaka: Ōsaka-fu Insatsu Kōgyō Kumiai, 2006), 10–13. Mack, *Manufacturing Modern Japanese Literature*, 26.
34. Itakura Masanobu, "Kyōkasho no Insatsu," in *Kindai Kyōiku o Sasaeta Kyōkasho*, ed. Insatsu Hakubutsukan (Tokyo: Toppan Insatsu, 2009), 17–24.
35. Fukuzawa's preface is dated December 1871; the first pamphlet was published in 1872.
36. Nishikawa Shunsaku, "Kaisetsu," in *Fukuzawa Yukichi Chosakushū*, by Fukuzawa Yukichi, vol. 3, *Gakumon no Susume*, 241–66 (Tokyo: Keio Gijuku Daigaku Shuppankai, 2002); Shindō Sakiko, ed., *Gakumon no Susume: Honbun to Sakuin* (Tokyo: Kasama Shoin, 1992), 310; Itakura, "Kyōkasho no Insatsu," 18. On Fukazawa's publishing business, see Giles Richter, "Marketing the Word: Publishing Entrepreneurs in Meiji Japan, 1870–1912" (Ph.D. diss., Columbia University, 1999), 131–65.
37. Fukuzawa, *Gakumon no Susume*, 7–8.
38. Fukuzawa Yukichi, *Seiyō no Jijō*, in *Fukuzawa Yukichi Chosakushū*, 1:38.
39. Shimizu, *Hon wa Nagareru*, 252.
40. On early newspapers, see also Takahashi Yasuo, *Media no Akebono: Meiji Kaikokuki no Shinbun Shuppan Monogatari* (Tokyo: Nihon Keizai Shinbunsha, 1994), 97–124, and Huffman, *Creating a Public*, 60, 145.
41. Asaoka Kunio, "Kindai no Kashihon'ya," in Yokota, *Shuppan to Ryūtsū*, 284–85; Shimizu, *Hon wa Nagareru*, 8.
42. Asaoka, "Kindai no Kashihon'ya," 291; Shimizu, *Hon wa Nagareru*, 26; Nagamine Shigetoshi, *"Dokusho Kokumin" no Tanjō: Meiji 30-nendai no Katsuji Media to Dokusho Bunka* (Tokyo: Nihon Editā Sukūru Shuppanbu, 2004), 14–20.
43. Yamaguchi Osamu, *Maejima Hisoka* (Tokyo: Yoshikawa Kōbunkan, 1990), 122–28; Shimizu, *Hon wa Nagareru*, 34, 48, 67–79; Huffman, *Creating a Public*, 56. On telegraph and postal networks, see Seth Jacobowitz, *Writing Technology in Meiji Japan: A Media History of Modern Japanese Literature and Visual Culture* (Cambridge, Mass.: Harvard University Asia Center, 2015), 43–64.
44. Shimizu, *Hon wa Nagareru*, 29, 37, 46.
45. Mack, *Manufacturing Modern Japanese Literature*, 26.
46. Nakahara Yūtarō et al., eds., *Insatsu Zasshi to Sono Jidai: Jikkyō Insatsu no Kingendaishi* (Tokyo: Insatsu Gakkai Shuppanbu, 2007), 11–13, 25–26.

47. Kajiyama Masafumi, "Meijiki Kentei Seido no Seiritsu to Hōkai: Kyōkasho Kokutei Seido e," in Insatsu Hakubutsukan, *Kindai Kyōiku o Sasaeta Kyōkasho*, 6–7; Ogata Hiromu, "Kindai Kyōiku Hatten Katei ni Miru Kyōkasho no Keifu," in Insatsu Hakubutsukan, *Kindai Kyōiku o Sasaeta Kyōkasho*, 25–27.
48. Itakura, *Motoki Shōzō*, 157–59; Kornicki, *The Book in Japan*, 165; Inaoka Masaru, "Meiji Shoki no Gakkō to Kyōkasho Shuppan," in Yokota, *Shuppan to Ryūtsū*, 258–59.
49. Shibano Kyōko, "Kokutei Kyōkasho Tokuyaku Hanbaisho to shite no Chihō Shoshi," in *Kokutei Kyōkasho wa ika ni Urareta ka: Kindai Shuppan Ryūtsū no Keisei*, ed. Wada Atsuhiko (Tokyo: Hitsuji Shobō, 2011), 99–100.
50. Huffman, *Creating a Public*, 199–223; Nagamine, *"Dokusho Kokumin" no Tanjō*, 23.
51. On contemporary reading practices, see Andrew Piper, *Book Was There: Reading in Electronic Times* (Chicago: University of Chicago Press, 2012).

1. PICTURES AND VOICES FROM A PAPER EMPIRE

1. James L. Huffman, *Creating a Public: People and Press in Meiji Japan* (Honolulu: University of Hawai`i Press, 1997), 150–99; Nagamine Shigetoshi, "Kindai Nihon no Zasshi to Dokusha," in *Mirion Serā Tanjō e!*, ed. Insatsu Hakubutsukan (Tokyo: Insatsu Hakubutsukan, 2008), 16–18.
2. Huffman, *Creating a Public*, 200–214; Jay Rubin, *Injurious to Public Morals: Writers and the Meiji State* (Seattle: University of Washington Press, 1984), 55.
3. Huffman, *Creating a Public*, 6, 50–58; Yamamoto Taketoshi, *Shinbun to Minshū: Nihongata Shinbun no Keisei Katei* (Tokyo: Kinokuniya Shoten, 1973), 57–64, 86–91; Rubin, *Injurious to Public Morals*, 15–16, 27.
4. Tamura Tetsuzō, *Kindai Shuppan Bunka o Kirihiraita Shuppan Ōkoku no Hikari to Kage: Hakubunkan Kōbō Rokujūnen* (Tokyo: Hōgaku Shoin, 2007), 7, 27. Tsuboya Zenshirō, *Hakubunkan Gojūnenshi* (Tokyo: Hakubunkan, 1937), 27. For a detailed discussion in English, see Giles Richter, "Marketing the Word: Publishing Entrepreneurs in Meiji Japan, 1870–1912" (Ph.D. diss., Columbia University, 1999), 200–219.
5. Tsuboya, *Hakubunkan Gojūnenshi*, 66–70. Ōhashi played a role in negotiations over the national textbook system of 1903. Kajiyama Masafumi, "Kokutei Kyōkasho Mondai to 'Taiyō,'" in *Zasshi "Taiyō" to Kokumin Bunka no Keisei*, ed. Suzuki Sadami (Tokyo: Shibunkaku Shuppan, 2001), 409.
6. Tsuboya, *Hakubunkan Gojūnenshi*, 5, 84; Huffman, *Creating a Public*, 199–223; Tamura, *Kindai Shuppan Bunka*, 38–39; Insatsu Hakubutsukan, *Mirion Serā Tanjō e!*, 53.
7. Kaneko Tsutomu, "Meiji Shuppankai no Hikari to Yami," in Suzuki, *Zasshi "Taiyō,"* 92–93; Tsuboya, *Hakubunkan Gojūnenshi*, 87–90; Torihara Manabu, *Nihon Shashinshi 1: Bakumatsu Ishin kara Kōdo Seichōki made* (Tokyo: Chūō Kōronsha Shinsha, 2013), 22.
8. Ozawa Takeshi, *Nihon no Shashinshi: Bakumatsu kara Meijiki made* (Tokyo: Nikkōru Kurabu, 1986), 174; Anne Wilkes Tucker et al., eds., *The History of Japanese Photography* (New Haven, Conn.: Yale University Press, 2003), 16–17; Itō Ippei,

Nihon Shashin Hattatsushi (Tokyo: Asahi Sonorama, 1975), 46–52; Terry Bennett, *Photography in Japan, 1853–1912* (Tokyo: Tuttle, 2006), 23.

9. Huffman, *Creating a Public*, 166, 175, 283.
10. Gyōda-shi Kyōdo Hakubutsukan, ed., *Hyakunen-mae ni Mita Nihon: Ogawa Isshin to Bakumatsu Meiji no Shashin* (Gyōda: Gyōda-shi Kyōdo Hakubutsukan, 2000), 15, 135; Tucker et al., *History of Japanese Photography*, 634; Ozawa, *Nihon no Shashinshi*, 135. See also Ogawa Kazumasa, *Nisshin Sensō Shashinchō*, 2 vols. (Tokyo: Hakubundō, 1895).
11. James R. Ryan, *Picturing Empire: Photography and the Visualization of the British Empire* (Chicago: University of Chicago Press, 1997), 11–27, 73–96.
12. Paul Virilio, *War and Cinema: The Logistics of Perception* (London: Verso, 1989), 7.
13. On *nishiki-e shinbun*, see Yoshimi Shun'ya and Kinoshita Naoyuki, eds., *Nyūsu no Tanjō: Kawaraban to Shinbun Nishikie no Jōhō Sekai* (Tokyo: Tōkyō Daigaku Sōgō Kenkyū Hakubutsukan, 1999), 102–4, 226–35, 308–10. On Kiyochika, see Henry D. Smith II, *Kobayashi Kiyochika: Artist of Meiji Japan* (Santa Barbara, Calif.: Santa Barbara Museum of Art, 1988).
14. Kōno Kensuke, *Shomotsu no Kindai: Media no Bungakushi* (Tokyo: Chikuma Shobō, 1992), 118–19.
15. Fukuda Kiyohito, "Kadai," in *Teihon Kunikida Doppo Zenshū*, vol. 5 (Tokyo: Gakushū Kenkyūsha, 1978), 614; Suzuki Sadami, "Meiji-ki '*Taiyō*' no Enkaku, oyobi Ichi," in Suzuki, *Zasshi "Taiyō,"* 8.
16. Fukuda, "Kadai," 607; Kuroiwa Hisako, *Henshūsha Kunikida Doppo no Jidai* (Tokyo: Kadokawa Gakugei Shuppan, 2007), 20–23.
17. Nakajima Reiko's seven-hundred-page study, *Kunikida Doppo no Kenkyū* (Tokyo: Ōfū Shoten, 2009), makes no mention of his career as a war reporter. A rare exception is Ono Matsuo, *Kunikida Doppo-ron* (Tokyo: Makino Shuppan, 2003), 106–40.
18. Kunikida Doppo, *Aitei Tsūshin*, in *Teihon Kunikida Doppo Zenshū*, 5:15.
19. Kuroiwa, *Henshūsha Kunikida Doppo*, 20; Ono, *Kunikida Doppo-ron*, 127.
20. Kunikida, *Aitei Tsūshin*, 15–16.
21. Kunikida, *Aitei Tsūshin*, 16.
22. Cited in Fukuda, "Kadai," 610.
23. Kunikida, *Aitei Tsūshin*, 39, 41. The entry is signed November 10.
24. Kunikida, *Aitei Tsūshin*, 80. An informative discussion of this passage appears in Ono, *Kunikida Doppo-ron*, 130–31.
25. Quoted in Fukuda, "Kadai," 608.
26. On Taiwan's camphor industry, see James Wheeler Davidson, *The Island of Formosa: Historical View from 1430 to 1900* (New York: Paragon, 1903), 397–443. I owe this fascinating connection to the insight of Toulouse-Antonin Roy.
27. Kuroiwa, *Henshūsha Kunikida Doppo*, 12, 58–59, 69, 78, 146.
28. Quoted in Kuroiwa, *Henshūsha Kunikida Doppo*, 63. Originally published as Yano Ryūkei, "Hakkan no Shui," *Tōyō Gahō* 1. no. 1 (March 1903).
29. Suzuki, *Zasshi "Taiyō,"* 6, 13; Insatsu Hakubutsukan, *Mirion Serā Tanjō e!*, 54–57; Tsuboya, *Hakubunkan Gojūnenshi*, 90; Tamura, *Kindai Shuppan Bunka*, 41; Ōwada Shigeru, "'*Taiyō*' Sōkangō no Hankyō," in Suzuki, *Zasshi "Taiyō,"* 43–44.
30. Kōno, *Shomotsu no Kindai*, 143–46; Tsubouchi Yūzō, "Henshūsha Ōhashi Otowa," in Suzuki, *Zasshi "Taiyō,"* 163.

31. Seki Hajime, *Shinbun Shōsetsu no Jidai: Media, Dokusha, Merodorama* (Tokyo: Shin'yōsha, 2007), 45. See also Yamazaki Yasuo, *Shun'yōdō Monogatari: Shun'yōdō o Meguru Meiji Bundan no Sakkatachi* (Tokyo: Shun'yōdō Shoten, 1969).
32. Quoted in Seki, *Shinbun Shōsetsu no Jidai*, 37; Seki, *Shinbun Shōsetsu no Jidai*, 50, 56, 80, 88, 196; Huffman, *Creating a Public*, 228–47.
33. Seki, *Shinbun Shōsetsu no Jidai*, 33, 53–60; Kōno, *Shomotsu no Kindai*, 57–61.
34. A parallel process played out in American commercial publishing at the same moment, featuring Japanese-influenced cover design. See R. John Williams, *The Buddha in the Machine: Art, Technology, and The Meeting of East and West* (New Haven, Conn.: Yale University Press, 2014), 13–44.
35. Suzuki, *Zasshi "Taiyō,"* ii.
36. Ōhashi Sahei, untitled foreword in *Taiyō*, no. 1 (January 1895): 2.
37. Ōhashi, foreword, 2.
38. Nagamine Shigetoshi, "Kindai Nihon no Zasshi," 17.
39. Ōhashi, foreword, 2.
40. Suzuki, *Zasshi "Taiyō,"* 17.
41. Nagamine Shigetoshi, *"Dokusho Kokumin" no Tanjō: Meiji 30-nendai no Katsuji Media to Dokusho Bunka* (Tokyo: Nihon Editā Sukūru Shuppanbu, 2004), 24; Nagamine, "Kindai Nihon no Zasshi," 17. See also Richter, "Marketing the Word," 200–219.
42. Suzuki, *Zasshi "Taiyō,"* 11; Ōwada, "'*Taiyō*' Sōkangō no Hankyō," 49.
43. Inoue Ken, "Meijiki '*Taiyō*' no Hon'yaku Bungaku Shōkai o Megutte," in Suzuki, *Zasshi "Taiyō,"* 435; Hayashi Masako, "'Taiyō wa Torusutoi 'Nichiro Hisenron' o Ika ni Tsutaeta ka," in Suzuki, *Zasshi "Taiyō,"* 469–71.
44. Huffman, *Creating a Public*, 225.
45. Tamura, *Kindai Shuppan Bunka*, 58.
46. Satō Takumi, *"Kingu" no Jidai: Kokumin Taishū Zasshi no Kōkyōsei* (Tokyo: Iwanami Shoten, 2002), 101, 103, 107.
47. Noma Seiji, *Noma Seiji Jiden*, in Shuppanjin no Ibun 3: *Kōdansha Noma Seiji* (Tokyo: Kurita Shoten, 1968), 1.
48. Miyatake Gaikotsu, *Meiji Enzetsushi* (Tokyo: Yūgensha, 1926), 6–15; Noma, *Noma Seiji Jiden*, 31.
49. Nakamura Kōya, *Noma Seiji-den* (Tokyo: Noma Seiji Denki Hensankai, 1944), 334; Satō, *"Kingu" no Jidai*, 339; Noma, *Noma Seiji Jiden*, 6.
50. Noma Seiji, "Hakkan no Ji," in *Yūben* 1, no. 1 (February 1910): 1–2.
51. Noma, *Noma Seiji Jiden*, 21.
52. Noma, "Hakkan no Ji," 1; Noma, *Noma Seiji Jiden*, 7.
53. Noma, *Noma Seiji Jiden*, 26.
54. Noma, "Hakkan no Ji," 2.
55. Haga Yaichi, "Yūben to Bungaku," *Yūben* 1, no. 2 (March, 1910): 124, 125.
56. Haga, "Yūben to Bungaku," 124.
57. Seth Jacobowitz, *Writing Technology in Meiji Japan: A Media History of Modern Japanese Literature and Visual Culture* (Cambridge, Mass.: Harvard University Asia Center, 2015), 116–42.
58. Haga, "Yūben to Bungaku," 125.
59. On visual media and performance arts, see Aaron Gerow, *Visions of Japanese Modernity: Articulations of Cinema, Nation, and Spectatorship, 1895–1925* (Berkeley: University of California Press, 2010), 27, 47.

60. Hyōdō Hiromi, *"Koe" no Kokumin Kokka: Naniwabushi ga Tsukuru Nihon Kindai* (Tokyo: Kōdansha, 2009), 8, 12, 22–23, 45, 81, 106–8, 185.
61. Hyōdō, *"Koe" no Kokumin Kokka*, 83, 97, 118; Jacobowitz, *Writing Technology in Meiji Japan*, 117–19, 198.
62. Noma, *Noma Seiji Jiden*, 104.
63. Miyatake, *Meiji Enzetsushi*, 22–23, 39–40; Hyōdō, *"Koe" no Kokumin Kokka*, 16, 47, 95, 119; Satō, *"Kingu" no Jidai*, 124.
64. Noma, *Noma Seiji Jiden*, 43–44.
65. Satō, *"Kingu" no Jidai*, 98–99.
66. See Kindai Bungaku Gōdō Kenkyūkai, ed., *Kōdansha Nettowāku to Dokusha* (Yokosuka: Kindai Bungaku Gōdō Kenkyūkai, 2006).
67. Hyōdō, *"Koe" no Kokumin Kokka*, 129.
68. Satō, *"Kingu" no Jidai*, ix, 149, 204.
69. Noma, *Noma Seiji Jiden*, 210.
70. Satō, *"Kingu" no Jidai*, 222.
71. Nagamine, *"Dokusho Kokumin" no Tanjō*, 206–15; Satō, *"Kingu" no Jidai*, 57.
72. Noma, *Noma Seiji Jiden*, 214.
73. Satō, *"Kingu" no Jidai*, 7–8.
74. Satō, *"Kingu" no Jidai*, 3, 5, 7–8. Originally published in the *Tōkyō Nichinichi Shinbun*, December 3, 1924.
75. Satō, *"Kingu" no Jidai*, 13, 64; Edward Mack, *Manufacturing Modern Japanese Literature: Publishing, Prizes, and the Ascription of Literary Value* (Durham, N.C.: Duke University Press, 2010), 92–93.
76. Unnumbered advertising pages and front matter, *Kingu* 1, no. 1 (January 1925).
77. "Santari Kingu no Shutsugen," *Kingu* 1, no. 1 (January 1925): 2–3. The founding editor of *Kingu* was Tanikawa Takurō; see Noma, *Noma Seiji Jiden*, 206.
78. "*Kingu* ga Yo ni Deru made no Kushin," *Kingu* 1, no. 1 (January 1925): 280.
79. See Satō, *"Kingu" no Jidai*, 199–287. See also Marc Steinberg, *Anime's Media Mix: Franchising Toys and Characters in Japan* (Minneapolis: University of Minnesota Press, 2012), and Henry Jenkins, *Convergence Culture: Where Old and New Media Collide* (New York: New York University Press, 2006).
80. See Satō, *"Kingu" no Jidai*, 323–88.

2. IWANAMI SHOTEN AND THE ENTERPRISE OF ETERNITY

1. Vanessa B. Ward, "The Spectre of the Left: Iwanami Shoten, Ideology and Publishing in Early Postwar Japan," *Japanese Studies* 26, no. 2 (Summer 2006): 171–84.
2. Toeda Hirokazu, *Iwanami Shigeo: Hikuku Kurashi, Takaku Omou* (Tokyo: Mineruva Shobō, 2013), 2–3. To distinguish the founder from the company, I refer to Iwanami Shigeo as "Shigeo" and the company as "Iwanami," following convention in Japanese scholarship.
3. Toeda, *Iwanami Shigeo*, 6–7; Abe Yoshishige, *Iwanami Shigeo-den* (Tokyo: Iwanami Shoten, 1957), 42.
4. Abe, *Iwanami Shigeo-den*, 73; Abe Yoshishige, "Iwanami to Watashi," in *Abe Yoshishige Senshū*, vol. 3 (Tokyo: Oyama Shoten, 1949), 153; Toeda, *Iwanami Shigeo*, 9–11.

5. Toeda, *Iwanami Shigeo*, 28–31.
6. Abe, *Iwanami Shigeo-den*, 113, 119; Toeda, *Iwanami Shigeo*, 32.
7. Abe, *Iwanami Shigeo-den*, 118, 124, 160; Abe, "Iwanami to Watashi," 160. Iwanami invested two thousand yen a year for four years.
8. Toeda, *Iwanami Shigeo*, 14–15; on Sōseki and Iwanami, see Toeda, *Iwanami Shigeo*, 51–60, and Andrew T. Kamei-Dyche, "The History of Books and Print Culture in Japan: The State of the Field," *Book History* 14 (2011).
9. Abe, *Iwanami Shigeo-den*, 120.
10. Toeda, *Iwanami Shigeo*, 35.
11. Toeda, *Iwanami Shigeo*, 39.
12. Toeda, *Iwanami Shigeo*, 62; Abe, *Iwanami Shigeo-den*, 123–25.
13. Abe, *Iwanami Shigeo-den*, 130.
14. Toeda, *Iwanami Shigeo*, 39–40, 103–6. *Kokoro* ran in the *Tōkyō Asahi Shinbun* from April to August of 1914. See also Gregory Golley, *When Our Eyes No Longer See: Realism, Science, and Ecology in Japanese Literary Modernism* (Cambridge, Mass.: Harvard University Asia Center, 2008).
15. Henri Poincaré, "The Value of Science," in *The Foundations of Science*, trans. George Halsted (New York: Science Press, 1913), 205. For a summary of the early years of Iwanami Shoten, see also Kōno Kensuke, *Monogatari Iwanami Shoten Hyakunenshi 1: Kyōyō no Tanjō* (Tokyo: Iwanami Shoten, 2013), 1–66.
16. "Kaidai," unattributed editor's note in pamphlet accompanying complete reprint of *Shichō* (Tokyo: Iwanami Shoten, 1981); Abe, *Iwanami Shigeo-den*, 140, 156; Abe, "Iwanami to Watashi," 162; Toeda, *Iwanami Shigeo*, 62, 89.
17. Abe, Abe, and Watsuji were active in the Mokuyōkai (Thursday Club) group of Sōseki's disciples; see Toeda, *Iwanami Shigeo*, 73.
18. Abe Jirō, "Hakkan no Ji," *Shichō* 1, no. 1 (May 1917): 1.
19. "Kaidai," 4.
20. Abe Jirō, "Hakkan no Ji," 2.
21. Abe Jirō, "Hakkan no Ji," 3.
22. Abe Jirō, "Hakkan no Ji," 3.
23. Abe Yoshishige, "Bonjin Bongo," *Shicho* 1, no. 1 (May 1917): 142–44.
24. Abe Yoshishige, "Bonjin Bongo," 143.
25. Abe Yoshishige, "Bonjin Bongo," 144–45. *Kyōyō* is glossed as *birudzungu*.
26. Unpaginated inside-front-cover advertisement, *Shichō* 1, no. 1 (May 1917).
27. Watsuji Tetsurō, "Nihon no Bunka ni tsuite," *Shichō* 1, no. 1 (May 1917): 90.
28. Watsuji's ideas have their antecedent in Okakura Kakuzō's (1862–1913) *The Ideals of the East* (1903). Watsuji develops the relationship between early Japan and Greco-Indian art and civilization in *Koji Junrei* (Pilgrimages to Ancient Temples), serialized in *Shichō* in 1918.
29. Watsuji, "Nihon no Bunka ni tsuite," 94.
30. See Rüdiger Safranski, *Romanticism: A German Affair*, trans. Robert Goodwin (Evanston, Ill.: Northwestern University Press, 2014).
31. Abe Yoshishige, "Shureiamahha to Doitsu Romanshugi," *Shicho* 1, no. 4 (August 1917): 94.
32. Toeda, *Iwanami Shigeo*, 62, 80; "Kaidai," 4–5. *Koji Junrei* ran in *Shichō* vol. 2, nos. 8–12, and vol. 3, no. 1. A noteworthy predecessor was *Shinshichō* (New Currents in Thought); Watsuji was an editor in the second installment in 1910–1911.

33. Abe Yoshishige, *Iwanami Shigeo-den*, 130; unnumbered inside-back-cover advertisement, *Shicho* 1, no. 1; unnumbered insert-page advertisement, *Shichō* 2 no. 4.
34. Unnumbered back-cover advertisement run across multiple issues of *Shichō*.
35. *Shisō* 1, no. 1, unnumbered inside front page.
36. On *Shichō* and *Shisō*, see also Kōno, *Monogatari Iwanami Shoten*, 144–67.
37. *Shisō* 1, no. 1, unnumbered inside front page.
38. Abe Yoshishige, "Iwanami to Watashi," 149; Toeda, *Iwanami Shigeo*, 102.
39. On *kyōyō*, see Karube Tadashi, *Utsuriyuku "Kyōyō"* (Tokyo: NTT Shuppan, 2007); Takeuchi Yō, *Taishū Modanizumu no Yume no Ato: Hōkō suru Kyōyō to Daigaku* (Tokyo: Shin'yōsha, 2001); and Tsutsui Kiyotada, *Nihongata "Kyōyō" no Unmei: Rekishi Shakaigakuteki Kōsatsu* (Tokyo: Iwanami Shoten, 2009).
40. Friedrich Nietzsche, *Ecce Homo*, trans. Anthony Ludovici, vol. 17 in *The Complete Works of Friedrich Nietzsche*, ed. Oscar Levy (New York: Macmillan, 1911), 36.
41. Abe Yoshishige, "Dokushoron," in *Abe Yoshishige Senshū*, vol. 4 (Tokyo: Oyama Shoten, 1949), 167, 168, 170.
42. Abe Yoshishige, "Dokushoron," 169, 171, 173.
43. Mack, *Manufacturing Modern Japanese Literature*, 51–91.
44. Seki Chūka, ed., *Zasshi "Kaizō" no Shijūnen* (Tokyo: Kōwadō, 1977), 99–101; Insatsu Hakubutsukan, ed., *Mirion Serā Tanjō e!* (Tokyo: Insatsu Hakubutsukan, 2008), 130.
45. Seki Chūka, *Zasshi "Kaizō,"* 99.
46. On the *enpon*, see Mack, *Manufacturing Modern Japanese Literature*, 91–138, and Christopher Keavney, *The Cultural Evolution of Postwar Japan: The Contributions of* Kaizō's *Yamamoto Sanehiko* (London: Palgrave Macmillan, 2013).
47. Seki Chūka, *Zasshi "Kaizō,"* 94–95; Satō Tsuji, "Rekuramu no Enkaku," *Shisō* 71 (September 1927): 93; Yamazaki Yasuo, *Eien no Jigyō: Iwanami Bunko Monogatari* (Tokyo: Hakuōsha, 1962), 17. Shinchōsha's series was released in 1929 but contracted earlier.
48. Toeda, *Iwanami Shigeo*, 141. Iwanami Bunko Henshūbu, *Iwanami Bunko no Hachijūnen*. (Tokyo: Iwanami Shoten, 2007), 401–2; Abe Yoshishige, *Iwanami Shigeo-den*, 162.
49. Yamazaki, *Eien no Jigyō*, 13. Nagamine Shigetoshi, *"Dokusho Kokumin" no Tanjō: Meiji 30-nendai no Katsuji Media to Dokusho Bunka* (Tokyo: Nihon Editā Sukūru Shuppanbu 2004), 25.
50. Iwanami Bunko Henshūbu, *Iwanami Bunko no Hachijūnen*, 2–3.
51. Yamazaki, *Eien no Jigyō*, 17; Toeda, *Iwanami Shigeo*, 134. The text of the essay is reprinted identically in all Iwanami Bunko volumes. References to the unpaginated text are cited as Miki Kiyoshi, "Dokushoshi ni Yosu."
52. Toeda, *Iwanami Shigeo*, 148.
53. Doi Mitsutomo, "Kokubungaku to Sekai Bungaku," *Shisō* 1, no. 1 (October 1921): 32, 35; Satō, "Rekuramu no Enkaku," 98; On publishing and the French Enlightenment, see Robert Darnton, *The Business of Enlightenment: A Publishing History of the* Encyclopédie *1775–1800* (Cambridge, Mass.: Belknap Press, 1979).
54. Doi, "Kokubungaku to Sekai Bungaku," 35, 82, 84. On canon formation, see Haruo Shirane and Tomi Suzuki, eds., *Inventing the Classics: Modernity, National Identity, and Japanese Literature* (Stanford, Calif.: Stanford University Press, 2000).

55. Abe Jirō, "Sekai Shichō no Imi," in *Iwanami Kōza Sekai Shichō*, vol. 1 (Tokyo: Iwanami Shoten, 1928), 5.
56. Miki, "Dokushoshi ni Yosu."
57. Kōno Kensuke, *Shomotsu no Kindai: Media no Bungakushi* (Tokyo: Chikuma Shobō, 1992).
58. Abe Yoshishige, *Iwanami Shigeo-den*, 159.
59. *Ōsaka Mainichi Shinbun*, October 18, 1927.
60. Miki, "Dokushoshi ni Yosu."
61. Miki, "Dokushoshi ni Yosu."
62. Miki, "Dokushoshi ni Yosu."
63. *Ōsaka Mainichi Shinbun*, October 18, 1927; Toeda, *Iwanami Shigeo*, 134; Nagamine, *"Dokusho Kokumin" no Tanjō*, 23.
64. Nagamine, *"Dokusho Kokumin" no Tanjō*, 23.
65. Yamazaki, *Eien no Jigyō*, 20–21.
66. Ward, "Spectre of the Left," 173–74.
67. Abe Yoshishige, *Iwanami Shigeo-den*, 166.
68. Miki Kiyoshi, "Shosoku Ittsu," *Shisō* 29 (March 1924): 110. Miki's letter is dated January 1, 1924.
69. Miki, "Shosoku Ittsu," 108–9.
70. Miki Kiyoshi, "Marukusushugi to Yuibutsuron," *Shisō* 69 (October 1927): 31. Miki would later produce the first Japanese translation of *The German Ideology* (as *Doicche Ideorogî*) for Iwanami Bunko in 1930.
71. Miki, "Shōsoku Ittsu," 115–16.
72. Miki, "Marukusushugi to Yuibutsuron," 36, 45–46.
73. Miki, "Marukusushugi to Yuibutsuron," 36. Miki does not cite Marx but includes the German in his text.
74. Submerged but not acknowledged in Miki's essay is the influence of Georg Lukács's *History and Class Consciousness* (1923), which was translated into Japanese by Mizutani Chōzaburō and published by Dōjinsha Shoten in January 1927 as *Kaikyū Ishiki to wa Nan zo ya: "Rekishiki to Kaishikyū Ishiki" Kaikyū Ishiki-ron*. On the early reception of Lukács in Japan, see Miriam Silverberg, *Changing Song: The Marxist Manifestos of Nakano Shigeharu* (Princeton, N.J.: Princeton University Press, 1990).
75. Nii Itaru, "Shuppan Shihonshugi to Chojutsuka," *Chūō Kōron*, April 1928, 58.
76. Ikuta Chōkō, *Shihonron Daiichi Bunsatsu* (Tokyo: En'yōsha, 1919), 7.
77. Takabatake Motoyuki, "Taishū Kōza: Marukusu no Shihonron," *Kaizō* 8, no. 11 (November 1927): 67. On this period in general, see Kōno, *Shomotsu no Kindai*, 295–306.
78. Yamazaki, *Eien no Jigyō*, 33. Volume 1 of Takabatake's translation was released by Shinchōsha in 1925, but the price remained well above Iwanami's or Kaizōsha's.
79. *Binbō Monogatari* was serialized in the *Ōsaka Asahi Shinbun* in 1916, published as a book in 1917, and went through thirty reprintings in two years; see Gail Lee Bernstein, *Japanese Marxist: A Portrait of Kawakami Hajime* (Cambridge, Mass.: Harvard University Press, 1976), 18; Kawakami Hajime, preface to *Chinrōdō to Shihon* (Tokyo: Iwanami Shoten, 1927), 6.
80. Yamazaki, *Eien no Jigyō*, 34.
81. *Tōkyō Asahi Shinbun*, September 23, 1927.

82. *Kaizō*, November 1927. The "November" issue of the magazine was actually released in October, as is the custom for periodicals in Japan.
83. *Kaizō*, November 1927.
84. Karl Marx, *Shihonron*, trans. Kawakami Hajime (Tokyo: Iwanami Shoten 1927–1928), 4.
85. Kawakami, preface to *Shihonron*, 6; Takabatake, "Taishū Kōza," 67.
86. *Kaizō*, March 1928.
87. Karl Marx, *Capital: A Critique of Political Economy*, trans. Ben Fowkes (New York: Penguin, 1990), 125.
88. Miki's wording is *seikatsu kōjō no shiryō*.
89. Marx, *Capital*, 125.
90. Iwanami released five volumes of Kawakami's translation between October 1927 and June 1929, with Miyakawa Minoru assisting on later volumes. Iwanami Bunko published a full translation by Sakisaka Itsurō in 1970; see Yamazaki, *Eien no Jigyō*, 35; Toeda, *Iwanami Shigeo*, 169.
91. Abe Yoshishige, *Iwanami Shigeo-den*, 175–78; Toeda, *Iwanami Shigeo*, 155–56. For more on the strike, see Kōno, *Monogatari Iwanami Shoten*, 281–94.
92. Abe Yoshishige, *Iwanami Shigeo-den*, 166.

3. THE TOPOGRAPHY OF TYPOGRAPHY

1. Yokomitsu Riichi, "Machi no Soko," in *Teihon Yokomitsu Riichi Zenshū*, ed. Hoshō Masao et al., vol. 2 (Tokyo: Kawade Shobō, 1981), 196. Originally published in *Bungei Jidai* 2, no. 8 (August 1925).
2. Natsume Sōseki, *Sanshirō*, in *Sōseki Zenshū*, vol. 7 (Tokyo: Iwanami Shoten, 1956), 82. The translation of this passage is from Natsume Sōseki, *Sanshirō*, trans. Jay Rubin (New York: Penguin Books, 2009), 76.
3. Leah Price, *How to Do Things With Books in Victorian England* (Princeton, N.J.: Princeton University Press, 2012), 19, 107.
4. See Hidenobu Jinnai, *Tokyo: A Spatial Anthropology*, trans. Kimiko Nishimura (Berkeley: University of California Press, 1995), 68–70.
5. Kabayama Kōichi, "Sekaishi no Naka no Insatsu Shuto Tokyo," in *Insatsu Toshi Tōkyō to Kindai Nihon*, ed. Insatsu Hakubutsukan (Tokyo: Toppan Insatsu, 2012), 11.
6. Suzuki Jun, "Insatsu ga Tsukutta Kindai Nihon," in Insatsu Hakubutsukan, *Insatsu Toshi Tōkyō*, 43, 49.
7. Iwakiri Shin'ichirō, "Insatsu Toshi Tōkyō no Meiji," in Insatsu Hakubutsukan, *Insatsu Toshi Tōkyō*, 106–17.
8. Nagamine Shigetoshi, *Modan Toshi no Dokusho Kūkan* (Tokyo: Nihon Editā Sukūru Shuppanbu, 2001), 4–5, 28, 31–33, 39.
9. Wada Keiko, "Kaidai," in *Maruzen to Yōsho*, ed. Wada Hirofumi and Wada Keiko, Korekushon Modan Toshi 79 (Tokyo: Yumani Shobō, 2012), 745–49; Maruzen Kabushikigaisha, ed., *Maruzen Hyakunenshi: Nihon Kindaika no Ayumi to tomo ni*, vol. 1 (Tokyo: Maruzen, 1981), 122–54; Kimura Ki, *Maruzen Gaishi* (Tokyo: Maruzen, 1969), 71.
10. Kimura, *Maruzen Gaishi*, 55–61; Wada, 745, 748, 758–759.

11. Wada, "Kaidai," 751. See Yoshimi Shun'ya, *Toshi no Doramaturugī: Tōkyō—Sakariba no Shakaishi.* (Tokyo: Kawade Shobō Shinsha, 2008), 220–25, 230–31.
12. Terada Torahiko, "Maruzen to Mitsukoshi," in *Terada Torahiko Zenshū*, vol. 7 (Tokyo: Iwanami Shoten, 1997), 12.
13. Terada, "Maruzen to Mitsukoshi," 12–14.
14. Akutagawa Ryūnosuke, "Aru Ahō no Isshō," in *Akutagawa Ryūnosuke Zenshū* vol. 16 (Tokyo: Iwanami Shoten, 1997), 38.
15. Akutagawa Ryūnosuke, "Haguruma," in *Akutagawa Ryūnosuke Zenshū*, vol. 15 (Tokyo: Iwanami Shoten, 1997), 57–58. See Seiji Lippit, *Topographies of Japanese Modernism* (New York: Columbia University Press, 2002), 55–57.
16. Kajii Motojirō, "Remon," in *Kajii Motojirō Zenshū*, vol. 1 (Tokyo: Chikuma Shobō, 1966), 8–9, 11, 13.
17. "Hakkan no Ji," *Manabi no Tomoshibi*, no. 1 (March 1897), unnumbered first page. The magazine was originally named *Manabi no Tomoshibi* with the English title *The Light of Knowledge* before being renamed *Gakutō*, the Sinitic reading of the same characters.
18. Kōno Toshirō, *Gakutō o Yomu* (Tokyo: Yūshōdō Shuppan, 2009), 7; Maruzen Kabushikigaisha, *Maruzen Hyakunenshi*, 363.
19. Nomura Takashi, *Uchida Roan-den* (Tokyo: Riburopōto, 1994), 316.
20. Nomura, *Uchida Roan-den*, 16–18, 21, 27, 67, 69. Roan used a variety of pen names, including Uchida Fuchian, Fuchian Shujin, Fuchi Sannin, and others. For consistency and clarity, I refer to him as Roan throughout.
21. Nomura, *Uchida Roan-den*, 136–37, 313–15.
22. Uchida Roan, "Keimōteki Dokushosetsu o Haisu," in *Uchida Roan Shomotsu Kankei Chosakushū*, ed. Yagi Sakichi et al., vol. 2 (Tokyo: Seishōdō, 1979), 219–21.
23. Natsume, *Sanshirō*, 83; translation from Rubin, 77.
24. Uchida Roan, "Tsundoku Sensei Raisan," in Yagi, *Uchida Roan Shomotsu*, 2:101–2.
25. Uchida Roan, "Shoseki no Hanashi," in Yagi, *Uchida Roan Shomotsu*, 2:60–62.
26. Uchida, "Tsundoku Sensei Raisan," 103.
27. Uchida, "Shoseki no Hanashi," 62.
28. Uchida, "Keimōteki Dokushosetsu o Haisu," 219, 226–27.
29. Uchida, "Keimōteki Dokushosetsu o Haisu," 219–21.
30. Uchida, "Keimōteki Dokushosetsu o Haisu," 219–20.
31. Uchida Roan, "Dokusho wa Bunkateki Kyōraku," in *Uchida Roan Shomotsu Kankei Chosakushū*, ed. Yagi Sakichi et al., vol. 3 (Tokyo: Seishōdō Shoten, 1979), 27.
32. Uchida Roan, "Dokusho wa Yūgi de aru," in Yagi, *Uchida Roan Shomotsu*, 2:241.
33. Uchida, "Keimōteki Dokushosetsu o Haisu," 222; Uchida, "Dokusho wa Yūgi de aru," 242.
34. Uchida, "Dokusho wa Yūgi de aru," 242, 244.
35. Uchida, "Keimōteki Dokushosetsu o Haisu," 223–24.
36. Uchida, "Dokusho wa Yūgi de aru," 245.
37. Uchida, "Keimōteki Dokushosetsu o Haisu," 229, 231–32.
38. Tōkyō Koshoseki Shōgyō Kyōdō Kumiai, ed., *Tōkyō Kosho Kumiai Gojūnenshi* (Tokyo: Tōkyō Koshoseki Shōgyō Kyōdō Kumiai, 1974), 4, 22, 28.
39. *Sanseidō no Hyakunen* (Tokyo: Sanseidō, 1982), 50–51.
40. Tōkyō Shosekishō Kumiai, ed., *Tōkyō Shosekishō Kumiai Gojūnenshi* (Tokyo: Tōkyō Shosekishō Kumiai, 1937), 28.

41. I use these names anachronistically, as they were formalized in 1930 following the amalgamation of multiple smaller unions. See Tōkyō Koshoseki Shōgyō Kyōdō Kumiai, ed., *Tōkyō Kosho Kumiai Gojūnenshi*, 20, 46–47, 207–10, 240.
42. Tatsuno Yutaka, "Shorō Shoton," in *Nihon no Meizuihitsu 36: Doku*, ed. Ibuse Masuji (Tokyo: Sakuhinsha, 1985), 48.
43. Ibuse Masuji, "Kami ya Hyōshi no Koto," *Hon*, no. 2 (April 1933), in Shoshi Shomoku Shirīzu, vol. 34, "*Hon*" (Tokyo: Yumani Shobō, 1993), 165–66.
44. Chiba Kameo, "Sōtei to Sakka no Kibun," *Shoshi*, no. 1 (February 1927), in Shoshi Shomoku Shirīzu, vol. 44, "*Shoshi*" (Tokyo: Yumani Shobō, 1997), 10–12.
45. Ozaki Kazuo, "Kosho Kaikodan," in Ibuse, *Nihon no Meizuihitsu 36*, 188.
46. Jean-Luc Nancy, *On the Commerce of Thinking: Of Books and Bookstores*, trans. David Wills (New York: Fordham University Press, 2009), 29.
47. Uchida Roan, "Shimi no Jiden," in *Uchida Roan Shomotsu Kankei Chosakushū*, ed. Yagi Sakichi et al., vol. 1 (Tokyo: Seishōdō, 1979), 210, 219, 222–25, 274. Serialized in *Tōnichi Yūkan* from May 4 to May 31, 1924.
48. Uchida, "Shimi no Jiden," 210, 216, 219.
49. Nancy, *On the Commerce of Thinking*, 35.
50. Kosho Chijin, "Wagahai wa Shomotsu de Aru," *Shomotsu Shumi* (*Philobiblon*) 1, nos. 1–3 (September–November 1932), in Shoshi Shomoku Shirīzu, vol. 34, "*Furuhon'ya*," 65, 67, 71.
51. Mizutani Futō, *Meiji Taishō Kosho Ka no Kenkyū* (Tokyo: Sunnansha, 1933), 17–19, 26–29. See also Brian Dowdle, "Why Saikaku Was Memorable but Bakin Was Unforgettable," *Journal of Japanese Studies* 42, no. 1 (Winter 2016): 92–106.
52. Ozaki, "Kosho Kaikodan," 187–88.
53. Tokushū Yūshō, "Shomotsu ni kansuru Koku no Konjaku," *Furuhon'ya: Bibliographia Japonica Antiqua*, no. 3 (November 1927), in Shoshi Shomoku Shirīzu, vol. 34, "*Furuhon'ya*," 171.
54. Tanmachi Shigeo, "Furuhon'yagyō no Honshitsu Kentō," in *Shomotsu Shumi: Philobiblon* 1, no. 2 (October 1932), in Shoshi Shomoku Shirīzu, vol. 34, "*Shomotsu Shumi: Philobiblon*," 127, 129, 130, 140.
55. Kobayashi Hideo, "Kottō," in *Nihon no Meizuihitsu Bekkan 34: Shūshū*, ed. Okumoto Daisaburō (Tokyo: Sakuhinsha, 1993), 93, 96.
56. Gustave Flaubert, *Bibliomania: A Tale* (London: Rodale Press, 1954), 28.
57. Originally published in *Le colibri* magazine in February 1837.
58. Flaubert, *Bibliomania*, 9–11, 14, 21.
59. Uchida Roan, "Tō kara," in Yagi, *Uchida Roan Shomotsu*, 2:398. Originally published in *Gakutō*, June 1917.
60. Uchida Roan, "Shoseki Shumi," in Yagi, *Uchida Roan Shomotsu*, 2:155. Originally published in *Gakutō*, September 1914.
61. John Klancher, "Wild Bibliography: The Rise and Fall of Book History in Nineteenth-Century Britain," in *Bookish Histories: Books, Literature, and Commercial Modernity, 1700–1900*, ed. Ina Ferris and Paul Keen (London: Palgrave Macmillan, 2009), 27.
62. See Kawahara Mankichi, *Kosho Sōwa* (Tokyo: Yumani Shobō, 2011). Originally published in 1936.
63. Saitō Shōzō, "Furuhon Mokuroku no Higeki," *Shomotsu Shunju* 1, no. 1 (October 1930), in Shoshi Shomoku Shirīzu, vol. 34, "*Shomotsu Shunju*," 27.

64. Klancher, "Wild Bibliography," 19, 24.
65. Shōseiro [Ichishima Kenkichi], "Horidashimono no Ben," *Shosai* 1, no. 4 (June 1926), in Shoshi Shomoku Shirīzu, vol. 34, "*Shosai*," 150.
66. Ozaki, "Kosho Kaikodan," 189.
67. Uchida Roan, "Hon'ya no Ude," in Yagi, *Uchida Roan Shomotsu*, 2:195–96.
68. Tamagawa Rōjin, "Furuhon'ya," *Furuhon'ya*, no. 2 (May 1927), in Shomoku Kankei Zasshi Sōsho, vol. 34 (Tokyo: Yumani Shobō, 1993), 94–95.
69. Tokushū, "Shomotsu ni kan suru Koku," 130.
70. *Hon'ya* 1, no. 1 (1915), in Shoshi Shomoku Shirīzu, vol. 106, "*Hon'ya*" (Tokyo: Yumani Shobō, 2014), 10.
71. Saitō, "Furuhon Mokuroku no Higeki," 10.
72. Uchida Roan, "Furuhon'ya no Mokuroku," in Yagi, *Uchida Roan Shomotsu*, 2:190. Originally published in *Furuhon'ya*, no. 3 (November 1927).
73. Uchida Roan, "Maruzen Enjō no Ki," in Yagi, *Uchida Roan Shomotsu*, 1:366–89. Originally included in Roan's diary. See also Edward Mack, *Manufacturing Modern Japanese Literature: Publishing, Prizes, and the Ascription of Literary Value* (Durham, N.C.: Duke University Press, 2010), 51–89.
74. Uchida Roan, "Tenseki no Haikyō," in Yagi, *Uchida Roan Shomotsu*, 1:106, 108, 155.
75. Uncredited editor's introduction, *Tenseki* 1, no. 1 (May 1915), in Shoshi Shomoku Shirīzu, vol. 44, "*Tenseki*," 26.
76. Ōtsuki Fumihiko, "Chinsho no Fukuhon no Hitsuyō," *Tenseki* 1, no. 1 (May 1915), in Shoshi Shomoku Shirīzu, vol. 44, "*Tenseki*," 35–37.
77. Yanagita Kunio, "Kosho Hozon to Kyōdo," "Chinsho no Fukuhon no Hitsuyō," *Tenseki* 1, no. 1 (May 1915), in Shoshi Shomoku Shirīzu, vol. 44, "*Tenseki*," 45.
78. Kida Jun'ichirō, *Koshogai o Aruku*, in *Kida Jun'ichirō Chosakushū*, vol. 3 (Tokyo: San'ichi Shobō, 1997), 130, 156.
79. Ganshōdō Shoten Kotenbu, ed., *Koshoseki Zaiko Mokuroku Nihon Shihen* (Tokyo: Ganshōdō Shoten, 1928), 1.
80. Yanagita Kunio, "Jō," in Ganshōdō Shoten Kotenbu, *Koshoseki Zaiko Mokuroku*, 3.
81. Miyazato Risshi and Satō Tetsuhiko, "Kaisetsu," in *Teikoku Toshokan Naikaku Kikanshitsu Kirokuka (Naikaku Bunko) / Kunaishō Toshoryō* (Tokyo: Yumani Shobō, 2010), 7–8, 12–13.
82. *Tōkyō Teikoku Daigaku Fuzoku Toshokan Zōhon Dainikai Tenrankai Mokuroku*, in *Meiji Taishōki Kisho Chinseki Shomoku Kaidaishū*, vol. 2 (Tokyo: Yumani Shobō, 2010), 4.
83. Nagamine, *Modan Toshi*, 6, 24–27. Kusano Masana, *Toshokan no Rekishi Nihon oyobi Kakkoku no Tosho to Toshokanshi* (Tokyo: Gakugei Tosho, 1971), 186–88. The Hibiya branch held nearly half a million volumes; see Ōsawa Satoshi, ed., *Toshokan to Dokusho*, Korekushon Modan Toshi Bunka 87 (Tokyo: Yumani Shobō, 2013), 136–39.
84. See Kusano, *Toshokan no Rekishi*, 134–37; Ōsawa Satoshi, "Kaisetsu," in Ōsawa, *Toshokan to Dokusho*, 598–99.
85. Katayama Sen, "Toshokan ni tsuite," *Taiyō* (December 1896), cited in Ishii Atsushi, ed., *Toshokanshi: Kindai Nihonhen* (Tokyo: Kyōiku Shiryō Shuppankai, 1989), 66, 68.
86. Ono Noriaki, *Nihon Toshokanshi* (Kyoto: Genbunsha, 1973), 231, 235; Ōsawa, "Kaisetsu," 601–3, 606.
87. Kusano, *Toshokan no Rekishi*, 198. The library was rebuilt in the modern style in 1893.

88. Uchida, "Tenseki no Haikyō," 123, 154. Ono Noriaki, *Nihon Toshokanshi*, 283–85.
89. Uchida Roan, "Toshokan no Fukkō to Bunken no Hozon," in Yagi, *Uchida Roan Shomotsu*, 1:329, 341; Ono Noriaki, *Nihon Toshokanshi*, 287.
90. Founded as the Meiji Jidai Shinbun Zasshi Hozonkan but soon renamed.
91. Gaikotsu published under a wide variety of pen names; I use Gaikotsu throughout for consistency.
92. Nishida Taketoshi, *Meiji Shinbun Zasshi Bunko no Omoide* (Tokyo: Rikiesuta no Kai, 2001), 9–10, 14.
93. Miyatake Gaikotsu, *Ichienpon Ryūkō no Dokugai to Sono Uramen*, in *Miyatake Gaikotsu Kono Naka ni Ari: Zasshi Shūsei*, vol. 23, *Minponshugi* (Tokyo: Yumani Shobō, 1995), 176–78, 183, 191–93.
94. Miyatake, *Ichienpon Ryūkō no Dokugai*, 223.
95. Miyatake Gaikotsu, "Jiko o Furikaerimiyo," *Meiji Kibun*, no. 1 (January 1925): 1.
96. Kimoto Itaru, *Hyōden Miyatake Gaikotsu* (Tokyo: Shakai Shisōsha, 1984), 513.
97. Miyatake, "Jiko o Furikaerimiyo," 1.
98. Kimoto, *Hyōden Miyatake Gaikotsu*, 535–36; Nishida, *Meiji Shinbun Zasshi*, 8, 12–13, 30–31.
99. Yoshino Sakuzō, "Hon'ya to no Shitashimi," in *Yoshino Sakuzō Senshū*, vol. 12 (Tokyo: Iwanami Shoten, 1995), 41–42. Originally published in *Isseidō Kosho Mokuroku*, November 1925; Yoshino Sakuzō, "Shiryō no Kishū—Meiji Bunka Kenkyūsha to shite," in *Yoshino Sakuzō Senshū*, 12:86. Originally published in *Tōkyō Asahi Shinbun*, June 24, 1931.
100. Yoshino Sakuzō, "*Meiji Bunka Zenshū* wa Ika ni Shite Hensan Sareta ka," in *Yoshino Sakuzō Senshū*, vol. 11 (Tokyo: Iwanami Shoten, 1995), 184.
101. Nishida, *Meiji Shinbun Zasshi*, 37–38, 60.
102. Nishida, *Meiji Shinbun Zasshi*, 7.
103. Nishida, *Meiji Shinbun Zasshi*, 28.
104. Ebihara Hachirō, *Meiji Bungaku Zakki* (Tokyo: Yumani Shobō, 1994), 397–98; Asaoka Kunio, "Shoshi Sakuseisha to shite no Ebihara Hachirō," in Ebihara, *Meiji Bungaku Zakki*, 111.
105. Asaoka, "Shoshi Sakuseisha," 111.
106. Asaoka, "Shoshi Sakuseisha," 186–89.
107. Asaoka, "Shoshi Sakuseisha," 398.

4. NEW AGE SENSATIONS

1. Marshall McLuhan, *The Gutenberg Galaxy: The Making of Typographic Man* (Toronto: University of Toronto Press, 1962), 35.
2. McLuhan, *The Gutenberg Galaxy*, 314.
3. McLuhan, *The Gutenberg Galaxy*, 153–54.
4. Ōsawa Satoshi, *Hihyō Media-ron: Senzenki Nihon no Rondan to Bundan* (Tokyo: Iwanami Shoten: 2015).
5. See Edward Mack, *Manufacturing Modern Japanese Literature: Publishing, Prizes, and the Ascription of Literary Value* (Durham, N.C.: Duke University Press, 2010), 187–97.

6. Toeda Hirokazu, "Kōkoku kara Mita Taishōki no Bungei Shunjū no Tenkai," *Kokubungaku Kenkyū* 148 (March 2006): 98–109; Toeda Hirokazu, "Shuppatsuki Bungei Shunjū no Media Senryaku," *Nihon Kindai Bungaku* 66 (May 15, 2002): 185–201.
7. Yokomitsu Riichi, "Bungei Jidai to Gokai," *Bungei Jidai* 1, no. 1 (October 1924): 15–16.
8. Kadono Torazō, *Kinseidō no Koro* (Tokyo: Wāku Tosho, 1972), 50, 73, 91, 127. See also Munakata Kazushige and Toeda Hirokazu, eds., *Kinseidō o Chūshin to Suru Taishō Shōwaki no Shuppan Shoshi to Bungaku ni kansuru Sōgō Kenkyū* (Tokyo: MEXT, 2007).
9. Kawabata Yasunari, "Sōkan no Ji," *Bungei Jidai* 1, no. 1 (October 1924): 6.
10. Kawabata, "Sōkan no Ji," 8. See also "Shinkankaku-ha Kisei Bundan Ronsō," in *Gendai Nihon Bungaku Ronsōshi*, ed. Hirano Ken, Odagiri Hideo, and Yamamoto Kenkichi, 1:293–382 (Tokyo: Miraisha, 2006).
11. Chiba Kameo, "Na wa Shosen Hitotsu no Gainen," *Bungei Jidai* 2, no. 7 (July 1925): 11.
12. Uncredited editors' contribution, "Henshū Kōki," *Bungei Jidai* 1, no. 1 (October 1924): 108.
13. Yokomitsu, "Bungei Jidai to Gokai," 16.
14. Kadono, *Kinseidō no Koro*, 70–71.
15. Kawabata Yasunari, "Bungei Jidai Sōkan Tōji," in *Bungei Jidai*, reissue suppl., ed. Odagiri Susumu (Tokyo: Nihon Kindai Bungakukan, 1967), 1; Kadono, *Kinseidō no Koro*, 7, 134.
16. Quoted in "Kaisetsu," in Hirano, Odagiri, and Yamamoto, *Gendai Nihon Bungaku Ronsōshi*, 1:9.
17. Kawabata, "Bungei Jidai Sōkan Tōji," 3.
18. Chiba Kameo, "Shinkankaku-ha no Tanjō," in *Kindai Nihon Bungaku Hyōron Taikei*, vol. 6, *Taishōki III Shōwaki I*, ed. Miyoshi Yukio (Tokyo: Kadokawa Shoten, 1973), 38–39. Originally published in *Seiki*, November 1924.
19. Kawabata Yasunari, "Atarashiki Seikatsu to Atarashiki Bungei," *Bungei Jidai* 1, no. 1 (October 1924): 6–10.
20. Chiba, "Shinkankaku-ha no Tanjō," 40.
21. Chiba, "Shinkankaku-ha no Tanjō," 40.
22. Hashizume Ken, "Daini Giteki Kōsatsu," *Bungei Jidai* 2, no. 7 (July 1925): 16.
23. Kawabata Yasunari, "Shinshin Sakka no Shinkeikō Kaisetsu," *Bungei Jidai* 2, no. 1 (January 1925): 4.
24. McLuhan, *The Gutenberg Galaxy*, 33.
25. Bungei Jidai Henshūbu, ed., *Bungei Shingo Jiten* (Tokyo: Kinseidō, 1926), 53.
26. Kataoka Teppei, "Tōan Hitotsu," *Bungei Jidai* 1, no. 1 (October 1924): 18.
27. Kawabata, "Shinshin Sakka no Shinkeikō Kaisetsu," 5.
28. Yokomitsu Riichi, "Kankaku Katsudō," *Bungei Jidai* 2. no. 2 (February 1925): 2–3. The original title is "Kankaku Katsudō—Kankaku Katsudō to Kankakuteki Sakubutsu ni taisuru Hinan e no Gyakusetsu" (Sensory Activity—A Retort to the Criticisms of Sensory Activity and Sensory Works). The essay appears in Yokomitsu's collected works as "Shinkankaku-ron" (Theory of New Sensation), a title appended later. A list of Yokomitsu's revisions is included in Hoshō Masao et al., eds., *Teihon Yokomitsu Riichi Zenshū*, vol. 13 (Tokyo: Kawade Shobō Shinsha, 1982),

619–21. Hereafter, the *Zenshū* is cited as *TYRZ*. I cite the text as it originally appeared in *Bungei Jidai*.

29. Yokomitsu, "Kankaku Katsudō," 3.
30. Yokomitsu, "Kankaku Katsudō," 5, 7.
31. Yokomitsu, "Kankaku Katsudō," 8.
32. Yokomitsu, "Kankaku Katsudō," 5.
33. Peter Bürger, *Theory of the Avant-Garde*, trans. Michael Shaw (Minneapolis: University of Minnesota Press, 1984), 20–34, 47. See also Kamiya Tadataka, *Nihon no Dada* (Sapporo: Kyōbunsha, 1987); Miryam Sas, *Fault Lines: Cultural Memory and Japanese Surrealism* (Stanford, Calif.: Stanford University Press, 2002); Gennifer Weisenfeld, *MAVO: Japanese Artists and the Avant-Garde* (Berkeley: University of California Press, 2002).
34. Yokomitsu Riichi, "Hae," in *TYRZ*, 1:189, 192. Originally published in *Bungei Shunjū* 1, no. 5 (May 1923).
35. Yokomitsu, "Hae," 193.
36. Futabatei Shimei, *Ukigumo*, in *Futabatei Shimei Zenshū*, vol. 1 (Tokyo: Chikuma Shobō, 1984), 25. On onomatopoeia and literature in Japan, see Otsubo Heiji, *Giseigo no Kenkyū* (Tokyo: Kazama Shobō, 2006).
37. Inoue Ken, Kamiya Tadataka, and Hatori Tetsuya, eds., *Yokomitsu Riichi Jiten* (Tokyo: Ōfū Shoten, 2002), 156–57; Komori Yōichi, *Kōzo to shite no Katari* (Tokyo: Shin'yōsha, 1988), 446.
38. See Inoue, Kamiya, and Hatori, *Yokomitsu Riichi Jiten*, 75–76. Shiga's influence is discussed in Yoshida Hiroo, "Yokomitsu Riichi to Shiga Naoya," *Kokubungaku Kaishaku to Kanshō* 48, no. 13 (October 1983): 67; Miyaguchi Noriyuki, "Yokomitsu Riichi 'Onmi' Shi-ron," *Nagoya Kindai Bungaku Kenkyū* 11 (1993); and Miyaguchi Noriyuki, "Yokomitsu Riichi 'Marukusu no Saiban' o Megutte—Shiga Naoya to no Kanren o Kangaeru Tame no Ichi Kōsatsu," *Yokomitsu Riichi Kenkyū* 5 (2007): 63–73.
39. Yokomitsu Riichi, "Onmi," in *TYRZ*, 1:310.
40. Yokomitsu, "Onmi," 311.
41. Yokomitsu, "Onmi," 319–20.
42. Yokomitsu Riichi, "Teki," in *TYRZ*, 1:266–67. Originally published in *Shinshōsetsu*, January 1924.
43. Yokomitsu Riichi, "Atama Narabi ni Hara," in *TYRZ*, 1:399. Originally published in *Bungei Jidai* 1, no. 1 (October 1924).
44. Yokomitsu, "Atama Narabi ni Hara," 396. My translation is adapted from Seiji Lippit, *Topographies of Japanese Modernism* (New York: Columbia University Press, 2002), 78.
45. Kataoka Teppei, "Wakaki Dokusha ni Uttau," *Bungei Jidai* 1, no. 3 (December 1924): 2, 6.
46. Yokomitsu, "Atama Narabi ni Hara," 396–97.
47. Yokomitsu, "Atama Narabi ni Hara," 396, 399.
48. Kataoka, "Wakaki Dokusha ni Uttau," 7.
49. Kataoka, "Wakaki Dokusha ni Uttau," 5.
50. "Nanakai no Undō" was published in *Bungei Shunjū* 5, no. 9 (September 1927). *Shanhai* appeared under various titles before being collated into the novel; on *Shanhai*, see Lippit, *Topographies of Japanese Modernism*, Gregory Golley, *When*

Our Eyes No Longer See: Realism, Science, and Ecology in Japanese Literary Modernism (Cambridge, Mass.: Harvard University Asia Center, 2008), 121–59; Dennis C. Washburn, *Shanghai: A Novel* (Ann Arbor: Center for Japanese Studies, University of Michigan, 2001); Yamamoto Ryōsuke, *Yokomitsu Riichi to Shōsetsu no Ronri* (Tokyo: Kasama Shoin, 2008), 191–230; Maeda Ai, *Toshi Kūkan no Naka no Bungaku* (Tokyo: Chikuma Shobō, 1982), 365–401; Komori, *Kōzo to shite no Katari*, 507–37; Toeda Hirokazu, "Kaizōsha to Shanhai," *Ajia Yūgaku* 62 (2004).

51. Yokomitsu Riichi, "Machi no Soko," in *TYRZ*, 2:192–93. Originally published in *Bungei Jidai* 2, no. 8 (August 1925).
52. David Harvey, *The Urban Experience* (Baltimore: Johns Hopkins University Press, 1989), 229; Yokomitsu, "Machi no Soko," 193.
53. Yokomitsu, "Machi no Soko," 194.
54. Yokomitsu, "Machi no Soko," 195.
55. Yokomitsu, "Machi no Soko," 195.
56. Lippit, *Topographies of Japanese Modernism*, 99.
57. Yokomitsu, "Machi no Soko," 196.
58. Yokomitsu, "Machi no Soko," 195–97.
59. Yokomitsu Riichi, "Moji ni tsuite—Keishiki to Mekanizumu ni tsuite," in *TYRZ*, 13:114–15. Originally published as "Keishiki to Mekanizumu ni tsuite" in *Sōsaku Gekkan*, March 1929.
60. Yokomitsu, "Moji ni tsuite," 116. These include "Yuibutsuronteki Bungakuron ni tsuite," *Sōsaku Gekkan*, February 1928; and "Aikyō to Marukushizumu ni tsuite," *Sōsaku Gekkan*, January 1929; as well as "Shinkankaku-ha to Konmunizumu Bungaku," *Shinchō*, January 1928. See also Komori, *Kōzo to shite no Katari*, 496–506; Yamamoto, *Yokomitsu Riichi*, 43–77; Golley, *When Our Eyes*, 57–61, 140–46.
61. Yokomitsu, "Moji ni tsuite," 116.
62. Quoted in Toeda Hirokazu, "Yokomitsu Riichi no 'Gengokan'—Sono Dōjidaiteki Haikei o Megutte," in *Kawabata Bungaku e no Shikai* 6, ed. Kawabata Bungaku Kenkyūkai (Tokyo: Kyōiku Shuppan Sentā, 1990–1991), 115. Originally published in Yokomitsu Riichi, "Bungei Jihyō," *Bungei Shunjū* 6, no. 12 (December 1928).
63. See Toeda Hirokazu, "1926 Nihon, Bungaku to Eiga no Sōgū," *Hikaku Bungaku Kenkyū* 92 (October 2008), and Aaron Gerow, *A Page of Madness: Cinema and Modernity in 1920s Japan* (Ann Arbor: Center for Japanese Studies, University of Michigan, 2008).
64. Representative is Usui Yoshimi, *Kindai Bungaku Ronsō*, vol. 1 (Tokyo: Chikuma Shobō, 1956), 263–86. A more nuanced analysis is in Mariko Shigeta Schimmel, "Estranged Twins of Revolution: An Examination of Japanese Modernist and Proletarian Literature" (Ph.D. diss., Yale University, 2006). The debate is compiled in Hirano, Odagiri, and Yamamoto, *Gendai Nihon Bungaku Ronsōshi*, 1:565–632.
65. Yokomitsu Riichi, "Bungei Jihyō (II)," in *TYRZ*, 13:151–52. Originally published in *Bungei Shunjū*, November 1928. Yokomitsu cites Kurahara's essay "Geijutsu Undō Tōmen no Kinkyū Mondai," in *Senki*, August 1928.
66. Kurahara Korehito, "Keishiki no Mondai," in Hirano, Odagiri, and Yamamoto, *Gendai Nihon Bungaku Ronsōshi*, 1:577. Originally published in the *Asahi Shinbun*, November 20, 1928.
67. Kurahara, "Keishiki no Mondai," 578.

68. Kurahara, "Puroretaria Geijutsu no Naiyō to Keishiki," in Nihon Puroretaria Bungaku Hyōronshū 4: *Kurahara Korehito-shū* (Tokyo: Shin-Nihon Shuppansha, 1990), 173.
69. Kurahara Korehito, "Puroretaria Rearizumu e no Michi," in *Kurahara Korehito-shū*, 116. See also Mats Karlsson, "Kurahara Korehito's Road to Proletarian Realism," *Japan Review* 20 (2008): 231–73.
70. See Kikuchi Kan, "Bungei Sakuhin no Naiyōteki Kachi," in Hirano, Odagiri, and Yamamoto, *Gendai Nihon Bungaku Ronsōshi*, 1:71–73. For an English summary, see Mack, *Manufacturing Modern Japanese Literature*, 146–51.
71. Nakagawa Yoichi, *Keishikishugi Geijutsuron* (Tokyo: Shinchōsha, 1930), 77, 123–25, 100–101.
72. Nakagawa Yoichi, "Hanauta ni yoru Keishikishugi Riron no Hatten," in Hirano, Odagiri, and Yamamoto, *Gendai Nihon Bungaku Ronsōshi*, 1:596. Originally published in *Bungei Shunjū*, February 1929.
73. Yokomitsu, "Yuibutsuronteki Bungakuron ni tsuite," in *TYRZ*, 13:98–99.
74. Yokomitsu, "Yuibutsuronteki Bungakuron ni tsuite," 100.
75. "Samazamanaru Ishō" was originally published in *Kaizō*, September 1929; "Ashiru to Kame no Ko (I)" was originally published in *Bungei Shunjū*, May 1930. In English, see Paul Anderer, *Literature of the Lost Home: Kobayashi Hideo—Literary Criticism, 1924–1939* (Stanford, Calif.: Stanford University Press, 1995), and James Dorsey, *Critical Aesthetics: Kobayashi Hideo, Modernity, and Wartime Japan* (Cambridge, Mass.: Harvard University Asia Center, 2009).
76. Kobayashi Hideo, "Samazamanaru Ishō," in *Kobayashi Hideo Zenshū*, vol. 1 (Tokyo: Shinchōsha, 2002), 150; Kobayashi Hideo, "Ashiru to Kame no Ko (I)," in *Kobayashi Hideo Zenshū*, 1:184.
77. Kobayashi, "Ashiru to Kame no Ko (I)," 179, 183–84.
78. Kobayashi, "Samazamanaru Ishō," 149–50.
79. Kobayashi, "Samazamanaru Ishō," 133.

5. BRAVE NEW WORDS

1. See Nanette Twine, *Language and the Modern State: The Reform of Written Japanese* (London: Routledge, 1991); Lee Yeonsuk, *"Kokugo" to iu Shisō* (Tokyo: Iwanami Shoten, 1996); Nanette Twine, "The Genbunitchi Movement: Its Origin, Development, and Conclusion," *Monumenta Nipponica* 33, no. 3 (Winter 1978): 333–356; Nanette Twine, "Toward Simplicity: Script Reform Movements in the Meiji Period," *Monumenta Nipponica* 38, no. 2 (Summer 1983): 115–32; Nanette Twine, "Standardizing Written Japanese: A Factor in Modernization," *Monumenta Nipponica* 43, no. 4 (Winter 1988): 429–54; Christopher Robins, "Revisiting Year One of Japanese National Language: Inoue Hisashi's Literary Challenge," *Japanese Language and Literature* 40, no. 1 (April 2006): 37–58.
2. Tsuchiya Michio, *Kokugo Mondai Ronsōshi* (Tokyo: Tamagawa Daigaku Shuppanbu, 2005), 46–52, 67–68; Paul Hendrix Clark, "The *Kokugo* Revolution: Ueda Kazutoshi, Language Reform, and Language Education in Meiji Japan (1868–1912)" (Ph.D. diss., University of Pittsburg, 2002), 5, 94–95, 136–37; Robins, "Revisiting Year One," 40.

3. Tsuchiya, *Kokugo Mondai Ronsōshi*, 84; Clark, "The *Kokugo* Revolution," 195; Konno Shinji, *Nihongo no Kindai: Hazusareta Kango* (Tokyo: Chikuma Shinsho, 2014). See also Yamaguchi Yōji, *Nihongo o Tsukutta Otoko: Ueda Mannen to Sono Jidai* (Tokyo: Shūeisha, 2016), 383–422.
4. Lee, "*Kokugo*," 73–86; Clark, "The *Kokugo* Revolution," 96; See also Yamaguchi, *Nihongo o Tsukutta Otoko*, 174–200.
5. Hoshina Kōichi, *Kokugogaku Shōshi* (Tokyo: Dai-Nihon Tosho, 1900), 368; Clark, "The *Kokugo* Revolution," 113–14.
6. Konno, *Nihongo no Kindai*, 173–79, 203–8, 213; Tsuchiya, *Kokugo Mondai Ronsōshi*, 72, 74, 88; Tsukishima Hiroshi, *Rekishiteki Kanazukai: Sono Seiritsu to Tokuchō* (Tokyo: Yoshikawa Kōbunkan, 2014), 146. See also Seth Jacobowitz, *Writing Technology in Meiji Japan: A Media History of Modern Japanese Literature and Visual Culture* (Cambridge, Mass.: Harvard University Asia Center, 2015), 116–42, 195–226.
7. Konno Shinji, *"Genkai" o Yomu: Kotoba no Umi to Meiji no Nihongo* (Tokyo: Kadokawa Gakugei Shuppan, 2014), 23, 34, 41–44; Fukumoto Kazuo, *Watakushi no Jishoron* (Tokyo: Kawade Shobō Shinsha, 1977), 23.
8. Konno, *"Genkai" o Yomu*, 57.
9. Clark, "The *Kokugo* Revolution," 180.
10. Tsukishima *Rekishiteki Kanazukai*, 115, 133–34, 147, 151; Tsuchiya, *Kokugo Mondai Ronsōshi*, 130.
11. Haga Yaichi, "Jō," in *Dai-Nihon Kokugo Jiten*, ed. Ueda Kazutoshi (Tokyo: Fuzanbō, 1915–1919), 2–3.
12. Toeda Hirokazu, "Yokomitsu Riichi no 'Gengokan'—Sono Dōjidaiteki Haikei o Megutte," in *Kawabata Bungaku e no Shikai* 6, ed. Kawabata Bungaku Kenkyūkai (Tokyo: Kyōiku Shuppan Sentā, 1990–1991), 114; Furuta Tōsaku, "Meiji Ikō no Kokuji Mondai no Tenkai," in *Kanji to Kokugo Mondai*, ed. Satō Kiyoji, Kanji Kōza 11 (Tokyo: Meiji Shoin, 1989); Nanette Gottlieb, *Kanji Politics: Language Policy and Japanese Script* (London: Kegan International, 1995), 23, 50, 70, 76–77; Tsukishima, *Rekishiteki Kanazukai*, 14; Tsuchiya, *Kokugo Mondai Ronsōshi*, 104–5, 145–47, 156; Lee, "*Kokugo*," 24–27; Clark, "The *Kokugo* Revolution," 39–40. On Maejima, see Jacobowitz, *Writing Technology in Meiji Japan*, 43–47.
13. Cited in Tsuchiya, *Kokugo Mondai Ronsōshi*, 127. Ōgai's statement is dated June 25, 1907.
14. Mori Ōgai, "Kanazukai no Iken," in *Ōgai Zenshū*, vol. 26 (Tokyo: Iwanami Shoten, 1973), 281, 284.
15. Lee, "*Kokugo*," 200–201.
16. A full list of the orthographic changes under the proposal is in Minami Kensaku, *Shinkanazukai to Jōyō Kanji no Jibiki* (Tokyo: Jitsugyō no Nihonsha, 1925).
17. George Bedell, "Kokugaku Grammatical Theory" (Ph.D. diss., MIT, 1968). Yamada Tadao et al., *Yamada Yoshio Nenpu: Fueisō* (Tokyo: Hōbunkan, 1959), 4–5.
18. Yamada Yoshio, "Renga Kenkyū no Jōsetsu," *Shiso* 67 (May 1927): 272. Bedell, "Kokugaku Grammatical Theory," 144–46; Brian Hurley, "Toward a New Modern Vernacular: Tanizaki Jun'ichirō, Yamada Yoshio, and Shōwa Restoration Thought," *Journal of Japanese Studies* 39, no. 2 (Summer 2013): 368–72.
19. Yamada Yoshio, "Monbushō no Kanazukai Kaitei-an o Ronzu," *Myōjō (II)* 2, no. 2 (February 1925): 4.

20. Yosano Hiroshi et al., "Kanazukai Kaitei-an Kōgi," *Myōjō (II)* 2, no. 2 (February 1925): 62, 69.
21. Yamada, "Monbushō no Kanazukai," 10.
22. Yosano et al., "Kanazukai Kaitei-an Kōgi," 61–63.
23. Yamada, "Monbushō no Kanazukai," 5.
24. Yamada, "Monbushō no Kanazukai," 10–11.
25. Yosano et al., "Kanazukai Kaitei-an Kōgi," 73. "PHONETIQUE" appears in roman capital letters without the accent mark in the original Japanese text.
26. As *Ippan Gengogaku Kōgi* by the linguist Kobayashi Hideo (1903–1978).
27. Quoted in Lee, *"Kokugo,"* 201; originally published in Hoshina Kōichi, *Kokugogaku Seigi* (Tokyo: Dōbunkan, 1910).
28. Yamada, "Monbushō no Kanazukai," 10.
29. Yamada, "Monbushō no Kanazukai," 10.
30. Quoted in Tsuchiya, *Kokugo Mondai Ronsōshi*, 155.
31. Akutagawa Ryūnosuke, "Monbushō no Kanazukai Kaitei-an ni tsuite," in *Akutagawa Ryūnosuke Zenshū*, vol. 12 (Tokyo: Iwanami Shoten, 1996), 118–19. Originally published in *Kaizō*, March 1925.
32. Kawabata Yasunari, "Bangai Hadōchō," *Bungei Jidai* 2, no. 3 (March 1925): 46.
33. Yamada, "Monbushō no Kanazukai," 15.
34. Kawabata, "Bangai Hadōchō," 46.
35. Kawabata Yasunari, "Gendai Sakka no Bunshō o Ronzu," cited in Toeda, "Yokomitsu Riichi no 'Gengokan,'" 123.
36. Satō Ichiei, "Kokugo Bungakugo Mondai no Hōkō—Shinkanazukai Mondai o Ijō Suru Hitobito ni Ataeru Kōkaijō," *Bungei Jidai* 2, no. 6 (June 1925): 93–94.
37. For an overview, see Kikuzawa Sueo, *Kokuji Mondai no Kenkyū* (Tokyo: Iwanami Shoten, 1931).
38. Takahashi Yasuo, *Media no Akebono: Meiji Kaikokuki no Shinbun Shuppan Monogatari* (Tokyo: Nihon Keizai Shinbunsha, 1994), 24–27, 31, 36, 43.
39. Takahashi, *Media no Akebono*, 48–53, 62. See also Insatsu Hakubutsukan, ed., *Katsuji Bunmei Kaika: Motoki Shōzō ga Kizuita Kindai* (Tokyo: Toppan Insatsu, 2003).
40. Kikuzawa, *Kokuji Mondai no Kenkyū*, 132.
41. Takahashi, *Media no Akebono*, 145; Tsuchiya, *Kokugo Mondai Ronsōshi*, 147.
42. A list of these conventions appears in Tamaru Takurō, *Rōmajibun no Kenkyū* (Tokyo: Nihon no Rōmajisha, 1920).
43. Kikuzawa, *Kokuji Mondai no Kenkyū*, 102.
44. See Tsuchiya, *Kokugo Mondai Ronsōshi*, 141.
45. Tamaru, *Rōmajibun no Kenkyū*, 18–19.
46. Tanakadate Aikitsu, "Rigaku Kyōkai Zasshi o Rōmaji nite Hatsuda suru no Hatsugi oyobi Rōmaji yōhō iken," in *Kuzu no Ne: Tanakadate Aikitsu Ronbun Basshū* (Tokyo: Nihon no Rōmajisha, 1938), 3. Originally published in *Rigaku Kyōkai Zasshi*, no. 16 (1885).
47. Tanakadate, "Rigaku Kyōkai Zasshi," 3–6.
48. Tanakadate Aikitsu, "Hatsuonkō," in *Kuzu no ne*, 19–21. Originally published in *Rigaku Kyōkai Zasshi*, no. 17 (1885). See also Jacobowitz, *Writing Technology in Meiji Japan*, 40–41.
49. See also Tanakadate Aikitsu, "Nihonshiki Rōmaji wa Gōritekinari," in *Kuzu no Ne*. Originally published in *Gakushikwai Geppō*, no. 506 (May 1930).

50. Tanakadate Aikitsu, "Japanese Writing and the Romazi Movement," in *Kuzu no Ne*, 144, 149. Originally published in *Transactions of the Japan Society of London* 17 (1920).
51. Tanakadate Aikitsu, "Gendai Bunka to Kokuzi," in *Kuzu no Ne*, 18. Originally published in *Gakushikwai Geppō*, no. 470 (May 1927).
52. Tanakadate, "Gendai Bunka to Kokuzi," 18–23.
53. Tanakadate Aikitsu et al., *Rōmaji Hitorigeiko* (Tokyo: Nihon no Rōmajisha, 1914), 2–3.
54. See Konno, *Nihongo no Kindai*.
55. Tanakadate et al., *Rōmaji Hitorigeiko*, 4–5.
56. Tanakadate et al., *Rōmaji Hitorigeiko*, 54–55, 58.
57. Sakurai Satoshi, *Rōmaji Shuchō no Hyakkojō, Rōmaji no Hantairon o Yaburu* (Osaka: Teikoku Rōmaji Kurabu, 1930), 1–11.
58. Sakurai, *Rōmaji Shuchō*, 19.
59. See Lee, "*Kokugo*."
60. The entries in *rōmaji* are from April 7, 1909 to June 16, 1909, plus several days thereafter; see Nagahama Isao, *Takuboku Nikki Kōkan Katei no Shinsō* (Tokyo: Shakai Hyōronsha, 2013), 19–20.
61. Donald Keene, *The First Modern Japanese: The Life of Ishikawa Takuboku* (New York: Columbia University Press, 2016), 136–40.
62. Ishikawa Takuboku, *Romazi Nikki*, in *Takuboku Zenshū*, vol. 15 (Tokyo: Iwanami Shoten, 1954), 5–6. Kuwabara Takeo, "Kaisetsu," in *Ishikawa Takuboku Rōmazi Nikki* (Tokyo: Iwanami Shoten, 1977), 246. Charles Shirō Inouye, "In the Scopic Regime of Discovery: Ishikawa Takuboku's *Rōmaji Nikki* and the Gendered Premise of Self-Identity," *Review of Japanese Culture and Society* 6 (December 1994): 13–14, 20.
63. Hamada Atsushi, *Kokugoshi no Shomondai* (Osaka: Izumi Shoin, 1986), 504–8.
64. Tanakadate, "Nihonshiki Rōmaji wa Gōritekinari," 48.
65. Kikuzawa cites Saussure in French.
66. Tanakadate, "Nihonshiki Rōmaji wa Gōritekinari," 49. The terms appear in English in the original essay.
67. Suehiro Izutarō, *Nihon Rōmajikai Panfuretto 5: Nihongo no Yukidzumari Mondai* (Tokyo: Nihon Rōmajikai, 1928), 1, 4.
68. Tamaru Takurō, *Nihon Rōmajikai Panfuretto 2: Nihongo no Sekaiteki Kakikata* (Tokyo: Nihon Rōmajikai, 1928), 3; Tōkyō Teikoku Daigaku Rōmajikai, *Rōmaji Nenpō 1932* (Tokyo: Nihon Rōmajikai Shuppanbu, 1931), 15.
69. Tanakadate, "Japanese Writing," 137, 139. See also Tōkyō Teikoku Daigaku Rōmajikai, *Rōmaji Nenpō 1932*, 12.
70. Tamaru, *Nihon Rōmajikai Panfuretto* 2, 3–5.
71. See Terry Martin, *The Affirmative Action Empire: Nations and Nationalism in the Soviet Union, 1923–1939* (Ithaca, N.Y.: Cornell University Press, 2001), 182–207; Nergis Ertürk, *Grammatology and Literary Modernity in Turkey* (Oxford: Oxford University Press, 2011), 89–94; Yurou Zhong, "Script Crisis and Literary Modernity in China, 1916–1958" (Ph.D. diss., Columbia University, 2014).
72. Tanakadate Aikitsu, "Hasigaki," in Kikuzawa, *Kokuji Mondai no Kenkyū*, iii–iv, vii.
73. Yamada Yoshio, "Jō," in Kikuzawa, *Kokuji Mondai no Kenkyū*, vi.
74. Kikuzawa, *Kokuji Mondai no Kenkyū*, 42.

75. Esther Schor, *Bridge of Words: Esperanto and the Dream of a Universal Language* (New York: Metropolitan Books, 2016), 3, 5, 10, 28–34, 59–77.
76. Ishiguro Yoshimi, *Esuperanto no Manabikata: Dokushū Sanjūnichi (Memlernolibro de Esperanto)* (Tokyo: Hakubunkan, 1931), 16.
77. Ian Rapley, "Green Star Japan: Language and Internationalism in the Japanese Esperanto Movement, 1905–1944" (Ph.D. diss., University of Oxford, 2013), 5. Sho Konishi, "Translingual World Order: Language Without Culture in Post-Russo-Japanese War Japan," *Journal of Asian Studies* 72, no. 1 (February 2013): 91.
78. Rapley, "Green Star Japan," 16, 37. The language was first introduced in "Sekaigo no Hyō" in the *Yomiuri Shinbun* on May 2, 1888, but it was not until after the Russo-Japanese War that the grammar and vocabulary were made available; Asahiga Noboru and Hagiwara Yōko, *Esuperanto Undō no Tenbō I (Perspektivo sur la Esperanto-Movado)* (Tokyo: Sekai Bunka Kenkyūkai, 1978), 199.
79. Konishi, "Translingual World Order," 99. See also Syozi Nobuhiko et al., eds., *El La Revuo Orienta: JEI Gojūnen no Ayumi 1; 1920–1936* (Tokyo: Japan Esperanto Institute, 1976).
80. Konishi, "Translingual World Order," 91, 94–100.
81. Kaneda Tsunesaburō, *Dokushū Jizai Esuperanto Kōgi (Lekcioj pri la lingvo Internacia Esperanto)* (Tokyo: Nihon Hyōronsha, 1922), 5, 17; Ishiguro, *Esuperanto no Manabikata*, 5, 10; Schor, *Bridge of Words*, 23. JEI founder Osaka Kenji makes a similar point in *Esuperanto Shōkei (Esperanto Kompleta Kurso por Japanoj)* (Tokyo: Esuperanto Gakkai, 1927), 1.
82. Ishiguro, *Esuperanto no Manabikata*, 10–12; Schor, *Bridge of Words*, 16, 81; Kaneda, *Dokushū Jizai Esuperanto Kōgi*, 13. See also Puroteraria Kagaku Kenkyūjo, ed., *Puroretaria Esuperanto Kōza (Proleta Kurso de Esperanto)* (Tokyo: Yōbunsha, 1968), 4; originally published in 1930.
83. Ishiguro, *Esuperanto no Manabikata*, 13; Kaneda, *Dokushū Jizai Esuperanto Kōgi*, 16.
84. "Esuperanto-yaku Sareta Nihon Bungaku Sakuhin," http://www.jei.or.jp/evento/2013/tradukajxoj.htm.
85. Hasegawa Futabatei, *Sekaigo (Esuperanto)* (Tokyo: Saiunkaku, 1906), 1–2; Rapley, "Green Star Japan," 46; Asahiga and Hagiwara, *Esuperanto Undō no Tenbō I*, 111; Konishi, "Translingual World Order," 110.
86. L. L. Zamenhof, *Sekaigo Dokuhon*, trans. Hasegawa Futabatei (Tokyo: Saiunkaku, 1906).
87. Cited in Asahiga and Hagiwara, *Esuperanto Undō no Tenbō I*, 111; Futabatei Shimei, *Esuperanto no Hanashi*, in Gendai Nihon Bungaku Taikei 1, *Seiji Shōsetsu Tsubouchi Shōyō Futabatei Shimei-shū* (Tokyo: Chikuma Shobō, 1971), 376; Konishi, "Translingual World Order," 100.
88. Schor, *Bridge of Words*, 71.
89. Asahiga and Hagiwara, *Esuperanto Undō no Tenbō I*, 117. See also Thomas W. Burkman, *Japan and the League of Nations: Empire and World Order, 1914–1938* (Honolulu: University of Hawai`i Press, 2008), 127–28.
90. Yanagita Kunio, "Jenēbu no Omoide," in *Yanagita Kunio Zenshū*, vol. 3 (Tokyo: Chikuma Shobō, 1989), 390, 394.
91. Yanagita, "Jenēbu no Omoide," 398; Nara Hiroshi, "Yanagita Kunio to Esuperanto," in Asahiga and Hagiwara, *Esuperanto Undō no Tenbō I*, 148.

92. Schor, *Bridge of Words*, 154. Konishi, "Translingual World Order," 105–6. On Esperanto and Baha'i, see Schor, *Bridge of Words*, 182–95.
93. Asahiga and Hagiwara, *Esuperanto Undō no Tenbō I*, 117.
94. Yanagita, "Jenēbu no Omoide," 395.
95. Yanagita Kunio, "Nihon ga Buntan Subeki Ninmu," *La Revuo Orienta* 8, no. 1 (January 1927); cited in Asahiga and Hagiwara, *Esuperanto Undō no Tenbō I*, 117–18.
96. Osaka, *Esuperanto Shōkei*, 148.
97. Zamenhof, *Sekaigo*, 4; Osaka, *Esuperanto Shōkei*, unpaginated preface page.
98. Asahiga and Hagiwara, *Esuperanto Undō no Tenbō I*, 64; Konishi, "Translingual World Order," 99–104.
99. Osaka Kenji and Akita Ujaku, *Mohan Esuperanto Dokushū (Memlernanto de Esperanto)* (Tokyo: Sōbunkaku, 1927), unpaginated preface page.
100. Osaka and Akita, *Mohan Esuperanto Dokushū*, unpaginated preface page.
101. Akita Ujaku, *Ujaku Jiden* (Tokyo: Shinhyōronsha, 1953), 14; Asahiga and Hagiwara, *Esuperanto Undō no Tenbō I*, 113; Akita Ujaku Kenkyūkai, *Zoku Akita Ujaku Sono Zenshigoto* (Tokyo: Kyōeisha Shuppan, 1976), 7–13.
102. Akita Ujaku Kenkyūkai, *Zoku Akita Ujaku*, 24–25; Asahiga and Hagiwara, *Esuperanto Undō no Tenbō I*, 113; Rapley, "Green Star Japan," 80. On Eroshenko, see Schor, *Bridge of Words*, 172–75, and Konishi, "Translingual World Order," 105–9.
103. Akita Ujaku Kenkyūkai, *Zoku Akita Ujaku*, 21, 36–37; Rapley, "Green Star Japan," 192. The quote is from Akita Ujaku, *Wakaki Souēto Roshiya* (Tokyo: Sōbunkaku, 1929), 102–3.
104. Akita, *Wakaki Souēto Roshiya*, 102.
105. Schor, *Bridge of Words*, 170–79.
106. Osaka and Akita, *Mohan Esuperanto Dokushū*, 83–85.
107. Puroretaria Kagaku Kenkyūjo, *Puroretaria Esuperanto Kōza*, 1, 2, 4.
108. Puroretaria Kagaku Kenkyūjo, *Puroretaria Esuperanto Kōza*, 7, 8.
109. Puroretaria Kagaku Kenkyūjo, *Puroretaria Esuperanto Kōza*, 9–10, 21, 53.
110. Schor, *Bridge of Words*, 64.
111. Takeuchi Jirō, *Puroretaria Esuperanto Undō ni tsuite* (Tokyo: Shihōshō Keijikyoku, 1939), 19–22, 46, 55, 233.
112. Schor, *Bridge of Words*, 153–55, 175–79; Takeuchi, *Puroretaria Esuperanto*, 241.
113. On this point, see Nanette Gottlieb, "Language and Politics: The Reversal of Postwar Script Reform Policy in Japan," *Journal of Asian Studies* 53, no. 4 (November 1994): 1175–98.

6. THE MEDIUM IS THE MASSES

1. Hayama Yoshiki, "Gokuchūki," in *Hayama Yoshiki Nikki* (Tokyo: Chikuma Shobō, 1971), 3–15. For a longer discussion of Hayama's diary, see Nathan Shockey, "Words Within Walls: Reading Hayama Yoshiki's Prison Diaries," in *Censorship, Media, and Literary Culture in Japan*, ed. Tomi Suzuki, Toeda Hirokazu, Hori Hikari, and Munakata Kazushige (Tokyo: Shin'yōsha, 2012), 124–26.
2. Hayama Yoshiki, "Daihyōsaku ni tsuite," in *Hayama Yoshiki Zenshū*, vol. 5 (Tokyo: Chikuma Shobō, 1976), 159. Originally published in *Kyūshū Bunka* 2, no. 5 (August 1935).

3. Hayama Yoshiki, "Inbaifu o Kaita Toki no Omoide," in *Hayama Yoshiki Zenshū*, 5:158. Originally published in *Bunshō Kurabu* 13, no. 7 (July 1928).
4. Hayama Yoshiki, "Rōgoku no Hannichi," in *Hayama Yoshiki Zenshū*, vol. 1 (Tokyo: Chikuma Shobō, 1975), 228–36. Originally published in *Bungei Sensen* 1, no. 5 (October 1924).
5. Hayama Yoshiki, "Inbaifu," in *Hayama Yoshiki Zenshū*, 1:236. Originally published in *Bungei Sensen* 2, no. 7 (November 1925).
6. Kuroiwa Hisako, *Pan to Pen: Shakaishugisha Sakai Toshihiko to "Baibunsha" no Tatakai* (Tokyo: Kōdansha, 2010), 97. On Christianity, radicalism, and Tolstoyan thought, see Sho Konishi, *Anarchist Modernity: Cooperatism and Japanese-Russian Intellectual Relations in Modern Japan* (Cambridge, Mass.: Harvard University Asia Center, 2013), 93–143.
7. Umemori Naoyuki, *Shoki Shakaishugi no Topogurafī: Ōsugi Sakae to Sono Jidai* (Tokyo: Yūshisha, 2016), 1–4, 14, 98–99; Umemori Naoyuki, "Heiminsha o Sekai e," in *Teikoku o Ute: Heiminsha Hyakunen Kokusai Shimupojiumu*, ed. Umemori Naoyuki (Tokyo: Ronsōsha, 2005), ii–iii; Ben Middleton, "Heiminsha to Gurōbarizumu," in Umemori, *Teikoku o Ute*, 12–13.
8. Kuroiwa, *Pan to Pen*, 107–13. On the birth of anti-imperialist thought in Japan, see Robert Tierney, *Monster of the Twentieth Century: Kōtoku Shūsui and Japan's First Anti-Imperialist Movement* (Berkeley: University of California Press, 2015), 1–12, 25–56.
9. The phrase appears in the paper's manifesto, attributed to Heiminsha *dōjin*; see Sakai Toshihiko, "Sengen," in *Sakai Toshihiko Zenshū*, vol. 3 (Tokyo: Hōritsu Bunkasha, 1970), 3. See also Kuroiwa, *Pan to Pen*, 115; Ōta Hideaki, "Sakai Toshihiko no Shisō Keisei to Hisenron," in *Sakai Toshihiko: Shoki Shakaishugi no Shisōken*, ed. Koshōji Toshiyasu (Tokyo: Ronsōsha, 2016), 49–56. On *Hisenron*, see Sho Konishi, "Translingual World Order: Language Without Culture in Post-Russo-Japanese War Japan," *Journal of Asian Studies* 72, no. 1 (February 2013), and Konishi, *Anarchist Modernity*, 142–208.
10. Yamaizumi Susumu, "Heiminsha no Hisenron to Torusutoi," in Umemori, *Teikoku o Ute*, 117–22. Tolstoy's essay, translated as "Nichirō Sensōron," was published August 7, 1904. See also Tierney, *Monster of the Twentieth Century*, 96–114.
11. Hasegawa Hiroshi, "*Nikkan Heimin Shinbun* Kaisetsu," in *Meiji Shakaishugi Shiryōshū*, ed. Rōdō Undōshi Kenkyūkai, vol. 4 (Tokyo: Meiji Bunken Shiryōkankōkai, 1961), 8–10.
12. Kuroiwa, *Pan to Pen*, 132–34.
13. Quoted in Kōno Kensuke, "Meijiki Bungakusha to Media Kisei no Kōbō," in Suzuki, Toeda, Hori, and Munakata, *Censorship, Media*, 59; see also Jay Rubin, *Injurious to Public Morals: Writers and the Meiji State* (Seattle: University of Washington Press, 1984), 15–31.
14. Kuroiwa, *Pan to Pen*, 43.
15. Umemori Naoyuki, "Nijūseiki no Shōnen kara Ojisan e—Sakai Toshihiko ni okeru 'Genbunitchi' 'Katei' 'Shakaishugi,'" in Koshōji, *Sakai Toshihiko*, 97–101; Umemori, *Shoki Shakaishugi no Topogurafī*, 276–80.
16. Sakai Toshihiko, *Genbun Itchi: Futsūbun*, in *Sakai Toshihiko Zenshū*, vol. 1 (Tokyo: Hōritsu Bunkasha, 1971), 497, 499.

17. Ishii Atsushi, *Nihon Kindai Kōkyō Toshokanshi no Kenkyū* (Tokyo: Nihon Toshokan Kyōkai, 1972), 213–15.
18. Yamaizumi Susumu, "Sakai Toshihiko to 'Fuyu no Jidai,'" in Umemori, *Teikoku o Ute*, 125–29.
19. Kuroiwa, *Pan to Pen*, 14, 75, 215–18, 253, 286–88.
20. Moriyama Shigeo, *Taigyaku Jiken Bungaku Sakkaron* (Tokyo: San'ichi Shobō, 1980), 31–33; Donald Keene, *The First Modern Japanese: The Life of Ishikawa Takuboku* (New York: Columbia University Press, 2016), 188–200.
21. Nagai Kafū, "Hanabi," in *Nagai Kafū Zenshū*, vol. 15 (Tokyo: Iwanami Shoten, 1963), 12; Moriyama, *Taigyaku Jiken*, 113–14, 123, 129.
22. Yamamoto Sanehiko, "Rasseru no Raichō," in Shuppanjin no Ibun 2: *Kaizōsha Yamamoto Sanehiko* (Tokyo: Kurita Shoten, 1968), 55.
23. Bertrand Russell, *Principles of Social Reconstruction* (London: Allen and Unwin, 1916), 224.
24. On Einstein in Japan, see Gregory Golley, *When Our Eyes No Longer See: Realism, Science, and Ecology in Japanese Literary Modernism* (Cambridge, Mass.: Harvard University Asia Center, 2008), 30–33.
25. Doi Bansui, "Kaizō no Dairei," *Kaizō* 1, no. 1 (April 1919): 48–49.
26. Tsubouchi Shōyō, "Shakai Kaizō to Engeki," *Kaizō* 1, no. 5 (August 1919): 91.
27. See Yamada Yoshio, "Shakai no Kisoteki Kaizō wa Fujin no Ninmu," *Kaizō* 1, no. 1 (April 1919); Kita Ikki, *Nihon Kaizō Hōan Taikō* (Tokyo: Nishida Mitsugi, 1926).
28. Matsubara Kazue, *Kaizōsha to Yamamoto Sanehiko* (Kagoshima: Nanpō Shinsha, 2002), 98; Seki Chūka et al., eds., *Zasshi "Kaizō" no Shijūnen* (Tokyo: Kōwadō, 1977), 17, 37, 44–45.
29. Kurokawa Iori, *Teikoku ni Kōsuru Shakai Undō: Daiichiji Nihon Kyōsantō no Shisō to Undō* (Tokyo: Yūgensha, 2014), 39–41.
30. Kurokawa, *Teikoku ni Kōsuru Shakai*, 37–38, 47; Kōno Kensuke, *Ken'etsu to Bungaku: 1920-nendai no Kōbō* (Tokyo: Kawade Shobō Shinsha, 2009), 53.
31. Obinata Sumio, "Home Ministry Censorship and the Publishing Culture of Pre-WWII Japan," in Suzuki, Toeda, Hori, and Munakata, *Censorship, Media*, 75–78; Kōno, *Ken'etsu to Bungaku*, 31–42, 56–59, 61–65. Jonathan Abel argues that the intellectual tendencies of *Kaizō* resulted in tighter restrictions than for centrist magazines; *Redacted: The Archive of Censorship in Transwar Japan* (Berkeley: University of California Press, 2012), 154–60.
32. Seki et al., *Zasshi "Kaizō" no Shijūnen*, 55.
33. Nagamine Shigetoshi, *Zasshi to Dokusha no Kindai* (Tokyo: Nihon Editā Sukūru Shuppanbu, 1997), 21–27.
34. Seki et al., *Zasshi "Kaizō" no Shijūnen*, 55.
35. Kurokawa, *Teikoku ni Kōsuru Shakai*, 36, 44–48.
36. Odagiri Susumu, "Kaisetsu," in *Tane Maku Hito Fukkokuban Bessatsu* (Tokyo: Nihon Kindai Bungaku Kenkyūjo, 1961), 8.
37. Imano Kenzō, "Kaisō no Naka kara," in Odagiri, *Tane Maku Hito Fukkokuban Bessatsu*, 4.
38. Tanemakisha, untitled editors' note, unpaginated inside cover, *Tane Maku Hito* 1, no. 1 (October 1921).

39. Odagiri, "Kaisetsu," 41.
40. Kōno, *Ken'etsu to Bungaku*, 95.
41. Ko Youngran, "Censorship Empires, Illegal Commodities," in Suzuki, Toeda, Hori, and Munakata, *Censorship, Media*, 127–31. See also Norma Field and Heather Bowen-Struyk, eds., *For Dignity, Justice, and Revolution: An Anthology of Japanese Proletarian Literature* (Chicago: University of Chicago Press, 2016), 4.
42. On censorship in Japan's colonies, see Kōno Kensuke, ed., *Ken'etsu no Teikoku: Bunka no Tōsei to Saiseisan* (Tokyo: Shin'yōsha, 2014).
43. See Mika Endo, "Pedagogical Experiments with Working Class Children in Prewar Japan" (Ph.D. diss., University of Chicago, 2011), 24–59; Field and Bowen-Struyk, *For Dignity, Justice, and Revolution*, 188–92.
44. Murayama Tomoyoshi, *Murayama Tomoyoshi Gurafikku no Shigoto* (Tokyo: Hon no Izumisha, 2001), 12–16; Yanase Masamu Kenkyūkai, ed., *Yanase Masamu: Hankotsu no Seishin to Jidai o Mitsumeru Me* (Tokyo: Yanase Masamu Kenkyūkai, 1999), 11–1, 35–37.
45. Germaine Hoston, *Marxism and the Crisis of Development in Prewar Japan* (Princeton, N.J.: Princeton University Press, 1986), 35–41, 65–68, 95–104.
46. For a summary of the massification debate, see Usui Yoshimi, *Kindai Bungaku Ronsō* (Tokyo: Chikuma Shobō, 1975), 1:231–48. For analysis, see Heather Bowen-Struyk, "Rethinking Japanese Proletarian Literature" (Ph.D. diss., University of Michigan, 2001), 126–39, and Kurihara Yukio, *Puroretaria Bungaku to Sono Jidai* (Tokyo: Impakuto Shuppankai, 2004), 82–109. On the capitalism debate, see Gavin Walker, *The Sublime Perversion of Capital: Marxist Theory and the Politics of History in Modern Japan* (Durham, N.C.: Duke University Press, 2016), 28–44.
47. See Ozaki Hotsuki, *Taishū Bungaku* (Tokyo: Kinokuniya Shoten, 1964), 19–60.
48. Hirabayashi Hatsunosuke, "Shōhin to shite no Kindai Shōsetsu," in *Hirabayashi Hatsunosuke Bungei Hyōron Zenshū*, vol. 1 (Tokyo: Bunsendō Shoten, 1975), 305.
49. Hirabayashi, "Shōhin to shite no Kindai Shōsetsu," 302, 308–9.
50. Nii Itaru, "Shuppan Shihonshugi to Chojutsuka," *Chūō Kōron*, April 1928, 58–59.
51. Takabatake Motoyuki, "Taishūshugi to Shihonshugi," *Chūō Kōron*, April 1928, 70–73.
52. Hasegawa Nyozekan, "Seijiteki Gainen to shite no Taishū," *Chūō Kōron*, April 1928, 68.
53. Aono Suekichi, "Taishō no Genjitsu ni tsuite," *Chūō Kōron*, April 1928, 74–76.
54. Takabatake, "Taishūshugi to Shihonshugi," 70–72.
55. Ōya Sōichi, "Shuppan Kakumei no Shōrisha," *Chūō Kōron*, December 1928, 246–47.
56. Takabatake Motoyuki, "Yonin Yoiro," *Chūō Kōron*, December 1928, 239.
57. Heibonsha Kyōiku Sangyō Sentā, ed., *Heibonsha Rokujūnenshi* (Tokyo: Heibonsha, 1974), 83–87, 92–93. The ad ran March 29, 1927.
58. Heibonsha Kyōiku Sangyō Sentā, *Heibonsha* Rokujūnenshi, 104–6.
59. I owe in full my attention to this crucial connection to Bowen-Struyk's important work in "Rethinking Japanese Proletarian Literature," 121–49. See also G. T. Shea, *Leftwing Literature in Japan: A Brief History of the Proletarian Literary Movement* (Tokyo: Hōsei University Press, 1964), 281.

60. Kawabata Yasunari, "Bungei Jihyō," *Bungei Shunjū*, August 1928; quoted in Uranishi Kazuhiko, "'Tokunaga Sunao'-hen Kaisetsu," in *Sakka no Jiden 68—Tokunaga Sunao*, ed. Uranishi Kazuhiko (Tokyo: Nihon Tosho Sentā, 1998), 274.
61. Tokunaga Sunao, "Watashi no Bungakuteki Jijoden"; quoted in Uranishi, *Sakka no Jiden 68*, 198–99.
62. Tokunaga, "Watashi no Bungakuteki Jijoden," 196–98.
63. Tokunaga, "Watashi no Bungakuteki Jijoden," 199.
64. Tokunaga, "Watashi no Bungakuteki Jijoden," 199–201.
65. Tokunaga, "Watashi no Bungakuteki Jijoden," 204–5.
66. Yokoyama Kazuo, *Nihon no Shuppan Insatsu Rōdō Undō Senzen Senchūhen*, vol. 1 (Tokyo: Nyūsusha, 1998), 227–28.
67. A narrative of the strike is in Yokoyama, *Nihon no Shuppan*, 491–589.
68. Yokoyama, *Nihon no Shuppan*, 220–31; Mizunuma Tatsuo, *Meiji Taishōki Jiritsuteki Rōdō Undō no Ashiato* (Tokyo: JCA, 1979), 110–15; Heibonsha Kyōiku Sangyō Sentā, *Nihon no Shuppan*, 59–67.
69. Tokunaga Sunao, "*Taiyō no Nai Machi* wa Ika ni Shite Seisaku Sareta ka," in *Kōki Puroretaria Bungaku Hyōronshū* 2 (Tokyo: Shin-Nihon Shuppansha, 1990), 246. Originally published in *Puroretaria Geijutsu Kyōtei*, no. 3 (April 1930).
70. Tokunaga, "*Taiyō no Nai Machi*," 249.
71. Tokunaga Sunao, *Taiyō no Nai Machi* (Tokyo: Senkisha, 1929), 3. In the original edition the prince's name is censored; it is restored in later editions as "Sesshō."
72. Tokunaga, *Taiyō no Nai Machi*, 3–6. My reading of this scene is informed by that of Kōno, *Shomotsu no Kindai*, 185–87.
73. Strike flyer, Kyōdō Insatsu Sōgi, February 1926 folder, Ōhara Institute for Social Research, Hōsei University.
74. Tokunaga, *Taiyō no Nai Machi*, 25–26.
75. Yokoyama *Nihon no Shuppan*, 523–25. See also Strike flyers, Shūeisha Sōgi, November 1926; Nisshin Insatsu Sōgi, September 1927; Kaishinsha Sōgi (undated) folder, Ōhara Institute for Social Research, Hōsei University.
76. Tokunaga, *Taiyō no Nai Machi*, 88–91. For a historical account of the negotiations, see Yokoyama, *Nihon no Shuppan*, 531–57.
77. Strike flyer, Kyōdō Insatsu Sōgi, February 1926 folder, Ōhara Institute for Social Research, Hōsei University.
78. Strike flyers, Yūrindō Insatsu Sōgi, May 1925; Sanseidō Insatsu Sōgi, June 1925; Seibidō Sōgi, August 1925 folder; and strike flyers, Heibonsha Sōgi, February 1929 folder, Ōhara Institute for Social Research, Hōsei University.
79. Yokoyama, *Nihon no Shuppan*, 663–66.
80. Strike flyers, Tōkyō Nichinichi Shinbun Sōgi, June 1930 folder; Kantō Shuppan Rōdō Kumiai folder (undated), Ōhara Institute for Social Research, Hōsei University; Shimura Akiko, *Gariban Monogatari* (Tokyo: Taishūkan Shoten, 2012), 56–67, 88–92, 96–98; Yokoyama, *Nihon no Shuppan*, 518.
81. Yokoyama, *Nihon no Shuppan*, 652.
82. Naimushō Keihokyoku, *Shuppan Keisatsu Gaikan* (Tokyo: Naimushō Keihokyoku, 1931).

CONCLUSION

1. Notable exceptions include the debate on the development of Japanese capitalism and critiques by Marxists like Uno Kōzō (1897–1977) and Tosaka Jun (1900–1945). See Gavin Walker, *The Sublime Perversion of Capital: Marxist Theory and the Politics of History in Modern Japan* (Durham, N.C.: Duke University Press, 2016), and Ken C. Kawashima et al., eds., *Tosaka Jun: A Critical Reader* (Ithaca, N.Y.: Cornell University Press, 2013).
2. On *shinsho*, see Kano Masanao, *Iwanami Shinsho no Rekishi* (Tokyo: Iwanami Shoten 2006), 1–65. For a fascinating discussion of magazine media and criticism in the 1930s, see Ōsawa Satoshi, *Hihyō Media-ron: Senzenki Nihon no Rondan to Bundan* (Tokyo: Iwanami Shoten, 2015).
3. See Mimasaka Tarō, Fujita Chikamasa, and Watanabe Kiyoshi, *Yokohama Jiken* (Tokyo: Nihon Editā Sukūru Shuppanbu, 1977), and Kuroda Hidetoshi, *Yokohama Jiken* (Tokyo: Kakugei Shorin, 1975).
4. Toeda Hirokazu, "The Home Ministry and GHQ/SCAP as Censors of Literature: Media Regulations and the Battle Over Expression in 1920s–1940s Japan," in *Censorship, Media, and Literary Culture in Japan*, ed. Tomi Suzuki, Toeda Hirokazu, Hori Hikari, and Munakata Kazushige (Tokyo: Shin'yōsha, 2012), 96–107; Yamamoto Taketoshi, *Senryōki Media Bunseki* (Tokyo: Hōsei Daigaku Shuppankyoku, 1996).
5. Adam Bronson, *One Hundred Million Philosophers: Science of Thought and the Culture of Democracy in Postwar Japan* (Honolulu: University of Hawai`i Press, 2016), 17–21.
6. See Atsuko Ueda et al, eds., *The Politics and Literature Debate in Postwar Japanese Criticism, 1945–52* (Lanham, Md.: Lexington Books, 2017), and Nanette Gottlieb, "Language and Politics: The Reversal of Postwar Script Reform Policy in Japan," *Journal of Asian Studies* 53, no. 4 (November 1994): 1175–98.
7. The title of an essay by Ara Masahito (1913–1979) published in *Kindai Bungaku*, March 1946.
8. For a nuanced discussion of the mixed character of contemporary reading practices, see Andrew Piper, *Book Was There: Reading in Electronic Times* (Chicago: University of Chicago Press, 2012).
9. On the concept of postprint, see N. Katherine Hayles and Jessica Pressman, "Making, Critique: A Media Framework," in *Comparative Textual Media: Transforming the Humanities in the Postprint Era*, ed. N. Katherine Hayles and Jessica Pressman (Minneapolis: University of Minnesota Press, 2013).
10. John B. Thompson, *Merchants of Culture: The Publishing Business in the Twenty-First Century* (New York: Plume, 2012), 313–76.
11. See, for example, Piper, *Book Was There*, 45–61.
12. N. Katherine Hayles, *How We Became Posthuman: Virtual Bodies in Cybernetics, Literature, and Informatics* (Chicago: University of Chicago Press, 1999), 2, 12–14, 42.
13. Bernard Stiegler, *Taking Care of Youth and the Generations*, trans. Stephen Barker (Stanford, Calif.: Stanford University Press, 2010), 17–22.
14. John Durham Peters, *The Marvelous Clouds: Toward a Philosophy of Elemental Media* (Chicago: University of Chicago Press, 2015), 326–29. See also John

Durham Peters, *Speaking into the Air: A History of the Idea of Communication* (Chicago: University of Chicago Press, 1999), 1–31.

15. Tung-Hui Hu, *A Prehistory of the Cloud* (Cambridge, Mass.: MIT Press, 2015), xiii. An exploration of the internet's physical infrastructure is in Andrew Blum, *Tubes: A Journey to the Center of the Internet* (New York: Ecco, 2012).
16. Kenneth Goldsmith, "The Artful Accidents of Google Books," *New Yorker*, December 4, 2013, https://www.newyorker.com/books/page-turner/the-artful-accidents-of-google-books; see also Piper, *Book Was There*, 1–23.

SELECTED BIBLIOGRAPHY

Abe Yoshishige. *Abe Yoshishige Senshū*. 5 vols. Tokyo: Oyama Shoten, 1948–1949.

——. *Iwanami Shigeo-den*. Tokyo: Iwanami Shoten, 1957.

Abel, Jonathan. *Redacted: The Archive of Censorship in Transwar Japan*. Berkeley: University of California Press, 2012.

Akita Ujaku. *Ujaku Jiden*. Tokyo: Shinhyōronsha, 1953.

——. *Wakaki Souēto Roshiya*. Tokyo: Sōbunkaku, 1929.

Akita Ujaku Kenkyūkai. *Zoku Akita Ujaku Sono Zenshigoto*. Tokyo: Kyōeisha Shuppan, 1976.

Akutagawa Ryūnosuke. *Akutagawa Ryūnosuke Zenshū*. 24 vols. Tokyo: Iwanami Shoten, 1995–1998.

Anderer, Paul. *Literature of the Lost Home: Kobayashi Hideo—Literary Criticism, 1924–1939*. Stanford, Calf.: Stanford University Press, 1995.

Anderson, Benedict. *Imagined Communities: Reflections on the Origin and Spread of Nationalism*. New York: Verso, 1991.

Anzai Ikurō and I Sūgyon, eds. *Kurarute Undō to "Tane Maku Hito": Hansen Bungaku Undō "Kurarute" no Nihon to Chōsen to no Tenkai*. Tokyo: Ochanomizu Shobō, 2004.

Aono Suekichi. *Aono Suekichi Senshū*. Tokyo: Kawade Shobō, 1950.

Asahiga Noboru and Hagiwara Yōko. *Esuperanto Undō no Tenbō I (Perspektivo sur la Esperanto-Movado)*. Tokyo: Sekai Bunka Kenkyūkai, 1978.

Barker, Nicholas, ed. *A Potencie of Life: Books in Society*. London: British Library, 1993.

Baron, Sabrina Alcorn, Eric N. Lindquist, and Eleanor Shevlin, eds. *Agent of Change: Print Culture Studies After Elizabeth L. Eisenstein*. Amherst: University of Massachusetts Press, 2007.

Beckmann, George M., and Okubo Genji. *The Japanese Communist Party, 1922–1945*. Stanford, Calif.: Stanford University Press, 1969.

Bedell, George. "Kokugaku Grammatical Theory." Ph.D. diss., MIT, 1968.

Benjamin, Walter. *Illuminations*. Trans. Harry Zohn. New York: Schocken Books, 1968.

——. *Reflections*. Trans. Edmund Jephcott. New York: Schocken Books, 1978.

——. *The Work of Art in the Age of Its Technological Reproducibility, and Other Writings on Media*. Ed. Michael W. Jennings, Brigid Doherty, and Thomas Y. Levin. Cambridge, Mass.: Belknap Press, 2008.

Bennett, Terry. *Photography in Japan, 1853–1912*. Tokyo: Tuttle, 2006.

Berman, Marshall. *All That Is Solid Melts Into Air*. New York: Viking, 1988.

Bernstein, Gail Lee. *Japanese Marxist: A Portrait of Kawakami Hajime*. Cambridge, Mass.: Harvard University Press, 1976.

Berry, Mary Elizabeth. *Japan in Print: Information and Nation in the Early Modern Period*. Berkeley: University of California Press, 2006.

Blair, Ann M. *Too Much to Know: Managing Scholarly Information Before the Modern Age*. New Haven, Conn.: Yale University Press, 2010.

Blum, Andrew. *Tubes: A Journey to the Center of the Internet*. New York: Ecco, 2012.

Bourdieu, Pierre. *The Field of Cultural Production: Essays on Art and Literature*. New York: Columbia University Press, 1993.

Bowen-Struyk, Heather. "Rethinking Japanese Proletarian Literature." Ph.D. diss., University of Michigan, 2001.

Brake, Laurel, ed. *Print in Transition, 1850–1910: Studies in Media and Book History*. London: Palgrave Macmillan, 2001.

Brokaw, Cynthia. *Commerce in Culture: The Sibao Book Trade in the Qing and Republican Periods*. Cambridge, Mass.: Harvard University Asia Center, 2007.

Bronson, Adam. *One Hundred Million Philosophers: Science of Thought and the Culture of Democracy in Postwar Japan*. Honolulu: University of Hawai`i Press, 2016.

Bungei Jidai Henshūbu, ed. *Bungei Shingo Jiten*. Tokyo: Kinseidō, 1926.

Bürger, Peter. *Theory of the Avant-Garde*. Trans. Michael Shaw. Minneapolis: University of Minnesota Press, 1984.

Burkman, Thomas W. *Japan and the League of Nations: Empire and World Order, 1914–1938*. Honolulu: University of Hawai`i Press, 2008.

Bush, Christopher. *Ideographic Modernism: China, Writing, Media*. Oxford: Oxford University Press, 2010.

Carter, Thomas Francis. *The Invention of Printing in China and Its Spread Westward*. New York: Columbia University Press, 1925.

Chartier, Roger. *On the Edge of the Cliff: History, Language, and Practices*. Trans. Lydia G. Cochrane. Baltimore: Johns Hopkins University Press, 1997.

——. *The Order of Books*. Stanford, Calif.: Stanford University Press, 1992.

Chia, Lucille. *Printing for Profit: The Commercial Publishers of Jianyang, Fujian (11th–17th Centuries)*. Cambridge, Mass.: Harvard University Asia Center, 2002.

Chiba Kameo. "Na wa Shosen Hitotsu no Gainen." *Bungei Jidai* 2, no. 7 (July 1925).

Chow, Kai-wing. *Publishing, Culture, and Power in Early Modern China*. Stanford, Calif.: Stanford University Press, 2004.

Clark, Paul Hendrix. "The *Kokugo* Revolution: Ueda Kazutoshi, Language Reform, and Language Education in Meiji Japan (1868– 1912)." Ph.D. diss., University of Pittsburgh, 2002.

Daniels, Robert V. *A Documentary History of Communism*. 2 vols. London: Tauris, 1985.

Danius, Sara. *The Senses of Modernism: Technology, Perception, and Aesthetics*. Ithaca, N.Y.: Cornell University Press, 2002.

Darnton, Robert. *The Business of Enlightenment: A Publishing History of the* Encyclopédie *1775–1800*. Cambridge, Mass.: Belknap Press, 1979.

——. *The Case for Books*. New York: Public Affairs, 2009.

——. "What Is the History of Books?" *Daedalus* 111, no. 3 (Summer 1982).

Darnton, Robert, and Daniel Roche, eds. *Revolution in Print: The Press in France, 1775–1800*. Berkeley: University of California Press, 1989.

Davis, Kenneth C. *Two-Bit Culture: The Paperbacking of America*. Boston: Houghton Mifflin, 1984.

DeFrancis, John. *Nationalism and Language Reform in China*. Princeton, N.J.: Princeton University Press, 1950.

Derrida, Jacques. *Dissemination*. Trans. Barbara Johnson. Chicago: University of Chicago Press, 1981.

——. *Paper Machine*. Trans. Rachel Bowlby. Stanford, Calif.: Stanford University Press, 2005.

Dewey, John. *Reconstruction in Philosophy*. New York: Holt, 1920.

Dickerman, Leah, ed. *Dada: Zurich, Berlin, Hannover, Cologne, New York, Paris*. Washington, D.C.: National Gallery of Art, 2005.

Dobrenko, Evgeny. *Aesthetics of Alienation: Reassessment of Early Soviet Cultural Theories*. Evanston, Ill.: Northwestern University Press, 2005.

Doi Bansui. "Kaizō no Dairei." *Kaizō* 1, no. 1 (April 1919).

Dōmeki Kyōzaburō. *Shinchōsha Kyūjūnen Shōshi*. Tokyo: Shinchōsha, 1986.

Dorsey, James. *Critical Aesthetics: Kobayashi Hideo, Modernity, and Wartime Japan*. Cambridge, Mass.: Harvard University Asia Center, 2009.

Dowdle, Brian. "Why Saikaku Was Memorable but Bakin Was Unforgettable." *Journal of Japanese Studies* 42, no. 1 (Winter 2016).

Drucker, Johanna. *The Alphabetic Labyrinth: The Letters in History and Imagination*. London: Thames and Hudson, 1995.

Ebihara Hachirō. *Meiji Bungaku Zakki*. Tokyo: Yumani Shobō, 1994.

Eisenstein, Elizabeth L. *The Printing Press as an Agent of Change: Communications and Cultural Transformations in Early Modern Europe*. 2 vols. Cambridge: Cambridge University. Press, 1979.

——. *The Printing Revolution in Early Modern Europe*. Cambridge: Cambridge University. Press, 2005.

Emmerich, Michael. *The Tale of Genji: Translation, Canonziation, and World Literature*. New York: Columbia University Press, 2013.

Endo, Mika. "Pedagogical Experiments with Working Class Children in Prewar Japan." Ph.D. diss., University of Chicago, 2011.

Ertürk, Nergis. *Grammatology and Literary Modernity in Turkey*. Oxford: Oxford University Press, 2011.

Febvre, Lucien, and Henri-Jean Martin. *The Coming of the Book: The Impact of Printing 1450–1800*. Trans. David Gerard. Ed. Geoffrey Nowell-Smith and David Wootton. London: N.L.B., 1976.

Ferris, Ina, and Paul Keen, eds. *Bookish Histories: Books, Literature, and Commercial Modernity, 1700–1900*. London: Palgrave Macmillan, 2009.

Field, Norma, and Heather Bowen-Struyk, eds. *For Dignity, Justice, and Revolution: An Anthology of Japanese Proletarian Literature*. Chicago: University of Chicago Press, 2016.

Flaubert, Gustave. *Bibliomania: A Tale*. London: Rodale Press, 1954.

Frederick, Sarah. *Turning Pages: Reading and Writing Women's Magazines in Interwar Japan*. Honolulu: University of Hawai`i Press, 2006.

Fukumoto Kazuo. *Watakushi no Jishoron*. Tokyo: Kawade Shobō Shinsha, 1977.

Fukuzawa Yukichi. *Autobiography of Yukichi Fukuzawa*. Trans. Eiichi Kiyooka. New York: Columbia University Press, 2007.

——. *Fukuzawa Yukichi Chosakushū*. 12 vols. Tokyo: Keio Daigaku Gijuku Shuppankai, 2002–2003.

Füssel, Stephan. *Gutenberg and the Impact of Printing*. Burlington, Vt.: Ashgate, 2005.

Futabatei Shimei. *Futabatei Shimei Zenshū*. 7 vols. Tokyo: Chikuma Shobō, 1984–1991.

Ganshōdō Shoten Kotenbu, ed. *Koshoseki Zaiko Mokuroku Nihon Shihen*. Tokyo: Ganshōdō Shoten, 1928.

Gardner, William. *Advertising Tower: Japanese Modernism and Modernity in the 1920s*. Cambridge, Mass.: Harvard University Asia Center, 2006.

Genette, Gérard. *Narrative Discourse: An Essay in Method*. Trans. Jane E. Lewin. Ithaca, N.Y.: Cornell University Press, 1983.

Gerow, Aaron. *A Page of Madness: Cinema and Modernity in 1920s Japan*. Ann Arbor: Center for Japanese Studies, University of Michigan, 2008.

——. *Visions of Japanese Modernity: Articulations of Cinema, Nation, and Spectatorship, 1895–1925*. Berkeley: University of California Press, 2010.

Gitelman, Lisa. *Always Already New: Media, History, and the Data of Culture*. Cambridge, Mass.: MIT Press, 2006.

Gladkov, Fyodor. *Cement: A Novel*. Trans. A. S. Arthur and C. Ashleigh. New York: Ungar, 1980.

Goldmann, Lucien. *Lukács and Heidegger: Towards a New Philosophy*. Trans. William Q. Boelhower. London: Routledge, 2009.

Goldsmith, Kenneth. "The Artful Accidents of Google Books." *New Yorker*, December 4, 2013. https://www.newyorker.com/books/page-turner/the-artful-accidents-of-google-books.

Golley, Gregory. *When Our Eyes No Longer See: Realism, Science, and Ecology in Japanese Literary Modernism*. Cambridge, Mass.: Harvard University Asia Center, 2008.

Goody, Jack, and Ian Watt. "The Consequences of Literacy." *Comparative Studies in Society and History* 5, no. 3 (April 1963).

Gordon, Andrew. *Labor and Imperial Democracy in Prewar Japan*. Berkeley: University of California Press, 1991.

Goto-Jones, Christopher S. *Political Philosophy in Japan: Nishida, the Kyoto School, and Co- Prosperity*. New York: Routledge, 2006.

Gottlieb, Nanette. *Kanji Politics: Language Policy and Japanese Script*. London: Kegan International, 1995.

——. "Language and Politics: The Reversal of Postwar Script Reform Policy in Japan." *Journal of Asian Studies* 53, no. 4 (November 1994).

Gumbrecht, Hans Ulrich. *In 1926: Living at the Edge of Time*. Cambridge, Mass.: Harvard University Press, 1997.

Gyōda-shi Kyōdo Hakubutsukan, ed. *Hyakunen-mae ni Mita Nihon: Ogawa Isshin to Bakumatsu Meiji no Shashin*. Gyōda: Gyōda-shi Kyōdo Hakubutsukan, 2000.
Hackforth, R., trans. *Plato's Phaedrus*. Cambridge: Cambridge University Press, 1952.
Hamada Atsushi. *Kokugoshi no Shomondai*. Osaka: Izumi Shoin, 1986.
Hansen, Mark B. N., and W. J. T. Mitchell, eds. *Critical Terms for Media Studies*. Chicago: University of Chicago Press, 2010.
Harootunian, H. D. *Overcome by Modernity: History, Culture, and Community in Interwar Japan*. Princeton, N.J.: Princeton University Press, 2000.
Haruhara Akihiko. *Nihon Shinbun Tsūshi*. Tokyo: Gendai Jānarizumu Shuppankai, 1974.
Harvey, David. *The Condition of Postmodernity*. Cambridge: Blackwell Publishing, 1990.
——. *The Urban Experience*. Baltimore: Johns Hopkins University Press, 1989.
Hasegawa Futabatei. *Sekaigo (Esuperanto)*. Tokyo: Saiunkaku, 1906.
Hasegawa Nyozekan. "Seijiteki Gainen to shite no Taishū." *Chūō Kōron*, April 1928.
Hashizume Ken. "Daini Giteki Kōsatsu." *Bungei Jidai* 2, no. 7 (July 1925).
Hatsuda Tōru. *Hyakkaten no Tanjō*. Tokyo: Sanseidō, 1993.
Havelock, Eric. *Preface to Plato*. Cambridge, Mass.: Belknap Press, 1963.
Hayama Yoshiki. *Hayama Yoshiki Nikki*. Tokyo: Chikuma Shobō, 1971.
——. *Hayama Yoshiki Zenshū*. 6 vols. Tokyo: Chikuma Shobō, 1975–1976.
Hayles, N. Katherine. *How We Became Posthuman: Virtual Bodies in Cybernetics, Literature, and Informatics*. Chicago: University of Chicago Press, 1999.
Hayles, N. Katherine, and Jessica Pressman, eds. *Comparative Textual Media: Transforming the Humanities in the Postprint Era*. Minneapolis: University of Minnesota Press, 2013.
Heibonsha Kyōiku Sangyō Sentā, ed. *Heibonsha Rokujūnenshi*. Tokyo: Heibonsha, 1974.
Heidegger, Martin. *Being and Time: A Translation of* Sein und Zeit. Trans. Joan Stambaugh. Albany: SUNY Press, 1996.
——. *The Question Concerning Technology and Other Essays*. Trans. William Lovitt. New York: Harper and Row, 1977.
——. *What Is Called Thinking?* Trans. J. Glenn Gray. New York: Harper Perennial, 1976.
Hennentai Taishō Bungaku Zenshū. 15 vols. Tokyo: Yumani Shobō, 2000–2003.
Hirabayashi Hatsunosuke. *Hirabayashi Hatsunosuke Bungei Hyōron Zenshū*. 3 vols. Tokyo: Bunsendō Shoten, 1975.
Hirano Ken, Odagiri Hideo, and Yamamoto Kenkichi, eds. *Gendai Nihon Bungaku Ronsōshi*. 3 vols. Tokyo: Miraisha, 2006.
Hōjō Tsunehisa. *Tane Maku Hito Kenkyū*. Tokyo: Ōfūsha, 1992.
Hoshina Kōichi. *Kokugogaku Shōshi*. Tokyo: Dai-Nihon Tosho, 1900.
Hoston, Germaine. *Marxism and the Crisis of Development in Prewar Japan*. Princeton, N.J.: Princeton University Press, 1986.
Hu, Tung-Hui. *A Prehistory of the Cloud*. Cambridge, Mass.: MIT Press, 2015.
Huffman, James L. *Creating a Public: People and Press in Meiji Japan*. Honolulu: University of Hawai'i Press, 1997.
Hurley, Brian. "Toward a New Modern Vernacular: Tanizaki Jun'ichirō, Yamada Yoshio, and Shōwa Restoration Thought." *Journal of Japanese Studies* 39, no. 2 (Summer 2013).

Huyssen, Andreas. *After the Great Divide: Modernism, Mass Culture, Postmodernism.* Bloomington: Indiana University Press, 1986.

Hyōdō Hiromi. *"Koe" no Kokumin Kokka: Naniwabushi no Tsukuru Nihon Kindai.* Tokyo: Kōdansha, 2009.

Ibuse Masuji, ed. *Nihon no Meizuihitsu 36: Doku.* Tokyo: Sakuhinsha, 1985.

Ichihara Minoru, ed. *Kikanshi no Rekishi: Senzen Senchū.* Osaka: Nihon Kikanshi Shuppan Sentā, 1999.

Iida Taizo, ed. *Iwanami Shigeo e no Tegami.* Tokyo: Iwanami Shoten, 2003.

Ikeda Hiroshi, ed. *"Taishū" no Tōjō: Hīrō to Dokusha no 20–30-nendai.* Tokyo: Impakuto Shuppankai, 1998.

Innis, Harold A. *The Bias of Communication.* Toronto: University. of Toronto Press, 2008.

——. *The Cod Fisheries: The History of an International Economy.* Toronto: University of Toronto Press, 1954.

——. *Empire and Communications.* Toronto: University of Toronto Press, 1972.

——. *The Fur Trade in Canada: An Introduction to Canadian Economic History.* Toronto: University of Toronto Press, 1999.

Inoue Ken, Kamiya Tadataka, and Hatori Tetsuya, eds. *Yokomitsu Riichi Jiten.* Tokyo: Ōfū Shoten, 2002.

Inouye, Charles Shirow. "In the Scopic Regime of Discovery: Ishikawa Takuboku's Rōmaji Nikki and the Gendered Premise of Self-Identity." *Review of Japanese Culture and Society* 6 (December 1994).

Insatsu Hakubutsukan, ed. *Edo Jidai no Insatsu Bunka.* Tokyo: Toppan Insatsu, 2000.

——. *Insatsu Toshi Tōkyō to Kindai Nihon.* Tokyo: Toppan Insatsu, 2012.

——. *Katsuji Bunmei Kaika: Motoki Shōzō ga Kizuita Kindai.* Tokyo: Toppan Insatsu, 2003.

——. *Kindai Kyōiku o Sasaeta Kyōkasho.* Tokyo: Toppan Insatsu, 2009.

——. *Mirion Serā Tanjō e: Meiji Taishō no Zasshi Media.* Tokyo: Tōkyō Shoseki, 2008.

Irokawa Daikichi. *Meiji Seishinshi.* 2 vols. Tokyo: Kōdansha, 1976.

——. *Shōwashi Sesōhen.* Tokyo: Shōgakukan, 1990.

Ishiguro Yoshimi. *Esuperanto no Manabikata: Dokushū Sanjūnichi (Memlernolibro de Esperanto).* Tokyo: Hakubunkan, 1931.

Ishihara Chiaki. *Dokusha wa Doko ni Iru ka: Shomotsu no Naka no Watashitachi.* Tokyo: Kawade Shobō Shinsha, 2009.

Ishii Atsushi. *Nihon Kindai Kōkyō Toshokanshi no Kenkyū.* Tokyo: Nihon Toshokan Kyōkai, 1972.

——, ed. *Toshokanshi: Kindai Nihonhen.* Tokyo: Kyōiku Shiryō Shuppankai, 1989.

Ishikawa Takuboku. *Takuboku Zenshū.* 16 vols. Tokyo: Iwanami Shoten, 1953–1954.

Itakura Masanobu. *Motoki Shōzō to Nihon no Kindai Katsuji.* Osaka: Ōsaka-fu Insatsu Kōgyō Kumiai, 2006.

Itō Ippei. *Nihon Shashin Hattatsushi.* Tokyo: Asahi Sonorama, 1975.

Itō Sei et al., eds. *Nihon Gendai Bungaku Zenshū Kōdanshaban.* Vols. 67 and 69. Tokyo: Kōdansha, 1968–1969.

Iwanami Bunko Henshūbu, ed. *Iwanami Bunko no Hachijūnen.* Tokyo: Iwanami Shoten, 2007.

Iwanami Kōza Nihongo 1: Nihongo to Kokugogaku. Tokyo: Iwanami Shoten, 1976.

Iwanami Kōza Sekai Shichō. 12 vols. Tokyo: Iwanami Shoten, 1928–1929.

Iwanami Shigeo. *Iwanami Shigeo: Shigeo Ibunshō.* Tokyo: Nihon Tosho Sentā, 1998.

Jacobowitz, Seth. *Writing Technology in Meiji Japan: A Media History of Modern Japanese Literature and Visual Culture.* Cambridge, Mass.: Harvard University Asia Center, 2015.

Jakobson, Roman. *My Futurist Years.* New York: Marsilio, 1997.

Jameson, Fredric. *Marxism and Form: Twentieth-Century Dialectical Theories of Literature.* Princeton, N.J.: Princeton University Press, 1974.

——. *The Political Unconscious: Narrative as a Socially Symbolic Act.* Ithaca, N.Y.: Cornell University Press, 1981.

——. *The Prison-House of Language: A Critical Account of Structuralism and Russian Formalism.* Princeton, N.J.: Princeton University Press, 1975.

Jay, Martin. *The Dialectical Imagination: A History of the Frankfurt School and the Institute of Social Research, 1923–1950.* Berkeley: University of California Press, 1996.

——. *Marxism and Totality: The Adventures of a Concept from Lukács to Habermas.* Berkeley: University of California Press, 1984.

Jenkins, Henry. *Convergence Culture: Where Old and New Media Collide.* New York: New York University Press, 2006.

Jinnai, Hidenobu. *Tokyo: A Spatial Anthropology.* Trans. Kimiko Nishimura. Berkeley: University of California Press, 1995.

Johns, Adrian. *The Nature of the Book: Print and Knowledge in the Making.* Chicago: University of Chicago Press, 1998.

Kadono Torazō. *Kinseidō no Koro.* Tokyo: Wāku Tosho, 1972.

Kagawa Toyohiko. *Shisen o Koete.* Tokyo: Kaizōsha, 1920.

Kajii Motojirō. *Kajii Motojirō Zenshū.* 3 vols. Tokyo: Chikuma Shobō, 1966.

Kamei-Dyche, Andrew T. "The History of Books and Print Culture in Japan: The State of the Field." *Book History* 14 (2011).

Kamiya Tadataka. *Nihon no Dada.* Sapporo: Kyōbunsha, 1987.

Kaneda Tsunesaburō. *Dokushū Jizai Esuperanto Kōgi (Lekcioj pri la lingvo Internacia Esperanto).* Tokyo: Nihon Hyōronsha, 1922.

Kano Masanao. *Iwanami Shinsho no Rekishi.* Tokyo: Iwanami Shoten, 2006.

Karatani Kōjin, ed. *Kindai Nihon no Hihyō.* 3 vols. Tokyo: Kōdansha, 1997.

——. *Marukusu, Sono Kanōsei no Chūshin.* Tokyo: Kōdansha, 1990.

——. *Origins of Modern Japanese Literature.* Trans. Brett deBary. Durham, N.C.: Duke University Press, 1993.

——. *Transcritique: On Kant and Marx.* Trans. Sabu Kohso. Cambridge, Mass.: MIT Press, 2005.

Karlsson, Mats. "Kurahara Korehito's Road to Proletarian Realism." *Japan Review* 20 (2008).

Karube Tadashi. *Hikari no Ryōgoku: Watsuji Tetsurō.* Tokyo: Sōbunsha, 1995.

——. *Utsuriyuku "Kyōyō."* Tokyo: NTT Shuppan, 2007.

Kataoka Teppei. *Kataoka Teppei Zenshū.* 9 vols. Tokyo: Nihon Tosho Sentā, 1995.

——. "Tōan Hitotsu." *Bungei Jidai* 1, no. 1 (October 1924).

——. "Wakaki Dokusha ni Uttau." *Bungei Jidai* 1, no. 3 (December 1924).

Katayama Sen. *The Labor Movement in Japan.* Chicago: Kerr, 1918.

Katō Masanobu and Matsumoto Takashi, eds. *Shōwa Zenki Nihongo no Mondaiten.* Tokyo: Meiji Shoin, 2007.

Kawabata Yasunari. "Atarashiki Seikatsu to Atarashiki Bungei." *Bungei Jidai* 1, no. 1 (October 1924).
——. "Bangai Hadōchō." *Bungei Jidai* 2, no. 3 (March 1925).
——. *Kawabata Yasunari Zenshū*. 35 vols. Tokyo: Shinchōsha, 1980–1984.
——. "Shinshin Sakka no Shinkeikō Kaisetsu." *Bungei Jidai* 2, no. 1 (January 1925).
——. "Sōkan no Ji." *Bungei Jidai* 1, no. 1 (October 1924).
Kawaguchi Takehiko. *Nihon Marukusushugi no Genryū—Sakai Toshihiko to Yamakawa Hitoshi*. Tokyo: Ariesu Shobō, 1983.
Kawahara Mankichi. *Kosho Sōwa*. Tokyo: Yumani Shobō, 2011.
Kawakami Hajime. *Binbō Monogatari*. Tokyo: Kōbundō Shoten, 1917.
Kawashima, Ken. *The Proletarian Gamble: Korean Workers in Interwar Japan*. Durham, N.C.: Duke University Press, 2009.
Kawashima, Ken C., et al., eds. *Tosaka Jun: A Critical Reader*. Ithaca, N.Y.: Cornell University Press, 2013.
Keavney, Christopher. *The Cultural Evolution of Postwar Japan: The Contributions of* Kaizō's *Yamamoto Sanehiko*. London: Palgrave Macmillan, 2013.
Kendall, Eugene. "Philosophy and Politics in Russian Social Democracy: Bogdanov, Lunacharsky, and the Crisis of Bolshevism, 1908–1909." Ph.D. diss., Columbia University, 1966.
Keene, Dennis. *Yokomitsu Riichi: Modernist*. New York: Columbia University Press, 1980.
Keene, Donald. *The First Modern Japanese: The Life of Ishikawa Takuboku*. New York: Columbia University Press, 2016.
Kida Jun'ichirō. *Kida Jun'ichirō Chosakushū*. 3 vols. Tokyo: San'ichi Shobō, 1997.
Kikuzawa Sueo. *Kokuji Mondai no Kenkyū*. Tokyo: Iwanami Shoten, 1931.
Kimoto Itaru. *Hyōden Miyatake Gaikotsu*. Tokyo: Shakai Shisōsha, 1984.
Kimura Ki. *Maruzen Gaishi*. Tokyo: Maruzen, 1969.
Kindai Bungaku Gōdō Kenkyūkai, ed. *Kōdansha Nettowāku to Dokusha*. Yokosuka: Kindai Bungaku Gōdō Kenkyūkai, 2006.
Kindai Bungaku Hyōron Taikei. 10 vols. Tokyo: Kadokawa Shoten, 1971–1975.
Kita Ikki. *Nihon Kaizō Hōan Taikō*. Tokyo: Nishida Mitsugi, 1926.
Kittler, Friedrich A. *Discourse Networks 1800/1900*. Trans. Michael Metteer with Chris Cullens. Stanford, Calif.: Stanford University Press, 1990.
——. *Gramophone, Film, Typewriter*. Trans. Geoffrey Winthrop-Young and Michael Wutz. Stanford, Calif.: Stanford University Press, 1999.
Kobayashi Hideo. *Kobayashi Hideo Zenshū*. 19 vols. Tokyo: Shinchōsha, 2001–2010.
Komaki Ōmi. *Aru Gendaishi: "Tane Maku Hito" Zengo*. Tokyo: Hōsei Daigaku Shuppankyoku, 1965.
Komori Yōichi. *Kōzō to shite no Katari*. Tokyo: Shin'yōsha, 1988.
Komori Yōichi, Kōno Kensuke, and Takahashi Osamu, eds. *Media, Hyōshō, Ideorogī: Meiji Sanjūnendai no Bunka Kenkyū*. Tokyo: Ozawa Shoten, 1997.
Konishi, Sho. *Anarchist Modernity: Cooperatism and Japanese-Russian Intellectual Relations in Modern Japan*. Cambridge, Mass.: Harvard University Asia Center, 2013.
——. "Translingual World Order: Language Without Culture in Post-Russo-Japanese War Japan." *Journal of Asian Studies* 72, no. 1 (February 2013).

Konno Shinji. *"Genkai" o Yomu: Kotoba no Umi to Meiji no Nihongo*. Tokyo: Kadokawa Gakugei Shuppan, 2014.

——. *Kanazukai no Rekishi: Nihongo o Kaku to iu Koto*. Tokyo: Chūō Kōron Shinsha, 2014.

——. *Nihongo no Kindai: Hazusareta Kango*. Tokyo: Chikuma Shinsho, 2014.

Kōno Kensuke, ed. *Ken'etsu no Teikoku: Bunka no Tōsei to Saiseisan*. Tokyo: Shin'yōsha, 2014.

——. *Ken'etsu to Bungaku: 1920-nendai no Kōbō*. Tokyo: Kawade Shobō Shinsha, 2009.

——. *Monogatari Iwanami Shoten Hyakunenshi 1: Kyōyō no Tanjō*. Tokyo: Iwanami Shoten, 2013.

——. *Shomotsu no Kindai: Media no Bungakushi*. Tokyo: Chikuma Shobō, 1992.

——. *Tōki to shite no Bungaku: Katsuji, Kenshō, Media*. Tokyo: Shin'yōsha, 2003.

Kōno Toshirō. *Gakutō o Yomu*. Tokyo: Yūshōdō Shuppan, 2009.

Kōno Toshirō and Hidaka Shōji, eds. *"Kaizō" Jikihitsu Genkō no Kenkyū*. Tokyo: Yūshōdō, 2007.

Konta Yōzō. *Edo no Hon'yasan: Kinsei Bunkashi no Sokumen*. Tokyo: Heibonsha, 2009.

Kornicki, Peter. *The Book in Japan: A Cultural History from the Beginnings to the Nineteenth Century*. Honolulu: University of Hawai`i Press, 2000.

Koshōji Toshiyasu, ed. *Sakai Toshihiko: Shoki Shakaishugi no Shisōken*. Tokyo: Ronsōsha, 2016.

Kunikida Doppo. *Teihon Kunikida Doppo Zenshū*. 11 vols. Tokyo: Gakushū Kenkyūsha, 1978.

Kurahara Korehito. *Puroretaria Geijutsu to Keishiki*. Tokyo: Yumani Shobō, 1991.

Kurihara Yukio. *Puroretaria Bungaku to Sono Jidai*. Tokyo: Impakuto Shuppankai, 2004.

Kuroda Hidetoshi. *Yokohama Jiken*. Tokyo: Kakugei Shorin, 1975.

Kuroiwa Hisako. *Henshūsha Kunikida Doppo no Jidai*. Tokyo: Kadokawa Gakugei Shuppan, 2007.

——. *Pan to Pen: Shakaishugisha Sakai Toshihiko to "Baibunsha" no Tatakai*. Tokyo: Kōdansha, 2010.

Kurokawa Iori. *Teikoku ni Kōsuru Shakai Undō: Daiichiji Nihon Kyōsantō no Shisō to Undō*. Tokyo: Yūgensha, 2014.

Kusano Masana. *Toshokan no Rekishi Nihon oyobi Kakkoku no Tosho to Toshokanshi*. Tokyo: Gakugei Tosho, 1971.

Lee Yeounsuk. *"Kokugo" to iu Shisō*. Tokyo: Iwanami Shoten, 1996.

Lefebvre, Henri. *The Production of Space*. Trans. Donald Nicholson-Smith. Oxford: Blackwell Publishing, 1991.

Lenin, V. I. *Imperialism: The Highest Stage of Capitalism; A Popular Outline*. New York: International Publishers, 1988.

Lewis, Michael. *Rioters and Citizens: Mass Protest in Imperial Japan*. Berkeley: University of California Press, 1990.

Lippit, Seiji. *Topographies of Japanese Modernism*. New York: Columbia University Press, 2002.

Liu, Lydia H. *The Freudian Robot: Digital Media and the Future of the Unconscious*. Chicago: University of Chicago Press, 2011.

——. *Translingual Practice: Literature, National Culture, and Translated Modernity—China, 1900–1937*. Stanford, Calif.: Stanford University Press, 1995.

Lukács, Georg. *History and Class Consciousness: Studies in Marxist Dialectics*. Trans. Rodney Livingstone. Cambridge, Mass.: MIT Press, 1971.

——. *Kaikyū Ishiki to wa Nan zo ya: "Rekishi to Kaikyū Ishiki" Kaikyū Ishikiron*. Trans. Mizutani Chōzaburō. Tokyo: Dōjinsha Shoten, 1927.

——. *Theory of the Novel: A Historico-Philosophical Essay on the Forms of Great Epic Literature*. Trans. Anna Bostock. Cambridge, Mass.: MIT Press, 1973.

Lunacharsky, Anatoly. *On Literature and Art*. Trans. Avril Pyman and Fainna Glagoleva. Moscow: Progress Publishers, 1965.

Lunn, Eugene. *Marxism and Modernism: An Historical Study of Lukács, Brecht, Benjamin, and Adorno*. Berkeley: University of California Press, 1984.

Lurie, David. *Realms of Literacy: Early Japan and the History of Writing*. Cambridge, Mass.: Harvard University Asia Center, 2011.

Mack, Edward. *Manufacturing Modern Japanese Literature: Publishing, Prizes, and the Ascription of Literary Value*. Durham, N.C.: Duke University Press, 2010.

Maeda Ai. *Kindai Dokusha no Seiritsu*. Tokyo: Yūseidō, 1973.

——. *Text and the City: Essays on Japanese Modernity*. Ed. James A. Fujii. Durham, N.C.: Duke University Press, 2004.

——. *Toshi Kūkan no Naka no Bungaku*. Tokyo: Chikuma Shobō, 1982.

Maeda Ai and Katō Hidetoshi. *Meiji Media-kō*. Tokyo: Chūō Kōron, 1983.

Manguel, Alberto. *A History of Reading*. New York: Penguin, 1997.

Marinetti, F. T. *Critical Writings*. Trans. Doug Thompson. New York: Farrar, Straus and Giroux, 2006.

Martin, Terry. *The Affirmative Action Empire: Nations and Nationalism in the Soviet Union, 1923–1939*. Ithaca, N.Y.: Cornell University Press, 2001.

Maruzen Kabushikigaisha, ed. *Maruzen Hyakunenshi: Nihon Kindaika no Ayumi to tomo ni*. 2 vols. Tokyo: Maruzen, 1981.

Marx, Karl. *Capital: A Critique of Political Economy*. Trans. Ben Fowkes. New York: Penguin, 1990.

——. *Chinrōdō to Shihon*. Trans. Kawakami Hajime. Tokyo: Iwanami Shoten, 1927.

——. *The 18th Brumaire of Louis Bonaparte*. New York: International Publishers, 1964.

——. *The Marx-Engels Reader: Second Edition*. Ed. Robert C. Tucker. New York: Norton, 1978.

——. *Shihonron*. Trans. Kawakami Hajime. Tokyo: Iwanami Shoten, 1927–1928.

——. *Shihonron*. Trans. Takabatake Motoyuki. Tokyo: Kaizōsha, 1927–1928.

——. *Shihonron Daiichi Bunsatsu*. Trans. Ikuta Chōkō. Tokyo: En'yōsha, 1919.

Marx, Karl, and Frederick Engels. *The Communist Manifesto: A Modern Edition*. New York: Verso, 1998.

——. *Doitche Ideorogī*. Trans. Miki Kiyoshi. Tokyo: Iwanami Shoten, 1930.

——. *The German Ideology*. Ed. C. J. Arthur. New York: International Publishers, 1970.

——. *Marukusu Engerusu Zenshū*. 34 vols. Tokyo: Kaizōsha, 1928–1935.

Matejka, Latislav, and Krystyna Pomorska, eds. *Readings in Russian Poetics: Formalist and Structuralist Views*. Ann Arbor: Michigan Slavic Publications, 1978.

Matsubara Kazue. *Kaizōsha to Yamamoto Sanehiko*. Kagoshima: Nanpō Shinsha, 2002.

McLuhan, Marshall. *The Gutenberg Galaxy: The Making of Typographic Man*. Toronto: University of Toronto Press, 1962.

——. *The Mechanical Bride: Folklore of Industrial Man*. Corte Madera, Calif.: Gingko Press, 2002.

——. *Understanding Media: The Extensions of Man*. Corte Madera, Calif.: Gingko Press, 2003.
Meiji Taishōki Kisho Chinseki Shomoku Kaidaishū. 7 vols. Tokyo: Yumani Shobō, 2010.
Miki Kiyoshi. "Dokushoshi ni Yosu." Tokyo: Iwanami Shoten, 1927.
——. "Marukusushugi to Yuibutsuron." *Shisō* 69 (October 1927).
——. *Miki Kiyoshi Zenshū*. 20 vols. Tokyo: Iwanami Shoten, 1966–1968.
Mimasaka Tarō, Fujita Chikamasa, and Watanabe Kiyoshi. *Yokohama Jiken*. Tokyo: Nihon Editā Sukūru Shuppanbu, 1977.
Minami Hiroshi, ed. *Nihon Modanizumu no "Hikari" to "Kage"—Kindai Shomin Seikatsushi 2: Sakariba Uramachi*. Tokyo: San'ichi Shobō, 1984.
Minami Kensaku. *Shinkanazukai to Jōyō Kanji no Jibiki*. Tokyo: Jitsugyō no Nihonsha, 1925.
Minato Chihiro. *Shomotsu no Hen: Gūguruberugu no Jidai*. Tokyo: Serika Shobō, 2010.
Miyaguchi Noriyuki. "Yokomitsu Riichi 'Marukusu no Saiban' o Megutte—Shiga Naoya to no Kanren o Kangaeru Tame no Ichi Kōsatsu." *Yokomitsu Riichi Kenkyū* 5 (2007).
——. "Yokomitsu Riichi 'Onmi' Shiron." *Nagoya Kindai Bungaku Kenkyū* 11 (1993).
Miyamoto Masao. *Ōsugi Sakae to Esuperanto Undō*. Tokyo: Kuroiro Sensensha, 1988.
Miyatake Gaikotsu. *Meiji Enzetsushi*. Tokyo: Yūgensha, 1926.
——, ed. *Meiji Kibun*. 6 vols. Tokyo: Hankyūdō, 1925–1926.
——. *Minponshugi*. Tokyo: Yumani Shobō, 1995.
Mizunuma Tatsuo. *Meiji Taishōki Jiritsuteki Rōdō Undō no Ashiato*. Tokyo: JCA, 1979.
Mizutani Futō. *Meiji Taishō Kosho Ka no Kenkyū*. Tokyo: Sunnansha, 1933.
Mori Ōgai. *Ōgai Zenshū*. 38 vols. Tokyo: Iwanami Shoten, 1973–1975.
Moriyama Shigeo. *Taigyaku Jiken Bungaku Sakkaron*. Tokyo: San'ichi Shobō, 1980.
Munakata Kazushige and Toeda Hirokazu, eds. *Kinseidō o Chūshin to Suru Taishō Shōwaki no Shuppan Shoshi to Bungaku ni kansuru Sōgō Kenkyū*. Tokyo: MEXT, 2007.
Murayama Tomoyoshi. *Murayama Tomoyoshi Gurafikku no Shigoto*. Tokyo: Hon no Izumisha, 2001.
Nagahama Isao. *Takuboku Nikki Kōkan Katei no Shinsō*. Tokyo: Shakai Hyōronsha, 2013.
Nagai Kafū. *Kafū Zenshū*. 28 vols. Tokyo: Iwanami Shoten, 1963–1965.
Nagamine Shigetoshi. *"Dokusho Kokumin" no Tanjō: Meiji 30-nendai no Katsuji Media to Dokusho Bunka*. Tokyo: Nihon Editā Sukūru Shuppanbu, 2004.
——. *Modan Toshi no Dokusho Kūkan*. Tokyo: Nihon Editā Sukūru Shuppanbu, 2001.
——. *Tōdaisei wa Donna Hon o Yonde Kita ka*. Tokyo: Heibonsha, 2007.
——. *Zasshi to Dokusha no Kindai*. Tokyo: Nihon Editā Sukūru Shuppanbu, 1997.
Naimushō Keihokyoku. *Shuppan Keisatsu Gaikan*. Tokyo: Naimushō Keihokyoku, 1931.
Nakagawa Yoichi. "Atarashii Byōki to Bungaku." *Bungei Jidai* 1, no. 1 (October 1924).
——. "Atarashiki Jidai no Tame ni." *Bungei Jidai* 2, no. 7 (July 1925).
——. *Keishikishugi Geijutsuron*. Tokyo: Shinchōsha, 1930.
Nakahara Yūtarō et al., eds. *Insatsu Zasshi to Sono Jidai: Jikkyō Insatsu no Kingendaishi*. Tokyo: Insatsu Gakkai Shuppanbu, 2007.
Nakajima Reiko. *Kunikida Doppo no Kenkyū*. Tokyo: Ōfū, 2009.
Nakamura Kōya. *Noma Seiji-den*. Tokyo: Noma Seiji Denki Hensankai, 1944.

Nancy, Jean-Luc. *On the Commerce of Thinking: Of Books and Bookstores*. Trans. David Willis. New York: Fordham University Press, 2009.

Narita Ryūichi. *Taishō Demokurashī*. Tokyo: Iwanami Shoten. 2007.

Natsume Sōseki. *Sanshirō*. Trans. Jay Rubin. New York: Penguin Books, 2009.

——. *Sōseki Zenshū*. 34 vols. Tokyo: Iwanami Shoten, 1956–1957.

Nietzsche, Friedrich. *Ecce Homo*. Trans. Anthony Ludovici. Vol. 17 in *The Complete Works of Friedrich Nietzsche*, ed. Oscar Levy. New York: Macmillan, 1911.

Nihon Bungaku Kenkyū Shiryō Sōsho: Yokomitsu Riichi to Shinkankaku-ha. Tokyo: Yūseidō, 1980.

Nihon Kindai Bungakukan, ed. *Bungei Kurabu Meijihen Sōmokuji*. Tokyo: Nihon Kindai Bungakukan, 2005.

Nihon Puroretaria Bungakushū. 40 vols. Tokyo: Shin-Nihon Shuppansha, 1984–1988.

Nihon Puroretaria Bungakushū Bekkan: Puroretaria Bungaku Shiryōshū, Nenpyō. Tokyo: Shin-Nihon Shuppansha, 1998.

Nihon Puroretaria Bungaku Hyōronshū. 7 vols. Tokyo: Shin-Nihon Shuppansha, 1991.

Nii Itaru. "Shuppan Shihonshugi to Chojutsuka." *Chūō Kōron*, April 1928.

Nishida Taketoshi. *Meiji Shinbun Zasshi Bunko no Omoide*. Tokyo: Rikiesuta no Kai, 2001.

Noma Seiji. *The Nine Magazines of Kodansha: The Autobiography of a Japanese Publisher*. New York: Vanguard Press, 1934.

——. Shuppanjin no Ibun 3: *Kōdansha Noma Seiji*. Tokyo: Kurita Shoten, 1968.

Nomura Takashi. *Uchida Roan-den*. Tokyo: Riburopōto, 1994.

Nonaka Jun. *Yokomitsu Riichi to Haisengo Bungaku*. Tokyo: Kasama Shoin, 2005.

Obi Toshito. *Shuppan to Shakai*. Tokyo: Genki Shobō, 2007.

Oda Hisashi. *Kōkoku Hyakunenshi: Taishō Shōwa*. Tokyo: Sekai Shisōsha, 1976.

Oda Mitsuo: *Shoten no Kindai: Hon ga Kagayaiteita Jidai*. Tokyo: Heibonsha, 2003.

Odagiri Hideo, ed. *Bungei Jidai (Fukkokuban)*. Nihon Kindai Bungakukan, 1967.

Ogawa Kazumasa. *Nisshin Sensō Shashinchō*. 2 vols. Tokyo: Hakubundō, 1895.

Ōji Seishi. *Ōji Seishi Sanrin Jigyōshi*. Tokyo: Ōji Seishi, 1976.

——. *Ōji Seishi Shashi*. Tokyo: Ōji Seishi, 2001.

Ōkubo Hitoshi, ed. *Ana-Boru Ronsō*. Tokyo: Dōjidaisha, 2005.

Okumoto Daisaburō, ed. *Nihon no Meizuihitsu Bekkan 34: Shūshū*. Tokyo: Sakuhinsha, 1993.

Omori, Kyoko. "Detecting Japanese Vernacular Modernism: *Shinseinen* Magazine and the Development of the *Tantei Shōsetsu* Genre, 1920–1931." Ph.D. diss., Ohio State University, 2003.

Ong, Walter J. *Orality and Literacy: The Technologizing of the Word*. London: Routledge, 2002.

Ono Matsuo. *Kunikida Doppo-ron*. Tokyo: Makino Shuppan, 2003.

Ono Noriaki. *Nihon Toshokanshi*. Kyoto: Genbunsha, 1973.

Osaka Kenji. *Esuperanto Shōkei (Esperanto Kompleta Kurso por Japanoj)*. Tokyo: Nihon Esuperanto Gakkai, 1927.

Osaka Kenji and Akita Ujaku. *Mohan Esuperanto Dokushū (Memlernanto de Esperanto)*. Tokyo: Sōbunkaku, 1927.

Ōsawa Satoshi. *Hihyō Media-ron: Senzenki Nihon no Rondan to Bundan*. Tokyo: Iwanami Shoten, 2015.

——, ed. *Toshokan to Dokusho*. Korekushon Modan Toshi Bunka 87. Tokyo: Yumani Shobō, 2013.

Otsubo Heiji. *Giseigo no Kenkyū*. Tokyo: Kazama Shobō, 2006.
Ōtsuki Fumihiko, ed. *Genkai*. Tokyo: Rinpei Shoten, 1904.
Ōwada Shigeru. *Shakai Bungaku 1920-nen Zengo—Hirabayashi Hatsunosuke to Dōjidai Bungaku*. Tokyo: Fuji Shuppan, 1992.
Ōya Sōichi. *Chūgakusei Nikki 1*. In *Ōya Sōichi Zenshū*, vol. 29. Tokyo: Sōyōsha, 1982.
——. "Shuppan Kakumei no Shōrisha." *Chūō Kōron*, December 1928.
Ozaki Hotsuki. *Taishū Bungaku*. Tokyo: Kinokuniya Shoten, 1964.
Ozawa Takeshi. *Nihon no Shashinshi: Bakumatsu kara Meijiki made*. Tokyo: Nikkōru Kurabu, 1986.
Park Byeng-sen. *Korean Printing from Its Origins to 1910*. Seoul: Jimoondang, 2003.
Perry, Samuel. *Recasting Red Culture in Proletarian Japan: Childhood, Korea, and the Historical Avant-Garde*. Honolulu: University of Hawai`i Press, 2014.
Peters, John Durham. *The Marvelous Clouds: Toward a Philosophy of Elemental Media*. Chicago: University of Chicago Press, 2015.
——. *Speaking into the Air: A History of the Idea of Communication*. Chicago: University of Chicago Press, 1999.
Piper, Andrew. *Book Was There: Reading in Electronic Times*. Chicago: University of Chicago Press, 2012.
——. *Dreaming in Books: The Making of the Bibliographic Imagination in the Romantic Age*. Chicago: University of Chicago Press, 2009.
Plekhanov, George V. *Fundamental Problems of Marxism*. New York: International Publishers, 1969.
Poincaré, Henri. *The Foundations of Science*. Trans. George Halsted. New York: Science Press, 1913.
Poovey, Mary. *Genres of the Credit Economy: Mediating Value in Eighteenth- and Nineteenth-Century Britain*. Chicago: University of Chicago Press, 2008.
Price, Leah. *How to Do Things With Books in Victorian England*. Princeton, N.J.: Princeton University Press, 2012.
Puroretaria Kagaku Kenkyūjo, ed. *Puroretaria Esuperanto Kōza (Proleta Kurso de Esperanto)*. Tokyo: Yōbunsha, 1968.
Rancière, Jacques. *Proletarian Nights: The Workers' Dream in Nineteenth-Century France*. Trans. John Drury. New York: Verso, 2012.
Rapley, Ian. "Green Star Japan: Language and Internationalism in the Japanese Esperanto Movement, 1905–1944." Ph.D. diss., University of Oxford, 2013.
Reed, Christopher A. *Gutenberg in Shanghai: Chinese Print Capitalism, 1876–1937*. Vancouver: University of British Columbia Press, 2005.
——. "Gutenberg and Modern Print Culture: The State of the Discipline II." *Book History* 10 (2007).
Richards, I. A. *Principles of Literary Criticism*. London: Routledge, 2001.
Richter, Giles. "Marketing the Word: Publishing Entrepreneurs in Meiji Japan, 1870–1912." Ph.D. diss., Columbia University, 1999.
Rimmon-Kenan, Shlomith. *Narrative Fiction: Contemporary Poetics*. London: Routledge, 1983.
Robins, Christopher. "Revisiting Year One of Japanese National Language: Inoue Hisashi's Literary Challenge." *Japanese Language and Literature* 40, no. 1 (April 2006).
Rousseau, Jean-Jacques. *Min'yakuron*. Trans. Hirabayashi Hatsunosuke. Tokyo: Iwanami Shoten, 1927.

——. *The Social Contract*. Trans. Maurice Cranston. New York: Penguin Books, 1968.

Rubin, Jay. *Injurious to Public Morals: Writers and the Meiji State*. Seattle: University of Washington Press, 1984.

Russell, Bertrand. *Principles of Social Reconstruction*. London: Allen and Unwin, 1916.

Ryan, James R. *Picturing Empire: Photography and the Visualization of the British Empire*. Chicago: University of Chicago Press, 1997.

Safranski, Rüdiger. *Romanticism: A German Affair*. Trans. Robert Goodwin. Evanston, Ill.: Northwestern University Press, 2014.

Sakai, Cécile. *Nihon no Taishū Bungaku*. Trans. Asahina Kōji. Tokyo: Heibonsha, 1997.

Sakai Toshihiko. *Sakai Toshihiko Zenshū*. 6 vols. Tokyo: Hōritsu Bunkasha, 1970–1971.

Sakurai Satoshi. *Rōmaji Shuchō no Hyakkojō, Rōmaji no Hantairon o Yaburu*. Osaka: Teikoku Rōmaji Kurabu, 1930.

Sanseidō no Hyakunen. Tokyo: Sanseidō, 1982.

Sas, Miryam. *Fault Lines: Cultural Memory and Japanese Surrealism*. Stanford, Calif.: Stanford University Press, 2002.

Satō Ichiei. "Kokugo Bungakugo Mondai no Hōkō—Shinkanazukai Mondai o Ijō Suru Hitobito ni Ataeru Kōkaijō." *Bungei Jidai* 2, no. 6 (June 1925).

Satō Kiyoji, ed. *Kanji to Kokugo Mondai*. Tokyo: Meiji Shoin, 1989.

Satō Takumi. *"Kingu" no Jidai: Kokumin Taishū Zasshi no Kōkyōsei*. Tokyo: Iwanami Shoten, 2002.

Satō Tsuji. "Rekuramu Bunko." *Shisō* 71 (September 1927).

Saussure, Ferdinand de. *Course in General Linguistics*. Trans. Wade Baskin. New York: McGraw-Hill, 1959.

Schiller, Friedrich. *On the Aesthetic Education of Man*. Trans. Reginald Snell. Mineola, N.Y.: Dover, 2004.

Schimmel, Mariko Shigeta. "Estranged Twins of Revolution: An Examination of Japanese Modernist and Proletarian Literature." Ph.D diss., Yale University, 2006.

Schor, Esther. *Bridge of Words: Esperanto and the Dream of a Universal Language*. New York: Metropolitan Books, 2016.

Seki Chūka et al., eds. *Zasshi "Kaizō" no Shijūnen*. Tokyo: Kōwadō, 1977.

Seki Hajime. *Shinbun Shōsetsu no Jidai: Media, Dokusha, Merodorama*. Tokyo: Shin'yōsha, 2007.

Shea, G. T. *Leftwing Literature in Japan: A Brief History of the Proletarian Literary Movement*. Tokyo: Hosei University Press, 1964.

Shell, Marc. *Money, Language, and Thought: Literary and Philosophic Economies from the Medieval to the Modern Era*. Baltimore: Johns Hopkins University Press, 1993.

Shibano Kyōko. *Shodana to Hiradai: Shuppan Ryūtsū to iu Media*. Tokyo: Kōbundō, 2009.

Shih, Shu-mei. *The Lure of the Modern: Writing Modernism in Semicolonial China, 1917–1937*. Berkeley: University of California Press, 2001.

Shimaya Seiichi. *Motoki Shōzō-den*. Tokyo: Rōbundō, 2001.

Shimizu Bunkichi. *Hon wa Nagareru: Shuppan Ryūtsū Kikō no Seiritsushi*. Tokyo: Nihon Editā Sukūru Shuppanbu, 1991.

Shimonaka Yasaburō. Shuppanjin no Ibun 8: *Heibonsha Shimonaka Yasaburō*. Tokyo: Kurita Shoten, 1968.

Shimura Akiko. *Gariban Monogatari*. Tokyo: Taishūkan Shoten, 2012.

Shindō Sakiko, ed. *Gakumon no Susume: Honbun to Sakuin*. Tokyo: Kasama Shoin, 1992.
Shirane, Haruo, ed. *Early Modern Japanese Literature: An Anthology, 1600–1900*. New York: Columbia University. Press, 2002.
——. *Traditional Japanese Literature: An Anthology, Beginnings to 1600*. New York: Columbia University Press, 2007.
Shirane, Haruo, and Tomi Suzuki, eds. *Inventing the Classics: Modernity, National Identity, and Japanese Literature*. Stanford, Calif.: Stanford University Press, 2000.
Shklovksy, Viktor. *Literature and Cinematography*. Trans. Irina Masinovsky. Champaign, Ill.: Dalkey Archive Press, 2008.
Shoshi Shomoku Shirīzu. 112 vols. Tokyo: Yumani Shobō, 1977–2017.
Siegert, Bernhard. *Relays: Literature as an Epoch of the Postal System*. Trans. Kevin Repp. Stanford, Calif.: Stanford University Press, 1999.
Silverberg, Miriam. *Changing Song: The Marxist Manifestos of Nakano Shigeharu*. Princeton, N.J.: Princeton University Press, 1990.
——. *Erotic Grotesque Nonsense: The Mass Culture of Japanese Modern Times*. Berkeley: University of California Press, 2006.
Simmel, Georg. *Simmel on Culture: Selected Writings*. Ed. David Frisby and Mike Featherstone. London: Sage Publications, 1997.
Smith, Henry Dewitt, II. *Japan's First Student Radicals*. Cambridge, Mass.: Harvard University Press, 1972.
——. *Kobayashi Kiyochika: Artist of Meiji Japan*. Santa Barbara, Calif.: Santa Barbara Museum of Art, 1988.
Steinberg, Marc. *Anime's Media Mix: Franchising Toys and Characters in Japan*. Minneapolis: University of Minnesota Press, 2012.
Stiegler, Bernard. *Taking Care of Youth and the Generations*. Trans. Stephen Barker. Stanford, Calif.: Stanford University Press, 2010.
Suehiro Izutarō. *Nihon Rōmajikai Panfuretto 5: Nihongo no Yukidzumari Mondai*. Tokyo: Nihon Rōmajikai, 1928.
Suga Hidemi. *Tantei no Kuritikku: Shōwa Bungaku no Rinkai*. Tokyo: Shichōsha, 1988.
Sugamoto Yasuyuki, ed. *Markusushugi*. Tokyo: Yumani Shobō, 2010.
——. *Modan Marukusushugi no Shinkuronishitī: Hirabayashi Hatsunosuke to Warutā Benyamin*. Tokyo: Sairyūsha, 2007.
Suzuki, Jun, and Ellis Tinois, eds. *Understanding Japanese Woodblock-Printed Illustrated Books: A Short Introduction to Their History, Bibliography and Format*. Leiden: Brill, 2013.
Suzuki Sadami. *Nihon no "Bungaku" Gainen*. Sakuhinsha, 1998.
——, ed. *Zasshi "Taiyō" to Kokumin Bunka no Keisei*. Kyoto: Shibunkaku Shuppan, 2001.
Suzuki, Tomi. *Narrating the Self: Fictions of Japanese Modernity*. Stanford, Calif.: Stanford University Press, 1996.
Suzuki, Tomi, Toeda Hirokazu, Hori Hikari, and Munakata Kazushige, eds. *Censorship, Media, and Literary Culture in Japan*. Tokyo: Shin'yōsha, 2012.
Syozi Nobuhiko et al., eds. *El La Revuo Orienta: JEI Gojūnen no Ayumi*. Tokyo: Japan Esperanto Institute, 1976.
Taguchi Ritsuo, ed. *Toshi*. Nihon Bungaku o Yomikaeru 12. Tokyo: Yūseidō, 1995.

Tai Michiru. "Purorettokaruto to shite no Rōmaji." *Bungei Sensen* 2, no. 1 (January 1925).

Tait, A. L. *Anatoly Lunacharsky: Poet of the Revolution (1875–1907)*. Birmingham, U.K.: Department of Russian Language and Literature, University of Birmingham, 1984.

Takabatake Motoyuki. "Taishū Kōza: Marukusu no *Shihonron*." *Kaizō*, November 1927.

——. "Taishūshugi to Shihonshugi." *Chūō Kōron*, April 1928.

——. "Yonin Yoiro." *Chūō Kōron*, December 1928.

Takahashi Yasuo. *Media no Akebono: Meiji Kaikokuki no Shinbun Shuppan Monogatari*. Tokyo: Nihon Keizai Shinbunsha, 1994.

Takeuchi Jirō. *Puroretaria Esuperanto Undō ni tsuite*. Tokyo: Shihōshō Keijikyoku, 1939.

Takeuchi Yō. *Kyōyōshugi no Botsuraku: Kawariyuku Erīto Gakusei Bunka*. Tokyo: Chūō Kōron Shinsha, 2003.

Tamaru Takurō. *Nihon Rōmajikai Panfuretto 2: Nihongo no Sekaiteki Kakikata*. Tokyo: Nihon Rōmajikai, 1928.

——. *Rōmajibun no Kenkyū*. Tokyo: Nihon no Rōmajisha, 1920.

Tamura Tetsuzō. *Hakubunkan: Shuppan Ōkoku no Hikari to Kage*. Tokyo: Hōgaku Shoin, 2007.

Tanakadate Aikitsu. *Kuzu no Ne: Tanakadate Aikitsu Ronbun Basshū*. Tokyo: Nihon no Rōmajisha, 1938.

Tanakadate Aikitsu et al. *Rōmaji Hitorigeiko*. Tokyo: Nihon no Rōmajisha, 1914.

Tane Maku Hito Bungei Sensen o Yomu Kai, ed. *Furontia no Bungaku—Zasshi Tane Maku Hito no Saikentō*. Tokyo: Tane Maku Hito Bungei Sensen o Yomu Kai, 2005.

Tatlock, Lynne, ed. *Publishing Culture and the "Reading Nation": German Book History in the Long Nineteenth Century*. Rochester, N.Y.: Camden House, 2010.

Teikoku Toshokan Naikaku Kikanshitsu Kirokuka (Naikaku Bunko) / Kunaishō Toshoryō. Tokyo: Yumani Shobō, 2010.

Terada Torahiko. *Terada Torahiko Zenshū*. 30 vols. Tokyo: Iwanami Shoten, 1996–1999.

Thompson, John B. *Merchants of Culture: The Publishing Business in the Twenty-First Century*. New York: Plume, 2012.

Thornber, Karen. *Empire of Texts in Motion: Chinese, Korean, and Taiwanese Transculturations of Japanese Literature*. Cambridge, Mass.: Harvard University Asia Center, 2009.

Tierney, Robert. *Monster of the Twentieth Century: Kōtoku Shūsui and Japan's First Anti-Imperialist Movement*. Berkeley: University of California Press, 2015.

Toeda Hirokazu. "Henshū Sareru Honbun." *Nihon Kindai Bungaku* 69 (2003).

——. "Hikisakareta Honbun." *Bungaku* 4, no. 3 (September 2003).

——. *Iwanami Shigeo: Hikuku Kurashi, Takaku Omou*. Tokyo: Mineruva Shobō, 2013.

——. "Kaizōsha to Shanhai." *Ajia Yūgaku* 62 (2004).

——. "Kōkoku kara Mita Taishōki no *Bungei Shunjū* no Tenkai." *Kokubungaku Kenkyū* 148 (March 2006).

——. "Kōsaku Suru Zasshi no Yukue." *Bungaku* 2, no. 4 (July 2001).

——. "1926 Nihon, Bungaku to Eiga no Sōgū." *Hikaku Bungaku Kenkyū* 92 (2008).

——. "Shinkankaku-ha no Hikari to Kage." *Bungaku* 3, no. 6 (November 2002).

——. "Shuppan Media to Sakka no Shinjidai." *Bungaku* 4, no. 2 (March 2003).

——. "Shuppatsuki *Bungei Shunjū* no Media Senryaku." *Nihon Kindai Bungaku* 66 (May 2002).

——. "Yokomitsu Riichi no 'Gengokan'—Sono Dōjidaiteki Haikei o Megutte." In *Kawabata Bungaku e no Shikai* 6, ed. Kawabata Bungaku Kenkyūkai. Tokyo: Kyōiku Shuppan Sentā, 1990–1991.

Tokunaga Sunao. *Taiyō no Nai Machi*. Tokyo: Nihon Kindai Bungakukan, 1971.

——. *Tokunaga Sunao Bungaku Senshū*. 2 vols. Kumamoto: Kumamoto Shuppan Bunka Kaikan, 2008.

Tōkyō Koshoseki Shōgyō Kyōdō Kumiai, ed. *Tōkyō Kosho Kumiai Gojūnenshi*. Tokyo: Tōkyō Koshoseki Shōgyō Kyōdō Kumiai, 1974.

Tōkyō Teikoku Daigaku Rōmajikai. *Rōmaji Nenpō 1932*. Tokyo: Nihon Rōmajikai Shuppanbu, 1931.

Torihara Manabu. *Nihon Shashinshi 1: Bakumatsu Ishin kara Kōdo Seichōki made*. Tokyo: Chūō Kōronsha Shinsha, 2013.

Tsien, Tsuen-Hsuin. *Paper and Printing*. Part 1 of *Science and Civilisation in China*, Ed. Joseph Needham, *Volume 5: Chemistry and Chemical Technology*. New York: Cambridge University Press, 1985.

Tsubouchi Shōyō. "Shakai Kaizō to Engeki." *Kaizō* 1, no. 5 (August 1919).

Tsuboya Zenshirō. *Hakubunkan Gojūnenshi*. Tokyo: Hakubunkan, 1937.

Tsuchiya Michio. *Kokugo Mondai Ronsōshi*. Tokyo: Tamagawa Daigaku Shuppanbu, 2005.

Tsuchiya Reiko. *Taishūshi no Genryū: Meijiki Koshinbun no Kenkyū*. Tokyo: Sekai Shisōsha, 2002.

Tsukishima Hiroshi. *Rekishiteki Kanazukai: Sono Seiritsu to Tokuchō*. Tokyo: Yoshikawa Kōbunkan, 2014.

Tsurumi Shunsuke. *Taishū Geijutsu*. Tokyo: Kawade Shinsho, 1954.

Tsutsui Kiyotada. *Nihongata "Kyōyō" no Unmei: Rekishi Shakaigakuteki Kōsatsu*. Tokyo: Iwanami Shoten, 2009.

Tucker, Anne Wilkes, et al., eds. *The History of Japanese Photography*. New Haven, Conn.: Yale University Press, 2003.

Twine, Nanette. "The Genbunitchi Movement: Its Origin, Development, and Conclusion." *Monumenta Nipponica* 33, no. 3 (Winter 1978).

——. *Language and the Modern State: The Reform of Written Japanese*. London: Routledge, 1991.

Uchida Roan. *Bungakusha to Naru Hō*. Tokyo: Tosho Shinbun, 1995.

——. *Uchida Roan Shomotsu Kankei Chosakushū*. Ed. Yagi Sakichi et al. 3 vols. Tokyo: Seishōdō, 1979.

Ueda, Atsuko, et al., eds. *The Politics and Literature Debate in Postwar Japanese Criticism, 1945–52*. Lanham, Md.: Lexington Books, 2017.

Ueda Kazutoshi, ed. *Dai-Nihon Kokugo Jiten*. Tokyo: Fuzanbō, 1915–1919.

Umemori Naoyuki. *Shoki Shakaishugi no Topogurafī: Ōsugi Sakae to Sono Jidai*. Tokyo: Yūshisha, 2016.

——, ed. *Teikoku o Ute: Heiminsha Hyakunen Kokusai Shimupojiumu*. Tokyo: Ronsōsha, 2005.

Unno Hiroshi. *Modan Toshi Shūyū—Nihon no 20-nendai o Tazunete*. Tokyo: San'yōsha, 1985.

——. *Modan Toshi Tōkyō*. Tokyo: Chūō Kōronsha, 1983.

Uranishi Kazuhiko, ed. *Sakka no Jiden 68—Tokunaga Sunao*. Tokyo: Nihon Tosho Sentā, 1998.

Usui Yoshimi. *Kindai Bungaku Ronsō*. 2 vols. Tokyo: Chikuma Shobō, 1975.
Virilio, Paul. *War and Cinema: The Logics of Perception*. London: Verso, 1989.
Vološinov, V. N. *Marxism and the Philosophy of Language*. Trans. Ladislav Matejka and I. R. Titunik. Cambridge, Mass.: Harvard University Press, 1986.
Wada Atsuhiko. *Dokusho no Rekishi o Tou: Shomotsu to Dokusha no Kindai*. Tokyo: Kasama Shoin, 2014.
——, ed. *Kokutei Kyōkasho wa ika ni Urareta ka: Kindai Shuppan Ryūtsū no Keisei*. Tokyo: Hitsuji Shobō, 2011.
Wada Hirofumi and Wada Keiko, eds. *Maruzen to Yōsho*. Korekushon Modan Toshi 79. Tokyo: Yumani Shobō, 2012.
Walker, Gavin. *The Sublime Perversion of Capital: Marxist Theory and the Politics of History in Modern Japan*. Durham, N.C.: Duke University Press, 2016.
Wallerstein, Immanuel. *Historical Capitalism*. New York: Verso, 1983.
Ward, Vanessa. B. "The Spectre of the Left: Iwanami Shoten, Ideology and Publishing in Early Postwar Japan." *Japanese Studies* 26, no. 2 (Summer 2006).
Weisenfeld, Gennifer. *MAVO: Japanese Artists and the Avant-Garde*. Berkeley: University of California Press, 2002.
Williams, Raymond. *Marxism and Literature*. Oxford: Oxford University Press, 1977.
Williams, R. John. *The Buddha in the Machine: Art, Technology, and the Meeting of East and West*. New Haven, Conn.: Yale University Press, 2014.
Wood, Frances. *The Diamond Sutra: The Story of the World's Earliest Dated Printed Book*. London: British Library, 2010.
Yamada Yoshio. *Kanazukai no Rekishi*. Tokyo: Hōbunkan, 1929.
——. *Kokugogakushiyō*. Tokyo: Iwanami Shoten, 1935.
——. "Monbushō no Kanazukai Kaitei-an o Ronzu." *Myōjō (II)* 2, no. 2 (February 1925).
——. "Renga Kenkyū no Jōsetsu." *Shisō* 67 (May 1927).
Yamaguchi Osamu. *Maejima Hisoka*. Tokyo: Yoshikawa Kōbunkan, 1990.
Yamaguchi Yōji. *Nihongo o Tsukutta Otoko: Ueda Mannen to Sono Jidai*. Tokyo: Shūeisha, 2016.
Yamamoto Masahide. *Genbun Itchi no Rekishi Ronkō*. Tokyo: Ōfūsha, 1971.
Yamamoto Ryōsuke. *Yokomitsu Riichi to Shōsetsu no Ronri*. Tokyo: Kasama Shoin, 2008.
Yamamoto Sanehiko. Shuppanjin no Ibun 2: *Kaizōsha Yamamoto Sanehiko*. Tokyo: Kurita Shoten, 1968.
Yamamoto Taketoshi. *Kindai Nihon no Shinbun Dokushasō*. Tokyo: Hōsei Daigaku Shuppankyoku, 1981.
——. *Kōkoku no Shakaishi*. Tokyo: Hōsei Daigaku Shuppankyoku, 1984.
——. *Senryōki Media Bunseki*. Tokyo: Hōsei Daigaku Shuppankyoku, 1996.
——, ed. *Shinbun, Zasshi, Shuppan*. Kyoto: Mineruva Shobō, 2005.
——. *Shinbun to Minshū: Nihongata Shinbun no Keisei Katei*. Tokyo: Kinokuniya Shoten, 1973.
Yamamoto Taketoshi and Tsuganezawa Toshihiro. *Nihon no Kōkoku: Hito, Jidai, Hyōgen*. Tokyo: Nihon Keizai Shinbunsha, 1986.
Yamamoto Yoshiaki. *Kane to Bungaku: Nihon Kindai Bungaku no Keizaishi*. Tokyo: Shinchōsha, 2013.
Yamazaki Yasuo. *Eien no Jigyō: Iwanami Bunko Monogatari*. Tokyo: Hakuōsha, 1962.

——. *Shun'yōdō Monogatari: Shun'yōdō o Meguru Meiji Bundan no Sakkatachi*. Tokyo: Shun'yōdō, 1969.

Yanagita Kunio. *Yanagita Kunio Zenshū*. 32 vols. Tokyo: Chikuma Shobō, 1989–1991.

Yanase Masamu Kenkyūkai, ed. *Yanase Masamu: Hankotsu no Seishi to Jidai o Mitsumeru Me*. Tokyo: Yanase Masamu Kenkyūkai, 1999.

Yokomitsu Riichi. "*Bungei Jidai* to Gokai." *Bungei Jidai* 1, no. 1 (October 1924).

——. "Kankaku Katsudō." *Bungei Jidai* 2, no. 2 (February 1925).

——. *"Love" and Other Stories of Yokomitsu Riichi*. Trans. Dennis Keene. Tokyo: Japan Foundation, 1974.

——. *Shanghai*. Trans. Dennis Washburn. Ann Arbor: Center for Japanese Studies, University of Michigan, 2001.

——. "Tada Namae Nomi ni tsuite." *Bungei Jidai* 2, no. 7 (July 1925).

——. *Teihon Yokomitsu Riichi Zenshū*. Ed. Hoshō Masao, Inoue Ken, and Kuritsubo Yukio. 16 vols. Tokyo: Kawade Shobō Shinsha, 1981–1987.

Yokota Fuyuhiko, ed. *Shuppan to Ryūtsū*. Tokyo: Heibonsha, 2016.

Yokoyama Kazuo. *Nihon no Shuppan Insatsu Rōdō Undō Senzen Senchūhen*. 2 vols. Tokyo: Nyūsusha, 1998.

Yosano Akiko. "Joshi Kaizō no Kisoteki Kōsatsu." *Kaizō* 1, no. 1 (April 1919).

Yosano Hiroshi et al. "Kanazukai Kaitei-an Kōgi." *Myōjō (II)* 2, no. 2 (February 1925).

Yoshida Hiroo. "Yokomitsu Riichi to Shiga Naoya." *Kokubungaku Kaishaku to Kanshō* 48, no. 13 (October 1983).

Yoshimi Shun'ya. *"Koe" no Shihonshugi: Denwa Rajio Chikuonki no Shakaishi*. Tokyo: Kōdansha, 1995.

——. *Toshi no Doramaturugī: Tōkyō—Sakariba no Shakaishi*. Tokyo: Kawade Shobō Shinsha, 2008.

Yoshimi Shun'ya and Kinoshita Naoyuki, eds. *Nyūsu no Tanjō: Kawaraban to Shinbun Nishikie no Jōhō Sekai*. Tokyo: Tōkyō Daigaku Sōgō Kenkyū Hakubutsukan, 1999.

Yoshino Sakuzō. *Yoshino Sakuzō Senshū*. 15 vols. Tokyo: Iwanami Shoten, 1995–1997.

Zamenhof, L. L. *Sekaigo Dokuhon*. Trans. Hasegawa Futabatei. Tokyo: Saiunkaku, 1906.

Zhang Xiumin, ed. *Katsuji Insatsu no Bunkashi: Kirishitanban, Kokatsujiban kara Shinjōyō Kanjihyō made*. Tokyo: Bensei Shuppan, 2009.

Zhong, Yurou. "Script Crisis and Literary Modernity in China, 1916–1958." Ph.D. diss., Columbia University, 2014.

Žižek, Slavoj. *The Sublime Object of Ideology*. New York: Verso, 1989.

INDEX

STUDIES OF THE WEATHERHEAD EAST ASIAN INSTITUTE
COLUMBIA UNIVERSITY

Selected Titles

(Complete list at: http://weai.columbia.edu/publications/studies-weai/)

Down and Out in Saigon: Stories of the Poor in a Colonial City, by Haydon Cherry. Yale University Press, 2019.

Beauty in the Age of Empire: Japan, Egypt, and the Global History of Aesthetic Education, by Raja Adal. Columbia University Press, 2019.

Mass Vaccination: Citizens' Bodies and State Power in Modern China, by Mary Augusta Brazelton. Cornell University Press, 2019.

Residual Futures: The Urban Ecologies of Literary and Visual Media of 1960s and 1970s Japan, by Franz Prichard. Columbia University Press, 2019.

The Making of Japanese Settler Colonialism: Malthusianism and Trans-Pacific Migration, 1868-1961, by Sidney Xu Lu. Cambridge University Press, 2019.

The Power of Print in Modern China: Intellectuals and Industrial Publishing from the end of Empire to Maoist State Socialism, by Robert Culp. Columbia University Press, 2019.

Beyond the Asylum: Mental Illness in French Colonial Vietnam, by Claire E. Edington. Cornell University Press, 2019.

Borderland Memories: Searching for Historical Identity in Post-Mao China, by Martin Fromm. Cambridge University Press, 2019.

Sovereignty Experiments: Korean Migrants and the Building of Borders in Northeast Asia, 1860 – 1949, by Alyssa M. Park. Cornell University Press, 2019.

The Greater East Asia Co-Prosperity Sphere: When Total Empire Met Total War, by Jeremy A. Yellen. Cornell University Press, 2019.

Thought Crime: Ideology and State Power in Interwar Japan, by Max Ward. Duke University Press, 2019.

Statebuilding by Imposition: Resistance and Control in Colonial Taiwan and the Philippines, by Reo Matsuzaki. Cornell University Press, 2019.

Nation-Empire: Ideology and Rural Youth Mobilization in Japan and Its Colonies, by Sayaka Chatani. Cornell University Press, 2019.

Fixing Landscape: A Techno-Poetic History of China's Three Gorges, by Corey Byrnes. Columbia University Press, 2019.

The Invention of Madness: State, Society, and the Insane in Modern China, by Emily Baum. University of Chicago Press, 2018.

Japan's Imperial Underworlds: Intimate Encounters at the Borders of Empire, by David Ambaras. Cambridge University Press, 2018.

Heroes and Toilers: Work as Life in Postwar North Korea, 1953–1961, by Cheehyung Harrison Kim. Columbia University Press, 2018.

Electrified Voices: How the Telephone, Phonograph, and Radio Shaped Modern Japan, 1868-1945, by Kerim Yasar. Columbia University Press, 2018.

Making Two Vietnams: War and Youth Identities, 1965–1975, by Olga Dror. Cambridge University Press, 2018.

A Misunderstood Friendship: Mao Zedong, Kim Il-sung, and Sino–North Korean Relations, 1949–1976, by Zhihua Shen and Yafeng Xia. Columbia University Press, 2018.

Playing by the Informal Rules: Why the Chinese Regime Remains Stable Despite Rising Protests, by Yao Li. Cambridge University Press, 2018.

Raising China's Revolutionaries: Modernizing Childhood for Cosmopolitan Nationalists and Liberated Comrades, by Margaret Mih Tillman. Columbia University Press, 2018.

Buddhas and Ancestors: Religion and Wealth in Fourteenth-Century Korea, by Juhn Y. Ahn. University of Washington Press, 2018.

Idly Scribbling Rhymers: Poetry, Print, and Community in Nineteenth Century Japan, by Robert Tuck. Columbia University Press, 2018.

China's War on Smuggling: Law, Economic Life, and the Making of the Modern State, 1842-1965, by Philip Thai. Columbia University Press, 2018.

Forging the Golden Urn: The Qing Empire and the Politics of Reincarnation in Tibet, by Max Oidtmann. Columbia University Press, 2018.

The Battle for Fortune: State-Led Development, Personhood, and Power among Tibetans in China, by Charlene Makley. Cornell University Press, 2018.

Aesthetic Life: Beauty and Art in Modern Japan, by Miya Elise Mizuta Lippit. Harvard University Asia Center, 2018.

Where the Party Rules: The Rank and File of China's Communist State, by Daniel Koss. Cambridge University Press, 2018.

Resurrecting Nagasaki: Reconstruction and the Formation of Atomic Narratives, by Chad R. Diehl. Cornell University Press, 2018.

China's Philological Turn: Scholars, Textualism, and the Dao in the Eighteenth Century, by Ori Sela. Columbia University Press, 2018.

Making Time: Astronomical Time Measurement in Tokugawa Japan, by Yulia Frumer. University of Chicago Press, 2018.

Mobilizing Without the Masses: Control and Contention in China, by Diana Fu. Cambridge University Press, 2018.

Post-Fascist Japan: Political Culture in Kamakura after the Second World War, by Laura Hein. Bloomsbury, 2018.

China's Conservative Revolution: The Quest for a New Order, 1927-1949, by Brian Tsui. Cambridge University Press, 2018.

Promiscuous Media: Film and Visual Culture in Imperial Japan, 1926-1945, by Hikari Hori. Cornell University Press, 2018.

The End of Japanese Cinema: Industrial Genres, National Times, and Media Ecologies, by Alexander Zahlten. Duke University Press, 2017.

The Chinese Typewriter: A History, by Thomas S. Mullaney. The MIT Press, 2017.

Forgotten Disease: Illnesses Transformed in Chinese Medicine, by Hilary A. Smith. Stanford University Press, 2017.

Borrowing Together: Microfinance and Cultivating Social Ties, by Becky Yang Hsu. Cambridge University Press, 2017.

Food of Sinful Demons: Meat, Vegetarianism, and the Limits of Buddhism in Tibet, by Geoffrey Barstow. Columbia University Press, 2017.

Youth For Nation: Culture and Protest in Cold War South Korea, by Charles R. Kim. University of Hawaii Press, 2017.

Socialist Cosmopolitanism: The Chinese Literary Universe, 1945-1965, by Nicolai Volland. Columbia University Press, 2017.

The Social Life of Inkstones: Artisans and Scholars in Early Qing China, by Dorothy Ko. University of Washington Press, 2017.

Darwin, Dharma, and the Divine: Evolutionary Theory and Religion in Modern Japan, by G. Clinton Godart. University of Hawaii Press, 2017.

Dictators and Their Secret Police: Coercive Institutions and State Violence, by Sheena Chestnut Greitens. Cambridge University Press, 2016.

The Cultural Revolution on Trial: Mao and the Gang of Four, by Alexander C. Cook. Cambridge University Press, 2016.

Inheritance of Loss: China, Japan, and the Political Economy of Redemption After Empire, by Yukiko Koga. University of Chicago Press, 2016.

Homecomings: The Belated Return of Japan's Lost Soldiers, by Yoshikuni Igarashi. Columbia University Press, 2016.

Samurai to Soldier: Remaking Military Service in Nineteenth-Century Japan, by D. Colin Jaundrill. Cornell University Press, 2016.

Ingram Content Group UK Ltd.
Milton Keynes UK
UKHW010856210523
422080UK00005B/199